P9-DGO-211

241412
Leach Library
Londonderry, NH 03053

DISCARD

Leach Library
276 Mammoth Road
Londonderry, NH 03053
Adult Services 432-1132
Children's Services 432-1127

LEACH LIBRARY
276 Mammoth Road
Londonderry, NH 03053

DISCARD

DYLAN
ON DYLAN
INTERVIEWS AND ENCOUNTERS
EDITED BY JEFF BURGER

CHICAGO REVIEW PRESS

An A Cappella Book

782.4216
DYL

18 May 09
B + T
30.00 (16.35

Copyright © 2018 by Jeff Burger
All rights reserved.
Published by Chicago Review Press Incorporated
814 North Franklin Street
Chicago, Illinois 60610

ISBN 978-0-912777-42-9

Library of Congress Cataloging-In-Publication Data
Are available from the Library of Congress.

A list of credits and copyright notices for the individual pieces in this collection can be found on pages 527–29.

Cover and interior design: Jonathan Hahn
Interior layout: Nord Compo

Printed in the United States of America
5 4 3 2 1

For Andre and Myriam,
from a proud father

CONTENTS

PREFACE

Google "Bob Dylan rarely gives interviews" and you'll discover dozens of articles that use that or a similar phrase—often in the introduction to a Dylan Q&A. Sometimes, as in a 1969 conversation with *Rolling Stone* editor Jann Wenner, it is Dylan himself who proclaims, "I don't give interviews."

This has never been even close to the truth. Granted, there have been periods of several years when he has met with journalists rarely or not at all. He has also complained about talking to the media, loudly and frequently, saying, for example, that "if you give one magazine an interview, then the other magazine wants an interview . . . so pretty soon you're in the interview business." He has said that his words get twisted by journalists, and that "performers feel that . . . a lot of times that their points are not taken the right way or they feel imposed upon to answer questions that have really little to do with why they fill halls or sell records."

But his complaints haven't stopped him from talking. Dylan has given numerous press conferences; spoken at length with countless large and small print publications and with broadcast media around the world; and even answered listeners' questions on call-in radio shows. There is far more Q&A material than any one book could accommodate.

Besides claiming that Dylan almost never grants interviews, journalists frequently say that when he does talk to them, he doesn't reveal much. His responses "are often vague, mystical, or testy," wrote Jon Bream in the *Minneapolis StarTribune* in 2013. He "has never spoken extensively about his early career," proclaimed the BBC in 2003. In no interview, "from what I can tell, did he reveal anything of substance about his nonpublic life," wrote Andrew Ferguson in London's *Weekly Standard* magazine in 2016.

After reading this book—which includes dozens of Dylan's most interesting interviews plus highlights from more than eighty other Q&As, encounters, and speeches—you'll understand why journalists make such comments. Like the Beatles, who offered silly answers to silly queries about their hairstyles and similarly trivial matters early in their careers, Dylan can be as evasive and abstruse as he is witty. Sometimes—especially in interviews that contain preposterous questions—he can be cranky and sarcastic. But when he's in the right mood, likes the interviewer, and hears intelligent questions, he often offers candid, revealing commentary about his groundbreaking music and creative process, and occasionally even about marriage, parenting, and other personal subjects.

You'll find such interviews in the pages that follow, along with ones in which Dylan's true feelings remain elusive, and I think you'll agree that while the former kind shed the most light, the latter can be just as colorful and entertaining. Indeed, Dylan is one of a small number of popular music artists who are nearly always as fascinating in conversation as they are on record.

His Q&As are particularly valuable because they offer one of the few non-musical glimpses we have into the mind of one of the most important performers and songwriters of the last hundred years. He rarely talks to audiences in concert, and he has never produced a full and proper autobiography. There is, of course, the terrific *Chronicles, Volume One.* But that memoir isn't nearly as confessional or wide-ranging as, say, Bruce Springsteen's; and while *Chronicles* was supposed to be a three-book project, we have yet to see a sequel to volume one, which appeared well over a decade ago. Dylan was reportedly working on volume two as far back as 2008, so it could appear at any moment, maybe even before this book hits the stores. But even if it does, I suspect we'll find in these interviews many otherwise unavailable clues to the man behind the music.

You have to read those clues carefully, though. Dylan said in 1986 that reporters sometimes "take quotations and turn things around and make you seem like a different kind of person . . . So you felt like you'd been suckered or something." But sometimes the reader gets suckered, too. A writer named Eduardo Bueno filed a Dylan tour feature in 1991 and found later that an editor had tried to pass it off as an interview, using some quotes from earlier articles and some that the singer had never even uttered. Then there was the case of *New Yorker* writer Jonah Lehrer, who resigned from that magazine in 2012 after admitting that he'd invented the Dylan quotes that appear in his book *Imagine: How Creativity Works*. (No, Jonah, that's not how it works.)

Dylan himself often speaks honestly to the press, but he, too, has at times tried to fool the public. "The press, I figured, you lied to it," he wrote in *Chronicles*, and some of the lies were big ones. The transcript of an ostensible 1965 press conference that appeared in the *Village Voice* was actually written by Dylan and the *Voice*'s J. R. Goddard. Dylan also told many tall tales about his teen years in early interviews. And when he didn't like what a *Playboy* editor did to the transcript of his 1965 conversation with Nat Hentoff, he rejected Hentoff's suggestion that he simply tell the magazine to cancel its publication of the interview. "I got a better idea," Dylan reportedly said. "I'm gonna make one up." And with some help from Hentoff, he did.

———————

The table of contents lists publication or broadcast dates, when available, but the full-length interviews here are arranged in the order that they were conducted. (I've indicated interview dates when no publication or broadcast date is available and in cases where a piece would appear to be out of sequence based on the publication or broadcast date.) Conversations that did not originally appear in print have been styled according to guidelines in *The Chicago Manual of Style*. I listened to audio recordings whenever possible, and in doing so, found many previous transcriptions to be incomplete and error-prone. I have done some minor editing to improve readability—for example, by deleting verbal ticks like "you know" as well as aborted, incoherent, and redundant phrases and sentences.

As for material that originated in print media, I have in most cases obtained copies of the publications and am presenting these features

exactly as they first appeared. Whether album and song titles are itali-
cized, placed in quotes, or simply written with initial caps, for example,
depends on how they are displayed in the original article; even when
punctuation or styling is at odds with all the rules I know, I've followed
The Chicago Manual of Style's guidelines about not altering previously
published material. I have, however, made rare exceptions to correct
obvious and egregious typos and spelling and punctuation mistakes and
have also used bracketed editor's notes to flag misstatements and explain
comments that seem unclear.

There isn't much repetition in these interviews. Dylan is highly
changeable, so the content and tone of conversations often differs dra-
matically, even when only weeks or months separate them. Moreover,
I have attempted to select interviews that mostly cover territory not
explored elsewhere in the same way or at all.

Still, as I noted in the preface to my last anthology, which featured
John Lennon's conversations, there are only two ways I could have
avoided all repetition. I could have excluded pieces that introduce any
redundancy, which would have meant cutting conversations that also
contain fascinating and fresh material; or I could have deleted sections
of interviews that cover subjects addressed elsewhere. Having concluded
that most fans would prefer unedited conversations, that's what I've opted
to present (with just a couple of exceptions, which are explained in my
introductions). Besides, I often find the occasional repetition enlightening,
in that it indicates topics of particular interest to Dylan or interviewers
and sometimes provides a new slant on familiar turf.

———————

It takes a lot of help to put together a book like this. I particularly want
to thank Yuval Taylor, my longtime editor at Chicago Review Press,
who enthusiastically signed on to this project as soon as I suggested it;
and managing editor Michelle Williams. Special thanks also to Gretchen
Day Bryant at the *SunSentinel*; Ken Charles at KNX; Tom Cording at
Columbia Legacy; Keith Cunningham at KLOS; Steven Finger at the *Los
Angeles Free Press*; Melissa Garza at Westwood One; Philomene Grandin,
daughter of Izzy Young; Tiffany Lintner at KMEL; Mark Moss at *Sing*

Out!; Dylan Scott at the *Minnesota Daily*; Nathaniel Shahan at the *Kenyon Collegian*; Mark Torres and Shawn Dellis at the Pacifica Foundation; Amanda Urban at ICM Partners; and all those who granted permission for use of their material in this anthology.

I also want to express my appreciation to journalist Jonathan Cott, who edited an excellent 2006 book of Dylan interviews that has recently been reissued. At one point, I discarded the possibility of preparing a Dylan anthology because Cott had already published one. As it turns out, though, it was he who wound up urging me to put together this book. "There are a lot of good interviews that I didn't get," he told me, and indeed there were. About two-thirds of the pieces that follow have not previously been anthologized anywhere and some of them have never before appeared in print. Some of the other Q&As—such as the early interviews with Paul Jay Robbins and Cynthia Gooding and the San Francisco press conference from 1965—have been excerpted elsewhere but not published in full.

Continued thanks to Ken Terry, my friend of nearly half a century, and to my many terrific coworkers at AIN Publications. I particularly want to acknowledge Jennifer Leach English, whose kindness and friendship I value more with each passing year; and Lysbeth McAleer, a first-rate professional who, as a bonus, couldn't be more fun to work with. I had planned to retire from my editorial job at AIN a couple of years ago; people like Jennifer and Lysbeth are among the biggest reasons why I have not done so.

Greatest thanks, as always, to my wife, Madeleine Beresford, and our children—who are now too old to fit that word—Andre and Myriam. I've had a fair amount of luck over the years, but nothing beats the good fortune of being able to share my life with these three wonderful people.

—JEFF BURGER
Ridgewood, New Jersey, 2018

"He [Frank Sinatra] was funny. We were standing out on his patio at night and he said to me, 'You and me, pal, we got blue eyes, we're from up there,' and he pointed to the stars. 'These other bums are from down here.' I remember thinking that he might be right."

—Bob Dylan, in an interview with Bill Flanagan, posted at bobdylan.com, March 22, 2017

IZZY YOUNG'S NOTEBOOK

Izzy Young | October 20, 1961–March 14, 1962 | *The Fiddler Now Upspoke* (UK)

Bob Dylan dropped out of the University of Minnesota in May 1960, around his nineteenth birthday. The following winter, he traveled to New York, where he began playing Greenwich Village clubs. Only about nine months later, famed producer John Hammond signed him to Columbia Records.

By then, Greenwich Village's Folklore Center had become a gathering place for Dylan and other leaders of the burgeoning folk-music movement. Izzy Young, who had founded the operation in 1957, apparently sensed that he was a witness to a historical moment, particularly regarding Dylan, because he kept a notebook where he recorded much of what the fledgling artist had to say to him. To my knowledge, only brief excerpts from the following material have ever been printed in any widely circulated publication.

The first notebook entry here dates from October 20, 1961—probably just weeks after the Hammond signing—when the artist was still five months away from release of his debut LP. The entry, which was used in the program for Dylan's Izzy Young–produced Carnegie Hall concert on November 4, 1961, opens with two paragraphs by the diarist. All the rest of the notes—which are today preserved in the Library of Congress—consist of Young's transcription of Dylan's comments, which the singer reportedly checked for accuracy. (Some clarifying words from Young are in parentheses; a few from me are in brackets.)

In his 2004 memoir, *Chronicles, Volume One*, Dylan wrote that Young would "ask me questions about myself like, where it was that I grew up and how did I get interested in folk music, where I discovered it, stuff like that. He'd then write about me in his diary. I couldn't imagine why. His questions were annoying, but I liked him because he was gracious to me and I tried to be considerate and forthcoming. I was very careful when talking to outsiders, but Izzy was okay and I answered him in plain talk."

1

"Plain talk" notwithstanding, some of Dylan's comments sound disjointed, some of his references are unclear, some of his lines seem more like notes than exact quotes, and some of the things he told Young are questionable or clearly false (such as the bit at the beginning about being raised in Gallup, New Mexico, and traveling with carnivals from age fourteen, a tale he spun for multiple early interviewers). Still, this is a rare window into Dylan's thoughts and life in a time before practically anyone knew his name—a time when he could recall recently knocking on record company doors, saying, "Howdy, I've written some songs," and being turned away. —Ed.

October 20, 1961

Bob Dylan was born in Duluth, Minnesota in 1941. He was raised in Gallup, NM and before he came to New York earlier this year, he lived in Iowa, South Dakota, North Dakota and Kansas. He started playing carnivals at the age of fourteen, accompanying himself on guitar and piano. He picked up harmonica about two years ago.

The University of Minnesota gave him a scholarship. He went there for some five months, attended a dozen lectures and then left. He learned many blues songs from a Chicago street singer named Arvella Gray. He also met a singer—Mance Lipscomb—from the Brazos River country of Texas, through a grandson that sang rock and roll. He listened a lot to Lipscomb and he heard Woody Guthrie's album of Dust Bowl ballads in South Dakota. In fact Bob Dylan has sung old jazz songs, sentimental cowboy songs and Top 40 hit parade stuff. He was always interested in singers and didn't know the term "folk music" until he came to New York.

[*In the remainder of Young's notebook entries, he is quoting Dylan, who is mostly referred to in the first person. —Ed.*]

It has to be called a name so they called it folk music. Very few people sing that way and it's being taken over by people who don't sing that way. It's all right but don't call it folk music. Stuff I do is nearer to folk music. Now I don't want to make a lot of money, want to get along. I want to reach more people and have a chance to sing the kind of music I sing. People have to be ready and have seen me once already.

People often say first time that it isn't folk music. My songs aren't easy to listen to. My favorite singers are Dave Van Ronk, Jack Elliott, Peter Stampfel, Jim Kweskin and Rick von Schmidt. I can offer songs that tell something of this America, no foreign songs. The songs of this land that aren't offered over TV and radio and very few records.

Groups are easy to be in. I've always learned the hard way. I will now, too. I dress the way I do because I want to dress this way and not because it is cheaper or easier.

I started writing my songs about four or five years ago. First song was to Brigitte Bardot, for piano. Thought if I wrote the song I'd sing it to her one day. Never met her. I've written some Hillbilly songs that Carl Perkins from Nashville sings. I write talking blues on topical things. *California Brown-Eyed Baby* has caught on. Noel Stookey [*aka Paul Stookey, of Peter, Paul, and Mary —Ed.*] gave me the idea for the *Bear Mountain Song* [*aka "Talking Bear Mountain Picnic Massacre Blues" —Ed.*] and I wrote it overnight but I wasn't there. Never sing it the same way twice because I never wrote it down.

No one is really influencing me now—but actually everything does. Can't think of anyone in particular now.

October 23, 1961

Played piano with Bobby Vee—would have been a millionaire if I'd stayed with him. Played piano Michigan Northwest to Montana. Sang for one dollar a day at Café Wha? [*an experience recounted in "Talkin' New York" on Dylan's debut LP —Ed.*], playing piano with Fred Neil. Bored stiff. It was warm and stayed a whole winter. Went to see *Raisin in the Sun*— Lou Gossett was in it. Dead Man's Hand or Aces and Eights. I believe in them. Believe in cards. Play a lot of cards. It's time to cash in when you get Aces and Eights. The other things I believe in are logical—the length of one's hair—less hair on the head more hair inside the head & vice versa. Crew cut all hair cluttering around the brain. Let my hair grow long to be wise and free to think. I have no religion. Tried a bunch of different religions. Churches are divided. Can't make up their minds neither can I. Never seen a God—can't say till I see one . . .

Got a free ride to NY—came to see Woody Guthrie—Came to the Folklore Center. Girl playing with banjo (Toni Mendell). O God, this is it, this is NY. Everyone's playing banjo faster than I've been playing guitar. Couldn't really play with them. Used to see Woody whenever I had enough money. Met him once before in California before I was really playing—think Jack Elliott was with him. I think [banjo player] Billy Faier was there, too. I was in Carmel, California—doing nothing. During the summer, Woody impressed me. Always made a point to see him again. Wrote a song to Woody in February of this year. [*"Song to Woody," which appears on Dylan's first album. —Ed.*] Was going to sing all Woody songs—Jack [Elliott] and Cisco [Houston] came out. Woody carries the paper I wrote the song on. Woody likes to hear his own songs. Woody likes my songs.

Haven't sung anything really funny. Woody doesn't like Joan Baez, or the Kingston Trio—Baez for her voice is too pretty and Trio because they can't be understood.

Sort of like NY, don't know really. I like to walk around, just walk around. Like to ride motorcycle—was a racer in North and South Dakota—Minnesota.

First guitar I had, strings were 2 inches away from the board—had a flat pick but couldn't play it. Got a Martin for a present. 6 or 7 years. No one ever taught me to play guitar or harmonica, or piano. Used to play sort of boogy woogyish type of stuff, played with rock n' roll songs. Never knew the names of the songs, but 12 bar blues, played along with them. A few coffee houses refused to let me play when I came to NY. Bob Shelton helped by writing an article [*"Bob Dylan: A Distinctive Folk Song Stylist," published September 29, 1961, in the* New York Times. —*Ed.*]—talked around—someone from Elektra came down but nothing happened. Bob Shelton been like a friend for a long time. Friends are pretty hard to come by in NY. Dave Van Ronk has helped me along in card games because he's always losing. I've been with Jack [Elliott]—we have an Island upstate NY—we saw the Island out in the lake—we named the Island Delliott Isle and swam back. Jack hasn't taught me any songs.

Jack doesn't know that many songs. He's had lots of chances. I went out to the Gleasons [*New Jersey couple Bob and Sidsel Gleason, at whose home Dylan made some early recordings. —Ed.*] and stayed out there for a while in East Orange. They have a lot of tapes—his [Dylan's] VD songs. [*A reference to songs on early Minneapolis tapes, such as "VD Blues," "VD Waltz," and "VD City." —Ed.*] Learned a bunch of those—sung them to Woody. Should get the rest from Harold Leventhal. [*Leventhal, a music manager, produced Dylan's concert at New York's Town Hall in April 1963. —Ed.*]

Met Jesse Fuller in Denver at the Exodus. I was playing in a stripper place. The Gilded Garter. Central City, a little mining town. Came down to Denver 2 summers ago—Jesse was playing downstairs. Upstairs was Don Crawford. Learned the way he does songs—mixed his style in with mine at the time. Before that there was a farmhand in Sioux Falls, S.D., who played the autoharp. Picked up his way of singing (Wilbur, never knew his last name).

Cowboy styles I learned from real cowboys. Can't remember their names. Met some in Cheyenne [Wyoming]. Cowboys nowadays go to Cowboy movies and sit there and criticize. Wear their hat this way or that—pick up their way of walking from the movie. Some of them. In Central City, Denver—the Tropics—played 20 minutes, strippers worked for 40 minutes with rock n' roll band. I'd play for 20 minutes again. Never stopped. One night I was about ready to strip myself. Only lasted a week and a half. Worst place I ever played. A full drag.

I have different ideas about folk music now. There's been no one around to cut records like the old Leadbelly, Houston & Guthrie. There are young people that are singing like that, but are being held back by commercial singers. People who have radio programs don't play. Jim Kweskin, Luke Faust aren't appreciated by enough people. Folkways is the only company that would record such stuff. Released Bill McAdoo's *Can't Let Little Children Starve To Death*. Liked title of song but hadn't heard it.

Went up to Folkways. I had written some songs. I says "Howdy, I've written some songs. Would you publish some songs"—wouldn't even look at them. I heard Folkways was good. [*Sing Out!* cofounder] Irwin

Silber didn't even talk to me. Never got to see [Folkways founder] Moe Asch. They just about said "Go" and I heard that *Sing Out!* was supposed to be helpful and friendly. Big heart. Charitable. I thought it was the wrong place and *Sing Out!* was on the door. Whoever told me that was wrong. It seems ironic I'm on a big label. The article came out on Thursday night—Bruce Langhorne and I backed up by Carolyn Hester. Showed the article to John Hammond—Come in and see me [he said]. I did. And he is recording me. He asked me what I do. I've got about 20 songs I want to record. Some stuff I've written. Some stuff I've discovered and some stuff I stole. That's about it.

Used to see girls from the Bronx, at Chicago, Antioch, with their gutstring guitars, singing *Pastures of Plenty*, no lipstick, Brotherhood songs. Struck me funny, not clowns, opened up a whole new world of people. I like the NY kind of girl now. Can't remember what the old kind was like. Can always tell a New Yorker out of town—want everyone to know they're from NY. I've seen it happen—first 4 or 5 days people just stare at me. Down South it's bad to say you're from NYC.

We played the new Bill McAdoo recording on Folkways. *Gonna Walk And Talk For My Freedom* with Pete Seeger on banjo. Beatniks: 10 years ago, a guy would get on a bus with a beard, long sideburns, a hat and people would say "look at the Rabbi". Some guy gets on a bus today. The same people say "look at the Beatnik". Played the Fifth Avenue Hotel for the Kiwanis Club. Got job through [folksinger] Kevin Krown—for no money (I don't like the McAdoo Record). A lot of different acts that night—dressed up like a clown—when someone would sing two clowns would perform. Jack just dropped in. Couldn't hear myself—a clown rolled up to pinch my cheek—kicked him in the nuts and no one saw. Rest of the clowns left me alone. Made Kevin Krown buy me 10 drinks. Met Krown in Denver, came through Chicago—never got back 75 cents owed him but stayed at his place.

OK but don't care for classical music. Don't go for any foreign music. I really like Irish music and Scottish music, too. Colleges are the best audiences, much better than nightclubs. NY is the best place for music.

School [University of Minnesota] was too—lived on the Mississippi River—about 10 feet away under a great bridge. I took some theater course. Said I had to take Science. Average credits is about 12—you can take 17 to 20. I enrolled with 26 credits. Narrowed it down to 20. Then down to 9. Couldn't even make that. Carnivals and fraternities—so much crap. So much phooey stuff. You might as well get out and live with some other people. A big hoax. Flunked out of anthropology—read a little, went to see the movies. One time I flunked out of English for teacher said I couldn't talk. Poetry we had to read, had to think about it for a long time. Poem should reach as many people as possible. I spent more time in Kansas City about 400 miles away. A girl friend was there. Went to High School in Upper Minnesota (Hibbing) a nothing little town.

Fargo in North Dakota—a lumberjack and mining town. Used to hop train. Big open pit. Lots of strikes there, lots of political stuff, a real mining town.

It's easy to criticize big money makers like Belafonte, Kingston Trio. Stuff he does is really like a popular singer—criticized by Jazz, Folk and Calypso people and he's making all the money. Won't criticize him until he sings one of my songs but then he'll make a lot of money for me. I liked Belafonte on the TV show.

Odetta: her and frustrated show singers—folk music is wide open for good voices. Instead of starting out at the bottom in Opera or Show or Jazz they start at the top in folk music.

Logan English—is one guy that if I don't have to see him—great—but the guy is just, Christ, every time I see him, his failure, singing folk music for there is, still trying. Logan's singing is one big bash of phooey. He's terrible. Lots of people sing simple—but Logan dwells on this—but no better—doesn't have it. Kills him but he sings Jimmie Rodgers—Peter LaFarge is a great songwriter.

Bruce Langhorne is great. Was at a party once, playing. Let me have a guitar, didn't have much fingers. I can't laugh. Read [Woody Guthrie's] *Bound for Glory* twice. Book should be taught to College kids—his poetry should be taught in English classes.

Got a bad deal from [gospel and folksinger] Brother John Sellers.

Highway 77—McKinley's bar in Kansas to the 5th Avenue Hotel in NYC.

We put on John Jacob [Niles's] new double record. I like him. Too much. Sort of. Niles is really great. I think he's a genius.

February 1, 1962

Wrote a song the other night *Ballad of Emmett Till*. After I wrote it someone said another song was written but not like it. I wrote it for CORE [Congress of Racial Equality]—I'm playing it Feb. 23. I think it's the best thing I've ever written. Only song I play with a capo. Stole the melody from Len Chandler—a song he wrote about a Colorado bus driver.

"born a black skinned boy
and he was born to die"

"just a reminder to remind your fellow men
that this kind of thing still lives today
in the ghost robed Klu [*sic*] Klux Klan"

I bought an apartment cost 350 dollars. Rent is 80 dollars. 161 W. 4th St., c/o Walker. Getting some money from Columbia. I'm supposed to be making all kinds of money. I seem, I don't play guitar if I don't feel like playing. I'd rather get drunk. I hate coffeehouses to play at. People come down to see freaks. Sometimes I'm in a bad mood. I don't like the idea too much. Carnival was different for I was with the same people. Entertainers in coffeehouses just don't have that togetherness.

Hope to stay in NY for a while. Might go down to New Orleans for the Mardi Gras. I like New York. At one time I said—if it wasn't for New York I'd move there. And I sort of like the town.

42nd St. That's about all. I went to Brooklyn Hospital. Seeing him [Woody Guthrie] steady for a year. I met him when I was thirteen. He likes my songs. You have to see the notes by Stacey Williams (A pseudonym used by Bob Shelton when writing liner notes). Never figured I'd play with Belafonte. I practice piano at Bob's house. Next album I'll play piano, guitar and harmonica. Writing a song called *The Death of Robert Johnson*. Columbia's [recordings are] the greatest of his work. Don't like to go up to John Hammond. Ivy League kids treat me like a king. At first I liked it. It gets sickening after a while. I took Len Chandler just to see what would happen. He couldn't believe it. [Leeds's] book comes out in

April with 13 songs. 3 arrangements. Hammond isn't a manager—more an advisor. I'm sort of disconnecting myself from the folk music scene. I've got a lot of friends in for that play. Too many guys want to make a big entertainment out of it with jazz and comedians.

30 year old guy Buffalo Bill—looks older. Why isn't he recorded? Moe Asch has a tape—"We've got guys from the South"—almost saying "he's not dead yet". [Folksinger and *Broadside* magazine coeditor] Gil Turner brought the tape to him. Curious to know how long the New Lost City Ramblers stayed at the Blue Angel.

Can't see the future. I hate to think about it. It's a drag to think about it. How could anyone notice if I were drunk. I'm inconspicuous.

February 17, 1962

Let Me Die In My Footsteps written while Gil Turner and I were in Toronto in Dec. 1961. I set out to say something about fallout and bomb-testing but I didn't want it to be a slogan song. Too many of the protest songs are bad music. Exception being *Which Side Are You On*. Most of the mining songs are good. Especially the bomb songs—usually awkward and with bad music. Which takes a stand—no beating around the bush.

Came to NYC in 1960—back to Oklahoma several times. Disastrous trip to California—no one liked me. Felt pretty low when I left. More than 20 songs.

February 22, 1962

Jesse Fuller—April 20, 21, 22—at Ann Arbor. Just me and Jesse Fuller. Concert at Goddard College. Billy James from Columbia Records doesn't want me to sign for too many things so as not to interfere with their plans until the record comes out. Left my life there. Waiting for my book to come out—more than the record. *Rambling Gambling Willy* is in the book. *Bear Mountain. Reminiscence Blues. Stand on the Highway. Poor Boy Blues. Talking NY. Song to Woody Guthrie.*

I wanted to write a song about 1 and a half years ago on Fallout Shelters to tune *So Long It's Been Good To Know You*. Song I wrote isn't like the rest of them.

Carolyn Hester's record will be out in May or next September. Mine is coming out in two weeks and she recorded two months before me.

Ernie Marrs [*a prolific Oklahoma-born songwriter who contributed frequently to* Broadside. *—Ed.*] is writing songs all over the place. I never even looked at them. To tell you the truth, except a few. They're pretty good, I guess.

I like Johnny Cash's songs. Because he's not trying to cover up. Writes real stuff. He writes a lot of songs. I think Woody Guthrie wrote better songs. I've seen some songs he never recorded.

Favorite Woody Guthrie songs? *Jack Hammer John. At the Mound of Your Grave. Slip Knot. Hard Traveling.* I like them all really. Except some of them are absurd. *Dirty Overalls* that's really good.

I just pick the melody out of the air sometimes.

Prestige Records, one of their guys—if Columbia doesn't—give me a call.

Folkways asked me for contemporary songs for an album of my own songs.

Bill McAdoo's albums are terrible. Writes songs to hold up a banner. He's just another Leon Bibb—same kind of voice. Don't think there's anything traditional about it. He's a nice guy, though.

Alan Lomax? I like him. He stuck around one night to hear me sing at the Bitter End. Ed McCurdy was MC. There was not time. I sang along with Bessy Jones at his house. We were sitting around eating apples.

Sure wish Cisco Houston was still alive. I really didn't know him. I liked him because he was real, just a singer.

Heard Bonny Dobson last night. [*Dobson, a Canadian folksinger, is best known for writing "Morning Dew." —Ed.*] She's OK, I guess. I heard Big Joe Williams when I was 9 or 10, in Chicago. I really didn't play so much. I just followed him around. I sung then. I got a cousin living in Chicago. He lives on the South Side. Funny thing. Big Joe Williams remembers it.

(After writing some lyrics about the Folklore Center.)

Good songwriter? I think Paul Anka is the worst songwriter. Saw some of his songs in the hit-parade book. I think Johnny Cash is the best songwriter.

Len Chandler—Ian and Sylvia have picked up some songs.

Strange Rain? I don't understand it. *Umbrella*? Why can't he say— don't shoot off those bombs. You ought to go to Nevada where all the stuff is going on. Go out there—you'll find some strange rain. I think dentists and scientists are together on this. How can you like a song you can't understand? In a foreign language. But this is our language. I should be able to understand it. Said he wouldn't understand it if I didn't explain.

March 14, 1962

Life and Death of Don White. Actually I wrote it a long time ago. I just finished it up. What's the story of the song? I'll sing it for you. Not a bunch of people suffering. One person. So it's justified. He was a common guy. No martyr or anything like that. But he had a right to be in an institution when he asked.

PM East (a New York weekly) in two weeks. No contract with Leeds exclusively. If I wrote to sell, I could do 20 a day. I'm just not. Can't see anything in it. Some of the songs passed off as songs! These are contemporary songs.

DYLAN ON

Getting Rich

"I just want to keep on singing and writing songs . . . I don't think about making a million dollars. If I had a lot of money what would I do? I would buy a couple of motorcycles, a few air-conditioners and four or five couches."

—from liner notes to *Bob Dylan*, released March 19, 1962

RADIO INTERVIEW

Cynthia Gooding | Early 1962 | *Folksinger's Choice*, WBAI-FM (New York)

This conversation, on listener-sponsored WBAI-FM, was one of Dylan's first extensive radio interviews, if not *the* first. (He had spoken with folksinger Oscar Brand on New York's WNYC the previous fall, but only briefly.)

Interviewer Cynthia Gooding, a folksinger herself, establishes excellent rapport with the young Dylan, who seems eager for her approval and asks, after nearly every song he performs for her, whether she likes it. She appears to grasp the extent of his talent and responds enthusiastically.

I have been unable to confirm the date of this conversation, whether it aired live, and if not, exactly when it did air. At least two sources cite March 11 as the interview or broadcast date, and WBAI's parent, Pacifica Radio, indicates that the station aired the show in March. However, WBAI's Amy Goodman has said only that the interview took place in "early 1962" and one of Dylan's comments suggests that it might have occurred in February. In any case, it's safe to say that the conversation happened only days or weeks before the March 19 release of Dylan's eponymous debut album. —Ed.

[Dylan performs "Lonesome Whistle Blues."]

Cynthia Gooding: That was Bob Dylan. Just one man doing all that. Playing the mouth harp and the guitar because, well, when you do this, you have to wear what another person might call a necklace.

Bob Dylan: Yeah.

Gooding: And then it's got joints so that you can bring the mouth harp up to where you can reach it to play it. Bob Dylan is . . . well, you must be twenty years old now, aren't you?

Dylan: Yeah, I must be twenty. [*Laughs.*]

Gooding: [*Laughs.*] Are you?

Dylan: Yeah. I'm twenty.

Gooding: When I first heard Bob Dylan it was about three years ago in Minneapolis, and at that time you were thinking of being a rock 'n' roll singer, weren't you?

Dylan: At that time, I was just sort of doin' nothin'. I was there.

Gooding: Well, you were studying.

Dylan: I was working, I guess. l was making pretend I was going to school out there. I'd just come in from South Dakota. That was about three years ago.

Gooding: Yeah?

Dylan: Yeah. I'd come there from Sioux Falls. That was about the only place you didn't have to go too far to find the Mississippi River. It runs right through the town.

[*Both laugh.*]

Gooding: You've sung now at Gerde's [Folk City] here in town, and have you sung at any of the coffeehouses?

Dylan: Yeah, I've sung at the Gaslight. That was a long time ago, though. I used to play down in the [Café] Wha, too. You know where that place is?

Gooding: Yeah, I didn't know you sang there.

Dylan: Yeah, during the afternoons. I played my harmonica for this guy there who was singing. He used to give me a dollar to play every day with him, from two o'clock in the afternoon until eight thirty at night. He gave me a dollar plus a cheeseburger.

Gooding: [*Laughs.*] A thin one or a thick one?

Dylan: I couldn't much tell in those days.

Gooding: Well, whatever got you off rock 'n' roll and on to folk music?

Dylan: I dunno. I wasn't calling it anything then; I wasn't really singing rock 'n' roll. I was singing Muddy Waters songs and I was writing songs, and I was singing Woody Guthrie songs. And I also sung Hank Williams songs and Johnny Cash, I think.

Gooding: Yeah, I think the ones that I heard were a couple of Johnny Cash songs.

Dylan: Yeah, this one I just sung for you is Hank Williams.

Gooding: It's a nice song, too.

Dylan: "Lonesome Whistle."

Gooding: Heartbreaking.

Dylan: Yeah.

Gooding: And you've been writing songs as long as you've been singing, huh?

Dylan: I guess you could say that. [*Apparently looks at Gooding's cigarettes.*] These are French ones, yeah?

Gooding: No, they are healthy cigarettes, because they've got a long filter and no tobacco.

Dylan: That's the kind I need.

Gooding: And now you're doing a record for Columbia?

Dylan: Yeah, I made it already. It's coming out next month. Or not next . . . yeah, it's coming out in March.

Gooding: And what's it going to be called?

Dylan: *Bob Dylan*, I think.

Gooding: That's a novel title for a record.

Dylan: Yeah, it's really strange.

Gooding: And this is one of the quickest rises in folk music, wouldn't you say?

Dylan: Yeah, but I really don't think of myself as a folksinger, because I don't really much play across the country, in any of these places. I'm not on a circuit like those other folksingers. I play once in a while. But I like more than just folk music, too. And I sing more than just folk music. A lot of people, they're just folk music, folk music, folk music. I like folk music like Hobart Smith stuff and all that but I don't sing much of that, and when I do it's probably a modified version of something. Not a modified version; I don't know how to explain it. It's just there's more to it, I think. Old-time jazz things. Jelly Roll Morton and stuff like that.

Gooding: Well, what I would like is for you to sing some songs from different parts of your short history. Short because you're only twenty now.

Dylan: Yeah, OK. Let's see. I'm looking for one.

Gooding: He has, I gather, a small part of his repertoire pasted to his guitar.

Dylan: Yeah. Well, actually, I don't even know some of these songs. I copied the best songs I could find down here from all these guitar players' lists. So I don't know a lot of these. It gives me something to do, though, on stage.

Gooding: Yeah, something to look at. [*Laughs.*]

Dylan: Yeah. Oh, you wanna hear a blues song?

Gooding: Sure.

Dylan: This one's called "Fixin' to Die."

[*Dylan performs "Fixin' to Die."*]

Gooding: That's a great song. How much of it is yours?

Dylan: I can't remember. My hands are cold. It's a pretty cold studio.

Gooding: The coldest studio! . . . You're a very good friend of John Lee Hooker's, aren't you?

Dylan: Yeah, I'm a friend of his.

Gooding: Do you sing any of his songs at all?

Dylan: Well, no. I sing one of Howlin' Wolf's. You wanna hear that one again?

Gooding: Well, first I wanna ask you, why don't you sing any of his [Hooker's]? Because I know you like him.

Dylan: I play harmonica with him, and I sing with him. But I don't sing any of his songs because—I might sing a version of one of them, but I don't sing any like he does because I don't think anybody sings any of his songs, to tell you the truth. He's a funny guy to sing like.

Gooding: Hard guy to sing like, too.

Dylan: I'll see if I can find a key here and do this one. I heard this one a long time ago. I never do it.

Gooding: This is the Howlin' Wolf song.

Dylan: Yeah.

[*Dylan performs "Smokestack Lightning."*]

Dylan: You like that?

Gooding: Yeah, I sure do. You're very brave to try and sing that kind of a Howlin' song.

Dylan: Yeah, it's Howlin' Wolf.

Gooding: Another of the singers that you're a very good friend of is Woody Guthrie.

Dylan: Yeah.

Gooding: His songs were some of the first ones that you sang.

Dylan: Yeah.

Gooding: Which ones do you sing of his? Or which do you like the best, perhaps I should say.

Dylan: Well, which ones you want to hear? Here, I'll sing you one.

Gooding: In order for Bob to put on his necklace, which is what he holds up the mouth harp with, he's gotta take his hat off. Then he puts on the necklace. Then he puts the hat back on. Then he screws up the necklace so that he can put the mouth harp in it. It's a complicated business. [*Laughs.*]

Dylan: The necklace gotta go around the collar.

Gooding: [*Laughs.*] Also, first, he decides what key he's gonna sing in and then he's gotta find the mouth harp that's in that key. And then he's gotta put the mouth harp in the necklace.

Dylan: Yeah. I'll sing you "Hard Travelin'." How's that one? Everybody sings it, but he [Guthrie] likes that one.

[*Dylan performs "Hard Travelin'."*]

Gooding: Nice! You started off slow but, boy, you ended up. [*Laughs.*]

Dylan: Yeah, that's a thing of mine there.

Gooding: Tell me about the songs that you've written yourself that you sing.

Dylan: I don't claim to call them folk songs or anything. I just call them contemporary songs. There's a lot of people who paint if they've got something that they wanna say. Or other people write. Well, I just write songs—same thing. You wanna hear one?

Gooding: Why, yes! That's just what I had in mind, Bob Dylan. Whatever made you think of that? [*Laughs.*]

Dylan: Well, let me see. What kind do you wanna hear? I got a new one I wrote.

Gooding: Yeah. You said you were gonna play some of your new ones for me.

Dylan: Yeah, I got a new one. This one's called "Emmett Till." Oh, by the way, I stole the melody from Len Chandler. And he's a funny guy. He's a folksinger guy. He uses a lot of funny chords when he plays and he always wants me to use some of these chords, trying to teach the new chords all the time. Well, he played me this one. He said, "Don't those chords sound nice?" And I said, "They sure do," so I stole the whole thing.

Gooding: That was his first mistake. [*Laughs.*]

Dylan: Yeah . . . Melody's his.

[*Dylan performs "The Death of Emmett Till."*]

Dylan: You like that one?

Gooding: It's one of the greatest contemporary ballads I've ever heard. It's *tremendous.*

Dylan: You think so?

Gooding: Oh, yes!

Dylan: Thanks!

Gooding: It's got some lines in it that just make you stop breathing. It's great. Have you sung that for Woody Guthrie?

Dylan: No. I'm gonna sing that for him next time. I just wrote that one last week, I think.

Gooding: Fine song. It makes me very proud. What's so magnificent about it to me is that it doesn't have any sense of being written. It doesn't have any of those little poetic contortions that mess up so many contemporary ballads. And you sing it so straight. That's fine.

Dylan: Wait till Len Chandler hears the melody, though.

[*Both laugh.*]

Gooding: He'll probably be very pleased with what you did to it. What song does he sing to it?

Dylan: He sings another one he wrote. He wrote about some bus driver out in Colorado that crashed a school bus with twenty-seven kids. That's a good one, too. It's a good song.

Gooding: What other songs are you gonna sing?

Dylan: You wanna hear another one?

Gooding: I want to hear *tons* more.

Dylan: OK, I never get a chance to sing. Let me just sing you a plain, ordinary one.

Gooding: Fine.

Dylan: I'll tune this one. It's open E. Oh, I got one! I got two of 'em. I broke my fingernail so it might slip a few times.

[*Dylan performs "Standing on the Highway."*]

Dylan: Like that?

Gooding: Yes, I do. You know, the eight of diamonds is delay, and the ace of spades is death so that sort of goes in with the two roads, doesn't it?

Dylan: I learned that from carnival.

Gooding: From who?

Dylan: Carnival. I used to travel with the carnival. I used to speak of those things all the time.

Gooding: Oh. You can read cards, too?

Dylan: I can't read cards. I really believe in palm reading, but for a bunch of personal experiences I don't believe too much in the cards. I like to think I don't believe too much in the cards, anyhow.

Gooding: [*Laughs.*] So you go out of your way not to get 'em read, so you won't believe them. How long were you with the carnival?

Dylan: I was with the carnival off and on six years.

Gooding: What were you doing?

Dylan: Oh, just about everything. I was a clean-up boy, I used to be on the main line, on the Ferris wheel, just run rides. I used to do all kinds of stuff like that.

Gooding: Didn't that interfere with your schooling?

Dylan: Well, I skipped a bunch of things, and I didn't go to school a bunch of years and I skipped this and skipped that.

Gooding: That's what I figured.

Dylan: All came out even, though.

Gooding: [*Laughs.*] You were gonna sing another blues, you said.

Dylan: Oh, yeah, I'll sing you this one. This is a nice slow one. I learned this . . . you know [folksinger] Ralph Rensler?

Gooding: Sure.

Dylan: Yeah, I learned this sort of thing from him. I got the idea from him. This isn't the blues, but . . . how much time we got?

Gooding: Oh, we've got half an hour.

Dylan: Oh, good.

[*Dylan performs "Roll On, John."*]

Gooding: That's a lonesome accompaniment, too. Oh, my!

Dylan: You like that one?

Gooding: It makes you feel even lonelier. How much of that last one was yours, by the way?

Dylan: Well, I dunno, maybe one or two verses.

Gooding: Where'd the rest of it come from?

Dylan: Well, like I say, I got the idea for "Roll On, John" from Ralph Rensler.

Gooding: Oh, I see.

Dylan: And then the rest just sort of fell together. Here's one I bet you'll remember. Yeah, I bet you'll know this one.

Gooding: Take the hat off, put on the necklace, put the hat back on. Nobody's ever seen Bob Dylan without his hat excepting when he's putting on his necklace. Is there a more dignified name for that thing?

Dylan: What—this?

Gooding: For the brace.

Dylan: Yeah. Harmonica holder. [*Laughs.*]

Gooding: Oh, I think necklace is better than that.

Dylan: Yeah. [*Laughs.*] This one here's an old jug-band song.

[*Dylan performs "Stealin'."*]

Dylan: Like that? That's called "Stealin'."

Gooding: I figured. [*Laughs.*] You haven't been playing the harmonica too long, have you?

Dylan: Oh, yeah. I been playing the harmonica for a long time. I just couldn't play 'em at the same time [as guitar]. I used to play the smaller Hohners. I never knew harmonica holders existed, the real kind like this. I used to play with a coat hanger. That never really held out so good so I used to put tape around it, and then it would hold out pretty good. They were smaller harmonicas than these. . . .

Gooding: At the carnival did you learn songs?

Dylan: No, I learned how to sing, though. That's more important.

Gooding: Yeah. You made up the songs even then?

Dylan: Actually, I wrote a song once I'm trying to find, a real good song I wrote about this lady I knew in the carnival. And they had a sideshow. This was Roy B. Thomas shows, and they had a freak show in it, and all the midgets and all that kind of stuff. Well, there was one lady in there in really bad shape. Like her skin had been all burned when she was a little baby, and it didn't grow right, and so she was like a freak. And all these people would pay money to come and to see and that really sort of got me. I mean, she didn't really look normal. She had this funny kind of skin and they passed her off as the elephant lady. And she was just burned completely since she was a baby.

And it's a funny thing about them. I know how those people think. Like when they wanna sell you stuff. You know, the spectators. And I don't see why people don't buy something, because they sell little cards of themselves, for like ten cents. They got a picture on it and it's got some story. A lot of them are very smart. A lot of them are great people.

But they got a funny thing in their minds. Here they are on the stage, they wanna make you have two thoughts. They wanna make you think that they don't feel bad about themselves. They want you to think that they just go on living every day and they don't ever think about what's bothering them, they don't ever think about their condition. And also they wanna make you feel sorry for them, and they gotta do that two ways. And I wrote a song for her a long time ago. And lost it some place. It's just about speaking from first person, like here I am, and sort of like, talking to you, and it was called, "Won't You Buy a Postcard?" That was the name of the song. Can't remember that one, though.

Gooding: There's a lot of circus literature about how freaks don't mind being freaks, but it's very hard to believe.

Dylan: Oh, yeah.

Gooding: You're absolutely right that they would have to look at it two ways at the same time. Did you manage to get both ways into the song?

Dylan: Yeah. I lost the song.

Gooding: I hope you find it, and when you find it, sing it for me.

Dylan: I got a verse here. . . . You know Ian and Sylvia?

Gooding: Sure. Ian and Sylvia are at the Bitter End club.

Dylan: I sort of borrowed this from—

Gooding: He's looking for a harmonica.

Dylan: I don't have to take the necklace off. You might have heard them do it. This is the same song. I used to do this one.

[*Dylan performs "Makes a Long-Time Man Feel Bad."*]

Dylan: You like that one?

Gooding: Boy, when you—

Dylan: That's got them funny chords in it.

Gooding: —really get going, there's a tremendous sort of push that you give things that's *wild*.

Dylan: Yeah, you really think so?

Gooding: [*Laughs.*] No, I was just talking.

Dylan: I'll take off my necklace.

Gooding: Without taking off your hat.

Dylan: No. I'm getting good at this.

Gooding: Yeah. After he takes off the necklace or puts it on, he's gotta fluff up the hat again every time.

Dylan: Yeah. I got it cleaned and blocked last week.

Gooding: [*Laughs.*] What did you wear on your head?

Dylan: Stetson. You seen me wear that Stetson.

Gooding: Oh, yeah, you were wearing somebody's Stetson.

Dylan: It was mine. I got that for a present.

Gooding: So why don't you wear it? 'Cause you like this one better?

Dylan: I like this one better. It's been with me longer.

Gooding: What happens when you take it off for any length of time? You go to sleep?

Dylan: Yeah.

Gooding: I see.

Dylan: Or else I'm in the bathroom or somethin'. Well, actually, just when I go to sleep. I wanted to sing "Baby, Please Don't Go" because I've wanted to hear how that sounded.

[*Dylan performs "Baby, Please Don't Go."*]

Gooding: That's a nice song, too. You said that you've written several new songs lately.

Dylan: Yeah.

Gooding: You've only sung one of them. You realize that? I know I'm working you very hard for this hour of the morning.

Dylan: Yeah, this really isn't a new one but this is one of the ones. You'll like it. I wrote this one before I got this Columbia Records thing. Just about when I got it. I like New York, but this is a song from one person's angle.

[*Dylan performs "Hard Times in New York Town."*]

Gooding: That's a very nice song, Bob Dylan. You've been listening to Bob Dylan playing and singing some of his songs and some of the songs that he's learned from other people. And thank you very, very much for coming down here and working so hard.

Dylan: It's my pleasure to come down.

Gooding: When you're rich and famous, are you gonna wear the hat, too?

Dylan: Oh, I'm never gonna become rich and famous.

Gooding: And you're never gonna take off the hat, either.

Dylan: No.

Gooding: And this has been *Folksinger's Choice*, and I'm Cynthia Gooding. I'll be here next week at the same time.

CONVERSATION

Izzy Young, Pete Seeger, Sis Cunningham, and Gil Turner | May 1962 (recording) | Unaired, WBAI-FM (New York)

Sources seem to agree that this discussion—taped for *Broadside* magazine's show on WBAI-FM—never aired. Like the Cynthia Gooding conversation, it took place quite early in the game. Dylan's debut album had been released only about two months earlier; and just weeks before this conversation, on April 16, he had finished writing "Blowin' in the Wind," which at this point carried the title "The Answer Is Blowin' in the Wind." Izzy Young hosted the show, which includes contributions from folksingers Pete Seeger, Sis Cunningham, and Gil Turner. —Ed.

Pete Seeger: I'd like to hear some of the songs that Bob Dylan's made up, because of all the people I've heard in America, he seems to be the most prolific. Bob, do you make the songs before breakfast every day or before supper?

Bob Dylan: I don't make up a song like that. Sometimes I could go about two weeks without making up a song.

Seeger: I don't believe it.

Dylan: Oh, yeah. . . . I write a lotta stuff. In fact, I wrote five songs last night, but I gave all the papers away someplace. It was in a place called the Bitter End. Some were just about what was happening on the stage. And I would never sing them any place. They were just for myself and for some other people. They might say, "Write a song about that" and I'd do it, but I don't sit around like a lot of people do, spread newspapers

24

all around, and pick something out to write a song about it. It's usually right there in my head before I start. That's the way I write. I mean, it might be a bad approach but I don't even consider that I wrote it when I got it done.

Seeger: Put it together.

Sis Cunningham: You made it up.

Dylan: Yeah, yeah. I just figure that I made it up or I got it someplace. The song was there before me, before I came along. I just sorta came and took it down with a pencil but it was all there before I came around. That's the way I feel about it.

Izzy Young: I feel about Bob Dylan's songs very often that Bob is actually a kind of folk mime. He represents all the people around. And all the ideas current are filtered down and they come out in poetry. For example, one song you wrote about that fellow that has to be put into an institution. What was his name . . . White?

Dylan: Oh, yeah. He's dead now.

Young: He's dead now. For example, in one line you say the institutions are overcrowded. And I just couldn't see that appearing on a traditional ballad stanza before you sang it. And it's actually the first modern folk song I can think of that uses the ideas of twentieth-century Freudian psychology, and the idea of people being afraid of life.

Gil Turner: Instead of talking about it, let's hear it. Could we hear that song?

Cunningham: Let him get tuned up while we're talking, anyway. We can let him give us an example of how these songs come to him and flow through him.

Turner: Well, I think this particular song is historical in that it's the first psychological song of the modern generation that I've heard.

Dylan: I took this from Bonnie Dobson's tune, "Peter Amberly," I think the name of it is.

[*Dylan performs "Ballad of Donald White."*]

Young: Thank you, Bob Dylan.

Seeger: I'd like to hear Bob sing another one of his songs.

Dylan: OK.

Seeger: You've got a whole batch of 'em. Bob, where were you raised?

Dylan: Gallup, New Mexico, and South Dakota.

Seeger: Holy mackerel. That's where you can go farther and see less than anywhere else.

Dylan: "Emmett Till" was supposed to be here. It's not in *Broadside*, though.

Seeger: Yeah, that's the one you've been promising to *Broadside* for a long time.

Dylan: OK. This is Len Chandler's tune. The funny thing about it was that Len, when he plays and sings, he uses a lot of chords, but he's really good. He uses his fingers all over, but he's good. And he's always trying to tell me to use more chords, and to sing a couple of songs in minor keys. Before I met him I never sang one song in minor key. And he taught me these chords, and he was singing the song to these chords. And I saw him do the chords, and I stole it from him. And he heard me doing it like that. He didn't care, though.

[Dylan performs "The Death of Emmett Till."]

Young: Topical songs have been the topic of the program this afternoon. We've just about reached the end of the program. And I'd like Bob Dylan to sing the last song, called, "The Answer Is Blowin' in the Wind."

Dylan: Oh, "The Answer Is Blowin' in the Wind"? That one? Oh, OK.

Young: Because I think being a topical song, it's just filled with poetry that people of all kinds will enjoy.

[Dylan performs "The Answer Is Blowin' in the Wind," with everyone joining in on the final chorus.]

Young: Thank you, Bob Dylan, Gil Turner, Pete Seeger, Sis Cunningham, and myself, Israel Young.

DYLAN ON

Supposedly Running Off to Chicago at Age Ten

"My folks didn't seem to mind [that I ran away] because I don't remember them saying anything. Maybe I was happy when I was little or I was unhappy, a million other kids were the same way. What difference does it make?"

—from interview with Edwin Miller, *Seventeen*, September 1962

DYLAN ON

His Gift

"I used to play the guitar when I was ten, so I figured, well, maybe my thing is playing the guitar . . . maybe that's my little gift, like somebody can make a cake, or somebody can saw a tree down and . . . nobody's really got the right to say that any of these gifts are any better than any other body's . . . And I'd say that this is exactly what my gift is. Maybe I got a better gift but as of right now I ain't found it."

—from interview with Studs Terkel, WFMT-FM (Chicago), May 1963

DYLAN ON

The Blues

"What made the real blues singers so great is that they were able to state all the problems they had; but at the same time, they were standing outside of them and could look at them. And in that way, they had them beat. What's depressing today is that many young singers are trying to get inside the blues, forgetting that those older singers used them to get outside their troubles."

—from liner notes to *The Freewheelin' Bob Dylan*, released May 27, 1963

DYLAN ON

What He Wanted to See

"The itch to move, to see, and hear, was always there. But I didn't want to see the atomic bathrooms and electronic bedrooms and souped-up can-openers; I wanted to watch and feel the people and the dust and ditches and the fields and fences."

—from interview with Sidney Fields, *New York Mirror*, September 12, 1963

DYLAN ON

Youth

"It's took me a long time to get young and now I consider myself young. And I'm proud of it. I'm proud that I'm young. And I only wish that all you people who are sitting out here today or tonight weren't here and I could see all kinds of faces with hair on their head and everything like that, everything leading to youngness. . . . It is not an old people's world. It has nothing to do with old people. . . . And I look down to see the people that are governing me and making my rules and they haven't got any hair on their head. I get very uptight about it."

—from speech at National Emergency Civil Rights Committee dinner, Americana Hotel, New York, December 13, 1963

DYLAN ON

Political Action

"It ain't nothin' just to walk around and sing. You have to step out a little, right? Take Joanie [Baez], man, she's still singin' about Mary Hamilton. I mean, where's that at? She's walked around on picket lines, she's got all kinds of feeling, so why ain't she steppin' out?"

—from interview with Richard Farina, *Mademoiselle*, August 1964

DYLAN ON

Changes in His Music

"These records I've made, I'll stand behind them, but some of that was jumping into the scene to be heard and a lot of it was because I didn't see anybody else doing that kind of thing. . . . You know—pointing to all the things that are wrong. Me, I don't want to write for people anymore. You know—be a spokesman. Like, I once wrote about Emmett Till in the first person, pretending I was him. From now on, I want to write them inside me, and to do that I'm going to have to get back to writing like I used to when I was ten—having everything come out naturally."

—from interview with Nat Hentoff, *New Yorker*, October 24, 1964

A DAY WITH BOB DYLAN

John Cocks | November 20, 1964 | *Kenyon Collegian* (Ohio)

Two and a half years separate the conversation with Izzy Young, Pete Seeger, and company from the following piece. It was a busy and productive time for Dylan.

In May 1963, fourteen months after his debut album had appeared, Columbia released *The Freewheelin' Bob Dylan*, a giant leap forward. Though the first LP mingles only two originals ("Talkin' New York" and "Song to Woody") with blues and folk covers, the situation reverses on *Freewheelin'*, which includes just two songs Dylan didn't write: "Corrina, Corrina," which dates from 1928, and "Honey, Just Allow Me One More Chance," a substantially reworked version of a 1927 recording by country blues singer Henry Thomas. The rest of the LP contains such now-classic originals as "Blowin' in the Wind," "Girl from the North Country," "Don't Think Twice, It's All Right," "Masters of War," and "A Hard Rain's A-Gonna Fall."

Critics understandably raved; this was a completely fresh voice, making music that wasn't like anything else out there. And it was no fluke: *The Times They Are A-Changin'*, which followed in January 1964, delivers a brilliant, all-originals mix of the political ("With God on Our Side" and "Only a Pawn in Their Game," for example) and the personal ("Boots of Spanish Leather"). A mere seven months after that, in August 1964, came *Another Side of Bob Dylan*, containing more indelible originals, among them "It Ain't Me, Babe," "My Back Pages," and "Chimes of Freedom."

These records didn't bring Dylan quite as much success as you might expect, given their latter-day reputations. In fact, his biggest claim to fame at this point was probably that Peter, Paul, and Mary had scored Top Ten hits with his "Blowin' in the Wind" and "Don't Think Twice, It's All Right." As for his own recordings, *Freewheelin'* topped charts in the United Kingdom but made it to only number twenty-two in the United States. *The*

Times They Are A-Changin' reached number twenty, and *Another Side* climbed just to number forty-three.

Three months after that last album's release, on November 6, 1964, Dylan stepped off an airplane in Columbus, Ohio, and headed for nearby Kenyon College, where he was scheduled to perform the next day. John "Jay" Cocks, a twenty-year-old student at the school who is today a well-known Hollywood screenwriter, wrote evocatively about the visit for the *Kenyon Collegian*.

As the story makes clear, these were still early days for Dylan. True, gaggles of teenage fans congregated around him after his concert. But he traveled with only one helper, who would share a room with him in a "small motel" near the college; and when this article appeared, the headline on a couple of carryover pages gave bigger billing to the student than the singer: "Jay Cocks Spends a Day with Folksinger," it read. —Ed.

Wearing high heel boots, a tailored pea-jacket without lapels, pegged dungarees of a kind of buffed azure, large sunglasses with squared edges, his dark, curly hair standing straight up on top and spilling over the upturned collar of his soiled white shirt, he caused a small stir when he got off the plane in Columbus. Businessmen nodded and smirked, the ground crew looked a little incredulous and a mother put a hand on her child's head and made him turn away. Bob Dylan came into the terminal taking long strides, walking hard on his heels and swaggering just a little. He saw us, smiled a nervous but friendly smile, and came over to introduce himself and his companion, a lanky, unshaven man named Victor [Maymudes, his road manager] who looked like a hip version of Abraham Lincoln. Dave Banks, who had organized the concert and who was Dylan's official reception committee, led Dylan and Victor to baggage claim. Along the way, Victor asked us how far we were from the school and where he and Dylan would be spending the night. Learning that Banks had reserved a room for them in a small motel seven miles from Kenyon, he smiled a little and said "Tryin' to keep us as far away from the school as you can, huh?"

The trip back from the airport was a quiet one. Both men seemed rather tired, Dylan especially, who was pale and nervous. He said he was right in the middle of a big concert tour which had been on for almost two months, and Victor reminisced about one memorable engagement in Cambridge. "They had this pep rally right before the concert," he said, "and they all came in sweaty and yellin'. Man, the audience was full of football players—*football* players." Banks mentioned that Kenyon hadn't won a single football game all year, and both men seemed enthusiastic. "Yeah? No kidden'?," Dylan said, and Victor flashed a gratified smile. They asked a lot of questions about the college, the *Review*, and girls. Victor was astonished to find the college was so small and that the girls were so far away. "Outside Cleveland?", he commented, "man, that's a *far* away to go for a chick." Dylan nodded sympathetically.

We talked a bit more then about Kenyon. "They really have to wear ties and stuff to the concert," Dylan asked, "ties? Well, I'm gonna tell them they can take them off. That's what I'm gonna do. Rules—man, that's why I never lasted long in college. Too many *rules*." He spoke quietly but with some animation, in an unmistakably mid-western accent.

Entering Mt. Vernon, Dylan asked if there was a liquor store around. "Nothin' strong—wine or somethin'. Beaujolais. Chianti's good. Yeah, or Almaden or anything just so it's red and dry."

Banks stopped to get some wine. Dylan was talking faster now, more excitedly, fingering his sideburns and running his hand nervously over the top of his head.

As we came into Gambier, Dylan pressed his face up against the car window. "Wow, great place for a school! Man, if I went here I'd be out in the woods all day gettin' drunk. Get me a chick," (and here he again smiled his nervous smile), "settle down, raise some kids." Banks drove the pair around the campus and stopped at Rosse Hall where the concert was to be given to show them the audio facilities. Victor didn't like the amplifier system ("Man, it's a *phonograph*") and Dylan was worried about making his entrance from the back of the hall and walking all the way to the stage in front. It was finally decided that he would use the classrooms in the basement for a dressing room and come in through the fire exit in front, facing the small College cemetery. "Strange set-up," he kept saying, "really strange set-up." He was pacing up and down, taking quick drags on a Chesterfield. "Look, try and get as many people in here as you can, O.K.? Let 'em sit on the floor, just try and let everybody in, O.K.?" Victor mentioned that they were both pretty hungry, so Banks suggested driving back into Mt. Vernon where Dylan wouldn't be recognized; even if he was noticed, Banks said, he would probably be taken for some crazy student anyway, and the worst that could happen was someone trying to pick a fight. "'S'all right, man," Dylan said, shrugging his narrow shoulders, "I'm ready for 'em."

Back in Mt. Vernon, both Dylan and Victor were convulsed by the public square. "Hey, man, look at that cat," Dylan said, pointing at a Civil War monument, "Who's he?" Victor leaned out the window and squinted: "Don't know—looks like General Custer from here." "Fantastic," Dylan said.

When we finally got to the motel and into the room, Dylan turned on the television and began to tune his Gibson guitar and sing while watching *Wanted: Dead or Alive*. Dave Banks went to take care of the luggage while Victor and I walked to a public phone booth to call out for some food. Dylan only wanted a salad, but Victor told me to order him something else. "Fish or somethin'. And some greens. He's gotta have some greens. Any kind, I don't know." The Rendezvous Restaurant, however, didn't have any greens. Victor smiled, shaking his head. "Wow—we'll just get him that fish plate or whatever it is. No greens—wow." The food would be ready in half-an-hour, so Banks and I left Dylan and Victor in the room watching Steve McQueen tackle some evil-looking Mexicans. Dylan was now completely absorbed in the program; Victor was trying to sleep.

When we returned with the food half-an-hour later, the television was still on, Victor sprawled on his bed, while Dylan clasped and unclasped his hands between his knees. The restaurant had cooked a good meal but had forgotten to include silverware. "Don't make no difference," Dylan and Victor said in chorus, "no difference," so we ate everything from home fried potatoes to salad with our fingers. Dylan poked around at his fried fish platter, but wolfed down the salad. "Greek salad in Mt. Vernon, Ohio," he said. "Crazy," wiped his fingers on his azure dungarees, lit a cigarette, and poured himself some more of the Almaden wine. He was interested in the article I was planning to write about him. "There's this one guy who writes for the *Post*, *The Saturday Evening Post*, you know, named Al Aronowitz. He was going to do this story on me for a year and a half but he couldn't do it. He's really a great guy. He knew it would be cut to shit by the *Post* and he wouldn't get to say what he'd want to be sayin', only what they wanted. And the guy really didn't want me to come out like that, you dig? But we tried to write it anyway, you know, together. I went up to his place one day and we sat down and began to write this story, about me meeting him in Central Park and everything. But we had to stop, because the thing was getting really weird, surrealistic, and the story never got written. The only other cat he won't do a story on is Paul Newman, because he don't want to ruin him by gettin' him all cut up."

While talking he constantly flexed his fingers and crossed and uncrossed his legs. Mentioning Paul Newman got him on the subject of acting. "For me, you know, acting is like the Marx Brothers, somethin' you can't learn. Like the Studio. In the early days it was good, before it became a big fad, but I went there and really got turned off. All these people—actors—they're all themselves, really, tryin' too hard to be someone else. You can't learn to be someone else. It's just gotta be inside. You dig what I'm tryin' to say?"

"Hey, Bob," Victor interrupted, switching off the TV, "we better get movin'." Dylan had been talking for forty-five minutes, and he had wanted to get out to the College before the concert to tune up. On the way, Dylan asked us to lock the door to the classroom he would be using to rehearse. He was worried about people coming in for autographs and an over-enthusiastic group of fans. Banks complied by driving his car across a space of bumpy lawn and up to the side door of the hall, where Victor hustled Dylan out and through the door past three or four gaping couples on their way to collect some early front row seats. We made sure the door was locked, and Victor and I took turns standing guard until Victor decided it was time to rig up the special microphones they had brought along. He went upstairs carrying a suitcase full of tubes and wire, while Dylan, in the next room, tuned up for three minutes by pounding out a wild rock and roll song on a grand piano and singing some gibberish lyrics.

Dave Banks knocked on the door and told Dylan that two people who said they were friends of his were upstairs. They had given their names as Bob and John. "Fantastic," said Dylan. "Hey Victor, go up and bring 'em down quick. Fantastic." I went back to join Dylan, who was pacing around in a circle.

All of a sudden the door crashed open and a soft-faced young man in black boots, trousers, coat, and gloves came running into the room screaming, "Hey, Bobby—hiya, baby," his long hair flapping like banners behind him. "Wow, fantastic," Dylan yelled, reeling backwards across the room, laughing and attempting to climb the wall, "whatya doin' here, Bob?"

"Driving out to the coast," said the newcomer, pumping Dylan's hand, "got this car and—hey, you know John. We're drivin' out together." He reintroduced Dylan to a tall, swallow-faced boy who had an expensive Japanese camera hanging around his neck. "Look at this place—I don't believe the set-up. Crazy."

"Yeah, I know. Hey, man, what're ya *doin'*."

"Man, like we have this car belongs to Al, you know, we're goin' out to the Coast. A Cobra—wow. We drove six hundred and fifty miles yesterday in ten hours. Took us thirty-five minutes to get through Pennsylvania. VAROOM—wow!"

Everyone laughed. "Hey listen, man, you gonna be out on the coast, give me a call. I'm gonna do some concert, Joanie [Baez] and me, so call."

"Yeah, yeah," Bob said. "What's happenin' out there?"

"Oh, Joanie and me's gonna do these concerts. Fantastic number of songs: we'll be out there for a while, but after all this shit we took I don't think it's much use doubling up on the hotel bills anymore, do you?"

"Yeah, yeah," Bob said again. "Listen, did you see the pictures from New York?" Dylan said that he hadn't. "Hey, John, I got 'em in the car. Go out and get 'em." John giggled and went running out. Victor returned from upstairs, reported that the microphones were all fixed and that the hall was about full, and greeted Bob, who said, "Hey, how about all the faggots they've got in this place?" John came back from the car holding some large photographs in his hand which he thrust at Dylan with a smile.

"Hey, these are really great," he said, looking through them. "This one's a little *bizarre* maybe, but I like it." He handed it to me. It was a picture of Bob, his hair trimmed in bangs, standing in front of a fever-ish abstract mural dressed in a woman's ensemble of matching [paisley] slacks and blouse, holding a tricycle in his left hand and turning the pedal. John grinned at me.

As the time for Dylan to go on approached, he became more ani-mated, more nervous. He paced and sometimes danced around the room gulping down wine from a small dixie cup and making large gestures with his hands. Around eight-thirty, Victor handed him his guitar, Dylan placed a black-wire harmonica holder around his neck, played a few chords, blew a few quick notes, and said "O.K. man, let's go." "Let's go—I'm comin' in through the graveyard, man."

We walked out and around the side of the auditorium, in front of the college cemetery and up some wobbly iron stairs to a fire exit. Several of the people standing near the door caught a glimpse of Dylan and began to nudge one another; one rather pudgy girl wearing an army surplus raincoat and blue tennis shoes even began primping her hair. Victor put his arm on Dylan's shoulder. Dylan nodded, straightened his shoulders, and walked into the hall to enthusiastic applause. He made no introduc-tions, starting in immediately to play his first song. But something was wrong with the amplifier system, and the music sounded like mosquitos caught in a net of Saran Wrap. Dylan finished the number and made a few sly comments while Victor replaced the microphone and someone from the college played with the amplifier system. Seemingly unfazed, Dylan proceeded, with better audio and the audience now completely with him. A predominantly conservative student body applauded at every derogatory mention of prejudice, injustice, segregation, or nuclear war-fare. Dylan, who had intended to sing only six songs for the first half, was apparently enjoying himself and added two more to the set. At intermission, he got a big hand.

Downstairs during the intermission, Dylan talked a lot, and drank more wine. He only half-jokingly spoke about the speaker system in the hall, about the songs and about the audience. There were a lot of people waiting to see him outside, but he was almost too wound up even to cope with friends who were already in the room with him. Victor said that except for the speaker system he thought it was going pretty well, although he was still worried about the crowds that would gather after the concert. "You'll see, man," he said, "you'll see."

For the second half of the concert, almost seventy-five people had left their seats and were sitting on the floor close to the stage. A path had to be cleared before Dylan could get on, but passing by one girl, he reached out, said "Hi" and touched her hair with his hand, which caused the people around her to laugh and applaud, while the girl herself simply—but audibly—sighed. For the rest of the concert she stared straight at Dylan, who by now was a little drunk, although he was performing as well as in the first half. After his last song Victor and I met him just as he got off the stage, and led him to the exit. He had gotten a standing ovation, and while we were persuading him to do an encore he kept repeating "They don't have to do *that*," nodding at the audience. He had unfastened the leather shoulder strap of his guitar, and the pudgy girl in the surplus raincoat rushed up to him, asking for "All I Really Want to Do," fumbling with the leather strap attempting to help him refasten it. He grinned at her, and went back on stage for the encore. Victor sent Bob and John downstairs to guard the entrance to the dressing room, he posted himself by the exit to block the pudgy girl and her companions and detailed me to get Dylan off the stage and through the crowd in the front row. Dylan finished up and, smiling, walked down into the audience and through the exit, Victor and I on either side.

We got him inside just before the crowd. Dylan was happy about the way the concert had gone, poured himself several congratulatory cups of wine and began to wonder about getting out of the building through the crowd and into the car which was waiting outside. He decided finally to wait twenty minutes or so, then make a break for it. At the outside door, Bob, wearing a pair of dark leather gloves which he kept rubbing together and up and down his thighs, was talking to a tall blonde man who kept repeating "Listen, Bobby invited me afterwards to . . ." He bent down and began to whisper in Bob's ear. Bob listened for a moment and pushed the man back.

"Listen, man, I don't want to hear about it. Go away."

"But, Bobby . . ."

"Listen, just go away, man. I don't want to talk about it. I don't want to hear about it. Just go away." He turned his attentions to the crowd which now must have been a hundred strong.

Victor meantime was packing the remainder of Dylan's clothes and equipment, and sticking the one surviving bottle of wine into his pocket. He looked tired; Dylan looked exhausted and drunk. "O.K.," Dylan almost sighed, "lead the way." We walked out of the classroom and towards the main door. When the crowd outside saw Dylan coming, many of them came forward to press their faces against the glass. As soon as I opened the door, Dylan stepped out and they all pressed forward.

"Bobby!"

"Hiya, Bobby!"

"Hey Bobby!"

"Hiya, Mr. Dylan."

"Hello, kid," Dylan said to a girl who was squirming against the door, "long time no see." In reply, she giggled and coughed. Walking through the crowd Dylan waved and shook a few hands. Another girl followed him all the way to the car, "I'm Billie Dylan's roommate from State," she announced, "Bob, you remember." Dylan said that he didn't remember. "Billie Dylan. From," the girl said, almost following him into the car. "Oh yeah," Dylan said, not very convincingly, "how is she?" "Great," the girl replied, "she says to tell you hello." "Fantastic," Dylan said. He slammed the door and we began to pull away. "Hey, Bobby, wait a minute," someone said, running frantically along side the car, "wait a minute." Bob looked around, rubbing his black leather gloves together. It was the blonde man whom he had pushed away a little earlier at the door. "Keep goin'" he said, "Keep drivin."

The morning was cold. In the frost and dust covering Banks's car, which had been parked outside Dylan's improvised dressing room the night before, we could still see outlines of little inscriptions written by some of the girls all over the hood, roof and windows: "Bobby," "Bobby," "Bobby Dylan," "Dylan," "Dylan," "Bobby Dylan." No one spoke much during the trip to the airport. Victor looked still asleep, and Dylan a little fuzzy.

About ten miles out of Mt. Vernon he folded his arms across his chest and, slinking down as much as he could in the Volkswagen, leaned his head back over the top of the seat and closed his eyes. All of a sudden, asleep, in that early morning, he looked very young.

Victor checked his baggage at the airport and we went for something to eat. Dylan, who looked a little more refreshed, spoke easily and with humor about his upcoming concerts. "Tomorrow we're goin' to Princeton, and Sunday to Bangor, Maine. Man, I don't know what's in Bangor, Maine. It's not a school or anything." I told him I didn't think the Chamber of Commerce had booked him, and he threw back his head and laughed for a long time. "Yeah, the Chamber of Commerce—wow!" For the first time since we had met him the day before he seemed completely at ease. "I'm gonna do these concerts out on the Coast, and Joanie's gonna be with me. Pretty soon we're gonna get billed together." He smiled that friendly vulnerable smile of his, but this time without a trace of nervousness. "I'm gonna be out there for a while."

The flight to New York was announced, and Banks and I walked them to the gate. The businessmen were staring again. When one of them turned to his companion nudging him and pointing at us, Dylan looked over his shoulder and waved. "It's alright man," he said, "I make more money than you do."

Banks thanked them both, and apologized for any embarrassing incidents that might have happened the previous evening. "That's O.K. man," Dylan replied, "wasn't nothin'."

"Look," Victor said, "we'll see you again, huh? If there's a concert somewhere, come back and see us."

We said we would if we could get past the crowds we hadn't thought would be around.

"Well, so long," Dylan said. "And thanks."

Banks and I watched them get on the plane. On their way, they passed two T.W.A. groundcrewmen wearing coveralls and white crashhelmets who turned and stared. One of them came up to us. "Hey, wasn't that that folksinger?"

We said that it was.

"Which one? The short one?"

Banks nodded.

"What's his name?" he asked.

"Bob Dylan," I said.

"Hey," he said, turning to his friend, "That was Bob Dylan."

DYLAN ON

Whether He Has an Important Philosophy to Share with the World

"Are you kidding? The world don't need me. Christ, I'm only five feet ten. [*Actually, five feet seven. —Ed.*] The world could get along fine without me. Don'cha know, everybody dies. It don't matter how important you think you are. Look at Shakespeare, Napoleon, Edgar Allan Poe, for that matter. They are all dead, right?"

—from pseudo-interview with J. R. Godard,
published in the *Village Voice* (New York), March 3, 1965

BOB DYLAN AS BOB DYLAN

Paul Jay Robbins | March and September 1965 (interview) | September 10, 17, and 24, 1965 | *Los Angeles Free Press*

The *Los Angeles Free Press*'s Paul Jay Robbins first met Dylan at a Columbia Records party on March 26, 1965, less than five months after the Kenyon College appearance. Just four days earlier, the label had issued his fifth album, *Bringing It All Back Home*—his first Top Ten hit in the United States and his second chart-topper in the United Kingdom—which contains "Mr. Tambourine Man," "Maggie's Farm," and "It's All Over Now, Baby Blue."

That would be plenty for most artists in any one year. As Robbins notes in his introduction, however, Dylan had already prepared album number six, the monumental *Highway 61 Revisited*, which would follow *Bringing It All Back Home* a mere five months later.

In part one of his piece, Robbins draws a vivid picture of how Dylan acts and talks at this stage of his career; the journalist also witnesses an early press party and press conference and a concert appearance with the Band. Then, in parts two and three, he offers the transcript of his extended and unusually straightforward March 27, 1965, conversation with the artist. —Ed.

Part One

In Dylan's sixth album, which will shortly be out, he sings a major poem called "Desolation Road." [*"Actually, "Desolation Row." Highway 61 Revisited, which contains it, in fact appeared less than two weeks before this article. —Ed.*] One stanza has to do with Ezra Pound and T.S. Eliot sitting in the captain's tower arguing for power while calypso dancers

41

leap on the deck and fishermen hold flowers. The image is relevant to any interview with Dylan, for it illustrates his basic attitude towards showplace words. It has to do with experiencing life, partaking of its unending facets and hangups and wonders instead of dryly discussing it. A typical Dylan interview is more an Absurdist Happening than a factfinding dialog. He presents himself in shatterproof totality—usually a somewhat bugged and bored mode of it—and lets components fall out as the interviewer pokes at it. He's not taciturn, he's simply aware of his absurd situation and the desperate clamor of folks who want to know how many times he rubs his eyes upon awakening and why.

I first met him at a promotion party thrown by Columbia Records in a highly selfconscious and slick hotel bar. The people were incompatible with anything Dylan stands for and I ate and drank free goodies and finally saw Dylan enter. He didn't so much enter the party as forcibly indulge himself in it. My fingers were sticky with free barbecued rib sauce as I shook his hand and he was a warm and halated [sic] human being. We talked a while (during which we composed a brief interview which was later run in the Free Press) and made a date to meet the next afternoon for a taped interview.

That second interview worked beautifully. Dylan became a purely natural person, candid and friendly—with indigenous exceptions. He is quite a nervous cat; his knee bobs like a yoyo, he darts at each sound, listens to all conversations at once, seems to enjoy doing more than two things at once. He is smallboned and very finely featured; he resembles an MGM idea of a Romantic Poet doomed by consumption. He speaks in a rambling chant of softspoken clip phrases. With brows raised and lids lowered, he leans forward into your words.

The purpose of the dialog was to get Bob Dylan down as Bob Dylan. I believe it was also his purpose. It is far too easy to suggest listening to his records to know where he is because much cannot come through songs. And the part which remains hidden is just that part, by definition, which his public wants to see.

Unwillingly, Dylan has been shoved or extruded onto the podium for all Hipdom. Being a person aware of his fallibility and fragmentary per-plexity—as well as of his freedom and the significance of individuality—it is hard for him to speak with certainty and weight. He constantly qualifies and insists on his ephemeral subjectivity, constantly underscores his right to privacy and unimportance. In doing so, he communicates a certain insecurity about his desired position in the fuzzy texture of his prefabricated and other-imaged life.

The taped interview lasted about 1½ hours. We stayed in his room and then went to the Santa Monica Civic Auditorium with him. After the concert, we went to a party given by his agent. All during this time I became exposed to the incessant gluts of hungry folk who beset and nibble at him. It must be rare for him to shut the bathroom door without a voice cutting through, "Hey, why are you sitting there like that? What does it mean?"

He returned here for a Hollywood Bowl engagement Sept. 3. The audience for this concert, as a whole, were not too receptive to the New Amplified Dylan. The first half was done with Dylan and his acoustic guitar laying out old songs and new in a clear, almost analytic voice. The second half found him backed by a group of musicians playing a tasty and unique brand of rock & roll. The lead guitarist, Robbie Robertson, was highly competent and inventive, but the group lacked the unity of a highly polished performance. This may be for the better; this group (and Dylan plans to keep working with them) carried a sparkling randomness in its actions and Dylan moves in it with comfort and joy.

I've heard Dylan playing electric guitar in private goofings off and asked why he didn't play lead guitar . . . he's certainly good enough. "Robbie does things I can't do which the songs need done."

Onstage, Dylan carries himself and his voice with an aloofness, a careful detachment from both his material and his audience. Is he interested in actively communicating his songs, in getting through to his audience? "I don't have to prove anything to anyone. Those people who dig me know where I'm at—I don't have to come on to them; I'm not a ballroom singer." What about those in the audience who aren't grooving with him? "I'm not interested in them."

His songs for this concert were a dappled barrel of easily accessible lyrics together with highly subtle and allusive strings of chanted jewels. The newer songs go quite deep in meanings and methods. Why the change towards this delicate structure of complexity? "My mistake was keeping my earlier stuff simple."

The above quotes are from a press conference held the day after the concert. The personnel for this tennis set were various representatives of major news periodicals and teenage fan mags. Dylan clearly wanted no part of the glib questioning—never does. He had been cajoled into presenting himself for dissection. After a long exchange of basically meaningless trivia, I asked Dylan if it were true that nothing of any consequence happened at these things, that it was all redundant and silly. He agreed. "Interviewers will write my scene and words from their own bags anyway, no matter what I say. I accept writers and photographers. I don't think it's necessary at all, but it happens anyway. I am really uninvolved."

The interview tolled leadenly on.

Q. Do you feel you're using more "urban imagery" than in the past? That your lyrics are becoming more sophisticated?

A. Well, I watch too much TV, I guess.

Q. What about Donovan?

A. I like everybody, I don't want to be petty.

Q. A word for your fans?

A. The lamppost leans on folded arms . . .

Q. What do you think of the New Bob Dylan?

A. What's your name?

Q. Dave Mopert.

A. Okay, what would you think if someone asked you what you think of the new Dave Mopert? What new Dave Mopert?

Q. Is Joan Baez still relevant?

A. She's one of the most relevant people I know.

Q. Do you feel you're living a real life?

A. What's that mean? If I'm not living it, who is? And if I'm not, whose life am I leading? Who's living mine? What's that?

Q. Do you feel you belong to your public now?

A. No. I don't have any responsibility to the people who are hung up on me. I'm only responsible for what I create—I didn't create them.

Q. Has your success infringed on your personal life?

A. What personal life? Hey, I have none.

This sort of ping-pong continued about an hour before the interviewers left. Many hostilities and befuddlements had been formed and blurted and I'm sure he'll be just as misquoted and little understood in the reports of this press set as in all the others.

After seeing this typical interview, I realized how lucky I had been to speak with him so easily and so openly. I also realized how essentially meaningless this transcription must be. He lays out many attitudes and concepts which, in their precise articulation and directness, will strike the public as shocking and unique. However, his larger meaning is to be found in his material. To know precisely what he thinks of Donovan or what year he began writing songs is extraneous. To make him come out for "No War Toys" or anti-police brutality is redundancy. Just listen to his songs.

However, we must shine flashlights down our hero's mouths and count their cavities. With that rider, what follows is probably the most meaningfully candid interview Dylan has ever indulged in. I only hope it will give you the deep understanding of and respect for Dylan which I gained.

Part Two

The introduction to this transcribed dialog was printed in last week's Free Press. The major point in Part One was that Dylan's privacy and complexity have been the targets for an all-out assault by reporters, photographers, fans, friends and enemies. His reaction to this attempt to reduce him to a known and predictable quantity comprises his public image as you probably know it—either from hearsay or reportage (both being equal and minus).

This interview is something of a rarity in that it is one of the very few—if any—in which Dylan volunteered to talk to and with his interviewer in a manner honest and meaningful. However, I do not claim to have caught Dylan in it—I have only caught a segment of his shadow on that day . . .

Robbins: I don't know whether to do a serious interview or carry on in that Absurdist way we talked last night.

Dylan: It'll be the same thing anyway, man.

R: Yeah. Okay . . . If you are a poet and write words arranged in some sort of rhythm, why do you switch at some point and write lyrics in a song so that you're singing the words as part of a Gestalt presence?

D: Well, I can't define that word poetry. I wouldn't even attempt it. At one time I thought that Robert Frost was poetry; other times I thought that Allen Ginsberg was poetry, sometimes I thought Francois Villon was poetry—but poetry isn't really confined to the printed page. Hey, then again, I don't believe in saying, "Look at that girl walking; isn't that poetry?" I'm not going to get insane about it. The lyrics to the songs . . . just so happens that it might be a little stranger than in most songs. I find it easy to write songs. I been writing songs for a long long time and the words to the songs aren't written out for just the paper; they're written so you can read it, you dig. If you take whatever there is to the song away—the beat, the melody—I could still recite it. I see nothing wrong with songs you can't do that with, either—songs that, if you took the beat and melody away, they wouldn't stand up. Because they're not supposed to do that, you know. Songs are songs . . . I don't believe in expecting too much out of any one thing.

R: Whatever happened to Blind Boy Grunt? (a name Dylan recorded a couple of his first folk sides under)

D: I was doing that four years ago. Now there's a lot of people writing songs on protest subjects. But it's taken some kind of a weird step. Hey, I'd rather listen to Jimmy Reed or Howlin' Wolf, man, or the Beatles, or Francois Hardy, than I would listen to any protest song singers—although

I haven't heard all the protest song singers there are. But the ones I've heard—there's this very emptiness which is like a song written "Let's hold hands and everything will be grand." I see no more to it than that. Just because someone mentions the word "bomb," I'm not going to go "Aaiee!," man, and start clapping.

R: It's that they just don't work anymore?

D: It's not that it don't work, it's that there are a lot of people afraid of the bomb, right. But there are a lot of other people who're afraid to be seen carrying a MODERN SCREEN magazine down the street, you know. Lot of people afraid to admit that they like Marlon Brando movies. . . . Hey, it's not that they don't work anymore but have you ever thought of a place where they DO work? What exactly DOES work?

R: They give a groovy feeling to the people who sing them, I guess that's about it. But what does work is the attitude, not the song. And there's just another attitude called for.

D: Yeah, but you have to be very hip to the fact about that attitude—you have to be hip to communication. Sure, you can make all sorts of protest songs and put them on a Folkways record. But who hears them? The people that do hear them are going to be agreeing with you anyway. You aren't going to get somebody to hear it who doesn't dig it. People don't listen to things they don't dig. If you can find a cat that can actually say, "Okay. I'm a changed man because I heard this one thing—or I just saw this one thing . . ." Hey, it don't necessarily happen that way all the time. It happens with a collage of experience which somebody can actually know by instinct what's right and wrong for him to do. Where he doesn't actually have to feel guilty about anything. A lot of people can act out of guilt. They act because they think somebody's looking at them. No matter what it is. There's people who do anything because of guilt . . .

R: And you don't want to be guilty?

D: It's not that I'm NOT guilty. I'm not any more guilty than you are. Like, I don't consider any elder generation guilty. I mean, they're having these trials at Nuremberg, right? Look at that and you can place it out. Cats say, "I had to kill all those people, or else they'd kill me." Now, who's to try them for that? Who are these judges that have got the right to try a cat? How do you know they wouldn't do the same thing?

R: This may be a side trip, but this thing about the Statute of Limitations running out and everybody wants to extend it? You remember, in ANIMAL FARM, what they wrote on the wall? "All animals are equal." But later they added, ". . . but some are more equal than others." It's the same thing in reverse. That some are less equal than others. Like Nazis are REALLY criminals, so let's REALLY get them; change any law just to nail them all.

D: Yeah, all that shit runs in the same category. Nobody digs revenge, right? But you have these cats from Israel who, after TWENTY years, are still trying to catch these cats, who're OLD cats, man, who have escaped. God knows they aren't going to go anywhere, they're not going to do anything. And you have these cats from Israel running around catching them. Spending twenty years out of their lives. You take that job away from them and they're no more or less than a baker. He's got his whole life tied up in one thing. It's a one-thought thing, without anything between: "That's what it is, and I'm going to get it." Anything between gets wiped all away. I can't make that, but I can't really put it down. Hey: I can't put ANYTHING down, because I don't have to be around any of it. I don't have to put people down which I don't like, because I don't have to be around any of those people. Of course, there is the giant great contradiction of What Do You Do. Hey, I don't know what you do, but all I can do is cast aside all the things NOT to do. I don't know where it's at, all I know is where it's NOT at. And as long as I know that, I don't really have to know, myself, where's it at. Everybody knows where it's at once in a while, but nobody can walk around all the time in a complete Utopia. Dig poetry. You were asking about poetry? Man, poetry is just bullshit, you know? I don't know about other countries, but in this one it's a total massacre. It's not poetry at all. People don't read poetry in this country—if they do, it offends them; they don't dig it. You go to school, man, and what kind of poetry do you read? You read Robert Frost's "The Two Roads," you read T.S. Eliot—you read all that bullshit and that's just bad, man, it's not good. It's not anything hard, it's all softboiled egg shit. And then, on top of it, they throw Shakespeare at some kid who can't read Shakespeare. Hey, everybody hates Shakespeare in high school, right? Who digs reading HAMLET, man? All they give you is IVANHOE, SILAS MARNER, TALE OF TWO CITIES—and they keep you away from things which you should do. You shouldn't even be there in school. You should find out from people. Dig; that's where it all starts. In the beginning—like from 13 to 19—that's where all the corruption is. These people all just overlook it, right? There's more V.D. in people 13 to 19 than there is in any other group, but they ain't going to ever say so. They're never going to go into the schools and give shots. But that's where it's at. It's all a hype, man.

R: Relating all this: if you put it in lyrics instead of poetry, you have a higher chance of hitting the people who have to be hit?

D: I do, but I don't expect anything from it, you dig? All I can do is be me—whoever that is—for those people that I do play to, and not come on with them, tell them I'm something that I'm not. I'm not going to tell them I'm the Great Cause Fighter or the Great Lover or Great Boy Genius or whatever. Because I'm not, man. Why mislead them? That's all just Madison Avenue, that's just selling. Sure Madison Avenue is selling me, but it's not really selling ME, 'cause I was hip to it before I got there.

R: Which brings up another thing. All the folk magazines and many folk people are very down on you. Do they put you down because you changed or—

D: It's that I'm successful and they want to be successful, man. It's jealousy. Hey, anybody with any kind of knowledge at all would know what I'm doing, would know by instinct what's happening here. Somebody who doesn't know that is still hung up with success and failure and good and bad . . . maybe he doesn't have a chick all the time . . . stuff like that. But I can't use comments, man. I don't take nothing like that seriously. If somebody praises me and says "How groovy you are!" it doesn't mean anything to me because I can usually sense where that person's at. And it's no compliment if someone who's a total freak comes up and says, "How groovy you are!" And it's the same if they don't dig me. Other kinds of people don't HAVE to say anything because, when you come down to it, it's all what's happening in the moment which counts. Who cares about tomorrow and yesterday? People don't live there; they live now.

R: I've a theory which I've been picking up and shaking out every so often. When I spoke with the Byrds, they were saying the same thing that I'm saying—a lot of people are saying it—you're talking it. It's why we have a new so-called rock & roll sound emerging, it's a synthesis of all things, a—

D: It's further than that, man. People know nowadays more than before. They've had so much to look at by now and know the bullshit of everything. People now don't even care about going to jail. So what? You're still with yourself as much as if you're out on the streets. There's still those who don't care about anything, but I got to think that anybody who doesn't hurt anybody, you can't put that person down, you dig, if that person's happy doing that.

R: But what if they freeze themselves into apathy? What if they don't care about anything at all anymore?

D: Whose problem is that? Your problem or theirs? No, it's not that, it's that nobody can learn by somebody else showing them or teaching them. People got to learn by themselves, going through something which relates. Sure, you say how do you make somebody know something . . . People know it by themselves; they can go through some kind of scene with other people and themselves which somehow will come out somewhere and it'll grind into them and be them. And all that just comes out of them somehow when they're faced up to the next thing.

R: It's like taking in until the time comes to put out, right. But people who don't care don't put anything out. It's a whole frozen thing where nothing's happening anywhere; it's just the maintenance of status quo, of existing circumstances, whatever they are . . .

D: People who don't care? Are you talking about gas station attendants or a Zen doctor, man? Hey, there's a lot of people who don't care; a lot don't care for different reasons. A lot care about some things and not about others, and some who don't care about anything. It's not up to me to make them care about something—it's up to me not to let them bring me down and not to bring them down. It's like the whole world has a little thing: it's being taught that when you get up in the morning, you have to go out and bring somebody down. You walk down the street and, unless you've brought somebody down, don't come home today, right? It's a circus world.

R: So who is it that you write and sing for?

D: Not writing and singing for anybody, to tell you the truth. Hey, really, I don't care what people say. I don't care what they make me seem to be or what they tell other people I am. If I did care about that, I'd tell you; I really have no concern with it. I don't even come in contact with these people. Hey, I dig people, though. But if somebody's going to come up to me and ask me some questions which have been on his mind for such a long time, all I can think of is, "Wow, man, what else can be in that person's head besides me? Am I that important, man, to be in a person's head for such a long time he's got to know this answer?" I mean, can that really straighten him out—if I tell him something? Hey, come on . . .

Here we'll break the interview and call it Part Two. The last section of this—which discusses Dylan's attitude about rock & roll, money and fame, Civil Rights, education, his new book, and a host of popular favorites—will be in next week's Free Press.

Part Three: Conclusion

Dylan, eyebrows up and lids down, spoke in intense staccato. He'd throw words out in rhythmic phrases, testing the articulation of his thought by speaking it. He would smoke distractedly, bob his knee as if dandling a kid, and diddle with his fingers . . . continually nervous. We'd been introduced by mutual friends and the talk had been straight and communicative for an hour or so. His nervousness wasn't irritation, it was restlessness. Dylan is a quester, a grower, a doer; and growth is a nonsleep engagement.

Off and on, during breaks and lulls, he'd negotiate a few licks and changes on his guitar; he had a concert that night. The discussion continued.

Robbins: A local disc jockey, Les Claypool, went through a whole thing on you one night, just couldn't get out of it. For maybe 45 minutes, he'd play a side of yours and then an ethnic side in which it was demonstrated that both melodies were the same. After each pair he'd say, "Well, you see what's happening . . . This kid is taking other people's melodies; he's not all that original. Not only that," he'd say, "but his songs are totally depressing and have no hope."

Dylan: Who's Les Claypool?

R: A folk jockey out here who has a long talk show on Saturday nights and an hour one each night, during which he plays highly ethnic sides.

D: He played THOSE songs? He didn't play something hopeful?

R: No, he was loading it to make his point. Anyway, it brings up an expected question: why do you use melodies that are already written?

D: I used to do that, when I was more or less in folk. I knew the melodies, they were already there. I did it because I liked the melodies. I did it when I really wasn't that popular and the songs weren't reaching that many people, and everybody around dug it. Man, I never introduced a song, "Here's the song I've stole the melody from, someplace." For me it wasn't that important; still isn't that important. I don't care about the melodies, man; the melodies are all traditional anyway. And if anybody wants to pick that out and say, "That's Bob Dylan," that's their thing, not mine. I mean, if they want to think that. Anybody with any sense at all, man; he says that I haven't any hope . . . Hey, I got FAITH. I know that there are people who're going to know that's total bullshit. I know the cat is just up tight. He hasn't really gotten into a good day and he has to pick on something. Groovy. He has to pick on me? Hey, if he can't pick on me, he picks on someone else. It don't matter. He doesn't step on me, 'cause I don't care. He's not coming up to me on the street and stepping on my head, man. Hey, I've only done that with very few of my songs, anyway. And then when I don't do it, everybody says they're rock & roll melodies. You can't satisfy the people—you just can't. You got to know, man: they just don't care about it.

R: Why is rock & roll coming in and folk music going out?

D: Folk music destroyed itself. Nobody destroyed it. Folk music is still here, it's always going to be here, if you want to dig it. It's not that it's going in or out. It's all the soft mellow shit, man, that's just being replaced by something that people know is there now. Hey, you must've heard rock & roll long before the Beatles, you must've discarded rock & roll around 1960. I did that in 1957. I couldn't make it as a rock & roll singer then. There were too many groups. I used to play piano. I made some records, too.

R: Okay. You've got a lot of bread now. And your way of life isn't like it was four or five years ago. It's much grander. Does that kind of thing tend to throw you off?

D: Well, the transition never came from working at it. I left where I'm from because there's nothing there. I come from Minnesota; there was nothing there. I'm not going to fake it and say I went out to see the world or I went out to conquer the world. Hey, when I left there, man, I knew one thing: I had to get out of there and not come back. Just from my senses I knew there was something more than Walt Disney movies. I was never turned on or off by money. I never considered the fact of money as anything really important. I could always play the guitar, you dig, and make friends—or fake friends. A lot of other people do other things and get to eat and sleep that way. Lot of people do a lot of things just to get around. You can find cats who get very scared, right? Who get married and settle down. But, after somebody's got something and sees it all around him, so he doesn't have to sleep out in the cold at night, that's all. The only thing is he don't die. But is he happy? There's nowhere to go. Okay, so I get the money, right? First of all, I had to move out of New York. Because everybody was coming down to see me—people which I didn't really dig. People coming in from weird-ass places. And I would think, for some reason, that I had to give them someplace to stay and all that. I found myself not really being by myself but just staying out of things I wanted to go to because people I knew would go there.

R: Do you find friends—real friends—are they recognizable anymore?

D: Oh, sure, man, I can tell somebody I dig right away. I don't have to go through anything with anybody. I'm just lucky that way.

R: Back to Protest Songs. The IWW's work is over now and the unions are pretty well established. What about the civil rights movement?

D: Well, it's okay now. It's proper. It's not "Commie" anymore. Harper's Bazaar can feature it, you can find it on the cover of Life. But when you get beneath it, like anything, you find there's bullshit tied up in it. The Negro Civil Rights Movement is proper now, but there's more to it than what's in Harper's Bazaar. There's more to it than picketing in Selma, right? There's people living in utter poverty in New York. And then again, you have this big Right to Vote. Which is groovy. You want all these Negroes to vote? Okay. I can't go over the boat and shout, "Hallelujah!" only because they want to vote. Who're they going to vote for? Just politicians; same as the white people put in their politicians. Anybody that wants to get into politics is a little greaky anyway. Hey, they're just going to vote, that's all they're going to do. I hate to say it like that, make it sound hard, but it's going to boil down to that.

R: What about the drive for education?

D: Education? They're going to school and learn about all the things the white private schools teach. The catechism, the whole thing. What're they going to learn? What's this education? Hey, the cat's much better off never going to school. The only thing against him is he can't be a doctor or a judge. Or he can't get a good job with the salesman's company. But that's the only thing wrong. If you want to say it's good that he gets an education and goes out and gets a job like that, groovy. I'm not going to do it.

R: In other words, the formal intake of factual knowledge—

D: Hey, I have no respect for factual knowledge, man. I don't care what anybody knows, I don't care if somebody's a living encyclopedia. Does that make him nice to talk to? Who cares if Washington was even the first president of the United States? You think anybody has actually ever been helped with this kind of knowledge?

R: Maybe through a test. Well, what's the answer?

D: There aren't any answers, man. Or any questions. You must read my book . . . there's a little part in there about that. It evolves into a thing where it mentions words like "Answer." I couldn't possibly rattle off the words I use for these, because you'd have to read the whole book to see why I use these specific words for Question and Answer. We'll have another interview after you read the book.

R: Yeah, you have a book coming out. What about it? The title?

D: Tentatively, "Bob Dylan Off the Record." But they tell me there's already books out with that "off the record" title. The book can't really be titled, that's the kind of book it is. I'm also going to write the reviews for it.

R: Why write a book instead of lyrics?

D: I've written some songs which are kind of far out, a long continuation of verses, stuff like that—but I haven't really gotten into writing a completely free song. Hey, you dig something like cut-ups? I mean, like William Burroughs?

R: Yeah. There's a cat in Paris who published a book with no pagination. The book comes in a box and you throw it in the air and, however it lands, you read it like that.

D: Yeah, that's where it's at. Because that's what it means, anyway. Okay, I wrote the book because there's a lot of stuff in there which I can't possibly sing . . . all the collages. I can't sing it because it gets too long or it goes too far out. I can only do it around a few people who would know. Because the majority of the audience—I don't care where they're from, how hip they are—I think it would just get totally lost. Something that had no rhyme, all cut up, no nothing, except something happening which is words.

R: You wrote the book to say something?

D: Yeah, but certainly not any kind of profound statement. The book don't begin or end.

R: But you had something to say. And you wanted to say it to somebody.

D: Yeah, I said it to myself. Only I'm lucky, because I could put it into a book. Now somebody else is going to be allowed to see what I said to myself.

R: You have four albums out now, with a fifth any day. Are these albums sequential in the way that you composed and sung them?

D: Yeah, I've got about two or three albums that I've never recorded, which are lost songs. They're old songs; I'll never record them. Some very groovy songs. Some old songs which I've written and sung maybe once in a concert and nobody else ever heard them. There are a lot of songs which could fill in between the records. It was growing from the first record to the second, then a head change on the third. And the fourth. The fifth I can't even tell you about.

R: So if I started with Album One, Side One, Band One, I could truthfully watch Bob Dylan grow?

D: No, you could watch Bob Dylan laughing to himself. Or you could see Bob Dylan going through changes. That's really the most.

R: What do you think of the Byrds? Do you think they're doing something different?

D: Yeah, they could. They're doing something really new now. It's like a danceable Bach sound. Like "Bells of Rhymney." They're cutting across all kinds of barriers which most people who sing aren't even hip to. They know it all. If they don't close their minds, they'll come up with something pretty fantastic.

The interview part was over. I stayed in the hotel room until we all left for the concert at which point he asked me if I wanted his guitar case. Since my cardboard case had long since fallen in, I took his. After the concert, we stopped back in his room before going to a party at his agents'. There he gave me two or three bottles of wine. It wasn't Bob Dylan handing out souvenirs or some sort of useable autograph, it was merely that he had something which he didn't necessarily need which I could use. It was a friendly gesture, an easy act done by someone who doesn't get much chance to be friendly with anyone except old friends.

When we left the concert, he insisted someone was following us and I felt this touch of paranoia to be a bit curious—until we actually discovered a car definitely following. There were also the groovy open friendly faces at the stage entrance when we went into the concert hall—hippies who wanted to get in free. Dylan said no and it also struck me as curious—until I realized what a continual Give is demanded of him, even by those who should know enough to make their own scenes.

Next time you hear a Dylan put-down story, remember that he's just as human as human beings are—and it's his very humanity which makes him the power he is.

DYLAN ON

How His Songwriting Was Changing

"The big difference is that the songs I was writing last year, songs like 'Ballad in Plain D,' they were what I call one-dimensional songs, but my new songs I'm trying to make more three-dimensional, you know, there's more symbolism, they're written on more than one level. . . . I wrote 'Hard Rain' while I was on the streets, I guess that was the first three-dimensional song I wrote. It took me about—oh, about two days."

—from interview with Jenny De Yong and Peter Roche, *Darts* (UK), May 1965

DYLAN ON

News Magazines

"If I want to find out anything, I'm not going to read *Time* magazine, I'm not gonna read *Newsweek*. I'm not gonna read any of these magazines. I mean, 'cause they just got too much to lose by printing the truth. You know that . . . They'd just go off the stands in a day if they printed really the truth . . . There's no ideas in *Time* magazine."

—from interview with Horace Judson of *Time* (US), London, May 9, 1965

DYLAN ON

Disc Weekly

"Listen, I couldn't care less what your paper writes about me. Your paper can write anything, don't you realize? The people that listen to me don't read your paper, you know, to listen to me. I'm not going to be known from your paper . . . You're using me. I'm an object to you. I went through this before in the United States, you know. There's nothing personal. I've nothing against you at all. I just don't want to be bothered with your paper, that's all. I just don't want to be a part of it. Why should I have to go along with something just so that somebody else can eat? Why don't you just say that my name is Kissenovitch? You know, and I came from Acapulco, Mexico. That my father was an escaped thief from South Africa. OK. You can say anything you want to say."

—from interview with Laurie Henshaw, *Disc Weekly* (UK), May 22, 1965

INTERVIEW

Nora Ephron and Susan Edmiston | August 1965 (interview) | Publication Unknown

As Paul Jay Robbins reported in part one of his *Los Angeles Free Press* series, a Hollywood Bowl audience in September 1965 had not been "too receptive to the New Amplified Dylan." And that wasn't the first time that plugging in had cost him some cheers: listeners also booed and cried "sellout!" when Dylan mingled folk with rock at the Newport Folk Festival in Rhode Island in July and at Forest Hills Tennis Stadium in New York that August.

Any rebellion was short-lived, however; in fact, it was during the latter half of 1965 that Dylan solidified his hold on a mass audience. At the end of August, he issued *Highway 61 Revisited*, which peaked in *Billboard* at number three and became his second bona fide hit album, thanks to rock landmarks such as the title cut, the lyrically stunning "Desolation Row," and "Like a Rolling Stone." The latter came out as a 45 in July and reached number two on the charts, becoming Dylan's first hit single; "Positively 4th Street" would follow in September and make it to number seven.

The month Columbia Records released *Highway 61 Revisited*, *New York Post* "Teen Talk" columnist Susan Edmiston got an appointment to interview Dylan. Nora Ephron—who would later break the news of the singer's November 1965 marriage to Sara Lownds and who would much later become a famous Hollywood screenwriter—was then a reporter at the *Post* and asked to come along.

"We both wrote pieces based on the interview," Edmiston told me. "I did a column and she did a large feature. Afterward, I took both of our notes and typed them up as an interview.

"I don't know how word of it got around," Edmiston continued, "but after I'd already agreed to the first publication, Jann Wenner [the editor and publisher] at *Rolling Stone* called me and tried to get me to give it to him instead. He offered to take me out to dinner, as if that was an incentive. I declined."

Today, Edmiston can't recall where this widely reprinted interview first appeared. Two sources cite a fanzine called *Positively Tie Dream* as the place of initial publication, but I've been unable to independently confirm that.

At any rate, you can see why Wenner would want the piece. Ephron and Edmiston hit Dylan with unusual questions, ranging from "Do you see the world as chaos?" to "Where did you get that shirt?" His answers suggest self-confidence, and a head full of ideas. —Ed.

This interview took place in late summer of 1965 in the office of Dylan's manager, Albert Grossman. Dylan had just been booed in the historic Forest Hills concert where he abandoned folk purity to the use of electric accompaniment. He was wearing a red-and-navy op-art shirt, a navy blazer, and pointy high-heeled boots. His face, so sharp and harsh when translated through media, was then infinitely soft and delicate. His hair was not bushy or electric or Afro; it was fine-spun soft froth like the foam of a wave. He looked like an underfed angel with a nose from the land of the Chosen People.

Some American folk singers—Carolyn Hester, for example—say that what you're now doing, the new sound, "folk rock," is liberating them.

Did Carolyn say that? You tell her she can come around and see me any time now that she's liberated.

Does labeling, using the term "folk rock," tend to obscure what's happening?

Yes.

It's like "pop gospel." What does the term mean to you?

Yeah, classical gospel could be the next trend. There's country rock, rockabilly. What does it mean to me? Folk rock. I've never even said that word. It has a hard gutter sound. Circusy atmosphere. It's nose-thumbing. Sound like you're looking down on what is . . . fantastic, great music.

The definition most often given of folk rock is the combination of the electronic sound of rock and roll with the meaningful lyrics of folk music. Does that sum up what you're doing?

Yes. It's very complicated to play with electricity. You play with other people. You're dealing with other people. Most people don't like to work with other people, it's more difficult. It takes a lot. Most people who don't like rock & roll can't relate to other people.

You mention the Apollo Theatre in Harlem on one of your album covers. Do you go there often?

Oh, I couldn't go up there. I used to go up there a lot about four years ago. I even wanted to play in one of the amateur nights, but I got scared. Bad things can happen to you. I saw what the audience did to a couple of guys they didn't like. And I would have had a couple things against me right away when I stepped out on the stage.

Who is Mr. Jones in "Ballad of a Thin Man"?

He's a real person. You know him, but not by that name.

Like Mr. Charlie?

No. He's more than Mr. Charlie. He's actually a person. Like I saw him come into the room one night and he looked like a camel. He proceeded to put his eyes in his pocket. I asked this guy who he was and he said, "That's Mr. Jones." Then I asked this cat, "Doesn't he do anything but put his eyes in his pocket?" And he told me, "He puts his nose on the ground." It's all there, it's a true story.

Where did you get that shirt?

California. Do you like it? You should see my others. You can't get clothes like that here. There are a lot of things out there we haven't got here.

Isn't California on the way here?

It's uptight here compared to there. Hollywood I mean. It's not really breathable here. It's like there's air out there. The Sunset Strip can't be compared to anything here, like 42nd Street. The people there look different, they look more like . . . you want to kiss them out there.

Do you spend a lot of time out there?

I don't have much time to spend anywhere. The same thing in England. In England everybody looks very hip East Side. They wear things . . . they don't wear things that bore you. They've got other hang-ups in other directions.

Do you consider yourself primarily a poet?

No. We have our ideas about poets. The word doesn't mean any more than the word "house." There are people who write _po_ems and people who write po_ems_. Other people write _poems_. Everybody who writes poems do you call them a poet? There's a certain kind of rhythm in some kind of way that's visible. You don't necessarily have to write to be a poet. Some people work in gas stations and they're poets. I don't call myself a poet because I don't like the word. I'm a trapeze artist.

What I meant was, do you think your words stand without the music?

They would stand but I don't read them. I'd rather sing them. I write things that aren't songs—I have a book coming out.

What is it?

It's a book of words.

Is it like the back of your albums? It seemed to me that the album copy you write is a lot like the writing of William Burroughs. Some of the accidental sentences—

Cut-ups.

Yes, and some of the imagery and anecdotes. I wondered if you had read anything by him.

I haven't read *Naked Lunch* but I read some of his shorter things in little magazines, foreign magazines. I read one in Rome. I know him. I don't really know him—I just met him once. I think he's a great man.

Burroughs keeps an album, a collection of photographs that illustrate his writing. Do you have anything similar to that?

I do that too. I have photographs of "Gates of Eden" and "It's All Over Now, Baby Blue." I saw them after I wrote the songs. People send me a lot of things and a lot of the things are pictures, so other people must have that idea too. I gotta admit, maybe I wouldn't have chosen them, but I can see what it is about the pictures.

I heard you used to play the piano for Buddy Holly.

No. I used to play the rock & roll piano, but I don't want to say who it was for because the cat will try to get hold of me. I don't want to see the cat. He'll try to reclaim the friendship. I did it a long time ago, when I was seventeen years old. I used to play country piano too.

This was before you became interested in folk music?

Yes. I became interested in folk music because I had to make it somehow. Obviously I'm not a hard-working cat. I played the guitar, that was all I did. I thought it was great music. Certainly I haven't turned my back on it or anything like that. There is—and I'm sure nobody realizes this, all the authorities who write about what it is and what it should be, when they say keep things simple, they should be easily understood—folk music is the only music where it isn't simple. It's never been simple. It's weird, man, full of legend, myth, Bible, and ghosts. I've never written anything hard to understand, not in my head anyway, and nothing as far out as some of the old songs. They were out of sight.

Like what songs?

"Little Brown Dog." "I bought a little brown dog, its face is all gray. Now I'm going to Turkey flying on my bottle." And "Nottemun Town," that's like a herd of ghosts passing through on the way to Tangiers. "Lord Edward," "Barbara Allen," they're full of myth.

And contradictions?

Yeah, contradictions.

And chaos?

Chaos, watermelon, clocks, everything.

You wrote on the back of one album, "I accept chaos but does chaos accept me?"

Chaos is a friend of mine. It's like I accept him, does he accept me?

Do you see the world as chaos?

Truth is chaos. Maybe beauty is chaos.

Poets like Eliot and Yeats—

I haven't read Yeats.

They saw the world as chaos, accepted it as chaos and attempted to bring order from it. Are you trying to do that?

No. It exists and that's all there is to it. It's been here longer than I have. What can I do about it? I don't know what the songs I write are. That's all I do is write songs, right? Write. I collect things too.

Monkey wrenches?

Where did you read about that? Has that been in print? I told this guy out on the coast that I collected monkey wrenches, all sizes and shapes of monkey wrenches, and he didn't believe me. I don't think you believe me either. And I collect the pictures too. Have you talked to Sonny and Cher?

No.

They're a drag. A cat got kicked out of a restaurant and he went home and wrote a song about it. [*A reference to Sonny Bono's solo hit, "Laugh at Me." —Ed.*]

They say your fan mail has radically increased since you switched sounds.

Yeah. I don't have time to read all of it, but I want you to put that I answer half of it. I don't really. A girl does that for me.

Does she save any for you—any particularly interesting letters?

She knows my head. Not the ones that just ask for pictures, there's a file for them. Not the ones that say, I want to make it with you, they go in another file. She saves two kinds. The violently put-down—

The ones that call you a sellout?

Yeah. Sellout, fink, Fascist, Red, everything in the book. I really dig those. And ones from old friends.

Like, "You don't remember me but I was in the fourth grade with you"?

No. I never had any friends then. These are letters from people who knew me in New York five, six years ago. My first fans. Not the people who call themselves my first fans. They came in three years ago, two years ago. They aren't really my first fans.

How do you feel about being booed at your concert at Forest Hills?

I thought it was great, I really did. If I said anything else I'd be a liar.

And at Newport Folk Festival?

That was different. They twisted the sound. They didn't like what I was going to play and they twisted the sound on me before I began.

I hear you are wearing a sellout jacket?

What kind of jacket is a sellout jacket?

Black leather.

I've had black leather jackets since I was five years old. I've been wearing black leather all my life.

I wonder if we could talk about electronic music and what made you decide to use it.

I was doing fine, you know, singing and playing my guitar. It was a sure thing, don't you understand, it was a sure thing. I was getting very bored with that. I couldn't go out and play like that. I was thinking of quitting. Out front it was a sure thing. I knew what the audience was gonna do, how they would react. It was very automatic. Your mind just drifts unless you can find some way to get in there and remain totally there. It's so much of a fight remaining totally there all by yourself. It takes too much. I'm not ready to cut that much out of my life. You can't have nobody around. You can't be bothered with anybody else's world. And I like people. What I'm doing now—it's a whole other thing. We're not playing rock music. It's not a hard sound. These people call it folk rock—if they want to call it that, something that simple, it's good for selling records. As far as it being what it is, I don't know what it is. I can't call it folk rock. It's a whole way of doing things. It has been picked up on, I've heard songs on the radio that have picked it up. I'm not talking about words. It's a certain feeling, and it's been on every single record I've ever made. That has not changed. I know it hasn't changed. As far as what I was totally, before, maybe I was pushing it a little then. I'm not pushing things now. I know it. I know very well how to do it. The problem of how I want to play something—I know it in front. I know what I am going to say, what I'm going to do. I don't have to work it out. The band I work with—they wouldn't be playing with me if they didn't play like I want them to. I have this song, "Queen Jane Approximately"—

Who is Queen Jane?

Queen Jane is a man.

Was there something that made you decide to change sounds? Your trip to England?

I like the sound. I like what I'm doing now. I would have done it before. It wasn't practical to do it before. I spend most of my time writing. I wouldn't have had the time. I had to get where I was going all alone. I don't know what I'm going to do next. I probably will record with strings some time, but it doesn't necessarily change. It's just a different color. And I know it's real. No matter what anybody says. They can boo till the end of time. I know that the music is real, more real than the boos.

How do you work?

Most of the time I work at night. I don't really like to think of it as work. I don't know how important it is. It's not important to the average cat who works eight hours a day. What does he care? The world can get along very well without it. I'm hip to that.

Sure, but the world can get along without any number of things.

I'll give you a comparison. Rudy Vallee. Now that was a lie, that was a downright lie. Rudy Vallee being popular. What kind of people could have dug him? You know, your grandmothers and mothers. But what kind of people were they? He was so sexless. If you want to find out about those times and you listen to his music you're not going to find out anything about the times. His music was a pipedream. All escapes. There are no more escapes. If you want to find out anything that's happening now, you have to listen to the music. I don't mean the words, although "Eve of Destruction" will tell you something about it. The words are not really gonna tell it, not really. You gotta listen to the Staples Singers, Smokey and the Miracles, Martha and the Vandellas. That's scary to a lot of people. It's sex that's involved. It's not hidden. It's real. You can overdo it. It's not only sex, it's a whole beautiful feeling.

But Negro rhythm and blues has been around underground for at least twelve years. What brought it out now?

The English did that. They brought it out. They hipped everybody. You read an interview asking who the Beatles' favorite singer was and they say Chuck Berry. You never used to hear Chuck Berry records on the radio, hard blues. The English did that. England is great and beautiful, though in other ways kinda messy. Though not outside London.

In what way messy?

There's a snobbishness. What you see people doing to other people. It's not only class. It's not that simple. It's a kind of Queen kind of thing. Some people are royalty and some are not. Here, man, somebody don't like you he tells you. There it's very tight, tight kinds of expressions, their whole tone of speaking changes. It's an everyday kind of thing. But the kids are a whole other thing. Great. They're just more free. I hope you don't think I take this too seriously—I just have a headache.

I think you started out to say that music was more in tune with what's happening than other art forms.

Great paintings shouldn't be in museums. Have you ever been in a museum? Museums are cemeteries. Paintings should be on the walls of restaurants, in dime stores, in gas stations, in men's rooms. Great paintings should be where people hang out. The only thing where it's happening is on radio and records, that's where people hang out. You can't see great paintings. You pay half a million and hang one in your house and one guest sees it. That's not art. That's a shame, a crime. Music is the only thing that's in tune with what's happening. It's not in book form, it's not on the stage. All this art they've been talking about is non-existent. It just remains on the shelf. It doesn't make anyone happier. Just think how many people would really feel great if they could see a Picasso in their daily diner. It's not the bomb that has to go, man, it's the museums.

DYLAN ON

The Vietnam War

"I don't do stuff like protest the war in Vietnam. Who's somebody to say no to another who wants to fight? . . . We all have to learn to take care of ourselves. We all have to learn judo to protect ourselves."

—from interview with Ann Carter, *Atlanta Journal*, October 10, 1965

PLAYBOY INTERVIEW:
BOB DYLAN

Nat Hentoff | Fall 1965 (interview) | March 1966 | *Playboy*

Journalist Nat Hentoff, who had previously interviewed Dylan for the *New Yorker*, met with him in the autumn of 1965 for a *Playboy* magazine Q&A. They talked for more than two hours, during which time Hentoff conducted what he would later call a "normal interview." What follows is not that interview, because as I note in the preface, Dylan didn't like what *Playboy*'s editors had done to the transcript.

"*Playboy* had a proviso that I should never have agreed to," Hentoff told John Whitehead of the Rutherford Institute in 2012. "When they were ready to run an interview, it had to be shown to the subject in case that person had something to object to. So one Saturday morning I was sitting ready to type and the phone rings. It's Bob Dylan. He is furious. 'They changed some of my stuff. I won't allow that.'"

Hentoff suggested that Dylan tell *Playboy* not to run the Q&A. Dylan's answer, as recalled by Hentoff to music journalist Clinton Heylin, was: "No. I got a better idea. I'm gonna make one up." And so he did, with Hentoff's help, right there on the phone. (The intro to the published piece says the conversation took place at a Columbia Records office in New York; in fact, that's where the original Q&A happened.)

As the new conversation got underway, Hentoff told Whitehead, "I realized I was going to be the straight guy. Dylan was improvising surrealistically and very funny."

Indeed, he was. The interview—billed in *Playboy* as "a candid conversation with the iconoclastic idol of the folk-rock set"—is loaded with classic Dylan wit. See, for example, his answer to a question about what made him "go the rock 'n' roll route," and the line where he sums up what his songs are "about."

Despite his successes to date, Dylan was apparently still not that big a deal at this point in the minds of *Playboy*'s editors, who put Hentoff's name on the cover but not the name of his interviewee. —Ed.

As a versatile musicologist and trenchant social commentator, Nat Hentoff brings uniquely pertinent credentials to . . . this month's controversial subject, about whom he writes:

"Less than five years ago, Bob Dylan was scuffling in New York—sleeping in friends' apartments on the Lower East Side and getting very occasional singing work at Gerde's Folk City, an unprepossessing bar for citybillies in the Village. With his leather cap, blue jeans and battered desert boots—his unvarying costume in those days—Dylan looked like an updated, undernourished Huck Finn. And like Huck, he had come out of the Midwest; he would have said 'escaped.' The son of Abraham Zimmerman, an appliance dealer, he was raised in Hibbing, Minnesota, a bleak mining town near the Canadian border. Though he ran away from home regularly between the ages of 10 and 18, young Zimmerman did manage to finish high school, and went on to spend about six months at the University of Minnesota in 1960. By then, he called himself Bob Dylan—in tribute to Dylan Thomas, according to legend; but actually after a gambling uncle whose last name was similar to Dylan.

"In the fall of that year, he came East to visit his idol, Woody Guthrie, in the New Jersey hospital where the Okie folk-singing bard was wasting away with a progressive disease of the nervous system. Dylan stayed and tried to scrape together a singing career. According to those who knew him then, he was shy and stubborn but basically friendly and, beneath the hipster stance, uncommonly gentle. But they argued about his voice. Some found its flat Midwestern tones gratingly mesmeric; others agreed with a Missouri folk singer who had likened the Dylan sound to that of 'a dog with his leg caught in barbed wire.' All agreed, however, that his songs were strangely personal and often disturbing, a pungent mixture of loneliness and defiance laced with traces of Guthrie, echoes of the Negro blues singers and more than a suggestion of country-and-western; but essentially Dylan was developing his own penetratingly distinctive style. Yet the voice was so harsh and the songs so bitterly scornful of conformity, race prejudice and

the mythology of the Cold War that most of his friends couldn't conceive of Dylan making it big even though folk music was already on the rise.

"They were wrong. In September of 1961, a music critic for The New York Times caught his act at Gerde's and hailed the scruffy l9-year-old Minnesotan as a significant new voice on the folk horizon. Around the same time, he was signed by Columbia Records, and his first album was released early the next year. Though it was far from a smash hit, concerts and club engagements gradually multiplied; and then Dylan scored his storied triumph at the Newport Folk Festival in 1962. His next LP began to move, and in the spring of 1963 came his first big single: 'Blowin' in the Wind.' That same spring he turned down a lucrative guest shot on 'The Ed Sullivan Show' because CBS wouldn't permit him to sing a mordant parody he'd written about the John Birch Society. For the nation's young, the Dylan image began to form: kind of a singing James Dean with over- tones of Holden Caulfeld; he was making it, but he wasn't selling out. His concerts began to attract overflow crowds, and his songs—in performances by him and other folk singers—were rushing onto the hit charts. One of them, 'The Times They Are A-Changin',' became an anthem for the rebel- lious young, who savored its message that adults don't know where it's at and can't tell their children what to do.

"By 1965 he had become a major phenomenon on the music scene. More and more folk performers, from Joan Baez to the Byrds, considered it mandatory to have an ample supply of Dylan songs in their repertoires; in one frantically appreciative month—last August—18 different recordings of Dylan ballads were pressed by singers other than the composer himself. More and more aspiring folk singers—and folk-song writers—have begun to sound like Dylan. The current surge of 'protest' songs by such long-haired, post-beat rock-'n'-rollers as Barry McGuire and Sonny and Cher is credited to Dylan. And the newest commercial boom, 'folk-rock,' a fusion of folk- like lyrics with an r-'n'-r beat and background, is an outgrowth in large part, of Dylan's recent decision—decried as a 'sellout' by folknik purists—to perform with a rock-'n'-roll combo rather than continue to accompany himself alone on the guitar. Backed by the big beat of the new group, Dylan tours England with as much tumultuous success as he does America, and the air play for his single records in both countries is rivaled only by that

of the Beatles, Herman's Hermits and the Rolling Stones on the Top 40 deejay shows. In the next 18 months, his income—from personal appearances, records and composer's royalties—is expected to exceed $1,000,000.

"Withal, Dylan seems outwardly much the same as he did during the lean years in Greenwich Village. His dress is still casual to the point of exoticism; his hair is still long and frizzy, and he is still no more likely to be seen wearing a necktie than a cutaway. But there have been changes. No longer protesting polemically against the bomb, race prejudice and conformity, his songs have become increasingly personal—a surrealistic amalgam of kafkaesque menace, corrosive satire and opaque sensuality. His lyrics are more crowded than ever with tumbling words and restless images, and they read more like free-verse poems than conventional lines. Adults still have difficulty digging his offbeat language—and its message of alienation—but the young continue to tune in and turn on.

"But there are other changes. Dylan has become elusive. He is no longer seen in his old haunts in the Village and on the Lower East Side. With few exceptions, he avoids interviewers, and in public, he is usually seen from afar at the epicenter of a protective coterie of tousle-topped young men dressed like him, and lissome, straight-haired young ladies who also seem to be dressed like him. His home base, if it can be called that, is a house his manager owns near Woodstock, a fashionable artists' colony in New York State, and he also enjoys the run of his manager's apartment on dignified Gramercy Park in New York City. There are tales told of Dylan the motorcyclist, the novelist, the maker of high-camp home movies; but except among his small circle of intimates, the 24-year-old folk hero is inscrutably aloof.

"It was only after a long period of evasion and hesitation that Dylan finally agreed to grant this 'Playboy Interview'—the longest he's ever given. We met him on the 10th floor of the new CBS and Columbia Records building in mid-Manhattan. The room was antiseptic: white walls with black trim, contemporary furniture with severe lines, avant-garde art chosen by committee, everything in order, neat desks, neat personnel. In this sterile setting, slouched in a chair across from us, Dylan struck a refreshingly discordant note—with his untamed brownish-blond mane brushing the collar of his tieless blue plaid shirt, in his black jacket, gray *vaudevillian-striped pipestem pants and well-worn blue-suede shoes. Sitting nearby—also long-haired, tieless and blackjacketed, but wearing faded jeans—was a stringy young man whom the singer identified only as Taco Pronto. As Dylan spoke—in a soft drawl, smiling only rarely and fleetingly, sipping tea and chainsmoking cigarettes—his unspeaking friend chuckled and nodded appreciatively from the side lines. Tense and guarded at first, Dylan gradually began to loosen up, then to open up, as he tried to tell us—albeit a bit surrealistically—just where he's been and where he's going. Under the circumstances, we chose to play straight man in our questions, believing that to have done otherwise would have stemmed the freewheeling flow of Dylan's responses."*

PLAYBOY: "Popular songs," you told a reporter last year, "are the only art form that describes the temper of the times. The only place where it's happening is on the radio and records. That's where the people hang out. It's not in books; it's not on the stage; it's not in the galleries. All this art they've been talking about, it just remains on the shelf. It doesn't make anyone happier." In view of the fact that more people than ever before are reading books and going to plays and art galleries, do you think that statement is borne out by the facts?

DYLAN: Statistics measure quantity, not quality. The people in the statistics are people who are very bored. Art, if there is such a thing, is in the bathrooms; everybody knows that. To go to an art gallery thing where you get free milk and doughnuts and where there is a rock-'n'-roll band playing: That's just a status affair. I'm not putting it down, mind you; but I spend a lot of time in the bathroom. I think museums are vulgar. They're all against sex. Anyhow, I didn't say that people "hang out" on the radio, I said they get "hung *up*" on the radio.

PLAYBOY: Why do you think rock 'n' roll has become such an international phenomenon?

DYLAN: I can't really think that there *is* any rock 'n' roll. Actually, when you think about it, anything that has no real existence is bound to become an international phenomenon. Anyway, what does it mean, rock 'n' roll? Does it mean Beatles, does it mean John Lee Hooker, Bobby

Vinton, Jerry Lewis' kid? What about Lawrence Welk? He must play a few rock-'n'-roll songs. Are all these people the same? Is Ricky Nelson like Otis Redding? Is Mick Jagger really Ma Rainey? I can tell by the way people hold their cigarettes if they like Ricky Nelson. I think it's fine to like Ricky Nelson: I couldn't care *less* if somebody likes Ricky Nelson. But I think we're getting off the track here. There isn't any Ricky Nelson. There isn't any Beatles; oh, I take that back: there are a lot of beetles. But there isn't any Bobby Vinton. Anyway, the word is not "international phenomenon"; the word is "parental nightmare."

PLAYBOY: In recent years, according to some critics, jazz has lost much of its appeal to the younger generation. Do you agree?

DYLAN: I don't think jazz has ever appealed to the younger generation. Anyway, I don't really know who this younger generation is. I don't think they could get into a jazz club anyway. But jazz is hard to follow; I mean you actually have to *like* jazz to follow it: and my motto is, never follow *anything*. I don't know what the motto of the younger generation is, but I would think they'd have to follow their parents. I mean, what would some parent say to his kid if the kid came home with a glass eye, a Charlie Mingus record and a pocketful of feathers? He'd say, "Who are you following?" And the poor kid would have to stand there with water in his shoes, a bow tie on his ear and soot pouring out of his belly button and say, "Jazz, Father, I've been following jazz." And his father would probably say, "Get a broom and clean up all that soot before you go to sleep." Then the kid's mother would tell her friends, "Oh yes, our little Donald, he's part of the younger generation, you know."

PLAYBOY: You used to say that you wanted to perform as little as possible, that you wanted to keep most of your time to yourself. Yet you're doing more concerts and cutting more records every year. Why? Is it the money?

DYLAN: Everything is changed now from before. Last spring. I guess I was going to quit singing. I was very drained, and the way things were going, it was a very draggy situation—I mean, when you do "Everybody Loves You for Your Black Eye," and meanwhile the back of your head is caving in. Anyway, I was playing a lot of songs I didn't want to play. I was singing words I didn't really want to sing. I don't mean words like "God" and "mother" and "President" and "suicide" and "meat cleaver." I mean simple little words like "if" and "hope" and "you." But "Like a Rolling Stone" changed it all: I didn't care anymore after that about writing books or poems or whatever. I mean it was something that I myself could dig. It's very tiring having other people tell you how much they dig you if you yourself don't dig you. It's also very deadly entertainment wise. Contrary to what some scary people think, I don't play with a band now for any kind of propaganda-type or commercial-type reasons. It's just that my songs are pictures and the band makes the sound of the pictures.

PLAYBOY: Do you feel that acquiring a combo and switching from folk to folk-rock has improved you as a performer?

DYLAN: I'm not interested in myself as a performer. Performers are people who perform for other people. Unlike actors, I know what I'm saying. It's very simple in my mind. It doesn't matter what kind of audience reaction this whole thing gets. What happens on the stage is straight. It doesn't expect any rewards or fines from any kind of outside agitators. It's ultra-simple, and would exist whether anybody was looking or not.

As far as folk and folk-rock are concerned, it doesn't matter what kind of nasty names people invent for the music. It could be called arsenic music, or perhaps Phaedra music. I don't think that such a word as folk-rock has anything to do with it. And folk music is a word I can't use. Folk music is a bunch of fat people. I have to think of all this as traditional music. Traditional music is based on hexagrams. It comes about from legends, Bibles, plagues, and it revolves around vegetables and death. There's nobody that's going to kill traditional music. All these songs about roses growing out of people's brains and lovers who are really geese and swans that turn into angels—they're not going to die. It's all those paranoid people who think that someone's going to come and take away their toilet paper—*they're* going to die. Songs like "Which Side Are You On?" and "I Love You, Porgy"—they're not folk-music songs; they're political songs. They're *already* dead. Obviously, death is not very universally accepted. I mean, you'd think that the traditional-music people could gather from their songs that mystery—just plain simple mystery—is a fact, a traditional fact. I listen to the old ballads; but I wouldn't go to a *party* and listen to the old ballads. I could give you descriptive detail of what they do to me, but some people would probably think my imagination had gone mad. It strikes me funny that people actually have the gall to think that I have some kind of fantastic imagination. It gets very lonesome. But anyway, traditional music is too unreal to die. It doesn't need to be protected. Nobody's going to hurt it. In that music is the only true, valid death you can feel today off a record player. But like anything else in great demand, people try to own it. It has to do with a purity thing. I think its meaninglessness is holy. Everybody knows that I'm not a folk singer.

PLAYBOY: Some of your old fans would agree with you—and not in a complimentary vein—since your debut with the rock-'n'-roll combo at last year's Newport Folk Festival, where many of them booed you loudly for "selling out" to commercial pop tastes. The early Bob Dylan, they felt, was the "pure" Bob Dylan. How do you feel about it?

DYLAN: I was kind of stunned. But I can't put anybody down for coming and booing: after all, they paid to get in. They could have been maybe a little quieter and not so persistent, though. There were a lot of old people there, too; lots of whole families had driven down from Vermont, lots of nurses and their parents, and well, like they just came to hear some relaxing hoedowns, you know, maybe an Indian polka or two. And just when everything's going all right, here I come on, and the whole place turns into a beer factory. There were a lot of people there who were very pleased that I got booed. I saw them afterward. I do resent somewhat, though, that everybody that booed said they did it because they were old fans.

PLAYBOY: What about their charge that you vulgarized your natural gifts?

DYLAN: What can I say? I'd like to *see* one of these so-called fans. I'd like to have him blindfolded and brought to me. It's like going out to the desert and screaming and then having little kids throw their sandbox at you. I'm only 24. These people that said this—were they Americans?

PLAYBOY: Americans or not, there were a lot of people who didn't like your new sound. In view of this widespread negative reaction, do you think you may have made a mistake in changing your style?

DYLAN: A mistake is to commit a misunderstanding. There could be no such thing, anyway, as this action. Either people understand or they *pretend* to understand—or else they really *don't* understand. What you're speaking of here is doing wrong things for selfish reasons. I don't know the word for that, unless it's suicide. In any case, it has nothing to do with my music.

PLAYBOY: Mistake or not, what made you decide to go the rock-'n'-roll route?

DYLAN: Carelessness. I lost my one true love. I started drinking. The first thing I know, I'm in a card game. Then I'm in a crap game. I wake up in a pool hall. Then this big Mexican lady drags me off the table, takes me to Philadelphia. She leaves me alone in her house, and it burns down. I wind up in Phoenix. I get a job as a Chinaman. I start working in a dime store, and move in with a 13-year-old girl. Then this big Mexican lady from Philadelphia comes in and burns the house down. I go down to Dallas. I get a job as a "before" in a Charles Atlas "before and after" ad. I move in with a delivery boy who can cook fantastic chili and hot dogs. Then this 13-year-old girl from Phoenix comes and burns the house down. The delivery boy—he ain't so mild: He gives her the knife, and the next thing I know I'm in Omaha. It's so cold there, by this time I'm robbing my own bicycles and frying my own fish. I stumble onto some luck and get a job as a carburetor out at the hot-rod races every Thursday night. I move in with a high school teacher who also does a little plumbing on the side, who ain't much to look at, but who's built a special kind of refrigerator that can turn newspaper into lettuce. Everything's going good until that delivery boy shows up and tries to knife me. Needless to say, he burned the house down, and I hit the road. The first guy that picked me up asked me if I wanted to be a star. What could I say?

PLAYBOY: And that's how you became a rock-'n'-roll singer?

DYLAN: No, that's how I got tuberculosis.

PLAYBOY: Let's turn the question around: Why have you stopped composing and singing protest songs?

DYLAN: I've stopped composing and singing anything that has either a reason to be written or a motive to be sung. Don't get me wrong, now. "Protest" is not my word. I've never thought of myself as such. The word "protest," I think, was made up for people undergoing surgery. It's an amusement-park word. A normal person in his righteous mind would have to have the hiccups to pronounce it honestly. The word "message" strikes me as having a hernia-like sound. It's just like the word "delicious." Also the word "marvelous." You know, the English can say "marvelous" pretty good. They can't say "raunchy" so good, though. Well, we each have our thing. Anyway, message songs, as everybody knows, are a drag. It's only college newspaper editors and single girls under 14 that could possibly have time for them.

PLAYBOY: You've said you think message songs are vulgar. Why?

DYLAN: Well, first of all, anybody that's got a message is going to learn from experience that they can't put it into a song. I mean it's just not going to come out the same message. After one or two of these unsuccessful attempts, one realizes that his resultant message, which is not even the same message he thought up and began with, he's now got to stick by it; because, after all, a song leaves your mouth just as soon as it leaves your hands. Are you following me?

PLAYBOY: Oh, perfectly.

DYLAN: Well, anyway, second of all, you've got to respect other people's right to also have a message themselves. Myself, what I'm going to do is rent Town Hall and put about 30 Western Union boys on the bill. I mean, then there'll *really* be some messages. People will be able to come and hear more messages than they've ever heard before in their life.

PLAYBOY: But your early ballads have been called "songs of passionate protest." Wouldn't that make them "message" music?

DYLAN: This is unimportant. Don't you understand? I've been writing since I was eight years old. I've been playing the guitar since I was ten. I was raised playing and writing whatever it was I had to play and write.

PLAYBOY: Would it be unfair to say, then, as some have, that you were motivated commercially rather than creatively in writing the kind of songs that made you popular?

DYLAN: All right, now, look. It's not all that deep. It's not a complicated thing. My motives, or whatever they are, were never commercial in the money sense of the word. It was more in the don't die-by-the-hacksaw sense of the word. I never did it for money. It happened, and I let it happen to me. There was no reason *not* to let it happen to me. I couldn't have written before what I write now, anyway. The songs used to be about what I felt and saw. Nothing of my own rhythmic vomit ever entered into it. Vomit is not romantic. I used to think songs are supposed to be romantic. And I didn't want to sing anything that was unspecific. Unspecific things have no sense of time. All of us people have no sense of time; it's a dimensional hangup. Anybody can be specific and obvious. That's always been the easy way. The leaders of the world take the easy way. It's not that it's so difficult to be unspecific and less obvious; it's just that there's nothing, absolutely nothing, to be specific and obvious *about.* My older songs, to say the least, were about nothing. The newer ones are about the same nothing—only as seen inside a bigger thing, perhaps called the nowhere. But this is all very constipated. I *do* know what my songs are about.

PLAYBOY: And what's that?

DYLAN: Oh, some are about four minutes; some are about five, and some, believe it or not, are about eleven or twelve.

PLAYBOY: Can't you be a bit more informative?

DYLAN: Nope.

PLAYBOY: All right. Let's change the subject. As you know, it's the age group from about 16 to 25 that listens to your songs. Why, in your opinion?

DYLAN: I don't see what's so strange about an age group like that listening to my songs. I'm hip enough to know that it ain't going to be the 85-to-90-year-olds. If the 85-to-90-year-olds *were* listening to me, they'd know that I can't tell them anything. The 16-to-25-year-olds, they probably know that I can't tell *them* anything either—and they know that *I* know it. It's a funny business. Obviously, I'm not an IBM computer any more than I'm an ashtray. I mean it's obvious to anyone who's ever slept in the back seat of a car that I'm just not a schoolteacher.

PLAYBOY: Even though you're not a schoolteacher, wouldn't you like to help the young people who dig you from turning into what some of their parents have become?

DYLAN: Well, I must say that I really don't know their parents. I really don't know if *anybody's* parents are so bad. Now, I hate to come on like a weakling or a coward, and I realize it might seem kind of irreligious, but I'm really not the right person to tramp around the country saving souls. I wouldn't run over anybody that was laying in the street, and I certainly wouldn't become a hangman. I wouldn't think twice about giving a starving man a cigarette. But I'm not a shepherd. And I'm not about to save anybody from fate, which I know nothing about. "Parents" is not the key word here. The key word is "destiny." I can't save them from that.

PLAYBOY: Still, thousands of young people look up to you as a kind of folk hero. Do you feel some sense of responsibility toward them?

DYLAN: I don't feel I have any responsibility, no. Whoever it is that listens to my songs owes *me* nothing. How could I possibly have any responsibility to any kind of thousands? What could possibly make me think that I owe anybody anything who just happens to be there? I've never written any song that begins with the words "I've gathered you here tonight . . ." I'm not about to tell anybody to be a good boy or a good girl and they'll go to heaven. I really don't know what the people who are on the receiving end of these songs think of me, anyway. It's horrible. I'll bet Tony Bennett doesn't have to go through this kind of thing. I wonder what Billy the Kid would have answered to such a question.

PLAYBOY: In their admiration for you, many young people have begun to imitate the way you dress—which one adult commentator has called "self-consciously oddball and defiantly sloppy." What's your reaction to that kind of put-down?

DYLAN: Bullshit. Oh, such bullshit. I know the fellow that said that. He used to come around here and get beat up all the time. He better watch it; some people are after him. They're going to strip him naked and stick him in Times Square. They're going to tie him up, and also put a thermometer in his mouth. Those kind of morbid ideas and remarks are so petty—I mean there's a *war* going on. People got rickets; everybody wants to start a riot; 40-year-old women are eating spinach by the carload; the doctors haven't got a cure for cancer—and here's some hillbilly talking about how he doesn't like somebody's clothes. Worse than that, it gets printed and innocent people have to read it. This is a terrible thing. And he's a terrible man. Obviously, he's just living off the fat of himself, and he's expecting his kids to take care of him. His kids probably listen to my records. Just because my clothes are too long, does that mean I'm unqualified for what I do?

PLAYBOY: No, but there are those who think it does—and many of them seem to feel the same way about your long hair. But compared with the shoulder-length coiffures worn by some of the male singing groups these days, your tonsorial tastes are on the conservative side. How do you feel about these far-out hair styles?

DYLAN: The thing that most people don't realize is that it's *warmer* to have long hair. Everybody wants to be warm. People with short hair freeze easily. Then they try to hide their coldness, and they get jealous of everybody that's warm. Then they become either barbers or Congressmen. A lot of prison wardens have short hair. Have you ever noticed that Abraham Lincoln's hair was much longer than John Wilkes Booth's?

PLAYBOY: Do you think Lincoln wore his hair long to keep his head warm?

DYLAN: Actually, I think it was for medical reasons, which are none of my business. But I guess if you figure it out, you realize that all of one's hair surrounds and lays on the brain inside your head. Mathematically speaking, the more of it you can get out of your head, the better. People who want free minds sometimes overlook the fact that you have to have an uncluttered brain. Obviously, if you get your hair on the outside of your head, your brain will be a little more freer. But all this talk about long hair is just a trick. It's been thought up by men and women who look like cigars—the anti-happiness committee. They're all freeloaders and cops. You can tell who they are: They're always carrying calendars, guns or scissors. They're all trying to get into your quicksand. They think you've got something. I don't know why Abe Lincoln had long hair.

PLAYBOY: Until your abandonment of "message" songs, you were considered not only a major voice in the student protest movement but a militant champion of the civil rights struggle. According to friends, you seemed to feel a special bond of kinship with the Student Nonviolent Coordinating Committee, which you actively supported both as a performer and as a worker. Why have you withdrawn from participation in all these causes? Have you lost interest in protest as well as in protest songs?

DYLAN: As far as SNCC is concerned, I knew some of the people in it, but I only knew them as people, not as of any part of something that was bigger or better than themselves. I didn't even know what civil rights *was* before I met some of them. I mean, I knew there were Negroes, and I knew there were a lot of people who don't *like* Negroes. But I got to admit that if I didn't know some of the SNCC people, I would have gone on thinking that Martin Luther King was really nothing more than some underprivileged war hero. I haven't lost any interest in protest since then. I just didn't have any interest in protest to begin with—any more than I did in war heroes. You can't lose what you've never had. Anyway, when you don't like your situation, you either leave it or else you overthrow it. You can't just stand around and whine about it. People just get aware of your noise; they really don't get aware of *you*. Even if they give you what you want, it's only because you're making too much noise. First thing you know, you want something else, and then you want something else, and then you want something else, until finally it isn't a joke anymore, and whoever you're protesting against finally gets all fed up and stomps on everybody. Sure, you can go around trying to bring up people who are lesser than you, but then don't forget, you're messing around with gravity. I don't fight gravity. I do believe in equality, but I also believe in distance.

PLAYBOY: Do you mean people keeping their racial distance?

DYLAN: I believe in people keeping everything they've got.

PLAYBOY: Some people might feel that you're trying to cop out of fighting for the things you believe in.

DYLAN: Those would be people who think I have some sort of responsibility toward *them*. They probably want me to help them make friends. I don't know. They probably either want to set me in their house and have me come out every hour and tell them what time it is, or else they just want to stick me in between the mattress. How could they possibly understand what I believe in?

PLAYBOY: Well, what *do* you believe in?

DYLAN: I already told you.

PLAYBOY: All right. Many of your folksinging colleagues remain actively involved in the fight for civil rights, free speech and withdrawal from Vietnam. Do you think they're wrong?

DYLAN: I don't think they're wrong, if that's what they see themselves doing. But don't think that what you've got out there is a bunch of little Buddhas all parading up and down. People that use God as a weapon should be amputated upon. You see it around here all the time: "Be good or God won't like you, and you'll go to hell." Things like that. People that march with slogans and things tend to take themselves a little too holy. It would be a drag if they, too, started using God as a weapon.

PLAYBOY: Do you think it's pointless to dedicate yourself to the cause of peace and racial equality?

DYLAN: Not pointless to dedicate yourself to peace and racial equality, but rather, it's pointless to dedicate yourself to the *cause*; that's *really* pointless. That's very unknowing. To say "cause of peace" is just like saying "hunk of butter." I mean, how can you listen to anybody who wants you to believe he's dedicated to the hunk and not to the butter? People who can't conceive of how others hurt, they're trying to change the world. They're all afraid to admit that they don't really know each other. They'll all probably be here long after we've gone, and we'll give birth to new ones. But they themselves—I don't think *they'll* give birth to *anything*.

PLAYBOY: You sound a bit fatalistic.

DYLAN: I'm not fatalistic. Bank tellers are fatalistic; clerks are fatalistic. I'm a farmer. Who ever heard of a fatalistic farmer? I'm not fatalistic. I smoke a lot of cigarettes, but that doesn't make me fatalistic.

PLAYBOY: You were quoted recently as saying that "songs can't save the world. I've gone through all that." We take it you don't share Pete Seeger's belief that songs can change people, that they can help build international understanding.

DYLAN: On the international understanding part, that's OK. But you have a translation problem there. Anybody with this kind of a level of thinking has to also think about this translation thing. But I don't believe songs can change people anyway. I'm not Pinocchio. I consider that an insult. I'm not part of that. I don't blame anybody for thinking that way. But I just don't donate any money to them. I don't consider them anything like unhip; they're more in the rubber-band category.

PLAYBOY: How do you feel about those who have risked imprisonment by burning their draft cards to signify their opposition to U. S. involvement in Vietnam, and by refusing—as your friend Joan Baez has done—to pay their income taxes as a protest against the Government's expenditures on war and weaponry? Do you think they're wasting their time?

DYLAN: Burning draft cards isn't going to end any war. It's not even going to save any lives. If someone can feel more honest with himself by burning his draft card, then that's great; but if he's just going to feel more important because he does it, then that's a drag. I really don't know too much about Joan Baez and her income-tax problems. The only thing I can tell you about Joan Baez is that she's not Belle Starr.

PLAYBOY: Writing about "beard-wearing draft-card burners and paci-fist income-tax evaders," one columnist called such protesters "no less outside society than the junkie, the homosexual or the mass murderer." What's your reaction?

DYLAN: I don't believe in those terms. They're too hysterical. They don't describe anything. Most people think that homosexual, gay, queer, queen, faggot are all the same words. Everybody thinks that a junkie is a dope freak. As far as I'm concerned, I don't consider myself outside of anything. I just consider myself *not around*.

PLAYBOY: Joan Baez recently opened a school in northern California for training civil rights workers in the philosophy and techniques of nonviolence. Are you in sympathy with that concept?

DYLAN: If you mean do I agree with it or not, I really don't see anything to be in agreement *with*. If you mean has it got my approval, I guess it does, but my approval really isn't going to do it any good. I don't know about other people's sympathy, but my sympathy runs to the lame and crippled and beautiful things. I have a feeling of loss of power—some-thing like a reincarnation feeling; I don't feel that for mechanical things like cars or schools. I'm sure it's a nice school, but if you're asking me would I go to it, I would have to say no.

PLAYBOY: As a college dropout in your freshman year, you seem to take a dim view of schooling in general, whatever the subject.

DYLAN: I really don't think about it.

PLAYBOY: Well, have you ever had any regrets about not completing college?

DYLAN: That would be ridiculous. Colleges are like old-age homes; except for the fact that more people die in colleges than in old-age homes, there's really no difference. People have one great blessing—obscurity—and not really too many people are thankful for it. Everybody is always taught to be thankful for their food and clothes and things like that, but not to be thankful for their obscurity. Schools don't teach that; they teach people to be rebels and lawyers. I'm not going to put down the teaching system; that would be too silly. It's just that it really doesn't have too much to teach. Colleges are part of the American institution; everybody respects them. They're very rich and influential, but they have nothing to do with survival. Everybody knows that.

PLAYBOY: Would you advise young people to skip college, then?

DYLAN: I wouldn't advise anybody to do anything. I certainly wouldn't advise somebody not to go to college; I just wouldn't pay his *way* through college.

PLAYBOY: Don't you think the things one learns in college can help enrich one's life?

DYLAN: I don't think anything like that is going to enrich my life, no—not my life, anyway. Things are going to happen whether I know why they happen or not. It just gets more complicated when you stick *yourself* into it. You don't find out why things move. You *let* them move; you *watch* them move; you stop them from moving: you start them moving. But you don't sit around and try to figure out *why* there's movement—unless, of course, you're just an innocent moron, or some wise old Japanese man. Out of all the people who just lay around and ask "Why?", how many do you figure really want to know?

PLAYBOY: Can you suggest a better use for the four years that would otherwise be spent in college?

DYLAN: Well, you could hang around in Italy; you could go to Mexico; you could become a dishwasher; you could even go to Arkansas. I don't know; there are thousands of things to do and places to go. Everybody thinks that you have to bang your head against the wall, but it's silly when you really think about it. I mean, here you have fantastic scientists working on ways to prolong human living, and then you have other people who take it for granted that you have to beat your head against the wall in order to be happy. You can't take everything you don't like as a personal insult. I guess you should go where your wants are bare, where you're invisible and not needed.

PLAYBOY: Would you classify sex among your wants, wherever you go?

DYLAN: Sex is a temporary thing; sex isn't love. You can get sex anywhere. If you're looking for someone to *love* you, now that's different. I guess you have to stay in college for that.

PLAYBOY: Since you didn't stay in college, does that mean you haven't found someone to love you?

DYLAN: Let's go on to the next question.

PLAYBOY: Do you have any difficulty relating to people—or vice versa?

DYLAN: Well, sometimes I have the feeling that other people want my *soul*. If I say to them, "I don't *have* a soul," they say, "I know that. You don't have to tell me that. Not me. How dumb do you think I am? I'm your *friend*." What can I say except that I'm sorry and I feel bad? I guess maybe feeling bad and paranoia are the same thing.

PLAYBOY: Paranoia is said to be one of the mental states sometimes induced by such hallucinogenic drugs as peyote and LSD. Considering the risks involved, do you think that experimentation with such drugs should be part of the growing up experience for a young person?

DYLAN: I wouldn't advise anybody to use drugs—certainly not the hard drugs; drugs are medicine. But opium and hash and pot—now, those things aren't drugs; they just bend your mind a little. I think *everybody's* mind should be bent once in a while. Not by LSD, though. LSD is medicine—a different kind of medicine. It makes you aware of the universe, so to speak; you realize how foolish *objects* are. But LSD is not for groovy people; it's for mad, hateful people who want revenge. It's for people who usually have heart attacks. They ought to use it at the Geneva Convention.

PLAYBOY: Are you concerned, as you approach 30, that you may begin to "go square," lose some of your openness to experience, become leery of change and new experiment?

DYLAN: No. But if it happens, then it happens. What can I say? There doesn't seem to *be* any tomorrow. Every time I wake up, no matter in what position, it's always been today. To look ahead and start worrying about trivial little things I can't really say has any more importance than looking back and *remembering* trivial little things. I'm not going to become any poetry instructor at any girls' school; I know *that* for sure. But that's about *all* I know for sure. I'll just keep doing these different things, I guess.

PLAYBOY: Such as?

DYLAN: Waking up in different positions.

PLAYBOY: What else?

DYLAN: I'm just like anybody else; I'll try anything once.

PLAYBOY: Including theft and murder?

DYLAN: I can't really say I *wouldn't* commit theft or murder and expect anybody to really believe me. I wouldn't believe anybody if they told *me* that.

PLAYBOY: By their mid-20s, most people have begun to settle into their niche, to find a place in society. But you've managed to remain inner-directed and uncommitted. What was it that spurred you to run away from home six times between the ages of ten and eighteen and finally to leave for good?

DYLAN: It was nothing; it was just an accident of geography. Like if I was born and raised in New York or Kansas City, I'm sure everything would have turned out different. But Hibbing, Minnesota, was just not the right place for me to stay and live. There really was nothing there. The only thing you could do there was be a miner, and even that kind of thing was getting less and less. The people that lived there—they're nice people; I've been all over the world since I left there, and they still stand out as being the least hung-up. The mines were just dying, that's all; but that's not their fault. *Everybody* about my age left there. It was no great romantic thing. It didn't take any great amount of thinking or individual genius, and there certainly wasn't any pride in it. I didn't run away from it; I just turned my back on it. It couldn't give me anything. It was very void-like. So leaving wasn't hard at all; it would have been much harder to stay. I didn't want to die there. As I think about it now, though, it wouldn't be such a bad place to go back to and die in. There's no place I feel closer to now, or get the feeling that I'm part of, except maybe New York; but I'm not a New Yorker. I'm North Dakota-Minnesota-Midwestern. I'm *that* color. I speak that way. I'm from someplace called Iron Range. My brains and feeling have come from there. I wouldn't amputate on a drowning man; *nobody* from out there would.

PLAYBOY: Today, you're on your way to becoming a millionaire. Do you feel in any danger of being trapped by all this affluence—by the things it can buy?

DYLAN: No, my world is very small. Money can't really improve it any; money can just keep it from being smothered.

PLAYBOY: Most big stars find it difficult to avoid getting involved, and sometimes entangled, in managing the business end of their careers. As a man with three thriving careers—as a concert performer, recording star and songwriter—do you ever feel boxed in by such noncreative responsibilities?

DYLAN: No, I've got other people to do that for me. They watch my money; they guard it. They keep their eyes on it at all times; they're supposed to be very smart when it comes to money. They know just what to do with my money. I pay them a lot of it. I don't really speak to them much, and they don't really speak to me at all, so I guess everything is all right.

PLAYBOY: If fortune hasn't trapped you, how about fame? Do you find that your celebrity makes it difficult to keep your private life intact?

DYLAN: My private life has been dangerous from the beginning. All this does is add a little atmosphere.

PLAYBOY: You used to enjoy wandering across the country—taking off on open-end trips, roughing it from town to town, with no particular destination in mind. But you seem to be doing much less of that these days. Why? Is it because you're too well known?

DYLAN: It's mainly because I have to be in Cincinnati Friday night, and the next night I got to be in Atlanta, and then the next night after that, I have to be in Buffalo. Then I have to write some more songs for a record album.

PLAYBOY: Do you get the chance to ride your motorcycle much anymore?

DYLAN: I'm still very patriotic to the highway, but I don't ride my motorcycle too much anymore, no.

PLAYBOY: How do you get your kicks these days, then?

DYLAN: I hire people to look into my eyes, and then I have them kick me.

PLAYBOY: And that's the way you get your kicks?

DYLAN: No. Then I *forgive* them; that's where my kicks come in.

PLAYBOY: You told an interviewer last year, "I've done everything I ever wanted to." If that's true, what do you have to look forward to?

DYLAN: Salvation. Just plain salvation.

PLAYBOY: Anything else?

DYLAN: Praying. I'd also like to start a cookbook magazine. And I've always wanted to be a boxing referee. I want to referee a heavyweight championship fight. Can you imagine that? Can you imagine any fighter in his right mind recognizing *me*?

PLAYBOY: If your popularity were to wane, would you welcome being anonymous again?

DYLAN: You mean welcome it, like I'd welcome some poor pilgrim coming in from the rain? No, I wouldn't welcome it; I'd accept it, though. Someday, obviously, I'm going to *have* to accept it.

PLAYBOY: Do you ever think about marrying, settling down, having a home, maybe living abroad? Are there any luxuries you'd like to have, say, a yacht or a Rolls-Royce?

DYLAN: No, I don't think about those things. If I felt like buying anything, I'd buy it. What you're asking me about is the future, *my* future. I'm the last person in the world to ask about my future.

PLAYBOY: Are you saying you're going to be passive and just let things happen to you?

DYLAN: Well, that's being very philosophical about it, but I guess it's true.

PLAYBOY: You once planned to write a novel. Do you still?

DYLAN: I don't think so. All my writing goes into the songs now. Other forms don't interest me anymore.

PLAYBOY: Do you have any unfulfilled ambitions?

DYLAN: Well, I guess I've always wanted to be Anthony Quinn in "La Strada." Not always—only for about six years now; it's not one of those childhood-dream things. Oh, and come to think of it, I guess I've always wanted to be Brigitte Bardot, too; but I don't really want to think about *that* too much.

PLAYBOY: Did you ever have the standard boyhood dream of growing up to be President?

DYLAN: No. When I was a boy, Harry Truman was President; who'd want to be Harry Truman?

PLAYBOY: Well, let's suppose that you were the President. What would you accomplish during your first thousand days?

DYLAN: Well, just for laughs, so long as you insist, the first thing I'd do is probably move the White House. Instead of being in Texas, it'd be on the East Side in New York. McGeorge Bundy would definitely have to change his name, and General McNamara would be forced to wear a coonskin cap and shades. I would immediately rewrite "The Star-Spangled Banner," and little school children, instead of memorizing "America the Beautiful," would have to memorize "Desolation Row" [one of Dylan's latest songs]. And I would immediately call for a showdown with Mao Tse-tung; I would fight him *personally*—and I'd get somebody to film it.

PLAYBOY: One final question: Even though you've more or less retired from political and social protest, can you conceive of any circumstance that might persuade you to reinvolve yourself?

DYLAN: No, not unless all the people in the world disappeared.

DYLAN ON

Whether "The Times They Are A-Changin'"
Concerns Generational Conflict

"That's not what I was saying. It happened maybe that those were the only words I could find to separate aliveness from deadness. It has nothing to do with age."

—from interview with Joseph Haas,
Chicago Daily News, November 27, 1965

PRESS CONFERENCE

December 3, 1965 | KQED-TV (San Francisco)

When Bob Dylan arrived in San Francisco for a five-concert series in December 1965, he was riding high. "Positively 4th Street," his catchy folk-rock follow-up to "Like a Rolling Stone," was ending a seven-week run in the Top Forty. Only a year earlier, he had been traveling on airliners with only one helper; now he flew privately and with an entourage. As for his personal life, less than two weeks earlier he had secretly married Sara Lownds, who was eight months pregnant with their first child.

Someone had suggested that Dylan hold a press conference in the studios of San Francisco public television station KQED, and he had readily agreed. In the audience for the event were poet Allen Ginsberg, rock promoter Bill Graham, and the Band's Robbie Robertson, along with reporters from several daily newspapers, local TV news crews, and some high school papers.

Critic Ralph J. Gleason, who would go on to cofound *Rolling Stone*, served as MC for the event. He later reported that Dylan "sat on a raised platform facing the cameras and the reporters and answered questions over a microphone, all the while smoking cigarettes and swinging his leg back and forth."

Many of the questions were as ridiculous as the ones aimed at the early Beatles, but Dylan seemed less annoyed than amused. He smiled and laughed often throughout the hour-long event and appeared to be having a great time toying with the reporters and their questions. —Ed.

Ralph J. Gleason: Ladies and gentlemen, I'd like to welcome you to the first KQED poets' conference—press conference. A poet who also happens to be a singer I figure you all know. . . . Mr. Dylan is a poet. He will answer questions about everything from atomic science to riddles and rhymes. Go! Who's first? Come on.

Reporter: I'd like to know about the cover of your forthcoming album, the one with "Subterranean Homesick Blues" in it. [*A reference to* Bringing It All Back Home, *which had actually been released the previous March. —Ed.*] I'd like to know about the meaning of the photograph of you wearing the Triumph T-shirt.

Bob Dylan: What would you want to know about it?

Reporter: Well, that's an equivalent photograph. It means something. It's got a philosophy in it. I'd like to know visually what it represents to you, because you're a part of that.

Dylan: I haven't really looked at it that much.

Reporter: I've thought about it a great deal.

Dylan: It was just taken one day when I was sitting on the steps. I don't really remember too much about it.

Reporter: Well, what about the motorcycle as an image in your song-writing? You seem to like that.

Dylan: Oh, we all like motorcycles to some degree.

Reporter: Do you think of yourself primarily as a singer or as a poet?

Dylan: Oh, I think of myself more as a song-and-dance man.

[*Laughter.*]

Reporter: Why?

Dylan: Oh, I don't think we have enough time to really go into that.

Reporter: You were quoted in the *Chicago Daily News* as saying that when you're really wasted you may enter into another field. How "wasted" is really wasted and do you foresee it?

Dylan: No, I don't foresee it, but it's more or less like a ruthless type of feeling. Very ruthless and intoxicated to some degree.

Reporter: The criticism that you've received for more or less leaving folk music for folk-rock hasn't seemed to bother you very much. Do you think you'll stick with folk-rock or are you going on into more writing?

Dylan: I don't play folk-rock.

Reporter: What would you call your music?

Dylan: I like to think of it more in terms of vision music. It's a mathematical music.

Reporter: Would you say that the words were more important than the music?

Dylan: The words are just as important as the music. There'd be no music without the words.

Reporter: Which do you do first, ordinarily?

Dylan: The words.

Reporter: Do you think there will ever be a time when you will paint or sculpt?

Dylan: Oh, yes. [*Laughs.*] Oh, sure.

Reporter: Do you think there will ever be a time when you'll be hung as a thief?

[*Laughter.*]

Dylan: You weren't supposed to say that. [*Laughs, then requests a match and lights cigarette.*]

Reporter: Bob, you said you always do your words first and you think of it as music. When you do the words, can you hear it?

Dylan: Yes. Oh, yes.

Reporter: Do you hear any music before you have words? Do you have any songs that you don't have words to yet?

Dylan: Sometimes, on very general instruments, not on the guitar, though. Maybe something like the harpsichord or the harmonica or autoharp, I might hear some kind of melody or tune which I would know the words to put to.

Reporter: You'd save that?

Dylan: Yes. Not with the guitar, though. The guitar is too hard an instrument. I don't really hear many melodies based on the guitar.

Reporter: Do you sit down just to write a song or do you just write them on inspiration?

Dylan: I more or less write it on a lot of things.

[*Laughter.*]

Reporter: What poets do you dig?

Dylan: Oh . . . [*Long pause.*] [Arthur] Rimbaud, I guess. W. C. Fields. The family . . . you know, the trapeze family in the circus? Smokey Robinson. Allen Ginsberg. Charlie Rich is a good poet.

Reporter: In a lot of your songs, you are hard on a lot of people. Like in "Like a Rolling Stone," you're pretty hard on the girl, and in "Positively 4th Street" you're pretty hard on a supposed friend. Are you hard on them because you want to torment them or because you want to change their lives and make them millionaires?

Dylan: I want to needle them.

[*Laughter.*]

Reporter: Do you still sing your older songs?

Dylan: No. I just saw a songbook last night. I don't really see too many of those things, but a lotta songs in those books I haven't even recorded. I've just written down, and put little tunes to and they published them. I haven't sung them, though. A lotta the songs I don't even know anymore, even the ones I did sing. There doesn't seem to be enough time.

Reporter: Did you change your program when you went to England?

Dylan: No, no, I finished it there. That was the end of my older program. I didn't change it. It was developed, and by the time we got there, I knew what was going to happen all the time. I knew how many encores there was, which songs they were going to clap loudest and all those kind of things.

Reporter: On a concert tour like this, do you do the same program night after night?

Dylan: Oh, sometimes it's different. I think we'll do the same one here, though.

Reporter: Did you in England do any of the songs like "Subterranean [Homesick Blues]"?

Dylan: No, I didn't work with a band there.

Reporter: Will you be working with a band here?

Dylan: Oh, yeah.

Reporter: In a recent *Broadside* interview, Phil Ochs said you should do films. Do you have any plans to do this?

Dylan: No, I don't. I do have plans to make a film but not because anybody said I should do them.

Reporter: How soon will this be?

Dylan: Next year, probably.

Reporter: Can you tell us what it will be about?

Dylan: It'll be just another song.

Reporter: Who are the people making films that you dig, particularly?

Dylan: [Francois] Truffaut. I really can't think of any more people. Italian movie directors, but not too many people in England or the United States which I really think that I would dig.

Reporter: You did a [Charlie] Chaplin bit as an exit line in one of your concerts once.

Dylan: I did? That must've been an accident. Have to stay away from that kind of thing.

[*Someone hands Dylan a photograph.*]

Oh, thank you very much. Was that taken right here with a Polaroid? [*Looks at photo, apparently of himself.*] Hmm. Good God, I must leave right away.

[*Laughter.*]

Reporter: What do you think of people that analyze your songs? Do they usually end up with the same meaning that you wrote or—

Dylan: I welcome them [*laughter*] with open arms.

Reporter: The University of California mimeographed the lyrics to all the songs from the last album and had a symposium discussing them. Do you welcome that?

Dylan: Oh, sure. I'm just kinda sad I'm not around to be a part of it but it was nice.

Reporter: It'd have been pretty wild if ya had been.

Dylan: Yeah.

Reporter: Mr. Dylan, Josh Dunson in his new book, *Freedom in the Air,* implies that you have sold out to commercial interests and the topical song movement. Do you have any comment, sir?

Dylan: Well, no comments, no arguments. I certainly don't feel guilty.

Reporter: If you were going to sell out to a commercial interest, which one would you choose?

[*Laughter.*]

Dylan: Ladies' garments. [*Thirty-nine years later, strangely enough, Dylan wound up being accused of selling out when he appeared in an ad for Victoria's Secret. —Ed.*]

[*Laughter.*]

Reporter: Bob, have you worked with any rock 'n' roll groups?

Dylan: Professionally?

Reporter: Or just sitting in or on concert tours with them or sitting in with their sessions.

Dylan: No, no. I don't usually play too much.

Reporter: Do you listen to other people's recordings of your songs?

Dylan: Sometimes. A few of them I've heard. I don't really come across it that much, though.

Reporter: Is it a strange experience?

Dylan: No. It's more or less like a heavenly kind of thing.

Reporter: What do you think of Joan Baez's interpretations of your earlier songs?

Dylan: I haven't heard her latest album or the one before that. She does 'em all right, I think.

Reporter: What about Donovan? "Colours." Do you think he's a good poet of love ballads?

Dylan: Nah. [*Pause.*] He's a nice guy, though.

[*Laughter.*]

Reporter: I'm shattered.

Dylan: Well, you needn't be.

Reporter: Are there any young folksingers or rock groups that you would recommend for us to hear?

Dylan: I'm glad you asked that. [*Laughter.*] Oh, yeah, the Sir Douglas Quintet I think are probably the best that are going to have a chance of reaching the commercial airways. They already have with a couple songs.

Reporter: What about Paul Butterfield's group?

Dylan: They're good.

Reporter: Mr. Dylan, you call yourself a completely disconnected person—

Dylan: No, I didn't call myself that. They sort of drilled those words in my mouth. I saw that paper.

Reporter: A-ha. How would you describe yourself? Have you analyzed why you appeal to people?

Dylan: I certainly haven't. No.

Reporter: Mr. Dylan, I know you dislike labels and probably rightly so, but for those of us who are well over thirty, could you label yourself and perhaps tell us what your role is?

Dylan: Well, I'd sort of label myself as "well under thirty." [*Laughter.*] And my role is to just stay here as long as I can.

[*Laughter.*]

Reporter: Phil Ochs wrote something in a recent *Broadside* magazine to the effect that you have twisted so many people's wigs that he feels that it becomes increasingly dangerous for you to perform in public before an audience.

Dylan: Well, that's the way it goes. I can't apologize, certainly.

Reporter: Did you envision the time when you would give five concerts in one area like this within ten days?

Dylan: No. No, this is all very new to me.

Reporter: If you were draftable at present, do you have any feelings of what your actions might be?

Dylan: No. I'd probably just do what had to be done.

Reporter: What would that be?

Dylan: Well, I don't know. I never really speak in terms of what if, so I don't really know.

Reporter: You're considered by many people to be symbolic of the protest movement in the country for the young people. Are you going to participate in the Vietnam Day Committee demonstration in front of the Fairmont Hotel tonight?

Dylan: No, I'll be busy tonight.

[*Laughter.*]

Reporter: Are you planning any demonstrations?

Dylan: Well, we thought of one. I don't know if it could be organized in time.

Reporter: Would you describe it?

Dylan: Well it was a demonstration where I make up the cards. You know, they have a group of protesters here, perhaps carrying cards with pictures of jack of diamonds and the ace of spades on them. Pictures of mules, maybe words and, oh, maybe about twenty-five, thirty thousand of these things printed up and just picket. Carry signs and picket in front of the post office.

Reporter: What words?

Dylan: Oh . . . camera [*laughter*], microphone [*laughter*], loose. Just words. Names of some famous people.

Reporter: Do you consider yourself a politician?

Dylan: Well, I guess so. I have my own party, though.

Reporter: Does it have a name?

Dylan: No. There's no presidents in the party. There's no presidents or vice presidents or secretaries or anything like that, so it makes it kinda hard to get in.

Reporter: Is there any right wing or left wing in that party?

Dylan: No. It's more or less in the center. Kind of on the uppity scale.

Reporter: Do you think your party could end the war with China?

Dylan: I don't know. I don't know if they have any people over there that would be in the same kind of party. So it might be kind of hard to infiltrate. I don't think my party would ever be approved by the White House or anything like that.

Reporter: Is there anyone else in your party?

Dylan: No. Most of us don't even know each other. It's hard to tell who's in it and who's not in it.

Reporter: Would you recognize them when you see them?

Dylan: Oh, you can recognize the people when you see them.

[*Laughter.*]

Reporter: Are there still tickets available for your concerts in this area?

Dylan: I would imagine so. At least some, I guess.

Reporter: How long do you think before you finally will quit?

Dylan: Gee, I don't know. I could answer that but it would mean something different probably for everybody, so we want to keep away from those kind of things.

Reporter: What did you mean when you said I don't think things will work out too easily . . .

Dylan: It's not that I don't think things can turn out. I don't think anything you plan ever turns out the way you plan it. That's all.

Reporter: Is that your philosophy?

Dylan: No, no. Doesn't mean anything.

Reporter: Do you think that it's fun to put on an audience?

Dylan: I don't know. I've never done it.

Reporter: I heard a song called "Baby, You Been on My Mind." Has it been recorded?

Dylan: No.

Reporter: Do you sing it in concert?

Dylan: No, I haven't.

Reporter: Are the concerts fun still?

Dylan: Yeah. Concerts are much more fun than they used to be.

Reporter: Do you consider them more important than your albums, for instance?

Dylan: No. It's just a kick to do it now. The albums are the most important.

Reporter: Because they reach more people?

Dylan: No, because it's all very concise, and it's easy to hear the words. There's no chance of the sound interfering, whereas we've played some concerts where sometimes they have very bad halls. You know, microphone systems so it's not that easy for somebody to come and just listen to a band as if they were listening to one person.

Reporter: Will you make all those lyrics of songs available in a book sometime?

Dylan: Oh, they all are, yeah.

Reporter: You say you no longer sing your older songs. Do you consider them less valid than the ones you're putting out now?

Dylan: No, I just consider them something else—in another time, another dimension. It would be kind of dishonest for me to sing them now, because I wouldn't really feel like singing them.

Reporter: What is the strangest thing that ever happened to you?

Dylan: You're gonna get it, man.

[*Laughter.*]

Reporter: But what is the weirdest thing that ever happened to you?

Dylan: I'll talk to you about it later. [*Laughter.*] I wouldn't do that to you.

Reporter: What areas of music that you haven't gotten into do you hope to get into?

Dylan: Writing a symphony with different melodies and different words, different ideas, all being the same, which just roll on top of each other and underneath each other.

Reporter: Mr. Dylan, when will you know that it's time to get out of the music field into another field?

Dylan: When I get very dragged.

Reporter: When you stop making money?

Dylan: No. When my teeth get better or, God . . . when I start to itch. When something just goes to a terrifying turn, and I know it's got nothing to do with anything and it's time to leave.

Reporter: You say you're gonna write symphonies. Is this in the terms that we think of symphonies?

Dylan: I'm not sure. Songs which are all written as a part of a symphony—different melodies, different changes—with words or without them. . . . I mean, they say that my songs are long now. Well, sometime I'm just gonna come up with one whole album, consisting of one song. I don't know who's going to buy it. That might be the time to leave.

Reporter: What's the longest song you've recorded?

Dylan: I don't know. I don't really check those things. They just turn out long. I guess I've recorded one about eleven, twelve minutes long. "[Ballad of] Hollis Brown" was pretty long on my second record [*Actually, on his third. —Ed.*] and "With God on Your Side" was kind of long. But none of them, I don't think, were as much into anything as "Desolation Row" was, and that was long, too. Songs shouldn't seem long. It just so happens that it looks that way on paper, that's all. The length of it doesn't really have anything to do with it.

Reporter: Doesn't this give you a problem in issuing records?

Dylan: No, they're just ready to do anything that I put down now, so they don't really care.

Reporter: But what happens if they have to cut a song in half, like "Subterranean Homesick Blues"?

Dylan: They didn't have to cut that in half.

Reporter: They didn't have to, but they did.

Dylan: No, they didn't. You're talking about "Like a Rolling Stone."

Reporter: Oh, yeah.

Dylan: They cut it in half for the disc jockeys. Well, you see, that song, it didn't matter for the disc jockeys if they had it cut in half because the other side was a continuation and if anybody was interested they could just turn it over. But we just made a song the other day which came out ten minutes long, and I thought of releasing it as a single but they would have cut it up but it wouldn't have worked that way, so we're not gonna turn it out as a single. It's called "Freeze Out." You'll hear it on the next album.

Bill Graham: Of all the people who record your compositions, who do you feel does most justice to what you're trying to say?

Dylan: I think Manfred Mann. They've done about three or four, and each one of them has been right in context with what the song was all about.

Reporter: What is your new book about?

Dylan: Oh, it's just about all kinds of different things. Rats, balloons. They're about the only things that come to my mind right now.

Reporter: Is that the same book that Macmillan—

Dylan: Yes, yes.

Reporter: Do press conferences oppress you?

Dylan: No, I don't really do too many of them. I wouldn't do it if I was oppressed or depressed. There's nothing wrong . . . it's just kind of silly to come up here, that's all.

Reporter: Mr. Dylan, how would you define folk music?

Dylan: How would I define folk music? As a constitutional replay of mass production.

Reporter: Do you call your songs folk songs?

Dylan: No, no.

Reporter: Are protests songs folk songs?

Dylan: I guess, if they're a constitutional replay of mass production.

[*Laughter.*]

Reporter: Do you prefer songs with a subtle or obvious message?

Dylan: I don't really prefer those kind of songs at all. Message . . . you mean like—

Reporter: Well, like "Eve of Destruction" and things like that.

Dylan: Do I prefer that to what?

Reporter: I don't know, but your songs are supposed to have a subtle message.

Dylan: Subtle message?

Reporter: Well, they're supposed to.

[*Laughter.*]

Dylan: Where'd you hear that?

[*Laughter.*]

Reporter: In a movie magazine.

[*Laughter.*]

Dylan: Oh, my God. Well, we don't discuss those things here.

Reporter: Are your songs ever about real people?

Dylan: Sure. They're all about real people.

Reporter: Particular ones?

Dylan: Particular people? Sure. I'm sure you've seen all the people in my songs at one time or another.

Reporter: Who's Mr. Jones?

Dylan: I'm not going to tell you his first name. I'd get sued.

[*Laughter.*]

Reporter: What does he do for a living?

Dylan: He's a pin boy. [*Laughter.*] He also wears suspenders.

[*Laughter.*]

Reporter: Can you explain your attraction as a performer and a writer ?

Dylan: Attraction to what?

[*Laughter.*]

Reporter: Your attraction, your mass popularity.

Dylan: No, no. I really have no idea. That's the truth. I always tell the truth.

Reporter: What are your personal hopes for the future, and what do you hope to change in the world?

Dylan: To be honest, I don't have any hopes for the future, and I just hope to have enough boots to be able to change them. That's all, really. It doesn't boil down to anything more than that. If it did, I would certainly tell you.

Reporter: What do you think of a question-and-answer session of this type, with you as the principal subject?

Dylan: Well, I think we all have different—I think I dropped an ash on myself somewhere; you'll see in a minute here—I'm not going to say anything about it, though. I . . . what was the question?

Reporter: What are you thinking about right now?

Dylan: I'm thinking about this ash.

[*Laughter.*]

Reporter: Right before that.

Dylan: The ash is creeping up on me somewhere. I've lost touch with myself so I can't tell where exactly it is.

Reporter: Was that an inadvertent evading of the question—what you feel about meetings of this kind, question-and-answer sessions—

Dylan: Oh, no, no. I just know in my own mind that we all have a different idea of all the words we're using, so I really can't take it too seriously. Like if I say the word "house," we're both going to see a different house. So we're using all these other words like "mass production" and "movie magazine" and we all have a different idea of these words, too, so I don't really know what we're saying here.

Reporter: Is it pointless?

Dylan: No, it's not pointless. If you want to do it, and you're there, it's not pointless. It doesn't hurt me any.

Reporter: Is there anything in addition to your songs that you want to say to people?

Dylan: Good luck.

Reporter: You don't say that in your songs.

Dylan: Oh, yes, I do. Every song tails off with "good luck, I hope you make it."

[*Laughter.*]

Reporter: What do you bother to write the poetry for if we all get different images and we don't know what you're talking about?

Dylan: Because I got nothing else to do, man.

[*Laughter.*]

Reporter: Do you have a rhyme for "orange"?

Dylan: A-ha. Just a rhyme for "orange"?

Reporter: Is it true that you were censored from singing on *The Ed Sullivan Show* because they wouldn't let you sing what you wanted to?

Dylan: I'll tell you the rhyme in a minute.

Reporter: Did they censor you from singing what you wanted to on *The Ed Sullivan Show*?

Dylan: Yes. It was a long time ago.

Reporter: What did you want to sing?

Dylan: I don't know, it was some song which I wanted to sing and they said I could sing. It's more to it than just censorship there. They actually said I could sing the song, but when we went through the rehearsal of it, the guy came back afterwards and said I have to change it and he said, "Can't you sing some folk song like the Clancy Brothers do?" And I didn't know any of their songs and so I couldn't be on the program. That's what it came down to.

Allen Ginsberg: Have you found that the texts of the interviews with you which have been published are accurate to the actual conversations?

Dylan: No. That's another reason I don't really give press interviews or anything, because even if you do something—there are a lot of people here, so they know what's going on—but if you just do it with one guy or a few guys, they just take it all out of context, split it up in the middle or just take what they want to use and they even ask you a question and you answer it and then it comes out in print that they just substitute another question for your answer. It's not really truthful to do that kind of thing, so I just don't do it. That's just a press problem there.

Reporter: Do you think the entire text of your news conference today should be printed in the newspaper?

Dylan: Oh, no, nothing like that. But this is just for the interviews, when they do interviews in places like Omaha or Cincinnati. I don't do it and then they write bad things.

Reporter: Well, isn't this partly because you are often inaudible? Like, for most of this dialogue or monologue you have been inaudible, and now when you're touched personally by the misquotation, your voice rises and we can hear you.

Dylan: Yeah, well, I just realized that maybe people in the back there can't hear me, that's all.

Reporter: I was going to ask you, in your songs you sing out—

Dylan: Yes, I do.

Reporter: —and whether in your conversations you cultivate—

Dylan: You see, the songs is what I do—write the songs and sing them and perform them. That's what I do. The performing part of it could end, but I'm gonna be writing these songs and singing them on records for . . . I see no end, right now. That's what I do. Anything else interferes with it, I mean anything trying to get on top, making something out of it which it isn't, it just brings me down, and it just makes it seem all very cheap.

Reporter: Well, it made me feel like you were almost doing a kind of penance of silence here—

Dylan: No, no.

Reporter: —for the first part—

Dylan: No, no, I'm not one of those kind of people at all.

Reporter: You don't need silence?

Dylan: No, no silence. It's always silent where I am.

Reporter: Mr. Dylan, when you're on a concert tour how many people travel in your party? Do you travel alone or do you have a—

Dylan: We travel with about twelve people now.

Reporter: Do the number of people seem to increase as you make more money?

Dylan: Oh, yes, of course.

[*Laughter.*]

Reporter: Is that known as Dylan's Law?

Reporter: Why do you need so many people when you travel?

Dylan: Well, we have five in the group. And we need other things. We have a lot of electronic equipment now, a lot of different things which have to be taken care of, so we need a lot of people. We have three road managers and things like that. We don't make any big public presentations, though. Like we never come into town in limousines or anything like that. We just go from place to place and do the shows.

Reporter: You fly in your own plane? Do you have a private plane?

Dylan: Yes, yes.

Reporter: Do you have to get in a certain type of mood to write your music?

Dylan: Yeah, I guess so. A certain type of mood, if you want to call it that.

Reporter: Do you find that you are perhaps more creative at a certain time of the day?

Dylan: Yes, yes, I feel that way.

Reporter: Like a night writer?

Dylan: I wouldn't say night has anything to do with it.

Reporter: Have you ever sung with the Beatles?

Dylan: No. Well, I think we may have messed around in London, but, no, I don't think anything serious.

Reporter: Have you ever played a dance?

Dylan: No. It's not that kind of music.

Reporter: It is.

Dylan: Well, what can I say? You must know more about the music then than I do. How long have *you* been playing it?

Reporter: Do you find that when you're writing you sort of free-associate often?

Dylan: No, it's all very clear and simple to me. These songs aren't complicated to me at all. I know what they all are all about. There's nothing hard to figure out for me. I wouldn't write anything I can't really see.

Reporter: I didn't mean it that way. I meant that when you're creating a song, are you doing it more or less on a subliminal level where you're letting your mind just flow? Where you're very conscious of each step, each word?

Dylan: No. No, that's the difference in the songs I write now. In the past year or so—in the last year and a half, maybe two, I don't know—but the songs before, up till one of those records . . . I wrote the fourth record in Greece, so there was a change there. But the records before that, I used to know what I wanted to say before I used to write the song, you see. All the stuff which I had written before which wasn't song was just on a piece of toilet paper when it comes out like that. That's the kind of stuff I never would sing because I know people just would not be ready for it. But I just went through that other thing of writing songs and I couldn't write like it anymore. It was just too easy and it wasn't really right. I would know what I wanted to say before I wrote the song and I would say it, and it never really would come out exactly the way I thought it would, but it came out, it touched it. But now, I just write a song, like I know that it's just going to be all right and I don't really know exactly what it's all about, but I do know the minute, the layers of what it's all about.

Reporter: What do you think about your song "It's Alright, Ma (I'm Only Bleeding)"? It happens to be my favorite one.

Dylan: God bless you, son. I haven't heard it for a long time. I couldn't even sing it for you probably.

Reporter: How long does it take you to write a song?

Dylan: Usually not too long a time, really. I might write all night and get one song out of a lot of different things I write.

Reporter: How many have you written?

Dylan: Well, there's one publisher that's got about a hundred. I've written about fifty others, I guess, so I got about 150 songs I've written.

Reporter: Have they all been published?

Dylan: Well, no. Some of the scraps haven't been published. But I find I can't really sing that anyway, because I forget it, so the songs I don't publish, I usually do forget.

Reporter: Have you ever taken these scraps, as you call them, and made them into a song?

Dylan: No, I've forgotten the scraps. I have to start over all the time. I can't really keep notes or anything like that.

Reporter: You can't go back to any of your earlier things and use them?

Dylan: No, no that wouldn't be right either.

Reporter: Do you get any help from the group that you play with when you write the songs?

Dylan: Robbie [Robertson], the lead guitar player, sometimes we play the guitars together, something might come up where I know it's gonna be right. I'll be just sitting around playing so I can write up some words. I don't get any kind of ideas, though, of what I want to . . . what's really going to happen here.

Reporter: Why do you think you're so popular?

Dylan: I don't know. I'm not a reporter, I'm not a newsman or anything. I'm not even a philosopher, so I have no idea. I would think other people would know, but I don't think I know. When you get too many people talking about the same thing it tends to clutter up things. Everybody asks me that so I realize they must be talking about it, so I'd rather stay out of it and make it easier for them. Then, when they get the answer, I hope they tell me.

[*Laughter.*]

Reporter: Has there been any more booing when you've played electric?

Dylan: Oh, there's booing. You can't tell where the booing's going to come up. Can't tell at all. It comes up in the weirdest, strangest places and when it comes up it's quite a thing in itself. I figure there's a little "boo" in all of us.

Reporter: Bob, where is Desolation Row?

Dylan: Where? Oh, that's someplace in Mexico. It's across the border. It's noted for its Coke factory. [*Laughter.*] Coca-Cola machines . . . sells a lotta Coca-Cola down there.

Reporter: Where is Highway 61?

Dylan: Highway 61 exists. That's out in the middle of the country. It runs down to the South, goes up north.

Reporter: Mr. Dylan, you seem very reluctant to talk about the fact that you're a most popular entertainer.

Dylan: Well, what do you want me to say about it?

Reporter: You seem almost embarrassed to admit that you're popular.

Dylan: Well, I'm not embarrassed. I mean, what do you want, exactly, for me to say? You want me to jump up and say "Hallelujah!" and crash the cameras or do something weird? Tell me, tell me. I'll go along with you. If I can't go along with you, I'll find somebody to go along with you.

Reporter: No, but you really have no idea as to why or no thoughts on why you are popular? That's what interests me.

Dylan: I just haven't really struggled for that. It happened, you know? It happened like anything else happens. Just a happening. You don't figure out happenings. You dig happenings. So I'm not going to even talk about it.

Reporter: Do you feel that part of the popularity is because of an identification of your audience with you or with what you're saying or what you've been writing about?

Dylan: I have no idea. I don't really come too much in contact.

Reporter: Does it make life more difficult?

Dylan: No, it certainly doesn't.

Reporter: Were you surprised the first time the boos came?

Dylan: Yeah, that was at Newport [Folk Festival]. Well, I did this very crazy thing. [*Laughter.*] So I didn't really know what was going to happen, but they certainly booed, I'll tell you that. You could hear it all over the place. I don't know who they were, though, and I'm certain whoever it was did it twice as loud as they normally would. They kind of quieted down some at Forest Hills [Tennis Stadium], although they did it there, too. They've done it just about all over except in Texas. They didn't boo us in Texas or in Atlanta or in Boston or in Ohio or in Minneapolis. But they've done it a lot of other places. I mean, they must be pretty rich to be able to go someplace and boo. [*Laughter.*] I couldn't afford it if I was in their shoes.

Reporter: Other than the booing, have the audiences changed? Do you get screaming? Do you get people rushing the stage?

Dylan: Oh, sometimes you get people rushing the stage, but you just turn 'em off very fast. Kick 'em in the head or something like that. [*Laughter.*] They get the picture.

Graham: Going back to what you said about not really being concerned and not really knowing why you are in the midst of this popularity. That is in direct opposition to what most people who reach this level of popularity say.

Dylan: Well, a lot of people start out and try to be stars, I would imagine. Like, however they have to be stars. I know a lot of those people. And they start out and they go into show business for many, many reasons—to be seen. This had nothing to do with it when I started. I started from New York City, and there just wasn't any of that around. It just happened.

Graham: Don't misunderstand me. I agree with your right not to have to care. My point is that it would be somewhat disappointing to the many people who think that you feel towards them the way they feel towards you and that's the reason for your popularity. That's what they think.

Dylan: Oh, well, I don't want to disappoint anybody. I mean, tell me what I should say. I'll certainly go along with anything, but I really don't have much of an idea.

Reporter: You have a poster there.

Dylan: Yeah, it's a poster somebody gave me. It looks pretty good. The Jefferson Airplane, John Handy Quintet, and Sam Thomas and the Mystery Trend and the Great Society are all playing at the Fillmore Auditorium Friday, December 10th, and I would like to go if I could. [*Laughter.*] But unfortunately, I won't be here, I don't think. But if I was here, I certainly would be there.

Reporter: Do you tour in the South?

Dylan: Yeah.

Reporter: What's more important to you—the way that your music and words sound, or the content, the message of the work?

Dylan: The whole thing while it's happening. It either happens or it doesn't happen. Just the thing which is happening at the time. That is the most important thing; there really isn't anything else. I don't know if I answered your question.

Reporter: Well, you mean it might happen one time, and it might not happen the next time with the same song?

Dylan: We've had some bad nights, but the records are always made of good cuts and in person most of the time it does come across. Most of the time we do feel like playing. That's important to me; the aftermath, and whatever happens before and after is not really important to me— just the time on the stage and the time that we're singing the songs and performing them. Or not really performing them even, just letting them be there.

Gleason: Bob, we promised to spring you at a certain time. It's now two o'clock. Thank you very much.

[*Applause.*]

PRESS CONFERENCE

December 16, 1965 | Los Angeles

Dylan must not have found his San Francisco press conference to be too distasteful an experience, because less than two weeks later, he subjected himself to another session with reporters, this time in Los Angeles. Here, journalists wasted no time in hitting him with absurd questions and Dylan, in fine form, was ready with appropriate answers. —Ed.

Aide to Dylan: I'd like to welcome everybody here this afternoon. At the far left is [publicist and talent scout] Billy James of Columbia Records. And I'm here just to sort of point fingers at people who've got questions. And Bob tells me that he has no formal statement. He said he would prefer not to answer any questions about science or trigonometry, which sort of blew the first ten that I had, so I would, if I may, lead it off with one question and then let you take it from there. Bob, these days, an awful lot of people are recording your songs, and I just wondered if you had any feelings of pride or horror or anything else about having your material done by other artists.

Bob Dylan: No.

Aide to Dylan: Anybody out there want to start off?

Reporter: Lately, in one of the national magazines, I read something about the protest singers, and I wonder if you could tell me, among the folksingers, how many would you say could be characterized as protest singers today?

Dylan: I don't understand. Could you ask the question again?

Reporter: Yeah. How many people who labor in the same musical vineyard in which you toil . . . how many are protest singers? That is, people who use their music and use the songs to protest the social state in which we live today—the matter of war, the matter of crime, or whatever it might be.

Dylan: How many?

Reporter: Yes, are there many who—

Dylan: Yeah, I think there's about 136.

[*Laughter.*]

Reporter: You say, "about 136"?

Dylan: Yeah.

Reporter: Or do you mean exactly 136?

Dylan: It's either 136 or 142.

Reporter: Are there, seriously? Can you name a few of them for me?

Dylan: Protest? You just want singers?

Reporter: How about Barry McGuire? Is he one? What is he?

Dylan: He'd be sort of a mixture of country and western and seventeenth-century literature music . . . Robert Goulet is a protest singer. All the attention has been given to everybody that that has long hair, but the truth of the matter is really that the protest singers are Eydie Gormé and Robert Goulet and Steve Lawrence. It's very obvious if you go beyond the word "protest."

Reporter: What does the word "protest" mean to you?

Dylan: It means singing when you really don't want to sing.

Reporter: Do you sing against your wishes?

Dylan: No.

Reporter: Do you sing protest songs?

Dylan: No.

Reporter: What do you sing?

Dylan: I sing all love songs.

Reporter: Is it true that you have changed your name? And if so, what was your real name?

Dylan: My real name was Kunezevitch. I changed it to avoid all these relatives that come up to you in different parts of the country and want tickets for concerts and stuff like that.

Reporter: Kunezevitch?

Dylan: Kunezevitch, yes.

Reporter: Was that your first or the last name?

Dylan: That was the first name. [*Laughter and applause.*] I don't really want to tell you what the last name was. [*Laughter.*]

Reporter: I've heard critics say that you have no real purpose in mind when you write a song except to shock people. Is that true?

Dylan: You know that's not true. You've heard the songs, haven't you?

Reporter: Yes.

Dylan: Well, you know that's not true then.

Reporter: I think "Puff the Magic Dragon" and "The [*sic*] Tambourine Man" were considered by some to be endorsements of marijuana smoking.

Dylan: Well, I didn't write "Puff the Magic Dragon." That's horrible. Whatever that is, I didn't write that. And, "Mr. Tambourine Man," there's no marijuana in that song. At least I never heard it before.

Reporter: Do you have a music background? What is your education?

Dylan: Same as everybody's. High school.

Reporter: Bob, if you were to put a label upon yourself, how would you characterize yourself? What kind of a singer *are* you?

Dylan: I'm more of a mathematical singer. I use words like most people use numbers. That's about the best I can do.

Reporter: Could you elaborate a little bit more on that? You're losing me there.

Dylan: Oh, I hate to do that. I can't elaborate on it any more than that. I could at another time. You really got me at a bad moment here.

Reporter: Bob, you and Joan Baez have become heroes of the new protest movement on college campuses.

Dylan: Oh, Jesus.

Reporter: I'd like to get your reaction to the student protest movement. A two-part question. The second part is whether you believe that there is a connection between the so-called New Left and the so-called new music.

Dylan: I don't know anything about the New Left or students very much at all. I don't really know any college students.

Reporter: I have a complaint against your vocals and I hear others and I read criticisms—

Dylan: Sorry. [*Giggles.*]

Reporter: I find it hard to get your words. You kind of mumble or you sort of slur and in the old days, you know, Sinatra on his fiftieth birthday, was complaining also about the new modern singers' enunciation and diction—

Dylan: Well, new modern singers are much too sick nowadays to—

Reporter: How about yourself? Are you sick in the same way? In terms of not comprehending the words and lyrics?

Dylan: I have a nervous disease. This keeps my words—if you want to pick on that, like you'd pick on a cripple . . .That's all I can say.

Reporter: You're not the only one. It's modern style. I'm just curious—

Dylan: It certainly isn't any style that's harmful to anybody. It's not gonna hurt anybody.

Reporter: Well, if they don't understand the words so easily.

Dylan: Well, it's not gonna hurt them not to understand the words.

Reporter: Bob, why is there such a widespread use of drugs among singers today?

Dylan: I don't know. Are you a singer?

[*Laughter.*]

Reporter: Am I wrong in assuming that or saying that?

Dylan: I don't know many of the other singers. I really don't know.

Reporter: Do you take drugs yourself?

Dylan: I don't even know what a drug is. I've never even seen a drug. I wouldn't know probably what one looked like if I saw one.

Reporter: Real way-out music and drugs seem to go together. Have any idea why that could be?

Dylan: I have no idea.

Reporter: Have you any intention of appearing at a Vietnam Day Committee benefit in San Francisco in a week or so?

Dylan: No. I'll be busy.

Reporter: Have you been asked?

Dylan: No.

Reporter: Bob, what'll be the next vogue in your opinion in the field of music in which you work?

Dylan: The next thing I'm gonna do?

Reporter: Anyone. What will catch on in your opinion?

Dylan: Gee, I don't know.

Reporter: What are you gonna do next? Something new and different?

Dylan: Yeah. I'm gonna write a symphony with words. Different words and songs going at the same time. I don't know if it's gonna be vogue.

Reporter: Can you explain a little bit more how you're gonna go about this? Will you have people reciting it all at once or what?

Dylan: Yeah. All at once everything's gonna happen. One song'll be playing here in one key, another song'll be in another key. There'll be sounds from out this way, other sounds from another track. It all depends on how many tracks I decide to use. Use ten tracks, you can use ten different things going on at the same time, which is really a symphony.

Reporter: Bob, what sort of technique do you use when you write songs? Or don't you call it any sort of technique? How do you do it? Do you play on the piano first or write the music down first or the lyrics? What do you do?

Dylan: No, I just sit down and next thing I know, it's there.

Reporter: How does it come there?

Dylan: I don't know. I just sit down and I write. And the next thing I know, it's there.

Reporter: Do you produce your own records and so forth?

Dylan: No, I don't.

Reporter: Who's your favorite producer? Do you have any?

Dylan: You mean an A&Rs man?

Reporter: Yeah, the one that does the whole job of background and music and instrumentation.

Dylan: I don't know of too many people really that do that. Phil Spector.

Reporter: Who does yours?

Dylan: Oh, Columbia Records. A fellow named Bob Johnston does it.

Reporter: He's very good.

Dylan: You know him?

Reporter: No, I don't know him but he's very good.

Reporter: Bob, do you have any movie plans coming up?

Dylan: Yeah.

Reporter: What would you like to do?

Dylan: [*Laughs.*] She's very excited. Just make a movie.

Reporter: Would you play yourself or would you actually act?

Dylan: No, I'm gonna play my mother.

[*Laughter.*]

Reporter: How would you do that?

Dylan: That's very simple, really, if you think about it.

Reporter: Would you think about it and tell us?

Dylan: No, no. I just do things. I don't think it out.

Reporter: What would you call the movie? Any idea?

Dylan: No. Uh, *Mother Revisited.*

[*Laughter.*]

Reporter: Is there any chance that you could be drafted? Or have you already been in the service?

Dylan: I've already gone through that a long time ago.

Reporter: Were you in the service?

Dylan: No.

Reporter: Why were you putting us and the rest of the world on so—

Dylan: I'm just trying to answer your questions as good as you can ask them.

Reporter: How do you like being with Columbia Records?

Dylan: I like being part of Columbia Records very much.

Reporter: How many songs have you written for music publishers?

Dylan: About 125.

Reporter: I'm sure you must have been asked a thousand times, "What are you trying to say in your music?" I don't understand one of the songs.

Dylan: Well, you shouldn't feel offended or anything. I'm not trying to say anything to you. If you don't get it, you don't have to really think about it, because it's not addressed to you.

Reporter: Whom are you addressing?

Dylan: They're not addressed to anybody.

Reporter: Are you trying to say something when you write? Or are you just entertaining?

Dylan: I'm just an entertainer. That's all.

Reporter: But what are you trying to say in your songs? Can you take a couple of songs—

Dylan: No, no. Obviously, I just can't try to tell you that.

Reporter: Do you really feel the things that you write and say?

Dylan: What's there to feel? Name me something.

Reporter: Did you feel "Mr. Jones" ["Ballad of a Thin Man"] when you wrote that?

Dylan: I guess so. I must have felt it.

Reporter: I think we're talking about—

Dylan: We're talking about two different things.

Reporter: No, we're talking about standard emotions. We're talking about pain or remorse or love or—

Dylan: I have none of those feelings at all.

Reporter: What sort of feelings do you have when you write a song?

Dylan: They're songs. I'm showing you my feelings. They're in the songs. I don't have to explain my feelings. I'm not on trial.

[*Laughter.*]

Reporter: Bob, do you feel the popularity of the English groups has helped to boost your own popularity?

Dylan: I can't really answer that. Maybe it has, maybe it hasn't. Who am I to say?

Reporter: What are some of the groups that you think are good and have a great future? Some of the popular groups.

Dylan: The Fugs. Have you heard the Fugs?

[*Laughter.*]

Reporter: Is it true that you dedicated your first song to [actress] Brigitte Bardot?

Dylan: Yes, it's true.

Reporter: Why did you do that? Are you a fan of Miss Bardot?

Dylan: Yes, of course.

Reporter: Why?

Dylan: Why? Do I have to answer *that*? [*Laughter.*] You gotta think for yourself a little bit.

Reporter: Are you here today voluntarily?

Dylan: Yes.

[*Laughter.*]

Reporter: Bob, a personal question here, and I hope you'll forgive it. But you sound and you look very tired. Are you ill or is this your normal state?

[*Laughter.*]

Dylan: I take it as an insult. I don't like to hear that kind of thing.

Reporter: I don't mean to offend you but we can hardly hear you and you look very—

Dylan: Well, I'm from New York City. You're all from California. This health thing. I feel quite embarrassed about it the same way you do probably. But I have no explanation for it.

Reporter: Bob, what about the nervous condition that you mentioned to us? Is that evident or—

Dylan: I keep that very well concealed.

[*Laughter.*]

Reporter: Are you taking medication for it?

Dylan: Oh, yes, medication. What do you mean—drugs? [*Laughter.*] What kind of questions are those? Come on.

Reporter: Bob, were you serious about the symphony?

Dylan: Yes, to some degree.

Reporter: Have you thought a lot—

Dylan: I have some ideas, yeah.

Reporter: What would be the influence of this symphony? You say you've heard Beethoven's Ninth, for example?

Dylan: No, there wouldn't be any influence by Beethoven's Ninth. I know what he does, though. I know the forms, I know the musical—

Reporter: What about the influences as a lyric writer or poet? You mentioned the influence by Guthrie but I don't hear the influence—

Dylan: No, that was more the voice of a romantic latter James Dean kind of thing. If I wanted influences, I would read somebody or listen to somebody because I would dig them. That would be the only reason I would.

Reporter: Who have you collected on records over the past ten years?

Dylan: That I personally like? Oh, Lotte Lenya. Ma Rainey, all those people. Modern singers. Sir Douglas Quintet. The Staple Singers. Some of the French singers.

Reporter: In the way of poetry, who have you collected?

Dylan: I haven't collected anybody. I get books sent to me from [San Francisco's] City Lights [bookstore]. And from New York bookstores, they send them to me. And I read those. I like a lot of the older poets, though, more than anybody around now.

Reporter: Bob, what is the reason for your visit to California?

Dylan: Oh, I'm here looking for some donkeys. [*Laughter.*] I'm making a movie about Jesus.

Reporter: Where are you making it?

Dylan: Back east.

Reporter: For whom or with whom?

Dylan: It's an independent film.

Reporter: What type of movie, Bob?

Dylan: I don't really want to talk about it. I'm sure everybody understands. That's why I'm here in California. Besides that, I'll be playing a few times here and there. But I'm really here on business.

Reporter: Do you prefer to live there than here?

Dylan: Yeah.

Reporter: Are the recording facilities better here than there?

Dylan: No.

Reporter: Where do you do most of your recording?

Dylan: New York City.

Reporter: Why do you like New York better than here?

Dylan: I don't know. I guess it's just the closed-in feeling. You get used to being closed in after a while and you realize that it's really true. You go other places and it's closed in but it's not really. There's more to deal with.

Reporter: Have you had interviews in New York similar to this?

Dylan: Yeah. Not really, though. I know all the reporters there.

Reporter: I was wondering if you had the same questions there as here.

Dylan: No.

Reporter: What kind of friends are you attracted to? What type of people do you like the best and like to be surrounded with, if anybody?

Dylan: Horrible people. I have a lot of friends which are thieves. I have a few.

Reporter: Are you planning on visiting Joan Baez's School of Nonviolence?

Dylan: No, no.

Reporter: What are your feelings about this kind of involvement in political activities by singers?

Dylan: You mean singers who are political?

Reporter: Mm-hmm.

Dylan: That's fine if they want to be political. It doesn't hurt anybody.

Reporter: Are you going to be? Many students are saying that you were far more political a few years ago.

Dylan: In the songs, you mean?

Reporter: Mm-hmm.

Dylan: Oh, if you know my history in New York City, you can see the reasons for a lot of that. It's not really political, anyway. It was just another thing from free writing. You see, I always wrote. I was on the East Side. When I came to make money, I just went over and sent folk songs that I wrote. So it was two different things. My attraction was to writing. Only lately, in the past two years, have I discovered that I could put them both together.

Reporter: You have any intention of getting involved in protest politics, à la Joan Baez?

Dylan: No. I have too many other things to do.

Reporter: Bob, a lot of people have labeled you establishment-protesting and called you the father of the protest movement.

Dylan: Well, I guess I am.

Reporter: Do you think there's a legitimate protest movement in music now?

Dylan: Yeah, but you know as well as anybody else what that means. Like what does it mean—protest? What are they protesting? People were protesting, writing those kind of songs, five years ago on the East Coast. Everybody out there was all about that. But I'm not really into what other people do that much.

Reporter: Why do you think kids are listening to you now? Why do you think they want to hear what you have to say?

Dylan: I really don't know. I just heard something a couple days ago that amazed me on this tape outside a concert I played in San Jose. There's this fifteen-year-old girl out there and she's being interviewed and she knew of poets like William Blake. She knew his works. And she was hip to all kinds of different things which people are usually not acquainted with at that age. So maybe it's just a new kind of person, a fifteen-year-old person. I don't know. I do know that person was more free in the mind than a twenty-two-year-old college kid.

Reporter: Well, there's a greater maturity among the very young nowadays. Why is that?

Dylan: I don't know. Maturity is not what I mean at all. Maturity's just a phony word.

Reporter: A special kind of maturity, though. A special kind of attitude is what you're saying?

Dylan: Yeah, an attitude.

Reporter: What is the attitude today among young people?

Dylan: Oh, God. I don't even know any young people. I don't really know.

Reporter: Well, when you said "attitude," what could that be?

Dylan: Well, you have a certain attitude, right? I bet you have an attitude, like you can be personally insulted, can't you? All right, well, there's an attitude among a certain crowd of people that can't be personally insulted. And they know, without thinking—

Reporter: Is that how you feel?

Dylan: No, that's just one . . . term. I'm not talking about how I feel. I'm telling you the truth. Forget it comes from me.

Reporter: Bob, I'd like to ask you about sexual freedom and so forth. This is a new bag today, and what's the reason for it?

Dylan: [*Laughs.*] This guy I thought was really hip when I looked at him. I don't know.

Reporter: You don't know?

Dylan: No.

Reporter: Well, do you participate in the new scene?

Dylan: I don't participate in anything. Nothing. I bet you couldn't name one thing that I participate in. Go ahead, I dare ya.

[*Laughter.*]

Reporter: Well, this press conference. No, that's what we're trying to find out.

Dylan: Well, hope you do.

Reporter: I imagine you get a lot of letters, a lot of reactions from people near you. Do you have a feeling that they do read you?

Dylan: Yeah, yeah. Some of the younger ones, too. Yeah, they do.

Reporter: I think you're more popular among the young crowd than you are among the older generation.

Reporter: Bob, you mentioned you sing mostly love songs. Is love important to you when you write your songs?

Dylan: No.

Reporter: Is it important to you when you sing songs?

Dylan: No.

Reporter: Do you enjoy performing as opposed to writing?

Dylan: I like to sing and play, yeah.

Reporter: I don't know whether you want to answer this, Bob. I work for *Variety* and we like to have dollars and cents in the paper. Can you tell me how much you make a month from your Columbia Records alone.

Dylan: I don't know how much I make.

Reporter: You don't get a breakdown?

Dylan: I have no idea what I make and I don't want to ever find out.

Reporter: You spend a lot?

Dylan: Yeah, I spend a lot, I guess.

Reporter: Maybe Billy James can answer that.

Dylan: No, he wouldn't answer that, either.

Reporter: What do you spend your money on? You seem to live a very simple, uncomplicated life. You don't seem to be interested in motorcars, girls, yachts . . .

Dylan: Well, that's the way it goes.

Reporter: So I'm trying to figure out what you spend money on.

Dylan: I spend money on whatever is there to spend money on that I want to buy.

Reporter: Do you have investments? Apartment houses?

Dylan: I don't know what happens to my money. When I want money, I go ask for it and I get it. And I spend it. And when I want more, I ask for it and I get it. That's all. It's very simple, really.

Reporter: On the back of one of your albums [*Another Side of Bob Dylan*], you said Dean Martin should apologize to the Rolling Stones. [*Martin had made jokes at the Stones' expense when they appeared on an episode of ABC-TV's* Hollywood Palace *variety show that he hosted. —Ed.*] Why—

Dylan: I don't know. How long ago was that?

Reporter: I don't know. A year ago?

Dylan: The Rolling Stones weren't heard of here yet. They were just in England and I saw a thing, some kind of a snobby thing. I don't know what it was. It had nothing to do with talent or anything.

Reporter: What do you think of the Byrds?

Dylan: I like the Byrds.

Reporter: The Byrds and the Fugs, your two favorites?

Dylan: The Byrds and the Fugs; you sure boil things down to simplicity. OK.

Reporter: Your original association with Columbia—did it come about through John Hammond's son? Or just how did you sign with Columbia?

Dylan: I made a record with Carolyn Hester who at that time was signed, about five years ago—

Reporter: Was Hammond—

Dylan: Yeah, he A&R'd it.

Reporter: And he suggested cutting an album or did you request cutting—

Dylan: No, he just heard me play the harmonica. He wanted to know if I wanted to make an album.

Reporter: Do you know Hammond Jr.?

Dylan: Yes.

Reporter: Have you ever worked with him?

Dylan: No.

Aide to Dylan: Thank you. Well, thank you very much. There's some more press information outside for anybody that needs it.

RADIO CONVERSATION

Bob Fass | January 26, 1966 | *Radio Unnameable*, WBAI-FM (New York)

Dylan's relationship with Bob Fass, host of listener-supported WBAI-FM's long-running *Radio Unnameable*, dates back to before the show began in 1963, when Fass and Carla Rotolo double-dated with Carla's sister Suze, who was then Dylan's girlfriend. Dylan subsequently appeared several times on Fass's all-night program, which was known for stream-of-consciousness conversation among guests and the listeners who phoned in. Not all of those listeners seemed to be playing with a full deck, and the minds of some of the rest appeared to be chemically altered.

Perhaps Dylan's most memorable appearance on the show came in the early hours of January 26, 1966, less than four months before the release of *Blonde on Blonde*, his superb seventh album. Dylan spent more than an hour and a half in the studio that night, talking to listeners over the phone. Also on hand were Victor Maymudes, who had been his tour manager in the early '60s, and Al Kooper, who had played with Dylan at Newport and on such classic tracks as "Like a Rolling Stone."

A full transcript of the session would consume a rather large portion of this book, so I'm offering only highlights below. —Ed.

Bob Fass: This is Bob Fass. We're back on here with *Radio Unnameable*. Remember I told you about ten minutes ago that we were gonna have somebody come up who wasn't Shirley Temple? Well, it's true. Say hello.

Bob Dylan: I . . . this is Shirley Temple?

Fass: Yeah?

Dylan: [*Laughs.*] No, come on, don't do this to me.

Fass: I'm sorry, what am I doing to you?

Dylan: I haven't come down to apologize for not being Shirley Temple.

Fass: You want me to introduce you like Mike Wallace?

Dylan: No, no, no, I wouldn't.

Fass: Uh, this is Bob Dylan.

[*After some additional conversation, they take a phone call.*]

Fass: All you hippy-dips from Forest Hills, here's your chance to call up and talk to Bob Dylan. OK? WBAI. Hello there.

Caller: Bob Fass?

Fass: Yeah, this is Bob Fass.

Caller: Oh, hi. Listen, I've just been listening, and I called a couple of times. I was wondering, is it possible to come over and take a couple of pictures?

Fass: No, it's not. I'm sorry. It's all right with me. You can take pictures of me but some other night. Bob Dylan shakes his head no.

Caller: He shakes his head no?

Fass: Yeah, the truth is that Bob Dylan isn't really here—

Caller: Oh, it's just a record.

Fass: —and he's sold his soul to the devil, and pictures don't appear. People point cameras at him and push buttons and nothing happens, and there are these blank emulsions.

Caller: Let me ask you one question, OK? Would you just tell him that it's my fifteen-year-old infatuated sister-in-law, and it's not for myself.

[*Laughter.*]

Dylan: Oh, of course, come right over.

Caller: She didn't make it to Forest Hills, and she didn't go to Antioch.

Dylan: My goodness.

Caller: You know, and it's rough all around.

Dylan: What can I do? What can I do?

Caller: And I promise a cup of coffee, also.

Dylan: Oh jeez, you make me feel terrible, I just can't begin to—

Caller: To make steps to go with the mustard.

Dylan: The mustache?

Caller: The mustard. And I also sent in fifteen dollars, you know, so—

Dylan: Oh, my goodness.

Fass: Did you send it to me or to Bob Dylan?

Caller: No, I sent it to you.

Fass: Oh, well, see, that doesn't do any good.

Caller: And I'm starving. It's not possible?

Dylan: Oh, well, all right. We'll see you again some other time. Thanks for calling.

Caller: It is possible or it's not possible?

Dylan: Huh? Is it possible what?

Caller: To take a picture or not?

Dylan: Oh, to take a picture up here?

Caller: Yeah.

Dylan: Oh, no, you wouldn't wanna do that, no, no.

Caller: I *would* like to do that!

Dylan: No, no. You really wouldn't. You'd be very disappointed.

———————————

Caller: May I speak to Mr. Dylan, please?

[*Laughter.*]

Dylan: Is this chick going out over the radio?

Fass: Yeah.

Dylan: [*Laughs.*] Can everybody else hear her voice?

Caller: Hello?

Dylan: Who's this?

Caller: I don't know.

Dylan: [*Laughs.*] All right.

Caller: Bob, did you ever share a TV dinner with anyone?

Dylan: Did I ever share a TV dinner with anyone?

Caller: Mm-hmm.

Dylan: Never! Never! No, no.

Caller: Would you share one with me?

Dylan: Insult after insult.

Fass: I'm sorry, I'm gonna have to close the telephone if you people keep making improper suggestions to my guests.

Caller: I thought it was a free-speech radio station.

Fass: Yes, but there are bounds of propriety. You can't shout free-speech dinner in a crowded theatre!

Caller: Oh, you cannot?

Dylan: It's true! God, that's pretty good! [*Laughs.*]

Caller: How about lots of TV dinners?

Fass: How about what?

Caller: How about lots of TV dinners?

Fass: That's compounding your conspiracy.

Dylan: Didn't I see you on Sixth Avenue?

Caller: I called up NBC concerning what they said about you!

Fass: What did they say about Mr. Dylan on NBC?

Caller: They didn't say anything about him, but they said something about BAI that I didn't like too much.

Fass: Uh-huh!

All: Ohh! Wooooooooh!

Fass: You know what we say about NBC!

Dylan: Yeah.

Fass: TV dinners to NBC.

Caller: OK. Bob wants two, but overcooked.

Fass: OK, anything else you want to say?

Caller: Is he happy?

Fass: That's a good question.

Caller: Are you?

Dylan: Who, Mr. Brill?

Caller: Bob!

Fass: That's my name. I'm Bob.

Caller: Are you happy?

Fass: No, his friends call him Bobby.

Caller: Well, who said I was his friend? Am I your friend? Am I?

Fass: Who are you talking to?

Caller: All of you.

Fass: All of us?

Dylan: True, everybody's your friend.

Fass: That's a very personal, individual question.

Dylan: It's not personal. No, it's just dumb.

Caller: Why is it dumb? Of course, I couldn't possibly be your friend, because you don't even know who I am.

Dylan: Oh, come on. I do, too!

Caller: You do not!

Dylan: Come on! I saw you the other day!

Caller: You did, huh?

Dylan: I did, yeah, and you know I did!

Caller: It's funny, 'cause I've never seen you.

Dylan: Well, nobody ever sees me.

Caller: Except on album covers. I'd like to, though, because I bet you're very nice.

Dylan: Well, that's fortunate. Most people don't even see those . . . huh?

Caller: —underneath it all.

Dylan: Underneath it all?

Caller: Um-hmm.

Fass: That sounds like a song.

Dylan: [*Sings.*] Underneath it all . . .

Caller: Would you make a record called "Underneath It All"? I bet you could.

Dylan: Would I make a record "Underneath It All"?

Caller: Yeah.

Fass: You have a peculiar love/hate relationship with your fans, I'm beginning to realize, like something out of [French novelist Jean] Genet.

Dylan: Oh, come on, all my fans have a sense of humor.

Fass: OK. Unless you can say something besides "TV dinner," we're gonna have to go on to another call.

Caller: Well, what can I say? Why don't you answer a question that I haven't asked? Something that you want to tell everybody but nobody asks you.

Dylan: I was waiting for somebody to ask me that!

Caller: Well, would you?

Dylan: Well, no, I won't.

———————

Fass: Who's calling, please?

Caller: Hello, my name is Frankenstein.

Fass: Yes?

Dylan: Yes? I don't believe him.

Caller: Can I speak to Bob Fass, please?

Fass: Yeah, I'm speaking, Mr. Stein.

Dylan: Are you gonna get any tea?

Caller: Hello. Yeah, oh, Frankenstein—that's my second name.

Fass: Do you want some tea with lemon? I wish someone would try to get some tea with lemon.

Caller: Hello.

Dylan: Yeah, OK, Mr. Frankenstein.

Caller: Yeah, well, I don't want to speak to Mr. Dylan.

Fass: You want to speak to me, right?

Caller: No, I wanna . . .

Fass: Yeah? Are you having trouble talking, sir?

Caller: Well . . .

Dylan: Say, Frankenstein, come on!

Caller: Can you get her phone number?

Fass: Can we what?

Caller: Can you get her phone number?

Fass: Whose phone number?

Caller: You see, I'm pretty hungry.

Fass: Uh-huh.

Dylan: No, no. Don't turn him off. He's hungry! Tell me, are you as hungry as a man in drag?

Caller: Yeah.

Dylan: Huh?

Caller: Yeah, well, she got a TV dinner there.

Dylan: Hey, hey, hey, come on now. Oh, you can't get an answer. How hungry are you?

Caller: Oh, I'm starvin'.

Fass: Oh?

Dylan: How hungry? About as hungry as a raccoon? A piece of flypaper that's balancing on a pair of earplugs—

Caller: Yeah—

Dylan: —out in Allen Ginsberg's kitchen? Are you that hungry?

Caller: I'm down outside your studio now.

Dylan: Huh?

Caller: I'm down outside your studio now. I'm waiting to throw snow-balls at you, but I'm so hungry, I'm sort of eating them.

Dylan: You're waiting to throw snowballs, huh? Well, this is all a joke here now. You just come up a little closer to that door, and you see what's gonna happen. If you come up just a little closer, you throw one at that door. We're not down there, but you just go ahead and do it!

Caller: I got a mob with me, too.

Dylan: Oh, groovy! [*Laughs.*]

Caller: And a small Irishman called Quill.

Dylan: Oh ho-ho! Very scary, very scary indeed but I'm not hungry.

Caller: Yeah, yeah, you wanna see us but—

Fass: So long, bye-bye.

Dylan: Why don't you say goodbye nicely to him and . . .

Fass: Goodbye nicely, sir.

Caller: Well, so long.

Fass: Nicely. WBAI.

Caller: Hello, is this Dial-a-Prayer?

Fass: [*Laughs.*] Yes, this is Dial-a-Prayer.

Dylan: Diaphragm?

Fass: Dial-a-Prayer!

Dylan: Oh.

Fass: That's where you sing from.

Dylan: Oh.

Fass: Yeah, hello. You'll have to turn your radio down, sir.

Dylan: I thought they were those things that chicks get. [*Laughs.*]

Fass: Hello? Hello? So long! WBAI.

Caller: Hello . . . Mr. Dylan, please.

Fass: Yes, the voice of sanity!

Dylan: Switch her right over here. This sounds very good.

Caller: Hello.

Dylan: Who is this?

Caller: Hello, who is this?

Dylan: Well, who is this?

Caller: This is Ann.

Dylan: Well, you have to say who it is because they have to all be marked down in a little book that has to go into the YMCA files.

Caller: Yeah, all right.

Dylan: So who is this, please?

Caller: This is Ann Wilkinson, sort of from Buffalo.

Dylan: Who?

Caller: Ann Wilkinson, sort of from Buffalo. I sort of met you there.

Dylan: [*Jokingly.*] Ann Wilkinson from Buffalo—oh, yes, of course.

Caller: I sort of burst in on one of your concerts at Kleinhans [Music Hall, in Buffalo, New York].

Dylan:. Was that you? One of the people who was beating on the window out there?

Caller: No, no, not there. I saw it from the sky.

Voice: A go-go dancer!

Caller: I wanted to wish you Merry Christmas.

Dylan: Well, thank you very much! How's your toe? [*Laughs.*]

Caller: I'm a bit late. I also wanted to know when "Visions of Johanna" is coming out.

Dylan: Oh, you heard that song?

Caller: Yeah, Al Kooper played it for me.

[*Laughter*].

Dylan: Oh, yeah, it's good, huh? [*Laughs.*]

———————

Fass: WBAI.

Caller: Good evening. I'd like to talk to Bob Dylan.

Fass: Why don't you?

Dylan: You have to give your name.

Caller: My name's Steve.

Dylan: Steve what?

Caller: It's Gitlin.

Dylan: Steve Dylan?

Caller: Gitlin.

Dylan: That was almost my name! [*Laughs.*]

Fass: What was it before it was Gitlin?

Caller: What was it before it was Gitlin? Gitlin!

Dylan: What do you have to say, Dylan?

Caller: Bob?

Dylan: [*Laughs.*] Come on. What else have you got to say?

Caller: Bob, I wish it were Dylan. To start off with, what do you think of the Byrds?

Dylan: The Fugs?

Caller: The Byrds!

Dylan: The Byrds! Oh, come on! Don't ask me these kinda questions. I like the Byrds, man. I like everybody! Come on, whaddaya mean?

Fass: Can somebody bring some water in here, please?

Dylan: Well, what do I think of Rosemary Clooney or Judy Garland's daughter? Rosa [*Actually Liza. —Ed.*] Minnelli?

Caller: What? What do you think about boys who have long hair? Do you think—

Dylan: Oh, you're Rosa Minnelli's boyfriend, I know who you are.

Fass: Boys with long hair, huh?

Caller: Do you think they should be made to be cut?

Dylan: Oh, what do you think?

Caller: Not really.

Dylan: Oh, well then, there you have it in a nutshell.

Fass: That's up to you.

Dylan: It's up to you. It's in your hands, man. Whatever you think, you tell your principal that.

Caller: Yeah, and if they flunk me out of school?

Dylan: Well, I don't know . . .

Fass: You don't wanna go to a school like that, do you?

Dylan: That depends what you wanna do, man. If you wanna go to school or if you don't wanna go to school. If you don't wanna go, you can try to help the school. But if you wanna go to school, you just better take your place and be quiet.

Caller: Uh-huh. Have you got a new album out?

Dylan: No, it won't be out . . . in about February.

Caller: Uh-huh. Where do you get your ideas for songs?

Dylan: No, no, this is over the limit.

Fass: We've got to go to another call. Thanks a lot.

Dylan: Goodbye now.

Fass: Bye-bye. WBAI.

Caller: Can I have Bob Dylan, please?

Fass: Can you what? Can you have him? No. Nobody can have him.

Dylan: You have to give your name. I'm sorry, sir.

Caller: Melvin Margoulis.

Dylan: Melvin Margoulis. I've seen you before.

Caller: I'm really Bob Dylan.

Dylan: Ha, ha. I know you are.

Caller: How do you know?

Dylan: I know everything.

Caller: Well, get that imposter off the radio then.

Dylan: Well, what can I do, man? He's sitting right here now . . .

Caller: No, but I'm really Dylan, by the way.

Fass: I think you have a very advanced case of schizophrenia. I'll go on to the next call.

Fass: WBAI.

Caller: Good morning.

Fass: Good morning.

Caller: First of all, Bob, I really like your program a whole lot. I usually call you up about this time some evenings to tell you that I'm doing a paper. And Mr. Dylan? I think your writing is real great, and you play the kazoo and guitar real great but it would be real greater if you could just kinda sing a little bit better.

Dylan: Huh? Well, I appreciate that! [*Laughs.*] I'm always looking for good, crisp, solid, good, solid, rock-bottom foundational criticism. And that just sinks it right in.

Caller: But I think your songs are really great.

Fass: You know, not everybody has the courage to tell Bob the truth.

Dylan: Not everybody has the courage to sing like I do! [*Laughs.*]

Caller: OK, thank you.

Caller: I'm not asking you to be a Phil Ochs. But like "God on Our Side." Or "Masters of War."

Dylan: Oh, God, man. "With God on Your Side" is contained in like two lines of something like "Desolation Row."

Caller: Yeah, right.

Dylan: If you can't pick it out, that's not my problem.

Caller: Yeah, yeah, right. But what I'm saying is it's a lot more subtle there. I think it is.

Fass: Wait a minute, which one do you think is more subtle?

Caller: Something like "Desolation Row."

Dylan: It's not more subtle. It's just more to the point. It doesn't spare you any time to string anything together. It is all together. It doesn't pretend like it has to do anything, that's all.

Caller: Yeah, well—

Dylan: Hey, I don't know. I can't talk about what I do. I'm not going to—

Caller: Well, no, no, no. Well, take, like, the Forest Hills concert.

Dylan: I don't do that. That's all.

Caller: You're not doing something now about it.

Dylan: About what?

Caller: Well, OK, yeah, there's very little anybody can do about—like, let's say, take the war. OK? There's very little anybody can do about it.

Dylan: So what can anybody do about it? It's a war.

Caller: Yeah, yeah, but you know, something.

Dylan: Hey, war has been around for a long time. What makes you think this is anything special?

Caller: Yeah, yeah. But, you know, guys are dying now.

Dylan: Of course they're dying. Guys have always died.

Caller: And it just seems like, a couple years back—

Dylan: No, no, it's none of my doings. I really do other things. I'm not like you.

Caller: Yeah, yeah. Well, I know, but—

Dylan: I'm very tied up in a lot of other daily exercises. And my mind just does not work—

Caller: Well, I realize that, but—

Dylan: —thinking about the troubles of the world. I mean, who am I to carry the world on my shoulders? Huh?

Caller: Like, when you were writing these more obvious protest—

Dylan: Yeah, well, all the stuff that I'm writing now . . . I just never wrote as songs, that's all.

Caller: Like, "Pawn in Their Game"—

Dylan: Yeah, well, I did it because that was the thing. There's no big hoax or any kind secret thing happening or any kind of plan from the beginning. I just did what was happening. I played rock and roll music when I was fifteen years old!

Caller: No, no, I'm not puttin' down your rock 'n' roll.

Dylan: Well, I quit doin' it, because I couldn't make it. It's just too hard. The music field is different now than it used to be. People who make money in it now are not necessarily old people where they used to be. They used to be just old people that smoked cigars and hung around in certain bars uptown, around Tin Pan Alley. That used to be the music thing. But it's not that anymore. I mean, no, don't put down rock and roll. I mean, I don't even know what it is. I don't play rock and roll, first of all, if you think I do.

Caller: I didn't put down rock and roll but, like, take March 17—

Dylan: Oh, where, this march—

Caller: Yeah, in Washington, this—

Dylan: Come on, I ain't going to march anywhere. I got things to do.

Caller: But hell. I mean . . . I'm sorry.

Dylan: Hey, listen, do you see me in politics? Or am I anybody's parents? Am I any mother or father to anybody? Who do you think I'm supposed to be responsible for? I didn't create any living person that walks around.

Caller: No, no . . . I'm not asking you to live like that. But if you felt enough about it two or three years ago, why not now? Or have you just changed?

Dylan: Well, I don't know what I was thinking about two or three years ago. I don't have to explain it to you. It's not so complicated, man. You don't even have to ask why. It's very simple, but I just don't feel like sitting here talking about it right now.

Caller: Oh, OK. I'm sorry.

Dylan: No, I'll talk to you some other time.

DYLAN ON

His Pastimes

"I have no pastimes. I have none at all. . . . I would love to say bowling or sailing or roller-skating or painting. I'd love to give you a hobby . . . but I can't really tell you anything. What I do is write and sing. I'd do it whether I'm getting paid for it or whether or not. I mean, that's all I do."

—from interview with Martin Bronstein,
Canadian Broadcasting Corporation, February 20, 1966

DYLAN ON

His Audience

"Playing on the stage is a kick for me now. It wasn't before, because I knew what I was doing then was just too empty. . . . It was just dead ambassadors who would come and see me and clap and say: 'Oh, groovy, I would like to meet him and have a cocktail. Perhaps I'll bring my son, Joseph, with me.' And the first thing you know, you've got about five or six little boys and girls hanging around with Coke bottles and ginger-ale bottles . . . and you're confronted by some ambassador who's got his hand in your pocket trying to shake your spine and give you compliments. I won't let anybody backstage anymore. Even to give me a compliment. I just don't care."

—from interview with Robert Shelton, March 1966, for *No Direction Home*, PBS-TV (US) and BBC Two (UK), September 26–27, 2005

RADIO INTERVIEW

Klas Burling | May 1, 1966 | Radio 3 (Sweden)

Bob Dylan was moving at a manic drug- and fame-fueled pace by the time he began the European leg of a world tour on April 29, 1966, at Stockholm, Sweden's Concert Hall—the very place where his Nobel Prize speech would be read half a century later. The day before the gig, he had an appointment to record an interview for Klas Burling's *Pop 66* radio program.

Burling told me that he waited a long time outside Dylan's large suite at the Flamingo hotel in Solna Municipality, near Stockholm. Finally, manager Albert Grossman opened the door to a darkened room with all curtains closed. There stood Dylan, dressed mostly in black and wearing sunglasses.

"He shook hands and said hello, but there was clearly something wrong with him," Burling recalled. "He was eight miles high, on another planet. Considering his state, I tried to keep my questions simple and be patient. Despite his arrogance, I felt sorry for him.

"Halfway through the interview," continued Burling, "Dylan took off his dark glasses. A scary sight. His eyes looked like small, dark, dried raisins. One question was replied to about two questions later."

Dylan became friendlier after the interview. "He had a record player in the suite and took out a test pressing of his forthcoming double LP, *Blonde on Blonde*," Burling said, "and he asked me to listen to the eleven-minute 'Sad-Eyed Lady of the Lowlands.'

"Dylan turned to me when it ended and said, 'Now, tell me, in one word only, what you think about it.' He looked proud and obviously wanted to hear something like 'fantastic.' My patience had run dry. I felt like kicking back, so I said, 'Long!'

"What to do with this disastrous interview? Back in the studio, I decided to make a few edits, to make Dylan seem less stupid and more comprehensible."

Added Burling: "This is in fact the only interview I have ever edited." —Ed.

Klas Burling: Very nice to see you in Stockholm, Bob Dylan. And I wonder . . . if you could explain a bit more about yourself and your kind of songs. What do you think of the protest-song tag?

Bob Dylan: I don't . . . oh, God. [*Laughs.*] No, no. I'm not gonna sit here and do that. I've been up all night, I've taken some pills, and I've eaten bad food and I've read the wrong things and I've been out for hundred-mile-an-hour car rides, and I'm just not gonna sit here and talk about myself as a protest singer or anything like that.

Burling: But the first things you did which got really famous on singles and things like that—for example, in England they released "The Times They Are A-Changin'." That was supposed to be a protest song, no?

Dylan: Oh, my God! How long ago was that?

Burling: A year ago.

Dylan: Yeah, well, come on, a year ago! [*Pauses.*] I'm not trying to be a bad fellow or anything, but I'd just be a liar or a fool to go on with all this business. I mean, I just can't help it if you're a year behind.

Burling: No, but that's the style—

Dylan: You don't expect me to be a year behind.

Burling: But that's the style you had then and then suddenly you changed to "Subterranean Homesick Blues" with the electric guitar and those things. Is there any special reason? I mean, the way you would tell about it yourself?

Dylan: No.

Burling: What would you call yourself, a poet or a singer? Or do you think that you write poems and then you put music to it?

Dylan: No . . . I don't know. It's so silly! I mean, you wouldn't ask these questions of a carpenter, would you? Or a plumber?

Burling: It would not be interesting in the same way, would it?

Dylan: I guess it would be. I mean, if it's interesting to me, it should be just as interesting to you.

Burling: Well, not as being a disc jockey, anyhow.

Dylan: What do you think Mozart would say to you if you ever come up to him and ask him these questions that you've been asking? What kind of questions would you ask him? "Tell me, Mr. Mozart . . ."

Burling: First of all, I wouldn't do it.

Dylan: How come you do it to me?

Burling: Well, because I'm interested in your records, and I think the Swedish audience is as well.

Dylan: I'm interested in the Swedish audiences, too, and Swedish people and all that kind of stuff, but I'm sure they don't wanna know all these dumb things.

Burling: No, well, they've read a lot of dumb things about you in the papers, I suppose, and I thought you could straighten them out yourself.

Dylan: I can't straighten them out. I don't think they have to be straightened out. I believe that they know. They *know*. Don't you know the Swedish people? I mean, they don't have to be *told*, they don't have to be explained to. You should know that. You can't tell Swedish people something which is self-explanatory. Swedish people are smarter than that.

Burling: Do you think so?

Dylan: Oh, of course.

Burling: Do you know many Swedes?

Dylan: I know plenty.

Burling: Yeah?

Dylan: I happen to be a Swede myself.

Burling: Oh, yeah, certainly.

Dylan: I happen to come from not too far away from here, my friend.

Burling: Should we try to listen to a song instead?

Dylan: We can try.

Burling: Yeah? Which one would you suggest then?

Dylan: You pick one out, any one you say. You realize I'm not trying to be a bad fellow. I'm just trying to make it along and get everything to be straight. You realize that?

Burling: Yeah, and that's why I asked you, and you had a chance to do it yourself.

Dylan: No, I don't want the chance to do it myself.

Burling: OK.

Dylan: I don't wanna do anything by myself . . . for what?

Burling: Or against what?

Dylan: Well, you know what it's against and what it's for. I don't need to tell you that. My songs are all mathematical songs. You know what that means, so I'm not gonna have to go into that. So this specific one here happens to be a protest song and it borders on the mathematical idea of things, and this specific one, "Rainy Day Women," happens to deal with a minority of cripples and Orientals, and the world in which they live. It's sort of a north Mexican kind of a thing, very protesty. Very, very protesty. And one of the protestiest of all things I've ever protested against in my protest years.

Burling: Do you really believe it?

Dylan: I don't have to believe it, I know it. I wrote it! I mean, I'm telling you I wrote it! I should know!

Burling: Yeah. Why that title? It's never mentioned in the song.

Dylan: Well, we never mention things that we love. Where I come from that's blasphemy. Blas-per-for-me, you know that word? Blas-per-for-me?

Burling: Yeah.

Dylan: It has to do with God.

Burling: Shall we have a listen to the song?

Dylan: OK.

Burling: Which is selling quite well in the States. And how do you feel about that?

Dylan: It's horrible.

Burling: It is?

Dylan: Yeah, because it is a protest song. We shouldn't really listen to protest songs.

Burling: Well, I see it in the way that a lot of people buy the record to listen to it, these radio stations and so on. So a lot of people could get the message in that case.

Dylan: Yeah. They do get the message. I'm glad they're getting the message.

Burling: How do you feel about earning a lot of money then, if you're not really concerned about it all?

Dylan: I like earning a lot of money.

Burling: From the start you didn't have much, but now you got a lot. What do you do with it?

Dylan: Nothing.

Burling: Not concerned?

Dylan: No. Somebody else handles it for me. I just do the same old things.

Burling: When you write a song, do you write the melody or the words first?

Dylan: I write it all, the melody and the words.

Burling: At the same time?

Dylan: Yeah. The melody is sort of unimportant, really. It comes natural.

Burling: Other artists used your songs and recorded them and got hits and things like that. How did you feel about that?

Dylan: Well, I didn't feel anything really. I felt happy.

Burling: Do you like to suddenly get famous then, first as a songwriter, and then also as a singer?

Dylan: Yeah, it's sort of all over, though. I don't have any interest anymore. I did have interest when I was thirteen, fourteen, fifteen to be a famous star and all that kind of stuff, but I been playing on the stage, following tent shows around, ever since I've been ten years old. That's fifteen years I've been doing what I've been doing. I mean, I know I'm doing better than anybody else does.

Burling: And nowadays, what is it you want to do?

Dylan: Nothing.

Burling: Nothing?

Dylan: No.

Burling: Do you enjoy traveling? Performing?

Dylan: Yeah, I like performing. I don't care to travel, though.

Burling: What about recordings?

Dylan: I like to record.

Burling: You got a group now, which I suppose you didn't have at the very start.

Dylan: Yes, I had a group at the very start. You must realize, I come from the United States. I don't know if you know what the United States is like. It's not like England at all. The people at my age now, twenty-five, twenty-six, everybody has grown up playing rock 'n' roll music.

Burling: You did it?

Dylan: Yes, 'cause it's the only kind of music you heard. I mean, everybody has done it, 'cause all you heard was rock 'n' roll and country and western and rhythm and blues music. Now at a certain time the whole field got taken over into some milk, and to Frankie Avalon, Fabian, and this kind of thing. That's not bad or anything, but there was nobody that you could look at and really want anything that they had or wanna be like them. So everybody got out of it. But nobody really lost that whole thing. And then folk music came in and was some kind of a substitute for a while, but it was only a substitute, don't you understand? That's all it was. Now it's different again, because of the English thing. And what the English thing did was, they just proved that you could make money playing the same old kind of music that you used to play.

Burling: Yeah, yeah.

Dylan: And that's the truth. That's not a lie. And it's not a come on or anything. But the English people can't play rock 'n' roll music.

Burling: How do you feel about the Beatles then?

Dylan: Oh, the Beatles are great, but they don't play rock 'n' roll.

Burling: You met them quite a few times as well in the States and in England.

Dylan: Yeah, I know the Beatles, they're not playing—

Burling: You don't think they play rock 'n' roll?

Dylan: No. Rock 'n' roll is just four beats . . . an extension of twelve-bar blues. And rock 'n' roll is a white, seventeen-year-old-kid music. That's all it is. Rock 'n' roll is a fake kind of attempt at sex.

Burling: But what would you call your style then? The music you sing?

Dylan: I don't know. I've never heard anybody that plays or sings like me, so I don't know.

Burling: There's no name for it that you would try to put on it yourself?

Dylan: Mathematical music.

Burling: Yeah? [*Laughs.*] OK, if you would like to choose a final song for this interview—

Dylan: You choose it.

Burling: There's no one particular that you would like more than another one?

Dylan: No. Well, I'd rather have you play "Tombstone Blues" than "Pretty Peggy-O." [*Laughs.*] But other than that, I'll let you make your own choice.

Burling: OK. Thanks a lot then.

DYLAN ON

What He'd Been Doing Since His July 29, 1966, Motorcycle Accident

"What I've been doin' mostly is seein' only a few close friends, readin' little 'bout the outside world. Porin' over books by people you never heard of. Thinkin' about where I'm goin' and why am I runnin' and am I mixed up too much and what am I knowin' and what am I givin' and what am I takin'. And mainly what I've been doin' is workin' on gettin' better and makin' better music, which is what my life is all about."

—from interview with Michael Iachetta,
New York Daily News, May 8, 1967

CONVERSATIONS WITH BOB DYLAN

John Cohen and Happy Traum | October/November 1968 | *Sing Out!*

Bob Dylan's life on the road, which appeared to be spinning out of control when he talked with Klas Burling on April 28, 1966, in Stockholm, came crashing to a halt—literally—three months later, on July 29. That's when he suffered his serious motorcycle accident.

As he explained in an interview for the *New York Daily News* (see previous page), everything changed in the wake of that crackup. Instead of putting out three albums of fresh and important material in little more than a year, as he had recently done, he spent a lot of time thinking about his life and goals and released nothing but a hits compilation for more than eighteen months. When he did reemerge with *John Wesley Harding* at the end of 1967, his voice had changed, his music had simplified, and his chief lyrical influences seemed to have shifted from drugs, musicians, and contemporary poets to Biblical parables. No longer touring, he was living a quiet life in Woodstock, New York.

That's where he met in June and July of 1968 with fellow musicians John Cohen and Happy Traum for three taped conversations. The transcripts, which the folk magazine *Sing Out!* published in its October/November issue, covered such subjects as politics, Dylan's new and old music, and the "unhealthy situations" that had preceded his accident.

By this time, he had perhaps realized that he couldn't afford to be reckless. He had responsibility for a two-year-old son and a baby daughter; and he also had an adopted six-year-old daughter from his wife's first marriage (to whom he briefly speaks during these conversations). Another child, Samuel, would arrive on July 30, 1968, right after the last of the talks with Traum and Cohen. —Ed.

JOHN: I didn't realize how good that film [*Eat the Document*, D.A. Pennebaker's documentary about Dylan's 1966 tour] was when I saw it last.

BOB: You thought it was good?

J: It wasn't finished—I liked it because of that. But I didn't see [Pennebaker's] "Don't Look Back."

B: It's just as well. The difference between the two would be in the editing . . . the eye. Mr. Pennebaker's eye put together "Don't Look Back," whereas someone else's eye put together this film which you saw.

J: Wasn't one of the "eyes" involved yours?

B: Not entirely. Don't forget, Mr. Pennebaker shot all the film, and Mr. [Jones] Alk was under direction from him. The (edited) cut was under the direction of, well . . . I was one of them. What we had to work with was not what you would conceive of if you were going shooting a film. What we were trying to do is to make a logical story out of this newsreel-type footage . . . to make a story which consisted of stars and starlets who were taking the roles of other people, just like a normal movie would do. We were trying to do the same thing with this footage. That's not what anyone else had in mind, but that is what myself and Mr. Alk had in mind. And we were very limited because the film was not shot by us, but by the eye, and we had come upon this decision to do this only after everything else failed. And in everything else failing, the film had been cut just to nothing. So we took it and tried to do it this way because it was a new method and it was new to us, and we were hoping to discover something. And we did. People might see it and say it's just a big mess. Well, it might seem like a mess, but it's not. It starts with a half hour of footage there, that is clean: the film is sloppy and it looks like a lot of cutting in it, thirty second cuts to ten second cuts. But what we tried to do was to construct a stage and an environment, taking it out and putting it together like a puzzle. And we did, that's the strange part about it. Now if we had the opportunity to re-shoot the camera under this procedure, we could really make a wonderful film.

J: I liked this quality of having things that would normally not be used, that would be discarded, suddenly put together in such a way . . .

B: Well, we had to do that because it's all we had. The reason it didn't get seen was that the program (TV) folded and by the time we handed it in, they had already a state-wide search begun to confiscate the film, because it was the property of ABC. So we were a little pressured here and there. What you saw was a rough work print.

J: What I liked was that the trip had such wildness, such insanity, it looked to me like things could only get worse, they couldn't get better while you were on such a thing. As the film built up, everything seemed to contribute to that. The nature of the crowds, the nature of the reporters . . . I don't know if it was the film, or if it was where we were sitting when we saw it, but . . . well I'm sure one person is capable of doing both things . . .

B: The subject and the director?

J: . . . Or the editor.

B: Well the editor and director were two different people.

J: Let's say the subject and one of the editors was the same person.

B: Well, you have a lot of major films where the subject himself might be the director. Marlon Brando. Charlie Chaplin. Frank Black.

J: But the nature of the person in the film . . . maybe to you that wasn't so wild.

B: I can imagine something a lot wilder . . . maybe not on a singing tour, but as a film. On the screen, what do you say is wild, and what do you say when wildness turns into chaos? Cecil B. DeMille made "Samson and Delilah" . . . that's pretty wild.

J: But that was a stage set . . . I had the feeling that your film was really happening. You didn't set up the reporters, . . . well, that girl who maybe jumps out the window, and maybe doesn't . . . it's hard to draw the line where play leaves off.

B: It's hard to do a tour, and in the after hours make a movie. What we were doing was to try to fulfill this contract, to make a television show, and the only time I had to do it was when I was on tour, because I was on tour all the time.

J: I never saw you perform when you were touring with an electric band, except the last time I saw you which was at Newport, in 1965, when the public first became fully aware of what you'd been writing and thinking. But by the time this movie was shot in England, why you were really flying . . . your hands going all over, above the mouth harp . . . I got the feeling that you don't necessarily have to predetermine these things, that they grow by themselves. When reporters ask such questions, and audiences scream at nothing, it invites you to become something that you didn't necessarily intend to be.

B: That's true, but I know quite a few people who accept it as a challenge. I used to see people who'd take off their tie and dangle it over the first row, and it would be almost hypnotic. P. J. Proby used to do that, there are people who actually invite it, who actually enjoy being pulled, you know . . . it's something having to do with contact. It's very athletic in a way.

J: I take that film as very different from the new record you made . . . it might be opposite sides of the same coin. I think it's great, that in the period of three years, you can be the same person who did both.

B: Well, you can do anything if it's your job. When I was touring, it was my line of work, to go out there and deliver those songs. You must accept that in some way. There's very little you can do about it. The only other thing to do is not do it. But you certainly can't tell what's going to happen when you go on the stage, because the audiences are so different. Years ago the audience used to be of one nature, but that's not true anymore.

J: You talked of it in the past—that *was* your job. But is it necessarily now your job?

B: It is in a way. I like to play music on the stage, I expect to be playing music endlessly. So this period of time now isn't important to me; I know I'm going to be performing again, it's just a matter of the right time. And I'll have different material—so there'll be a change there.

J: I recall a conversation we had in 1962 . . . I don't know if I was seeing something, or wishing something on you—but I had just come back from Kentucky and you showed me "Hard Rain," at Gerde's or upstairs at the Gaslight . . .

B: I believe at the time, you were wondering how it fit into music. How I was going to sing it.

J: That was my initial reaction. That's really ancient history now because a whole aesthetic, a whole other approach has come into music since then, to make it very possible to sing that kind of song.

B: Yes, that's right.

J: Before then it wasn't so possible. The question I asked you on seeing this stream of words was, if you were going to write things like that, then why do you need Woody Guthrie? How about Rimbaud? And you didn't know Rimbaud . . . yet.

B: No, not until a few years ago.

J: Back then, you and Allen Ginsberg met.

B: Al Aronowitz, a reporter from the *Saturday Evening Post*, introduced me to Allen Ginsberg and his friend Peter Orlovsky, above a bookstore on 8th Street, in the fall of '64 or '65. I'd heard his name for many years. At that time these two fellows had just gotten back from a trip to India. Their knapsacks were in the corner and they were cooking a dinner at the time. I saw him again at Washington Square, at a party . . .

J: At that time, for you, was there a stronger leaning towards poetry, and the kind of thing that Allen had dealt with? . . . as opposed to what Woody had dealt with.

B: Well, the language which they were writing, you could read off the paper, and somehow it would begin some kind of tune in your mind. I don't really know what it was, but you could see it was possible to do more than what . . . not more . . . something different than what Woody and people like Aunt Molly Jackson and Jim Garland did. The subject matter of all their songs wasn't really accurate for me; I could see that they'd written thousands of songs, but it was all with the same heartfelt subject matter . . . whereas that subject matter did not exist then, and I knew it. There was a sort of semi-feeling of it existing, but as you looked around at the people, it didn't really exist the way it probably existed back then, there was no real movement, there was only organized movement.

There wasn't any type of movement which was a day by day, liveable movement. When that subject matter wasn't there anymore for me, the only thing that was there was the style. The idea of this type of song which you can live with in some kind of way, which you don't feel embarrassed twenty minutes after you've sung it; that type of song where you don't have to question yourself . . . where you're just wasting your time.

J: I don't know which was the cart and which was the horse, but people were asking about your music (and Phil Ochs' and others'), "Is this stuff poetry or is this song?"

B: Yes, well you always have people asking questions.

J: What I'm trying to get at is whether you were reading a lot then, books, literature? Were your thoughts outside of music?

B: No, my mind was with the music. I tried to read, but I usually would lay the book down. I never have been a fast reader. My thoughts weren't about reading, no . . . they were just about that feeling that was in the air. I tried to somehow get a hold of that, and write that down, and using my musical training to sort of guide it by, and in the end, have something I could do for a living.

J: Training!

B: Yes, training. You have to have some. I can remember traveling through towns, and if somebody played the guitar, that's who you went to see. You didn't necessarily go to meet them, you just went necessarily to watch them, listen to them, and if possible, learn how to do something . . . whatever he was doing. And usually at that time it was quite a selfish type of thing. You could see the people, and if you knew you could do what they were doing, with just a little practice, and you were looking for something else, you could just move on. But when it was down at the bottom, everyone played the guitar, when you knew that they knew more than you, well, you just had to listen to everybody. It wasn't necessarily a song; it was technique and style, and tricks and all those combinations which go together—which I certainly spent a lot of hours just trying to do what other people have been doing. That's what I mean by training.

J: It's hard for me, because this is an interview and can't be just a conversation . . . like the tape recorder is a third element . . . I can't just say to your face that you did something great, that I admire you . . .

B: Well in my mind, let me tell you John, I can see a thousand people who I think are great, but I've given up mentioning any names anymore. Every time I tell somebody who I think is pretty good, they just shrug their shoulders . . . and so I now do the same thing. Take a fellow like Doc Watson, the fellow can play the guitar with such ability . . . just like water running. Now where do you place somebody like that in this current flow of music? Now he doesn't use any tricks. But that has to do with age, I imagine, like how long he lives.

J: I think it's also got to do with the age he comes from, he doesn't come from yours or mine.

B: No, but I'm a firm believer in the longer you live, the better you get.

J: But Doc is different from you and me. I know people who hate your voice. They can't stand that sound, that kind of singing, that grating. The existence of your voice and people like you, like Roscoe Holcomb, it challenges their very existence. They can't conceive of that voice in the same breath as their own lives.

B: Well my voice is one thing, but someone actually having hate for Roscoe Holcomb's voice, that beautiful high tenor, I can't see that. What's the difference between Roscoe Holcomb's voice and Bill Monroe's?

J: I don't think Bill likes Roscoe's voice. Bill sings with such control. Roscoe's voice is so uncontrolled.

B: Well Bill Monroe is most likely one of the best, but Roscoe does have a certain untamed sense of control which also makes him one of the best.

J: I don't think Doc Watson's voice and your voice are compatible, it doesn't bother me.

B: No, no . . . maybe someday, though.

J: I'd like to talk about the material in the songs.

B: All right.

J: Well, I mean your music is fine, it's complete . . . but what I'm asking about is the development of your thoughts . . . which could be called "words." That's why I was asking about poetry and literature. Where do these things come upon a person? Maybe nobody asks you that.

B: No, nobody does, but . . . who said that, it wasn't Benjamin Franklin, it was somebody else. No, I think it was Benjamin Franklin. He said (I'm not quoting it right) something like, "For a man to be—(something or other)—at ease, he must not tell all he knows, nor say all he sees." Whoever said that certainly I don't think was trying to cover up anything.

J: I once got a fortune cookie that said "Clear water hides nothing" . . . Three or four years ago, there was an interview with you in *Playboy*. One particular thought stuck with me. You said it was very important that "Barbara Allen" had a rose grow out of her head, and that a girl could become a swan.

B: That's for all those people to say, "Why do you write all these songs about mystery and magic and Biblical intonations? Why do you do all that? Folk music doesn't have any of that." There's no answer for a question like that, because the people who ask them are just wrong.

J: They say folk music doesn't have this quality. Does rock and roll music have it?

B: Well, I don't know what rock and roll music is supposed to represent. It isn't that defined as a music. Rock and roll is dance music, perhaps an extension of the blues forms. It's live music; nowadays they have these big speakers, and they play it so loud that it might seem live. But it's got rhythm . . . I mean if you're riding in your car, rock and roll stations playing, you can sort of get into that rhythm for three minutes—and you lose three minutes. It's all gone by and you don't have to think about anything. And it's got a nice place; in a way this place is not necessarily in every road you turn, it's just pleasant music.

J: You're part of it aren't you? Or it's part of you.

B: Well, music is part of me, yes.

J: From what I saw in that film, you were really in it.

B: I was in it because it's what I've always done. I was trying to make the two things go together when I was on those concerts. I played the first half acoustically, second half with a band, somehow thinking that it was going to be two kinds of music.

J: So acoustic would mean "folk" and band would mean "rock and roll" at that moment?

B: Yes, rock and roll is working music. You have to work at it. You just can't sit down in a chair and play rock and roll music. You can do that with a certain kind of blues music, you can sit down and play it . . . you may have to lean forward a little.

J: Like a ballad, or one of your "dreams"?

B: Yes, you can think about it, you don't necessarily have to be in action to think about it. Rock and roll is hard to visualize unless you're actually doing it. . . . Actually too, we're talking about something which is for the most part just a commercial item; it's like boats and brooms, it's like hardware, people sell it, so that's what we're talking about. In the other sense of the way which you'd think about it, it's impossible.

J: But the kids who are getting into it today, they don't want to sell brooms.

B: It's an interesting field . . .

(aside to daughter)

Hello, did you just get home? Well maybe you better ask mamma. How was school? You learn anything? Well that's good. "My shoes hurt right here." Well, we'll see what we can do about it.

J: Could we talk about your new record *John Wesley Harding*?

B: There were three sessions: September, October and December, so it's not even a year old. I know that the concepts are imbedded now, whereas before that record I was just trying to see all of which I could do, trying to structure this and that. Every record was more or less for impact. Why, I did one song on a whole side of an album! It could happen to anybody. One just doesn't think of those things though, when one sees that other things can be done. It was spontaneously brought out, all those seven record albums. It was generously done, the material was all there. Now, I like to think that I can do it, do it better, on my own terms, and I'll do whatever it is I can do. I used to slight it off all the time. I used to get a good phrase or a verse, and then have to carry it to write something off the top of the head and stick it in the middle, to lead this into that. Now as I hear all the old material that was done, I can see the whole thing. I can't see how to perfect it, but I can see what I've done. Now I can go from line to line, whereas yesterday it was from thought to thought. Then of course, there are times you just pick up an instrument—something will come, like a tune or some kind of wild line will come into your head and you'll develop that. If it's a tune on a piano or guitar—you'll just uuuuuhhhh (hum) whatever it brings out in the voice, you'll write those words down. And they might not mean anything to you at all, and you just go on, and that will be what happens. Now I don't do that anymore. If I do it, I just keep it for myself. So I have a big lineup of songs which I'll never use. On the new record, it's more concise. Here I am not interested in taking up that much of anybody's time.

J: That's why I gave you Kafka's *Parables and Paradoxes*, because those stories really get to the heart of the matter, and yet you can never really decipher them.

B: Yes, but the only parables that I know are the Biblical parables. I've seen others. Khalil Gibran perhaps. . . . It has a funny aspect to it—you certainly wouldn't find it in the Bible—this type of soul. Now Mr. Kafka comes off a little closer to that. Gibran, the words are all mighty but the strength is turned into that of a contrary direction. There used to be this disc jockey, Rosko. I don't recall his last name. Sometimes at night, the radio would be on and Rosko would be reciting this poetry of Khalil Gibran. It was a radiant feeling, coming across it on the radio. His voice was that of the inner voice in the night.

J: When did you read the Bible parables?

B: I have always read the Bible, though not necessarily always the parables.

J: I don't think you're the kind who goes to the hotel, where the Gideons leave a Bible, and you pick it up.

B: Well, you never know.

J: What about Blake, did you ever read . . .?

B: I have tried. Same with Dante, and Rilke. I understand what's there, it's just that the connection sometimes does not connect . . . Blake did come up with some bold lines though.

J : A feeling I got from watching the film—which I hadn't considered much before folk music and rock & roll got so mixed together—is about this personal thing of put ons, as a personal relationship. Like with the press, they ask such idiotic questions that they are answered by put ons.

B: The only thing there, is that that becomes a game in itself. The only way to not get involved in that is not to do it, because it'll happen every time. It even happens with the housewives who might be asked certain questions.

J: It's become a way of imparting information. Like someone will come with an idea, a whole thesis, and then they'll ask, "Is this so?" and you might not have thought of it before, but you can crawl on top of it.

B: It's this question and answer business. I can't see the importance of it. There's so many reporters now. That's an occupation in itself. You don't have to be any good at it at all. You get to go to fancy places. It's all on somebody else.

J: Ridiculous questions get ridiculous answers, and the ridiculous response becomes the great moment.

B: Yes, well you have to be able to do that now. I don't know who started that, but it happens to everybody.

J: I wouldn't have mentioned it, but to me, you've moved away from it . . . gotten beyond it.

B: I don't know if I've gotten beyond it. I just don't do it anymore, because that's what you end up doing. You end up wondering what you're doing.

J: Hey. In the film, was that John Lennon with you in the car, where you're holding your head? He was saying something funny, but it was more than that . . . it was thoughtful.

B: He said "Money." . . .

J: Do you see the Beatles when you go there or they come here? There seems to be a mutual respect between your musics—without one dominating the other.

D: I see them here and there.

J: I fear that many of the creative young musicians today may look back at themselves ten years from now and say "We were just under the tent of the Beatles." But you're not.

B: Well, what they do . . . they work much more with the studio equipment, they take advantage of the new sound inventions of the past year or two. Whereas I don't know anything about it. I just do the songs, and sing them and that's all.

J: Do you think they are more British or International?

B: They're British, I suppose, but you can't say they've carried on with their poetic legacy, whereas the Incredible String Band who wrote this "October Song" . . . that was quite good.

J: As a finished thing—or did it reach you?

B: As a finished song it's quite good.

J: Is there much music now that you hear, that reaches you?

B: Those old songs reach me. I don't hear them as often as I used to. But like this other week, I heard on the radio Buell Kazee and he reached me. There's a lot. . . Scrapper Blackwell, Leroy Carr, Jack Dupree, Lonnie Johnson, James Ferris, Jelly Roll Morton, Buddy Bolden, Ian and Sylvia, Benny Fergusen, Tom Rush, Charlie Pride, Porter Wagoner, The Clancy Brothers and Tommy Makem. . . . Everything reaches me in one way or another.

J: How do you view the music business?

B: I don't exactly view it at all. Hearing it and doing it, I'll take part in that—but talking about it . . . there's not much I can contribute to it.

J: I recall in *Billboard*, a full-page ad of you with electric guitar like in the movie. . . .

B: Sure, I was doing that.

J: I'm interested how you talk of it in the past tense, as if you don't know what's coming next.

B: Well, I don't in a sense . . . But I've been toying with some ridiculous ideas—just so strange and foreign to me, as a month ago. Now some of the ideas—I'll tell you about them—after we shut off this tape recorder.

J: I was pleased that you know the music of Dillard Chandler, and that you were familiar with some unaccompanied ballads on a New Lost City Ramblers record. Do you think you'll ever try to write like a ballad?

B: Yes, I hope so. Tom Paxton just did one called "The Cardinal," quite interesting . . . it's very clean . . . sings it unaccompanied. The thing about the ballad is that you have to be conscious of the width of it at all times, in order to write one. You could take a true story, write it up as a ballad, or you can write it up in three verses. The difference would be, what are you singing it for, what is it to be used for. The uses of a ballad have changed to such a degree. When they were singing years ago, it would be as entertainment . . . a fellow could sit down and sing a song for half an hour, and everybody could listen, and you could form opinions. You'd be waiting to see how it ended, what happened to this person or that person. It would be like going to a movie. But now we have movies, so why does someone want to sit around for a half hour listening to a ballad? Unless the story was of such a nature that you couldn't find it in a movie. And after you heard it, it would have to be good enough so that you could sing it again tomorrow night, and people would be listening to hear the story again. It's because they want to hear that story, not because they want to check out the singer's pants. Because they would have a conscious knowledge of how the story felt and they would be a part of that feeling . . . like they would want to feel it again, so to speak.

J: It must be terrific to try to write within those dimensions.

B: Well once you set it up in your mind, you don't have to think about it any more. If it wants to come, it will come.

J: Take a song like "The Wicked Messenger." Does that fit?

B: In a sense, but the ballad form isn't there. Well the scope is there actually, but in a more compressed sense. The scope opens up, just by a few little tricks. I know why it opens up, but in a ballad in the true sense, it wouldn't open up that way. It does not reach the proportions I had intended for it.

J: Have you ever written a ballad?

B: I believe on my second record album, *Boots of Spanish Leather.* [*That song actually appeared on Dylan's third album,* The Times They Are A-Changin'. —*Ed.*]

J: Then most of the songs on *John Wesley Harding*, you don't consider as ballads.

B: Well I do, but not in the traditional sense. I haven't fulfilled the balladeer's job. A balladeer can sit down and sing three ballads for an hour and a half. See, on the album, you have to think about it after you hear it, that's what takes up the time, but with a ballad, you don't necessarily have to think about it after you hear it, it can all unfold to you. These melodies on the *John Wesley Harding* album lack this traditional sense of time. As with the third verse of "The Wicked Messenger," which opens it up, and then the time schedule takes a jump and soon the song becomes wider. One realizes that when one hears it, but one might have to adapt to it. But we are not hearing anything that isn't there; anything we can imagine is really there. The same thing is true of the song "All Along the Watchtower," which opens up in a slightly different way, in a stranger way, for here we have the cycle of events working in a rather reverse order.

———————

J: One suggested interpretation of "Dear Landlord" is that you wrote it to bring out the line "each one has his own special gift" . . .

B: I don't know about that. These songs might lay around in your head for two or three years, and you're always writing about something previous. You learn to do that, so that the song would not tend to be a reaction, something contemporary would make it a reaction. I don't know what it seems to explain any more than anybody else. But you always have to consider that I would write the song for somebody else. He might say something, or behave in a certain manner, or come right out and offer information like that. And if it's striking enough, it might find an opening. And don't forget now John, I'll tell you another discovery I've made. When the songs are done by anybody on a record, on a strange level the songs are done for somebody, about somebody and to somebody. Usually that person is the somebody who is singing that song. Hear all the records which have ever been made and it kinda comes down to that after a while.

J: Could you talk about where you were going when you first started out from home?

B: As I think about it, it's confusing to me to think of how I reached whatever place this is. I tend not to wonder about it anyway. It's true, I have no goal so to speak. I don't have any more intentions than you do.

J: I intend to do my work.

B: Yes, me too, and to make the work interesting enough, in order to keep doing it.

That's what has kept it up so far. I really can't do it if it's not interesting. My intention would be not to think about it, not to speak about it, or remember any of it that might tend to block it up somehow. I've discovered this from the past anyway. There was one thing I tried to do which wasn't a good idea for me. I tried to write another "Mr. Tambourine Man." It's the only song I tried to write "another one." But after enough going at it, it just began bothering me, so I dropped it. I don't do that anymore.

J: A danger of such a position is that you can be accused of only living in the present. People will say you're just living for the minute—with no plan and no care for the past.

B: I have more memories for the past than for the future. I wouldn't think about the future. I would only have expectations, and they'd all be very good. For the past I just have those memories. We were just talking of this "past" business the other night. Say this room is empty now, except with just myself. Now you enter the room, but you're bound to leave, and when you do, what's to guarantee that you've even been in this room. But yet you were in this room, if I want to reconstruct it, sit here for the rest of the day . . . if I take enough notes while you are in the room, I could possibly sit here for a week, with you in the room . . . something like that anyway.

J: It's elusive. Anyway, back to the thought of "each one has his own special gift."

B: That would be . . . just a fact.

J: But if everybody felt it, perhaps the American army wouldn't be so capable of killing, and Kennedy might not be killed—King might not be killed.

B: But we're talking now about things which have always happened since the beginning of time, the specific name or deed isn't any different than that which has happened previous to this. Progress hasn't contributed anything but changing face . . . and changing situations of money, wealth . . . that's not progress, really. Progress for disease—that's progress . . . but putting in a new highway through a backyard is getting rid of the old things.

J: The real progress each person makes is not going outwards, but going inwards. I have the feeling that a change has come over you . . . you seem to have discovered that same idea.

B: Well, I discover ideas here and there, but I can't put them into words.

J: You mean, that by the time they are songs, they're said?

B: Well, the songs are a funny thing. If I didn't have the recording contract and I didn't have to fulfill a certain amount of records, I don't really know if I'd write down another song as long as I lived. I'm just content enough to play just anything I know. But seeing as how I do have this contract, I figure my obligation is to fill it, not in just recording songs, but the best songs I can possibly record. Believe me, I look around. I don't care if I record my own songs, but I can't sometimes find enough songs to put on an album, so then I've got to do it all with my songs. I didn't want to record this last album. I was going to do a whole album of other people's songs, but I couldn't find enough. The song has to be of a certain quality for me to sing and put on a record. One aspect it would have to have is that it didn't repeat itself. I shy away from those songs which repeat phrases, bars and verses, bridges . . . so right there it leaves out about nine-tenths of all the contemporary material being written, and the folk songs are just about the only ones that don't . . . the narrative ones, or the ones with a chorus like "Ruben's Train." I don't know, maybe then too I'm just too lazy to look hard enough.

J: Do you consider that there's been a change of pace in your life over the past three years?

B: "Change of pace" if you mean what I was doing before. I was touring for a couple of years. That's a fast pace, plus we were doing a whole show, no other acts. It's pretty straining to do a show like that, plus a lot of really unhealthy situations rise up. I was just going out there performing these songs. Everyone else was having a good time. Right now I don't think about it anymore. I did it, and I did it enough to know that there must be something else to do.

J: In a way, you had the opportunity to move into it and move out of it at your own choice.

B: It wasn't my own choice. I was more or less being pushed into it—pushed in and carried out.

(enter Happy Traum)

HT: Has anyone picked up on your new approach—like on the album, clear songs and very personal, as opposed to the psychedelic sounds?

B: I don't know.

HT: What do you know?

B: What I do know is that I put myself out of the songs. I'm not in the songs anymore, I'm just there singing them, and I'm not personally connected with them. I write them all now at a different time than when I record them. It used to be, if I would sing, I'd get a verse and go on and wait for it to come out as the music was there, and sure enough, something would come out, but in the end, I would be deluded in those songs. Besides singing them, I'd be in there acting them out—just pulling them off. Now I have enough time to write the song and not think about being in it. Just write it for somebody else to sing, then do it—like an acetate. At the moment, people are singing a simpler song. It's possible in Nashville to do that.

J: I heard "Blowin' in the Wind" played on the radio after the most recent assassination.

B: By who?

J: It was Muzak style . . . music to console yourself by.

B: Airplane style.

J: Do you think you'll ever get a job playing for Muzak? The best musicians do that work, Bob.

B: Well I'd give it a try if they ask.

J: No one calls you into the studio to "Lay down some music" as they say.

B: Before I did the new album, I was waiting to meet someone who would figure out what they would want me to do. Does anybody want any songs written about anything? Could Bob be commissioned, by anybody? Nobody came up with anything, so I went ahead and did something else.

J: For a while a number of years ago, the songs you were writing, and that others were writing along similar lines, were played a lot on popular radio. Today it's not completely disappeared, but it certainly is going in some other direction.

B: You just about have to cut something tailor-made for the popular radio. You can't do it with just half a mind. You must be conscious of what you're involved in. I get over-anxious when I hear myself on the radio, anyway. I don't mind the record album, but it's the record company, my A&R man, Bob Johnston—he would pick out what's to be played on the radio.

H: Did you ever make a song just to be a single?

B: Yes I did. But it wasn't very amusing because it took me away from the album. The album commands a different sort of attention than a single does. Singles just pile up and pile up; they're only good for the present. The trend in the old days was that unless you had a hit single, you couldn't do very well with an album. And when you had that album, you just filled it up. But now albums are very important.

J: You've tried movies and books . . .

B: In both cases, in shallow water.

J: In that book of photographs of you [Bob Dylan, *by Daniel Kramer* —Ed.] that was published, when I finished looking at it, I came away knowing not one bit more than when I started.

B: Yes, well what can you know about anybody? Book or photographs, they don't tell you too much about a person.

H: For years now, people have been analyzing and pulling apart your songs. People take lines out of context and use them to illustrate points, like on "Quinn, the Eskimo" . . . I've heard some kids say that Quinn is the "bringer of drugs." Whatever you meant doesn't matter . . . the kids say "Dylan is really into this drug thing . . . when the drugs come, everybody is happy." This kind of thing is always happening with all of your songs.

B: Well, that's not my concern.

J: Many of the songs have set up conditions where people can read whatever they want into them.

H: People pull them apart and analyze them.

B: It's not every one who does that—just a certain kind. People I come in contact with don't have any questions.

H: Perhaps that's come back lately in the very spontaneous art, in the whole multi-media kind of thing. Response to impulses . . . you can't respond any other way.

J: I think it's to anyone's favor that they can follow what's on their mind, what comes from within them, rather than getting swept up in all these other possibilities . . . which might be just a reaction against the analytic approach anyway. There is another way . . . someone might just follow his inner course . . . without being unaware of what is going on. Bob, how do you respond to multi-media?

B: When you say multi-media, would that be like the clothes stores?

J: Never having been to one, I'll say yes.

B: I've never been to one either.

H: It's also stage presentations where music, dance, lights and the rest are jumbled together, piled on the viewer, where all the senses are used.

J: In that context of multi-media, where are you?

B: Well I'm a very simple man. I take one, maybe two . . . too much just confuses me. I just can't master confusion. If I don't know what's happening and everyone who goes and tells me just says that they don't know what happened any more than I do, and they were there, then I'd say that I didn't know where we were.

H: Do you feel the same way about the psychedelic sound on records?

B: No, I don't.

H: A lot of the music today is not only very loud and very fast, but it's structured in such a way that a lot of instruments are playing at once, with a lot of distortion.

B: That's fine. A lot of people playing it.

H: You seem to have made a conscious effort away from that on your last record.

B: It was a conscious effort just to begin again. It wasn't a conscious effort to go in a certain direction, but rather like put up or shut up so-to-speak. So that's all.

J: I see that picture of Muhammed Ali here. Do you know him?

B: No, I've seen him perform a few times.

H: Do you follow the fights?

B: Not any more. When he came down to Bleecker Street to read his poetry, you would have wished you were there.

J: He really made a point that lasted afterwards—beyond that someone got conked.

H: Not being particularly interested in fighting, what impressed me is how he stayed true to himself—his own stand as a human being was more important to himself than the championship.

J: Could you talk about some of the diverse elements which go into making up one of your songs, using a song from which you have some distance?

B: Well, there's not much we could talk about—that's the strange aspect about the whole thing. There's nothing you can see. I wouldn't know where to begin.

J: Take a song like "I Pity the Poor Immigrant." There might have been a germ that started it.

B: Yes, the first line.

J: What experience might have triggered that? Like you kicked the cat who ran away, who said "Ouch!" which reminded you of an immigrant.

B: To tell you the truth, I have no idea how it comes into my mind.

J: You've said there was a person usually in it.

B: Well, we're all in it. They're not any specific people . . . say, someone kicks the cat, and the cat writes a song about it. It might seem that way, during some of the songs, and in some of the poetry that's being passed around now-a-days. But it's not really that way.

J: You said that often a song is written for a certain person.

B: That's for a person, not about him. You know, you might sometimes be with someone who's got no song to sing, and I believe you can help someone out, that's the extent of it really.

J: Well, "Quinn the Eskimo" wasn't that way.

B: You see, it's all grown so serious, the writing-song business. It's not that serious. The songs don't painfully come out. They come out in a trick or two, or from something you might overhear. I'm just like any other songwriter, you pick up the things that are given to you. "Quinn the Eskimo," I can't remember how that came about. I know the phrase came about, I believe someone was just talking about Quinn, the Eskimo.

J: Someone told me there was once a movie with Anthony Quinn playing an Eskimo. Did you know of that?

B: I didn't see the movie.

J: But that could have triggered it.

B: Of course.

J: This makes a lot of sense, in the sense that you can travel down a road, and see two signs advertising separate things, but where two words come together, it will make a new meaning which will trigger off something.

B: Well, what the songwriter does, is just connect the ends. The ends that he sees are the ones that are given to him and he connects them.

H: It seems that people are bombarded all the time with random thoughts and outside impulses, and it takes the songwriter to pick something out and create a song out of them.

B: It's like this painter who lives around here—he paints the area in a radius of twenty miles, he paints bright strong pictures. He might take a barn from twenty miles away, and hook it up with a brook right next door, then with a car ten miles away, and with the sky on some certain day, and the light on the trees from another certain day. A person passing by will be painted alongside someone ten miles away. And in the end he'll have this composite picture of something which you can't say exists in his mind. It's not that he started off willfully painting this picture from all his experience. . . . That's more or less what I do.

J: Which and where is Highway 61?

B: I knew at one time, but at this time it seems so far away I wouldn't even attempt it. It's out there, it's a dividing line.

J: Is it a physical Highway 61?

B: Oh yes, it goes from where I used to live . . . I used to live related to that highway. It ran right through my home town in Minnesota. I travelled it for a long period of time actually. It goes down the middle of the country, sort of southwest.

J: I think there is an old blues about Highway 61.

B: Same highway, lot of famous people came off that highway.

J: Can you keep contact with the young audiences who perhaps buy most of your records?

B: That's a vague notion, that one must keep contact with a certain illusion of people which are sort of undefinable. The most you can do is satisfy yourself. If you satisfy yourself then you don't have to worry about remembering anything. If you don't satisfy yourself, and you don't know why you're doing what you do, you begin to lose contact. If you're doing it for *them* instead of you, you're likely not in contact with them. You can't pretend you're in contact with something you're not. I don't really know who I'm in contact with, but I don't think it's important.

J: Well, on the airplanes, they have these seven channels of stereo, and your music is marked as "for the kids" rather than anywhere else, and it sort of bothered me. Do you have a chance to meet the kids?

B: I always like to meet the kids.

J: Do you get a chance?

B: Not so much when I'm touring as when I'm not touring. When you're touring, you don't get a chance to meet anybody. I've just been meeting people again in the last few years.

J: It's a strange phenomenon, for you reach them the most when you are on tour yet you can't reach them at all.

B: Well yes, but the next time I go out, it's going to be a little bit more understandable. Next time out, my hopes are to play the music in a different way.

H: How can you get around the problems you encountered last time?

BD: I'm not really aware of those problems. I know they exist because it was very straining, and that's not the way work should be. But it's a situation that's pretty much all over . . . the screaming. Even some musician like Jimi Hendrix gets people seeing him who aren't coming there to scream—they're coming to hear him.

H: Do you see any way you can approach your music in a public way, that would give a different perspective to an audience?

B: Yes. Just playing the songs. See, the last time we went out, we made too much of a production of the songs. They were all longer, they were all my own songs, not too much thought had gone into the program, it just evolved itself from when I was playing single.

J: And the film we've been discussing, is that a fair summary of that kind of tour?

B: Yes it was. I hope people get a chance to see that film.

J: Why do you think your music appeals to American Indians?

B: I would hope that it appeals to everybody.

J: I know suburban people who can't stand it.

B: Well, I wish there was more I could do about that.

J: We just heard your record being played at an elegant store in New York City, as the background for people shopping.

H: Pete Seeger told me the *John Wesley Harding* album is great to skate to. He said some records are good to skate to and some aren't, and that's a good one.

B: I'm awfully glad he feels that way about it.

J: What is your relationship to student groups, or black militants, like the kids at Columbia or at Berkeley?

B: If I met them at all, I would meet them individually; I have no special relationship to any group.

J: Do you follow these events, even from a distance, like reading a newspaper?

B: Just like anyone else. I know just as much about it as the lady across the street does, and she probably knows quite a bit. Just reading the papers, talking to the neighbors, and so forth.

J: These groups feel more about you than they do about that lady next door.

B: I can assure you I feel the same thing. There are people who are involved in it and people who are not. You see, to be involved, you just about have to be there, I couldn't think about it any other way.

J: Someone like Pete Seeger, who is different from all of us in this room, he reaches out.

B: But how much of a part of it is he?

H: Do you foresee a time when you're going to have to take some kind of a position?

B: No.

H: You don't think that events will ever reach you?

B: It's not that events won't reach me, it's more a case of what I, myself would reach for. The decisions I would have to make are my own decisions, just like anyone else has to make his own. It doesn't necessarily mean that any position must be taken.

J: Although I asked it, this is not really the kind of question I'm really concerned with. After all, if someone asked me, I could only say I do what I can, I sing my own music, and if they like to hear it, well, fine.

B: Yes, but I don't know ... What was the question again? You must define it better.

H: I think that every day we get closer to having to make a choice.

B: How so?

H: I think that events of the world are getting closer to us, they're as close as the nearest ghetto.

B: Where's the nearest ghetto?

H: Maybe down the block. Events are moving on a mass scale.

B: What events?

H: War, racial problems, violence in the streets.

J: Here's a funny aspect; we're talking like this here, but in a strange way, Bob has gone further than you or I in getting into such places. I just have heard from Izzy Young that the songs they were singing at Resurrection City were "Blowin' in the Wind" and "The Times They Are [A-] Changin'." So in a sense by maintaining his own individual position, Bob and his songs are in the ghetto, and the people there are singing them—to them they mean action.

H: Well, the kids at Columbia University are taking a particular stand on what they see as the existing evils. They're trying to get their own say in the world, and in a way trying to overcome the people ruling them, and there are powerful people who are running the show. They can be called the establishment, and they are the same people who make wars, that build the missiles, that manufacture the instruments of death.

B: Well, that's just the way the world is going.

H: The students are trying to make it go another way.

B: Well, I'm for the students of course, they're going to be taking over the world. The people who they're fighting are old people, old ideas. They don't have to fight, they can sit back and wait.

H: The old ideas have the guns, though.

J: Perhaps the challenge is to make sure that the young minds growing up remain open enough so that *they* don't become the establishment that they are fighting.

B: You read about these rebels in the cartoons, people who were rebels in the twenties, in the thirties, and they have children who are rebels, and they forget that they were rebels. Do you think that those who are rioting today will somehow have to hold their kids back from doing the same thing?

J: Are your day-to-day contacts among the artists, crusaders, businessmen or lumberjacks?

B: Among the artists and lumberjacks.

J: Crusaders?

B: Well, you mean the people who are going from here to there, the men in long brown robes and little ivy twines on their head? I know quite a few crusaders but don't have much contact with them.

J: How about leaders of the student groups? Did you know Malcolm X, or the kids from SNCC?

B: I used to know some of them.

J: Social crusaders, someone like Norman Mailer.

B: No.

J: What about businessmen?

B: I get a lot of visitors and see a lot of people, and who's a businessman? I'm sure a whole lot of businessmen have passed by the past few hours, but my recollection really isn't that brilliant.

J: Does your management serve as a buffer in translating your artistic works into business?

B: I'm just very thankful that my management is there to serve what purpose a management serves. Every artist must have one these days.

J: Would you talk of any of the positive things that drugs have to offer, how they might have affected your work?

B: I wouldn't think they have anything to offer. I'm speaking about drugs in the everyday sense of the word. From my own experience they would have nothing positive to offer, but I'm not speaking for anyone else. Someone else might see them offering a great deal.

J: But in the way of insights or new combinations, it never affected you that way?

B: No, you get those same insights over a period of time anyway.

J: For a while you were working on a book, they gave it a name *Tarantula*. Have you tried any other writing since then, or did you learn anything from the experience of trying?

B: Yes, I do have a book in me, it'll be out sometime. MacMillan will publish it.

J: Did you learn from the one you did reject?

B: I learned not to do a book like that. That book was the kind of thing where the contract comes in before the book is written, so you have to fulfill the contract.

J: In thinking over this interview thus far, it seems like that has happened to you several times over the recent years, not necessarily of your choosing.

B: Yes, that's true. But it happens to other people and they come through. Dostoevsky did it, he had a weekly number of words to get in. I understand Frederick Murrey does it, and John Updike must . . . For someone else it might be exactly what they always had wished.

J: In trying to write it, was it a difficulty of structure or concept?

B: No, there was no difficulty in writing it at all. It just wasn't a book, it was just a nuisance. It didn't have that certain quality which now I think a book should have. It didn't have any structure at all, it was just one flow. It flowed for ninety pages.

J: I'm thinking of a parallel. You know some of these old crazy talking blues? They go on where just the last phrase of a sentence connects up to the next sentence, but the two thoughts aren't related. "Slipping up and down the mantel piece, feet in a bucket of grease, hunting matches, etc." Did it go that way?

B: More or less. They were short little lines, nothing within a big framework. I couldn't even conceive of doing anything in a big framework at that time. I was doing something else.

H: Do you think future writings will use the poetic form or the novel?

B: I think it will have everything in it.

J: Listening to the car radio, I heard that you have a song on the country music stations, "I'll Be Your Baby Tonight." I can't remember the singer's name, but I understand that Burl Ives has also recorded it.

B: A lot of people record them, they always do a good job.

J: When did you first hear Burl Ives?

B: I first heard Burl Ives when I was knee-high to a grasshopper.

J: Was that folk music to you when you first heard it?

B: Yes, I guess everybody's heard those old Burl Ives records on Decca, with a picture of him in a striped T-shirt, holding a guitar up to his ear, just wailing.

J: Did you know that his first recordings were for Moe Asch (of Folkways records)? Alan Lomax had brought him in. Who made the first recordings you are on?

B: I recorded with Big Joe Williams.

J: Where did this Blind Boy Grunt thing come in?

B: Someone told me to come down 'cause they were doing some kind of an album. So I was there and singing this song, and it only had a couple of verses and that's all, so someone in the control booth said, "Do some more." I said well, there is no more, I can't sing any more. The fellow says "If you can't sing, GRUNT." So I said "Grunt?" Then someone else sitting at a desk to my left says, "What name shall I put down on this record?" And I said "Grunt." She said "Just Grunt?" Then the fellow in the control booth said "Grunt." Somebody came in the door then and said "Was that Blind Boy Grunt?" and the lady at the desk said "Yes it was."

J: Was this Moe Asch and Marion Distler?

B: It could have been.

———————————

J: My last question is really a rehash of one aspect we've already discussed; at the moment, your songs aren't as socially or politically applicable as they were earlier.

B: As they were earlier? Could it be that they are just as social and political, only that no one cares to . . . let's start with the question again. (J. repeats question.) Probably that is because no one cares to see it the way I'm seeing it now, whereas before, I saw it the way they saw it.

H: You hear a lot about the word "engaged" artists. Painters, film makers, actors, they're actively involved in current events, through their art.

B: Well, even Michelangelo though . . .

H: Many artists feel that at this particular time in history, they can't just do their thing without regarding the larger scale around them.

B: The thing is, if you can get the scales around you in whatever you create, that's nice. If you physically have to go out there and experience it time and time again, you're talking about something else.

H: Probably the most pressing thing going on in a political sense, is the war. Now I'm not saying any artist or group of artists can change the course of the war, but they still feel it their responsibility to say something.

B: I know some very good artists who are for the war.

H: Well I'm just talking about the ones who are against it.

B: That's like what I'm talking about; it's for or against the war. That really doesn't exist. It's not for or against the war. I'm speaking of a certain painter, and he's all for the war. He's just about ready to go over there himself. And I can comprehend him.

H: Why can't you argue with him?

B: I can see what goes into his paintings, and why should I?

H: I don't understand how that relates to whether a position should be taken.

B: Well, there's nothing for us to talk about really.

J: Someone just told me that the poet and artist William Blake harboured Tom Paine when it was dangerous to do so. Yet Blake's artistic production was mystical and introspective.

H: Well, he separated his work from his other activity. My feeling is that with a person who is for the war and ready to go over there, I don't think it would be possible for you and him to share the same basic values.

B: I've known him for a long time, he's a gentleman and I admire him, he's a friend of mine. People just have their views. Anyway, how do you know I'm not, as you say, for the war?

J: Is this comparable? I was working on a fireplace with an old local stone mason last summer, while running off to sing at the New Politics Convention. When I returned I was chopping rocks with him, and he says, "All the trouble today is caused by people like Martin Luther King." Now I respect that man, not for his comments on Dr. King, but for his work with stone, his outlook on his craft, and on work and life, in the terms he sees it. It is a dilemma.

H: I think it is the easy way out, to say that. You have to feel strongly about your own ideas, even if you can respect someone else for their ideas. (to Bob) I don't feel there is that much difference between your work now and your earlier work. I can see a continuity of ideas, although they're not politically as black and white as they once were. "Masters of War" was a pretty black and white song. It wasn't too equivocal. You took a stand.

B: That was an easy thing to do. There were thousands and thousands of people just wanting that song, so I wrote it up. What I'm doing now isn't more difficult, but I no longer have the capacity to feed this force which is needing all these songs. I know the force exists but my insight has turned into something else. I might meet one person now, and the same thing can happen between that person (and myself) that used to happen between thousands.

J: This leads right to the last statement on my interview list: On your latest album, the focus has become more on the individual, axioms and ideas about living, rather than about society's doings or indictments of groups of people. In other words, it's more of how one individual is to act.

B: Yes, in a way . . . in a way. I would imagine that's just the way we grow.

DYLAN ON

His Early Songs

"Those songs were all written in the New York atmosphere. I'd never have written any of them—or sung them the way I did—if I hadn't been sitting around listening to performers in New York cafés and the talk in all the dingy parlors. When I got to New York, it was obvious that something was going on—folk music—and I did my best to learn and play it. I was just there at the right time with pen in hand."

—from interview with Hubert Saul, *Newsweek*, April 4, 1969

PRESS CONFERENCE

August 27, 1969 | Isle of Wight, England

As it turned out, *John Wesley Harding* did not mark a return to a heavy recording schedule. It took Dylan nearly a year and a half to issue a follow-up and, when he did, in April 1969, the LP proved as surprising as any he had issued to date. Recorded in Nashville with the cream of its studio musicians, *Nashville Skyline* found Dylan immersed in traditional country music. His voice sounded completely different, and so did his songs, which took him further into the territory he'd flirted with on *John Wesley Harding*'s "I'll Be Your Baby Tonight."

Four months after *Nashville Skyline*'s release came another surprise: Dylan performed at the Isle of Wight Festival in England. It was his first paid performance since his motorcycle accident three years earlier (though he had appeared at a Woody Guthrie tribute in January 1968, on the *Johnny Cash Show* in June 1969, and at a Band gig the following month). It would also be his last public performance for two years.

This press conference, at the now-demolished Halland Hotel, took place on the Isle of Wight four days before the gig there. Probably the most remarkable thing about this brief session with the media is how unremarkable it is. Dylan provides direct albeit mostly unrevealing answers, and he seems to have lost his interest in sparring with or putting on reporters. At the end, someone asks him whether he "has a personal message for the kids today." His answer sounds as if it is a message he has sent to himself. —Ed.

Ronnie Burns [of BBC TV South]: Why did you come to the Isle of Wight?

Bob Dylan: I wanted to see the home of [British poet] Alfred, Lord Tennyson.

Burns: Why?

Dylan: Just curious.

Reporter: With, say, seventy-five thousand or a hundred thousand teenagers, there could possibly be some sort of drugs problem. Are you concerned about it or do you feel it doesn't concern you at all?

Dylan: I hope there isn't any.

Burns: Can you tell us your general views on drug taking among teenagers and young people these days?

Dylan: I don't have any of those views. I wish I did. I'd be glad to share them with you, but I think everyone should lead their own life.

Burns: You used to, I believe, make public pronouncements on your views on things, like Vietnam, and it has been noticed in certain quarters you haven't been doing this recently, making your views known on big political and international issues. Is this deliberate policy on your part?

Dylan: No. I think that's more a rumor than a fact. You check your old newspapers. You won't be able to find too many statements I've made on those issues.

Burns: I've heard it said here today by some of your fans that the new Bob Dylan is a bit of a square. Is this true? [*Laughter.*]

Dylan: You'll have to ask the fans.

Lon Goddard [of London's *Record Mirror*]: Do you feel your days of protesting are over?

Dylan: I don't want to protest anymore. I never said I'm an angry young man.

Goddard: Can you tell us exactly what happened when you suffered an accident a while ago?

Dylan: It's true I suffered a broken neck. It's awful hard to explain. I have to take it easy sometimes.

Reporter: Do you think you have changed very much since we last saw you in London? Your clothes and hair have changed.

Dylan: I believe there's a conscious thing since the accident. I haven't really changed. It had more to do with the show I was doing than anything else. It really had nothing to do with me personally. That stuff was all for publicity. I don't do that kind of thing anymore.

Reporter: Can you tell us what songs you will be performing?

Dylan: Everything we will do is on record. I'm not going to sing anything new. Things you will have heard before but with new arrangements.

Reporter: Because of your lack of public appearances, do you still like doing shows?

Dylan: We appeared a month ago in St. Louis. [*A reference to a July 14 surprise appearance at the Mississippi River Festival, in Edwardsville, Missouri, near St. Louis, where the Band headlined. —Ed.*] The more shows the better.

Reporter: Who are you looking forward to meeting while you're here?

Dylan: I'm hoping to meet anybody who's around. I'd like to meet the Who and maybe Georgie Fame.

Reporter: What about the Beatles?

Dylan: George Harrison has come to visit me. The Beatles have asked me to work with them. I love the Beatles and I think it would be a good idea to do a jam session.

Reporter: What about reports that various people will perform with you on stage?

Dylan: Great, great.

Reporter: Do you feel that cameras are like guns?

Dylan: I don't know.

Goddard: Do you feel this change that has come over you and your music is due to domestic effects? Are you chiefly a family man now?

Dylan: I would think so.

Reporter: There is a very large crowd expected here for your performance. Any comments on that?

Dylan: I just hope it's a good show.

Reporter: Do you have a personal message for the kids today?

Dylan: Take it easy and do your job well.

Reporter: What exactly then is your position on politics and music?

Dylan: My job is to play music. I think I've answered enough questions.

DYLAN ON

Why His Voice Sounds Different on *Nashville Skyline*

"I stopped smoking. When I stopped smoking, my voice changed—so drastically, I couldn't believe it myself. That's true. I tell you, you stop smoking those cigarettes [*laughs*] and you'll be able to sing like Caruso."

—from interview with Jann Wenner, *Rolling Stone*, November 29, 1969

DYLAN ON

Performing to Survive

"I had to hold a lot of things back before [in the period prior to the recording of *The Times They Are A-Changin'*]. That's why I was doing other kinds of writing, because I could of never got away with it in song. People would never understand, they would have killed me. I would have been dead, they would have chased me off the stage, I would have been a total failure. I held it back because I had to survive, I had to make it back then, I couldn't go too far out. If somebody was going to give me three hundred dollars for doing a certain thing, it wouldn't be too hard to do that thing. I'd just do it. My ideals aren't that important to me, what you might call ideals. I didn't really care. I didn't have what people call ideals. So it didn't matter a damn. I needed bread, and I had to scuffle. That's all. But I don't have to scuffle anymore. I can do it my way now."

—from *Bob Dylan: An Intimate Biography* by Anthony Scaduto, 1971

DYLAN ON

His 1974 Tour

"The last tour we did, in 1965–'66, was like a hurricane. This one is more like a hard rain. The last tour, we were going all the time, even when we weren't going. We were always doing something else, which is just as draining as performing. We were looking for Loch Ness monsters, staying up for four days running—and making all those 8 o'clock curtains, besides. There won't be any of that on this tour—for me, anyway."

—from interview with John Rockwell, *New York Times*, January 8, 1974

DYLAN ON

Publicity and the Public

"All this publicity. Sometimes I think they're talking about somebody else. I take it as it comes but I'm not certain it's beneficial to my life. . . . I try not to deal with the audience response. Too synthetic. Besides, it would be more than I could handle. I'm just basically interested in real things."

—from interview with David DeVoss, *Time*, January 21, 1974

DYLAN ON

Fame

"Fame threw me for a loop at first. Until I learned how to swim with it and until I learned to turn it around—so you can just throw it in the closet and pick it up when you need it. . . . The turning point was back in Woodstock. A little after the accident. Sitting around one night under a full moon, looked out into the bleak woods and I said, 'Something's gotta change.'"

—from interview with Ben Fong-Torres, *Rolling Stone*, February 14, 1974

RADIO INTERVIEW

Mary Travers | April 20, 1975 | *Mary Travers and Friend*, KNX-FM (Los Angeles)

The first half of the 1970s marked a career low point for Dylan, whose record releases garnered much less acclaim than his earlier LPs had enjoyed. June 1970 brought *Self Portrait*, a covers-dominated double album whose review in *Rolling Stone* by Greil Marcus famously began, "What is this shit?" *New Morning*, which followed four months later, was better but the next few years delivered only *Greatest Hits, Vol. II,* with a few previously unreleased tracks; the instrumentals-heavy *Pat Garrett & Billy the Kid*, which did include the memorable "Knockin' on Heaven's Door"; the disastrous *Dylan*, a thrown-together package that was widely viewed as Columbia Records' revenge for his departure from the label; the relatively so-so (although chart-topping) *Planet Waves*; and *Before the Flood*, a document of his 1974 return to touring with the Band after about seven years away from the road.

But 1975 was another story. Having re-signed to Columbia Records, Dylan in January offered *Blood on the Tracks*, an album that many fans and critics (including this one) still regard as a highlight of his entire career. Five months later, the label issued the first official version of the often-bootlegged *Basement Tapes*, a series of wonderful informal recordings that Dylan had made with the Band near Woodstock, New York, in the late '60s. In between those two releases, in early 1975, he gave his first broadcast interview in years, to Mary Travers, whose group Peter, Paul, and Mary had been instrumental in popularizing his early work. Travers talked with Dylan in Oakland, California; her program originated from KNX-FM in Los Angeles and was syndicated nationally.

I was disappointed by this much-anticipated interview when it aired in April 1975. "With Travers playing some forty minutes of music, running commercials, and carrying on extended monologues," I wrote after the broadcast, "it's a wonder Dylan had time to say anything on the hour-long program."

A shortage of time wasn't the only problem. Granted, Dylan doesn't seem eager to volunteer much commentary, and there are indications that boundaries have been set for the conversation. (Travers implies at the beginning that the exchanges will be limited to "musical questions" and, later, when he says, "I think we might be crossing a line here," she quickly responds, "OK, we'll drop that.") Still, Dylan does appear willing to answer intelligent questions, and Travers, who is clearly unprepared, doesn't take much advantage of that willingness.

She begins the first aired Dylan interview in ages by asking him a yes/no question ("Did you ever meet him [Woody Guthrie]?") that he has already answered many times. And you don't spark great dialogue with observations like these: "I suppose Peter, Paul, and Mary and Pete Seeger and the Weavers and yourself even were caught up in that social commentary," or "You wrote a lot of good topical songs." Most such comments elicited from Dylan the response they deserved: "Mm-hmm."

All that said, the interview seems a good deal more interesting to me today than it did when it aired. I still think Travers fell short, but in retrospect, some of Dylan's answers are as memorable as they are brief. Note, for example, his observations about cover versions of "Just Like a Woman" as well as his reaction when Travers mentions having "enjoyed" *Blood on the Tracks*. —Ed.

Mary Travers: Hi. This is Mary Travers and you're listening to *Mary Travers and Friend*. And tonight's guest is Bob Dylan. We're here in the studio with Bob and there are a lot of good musical questions to talk about. First, I'd like to talk a little bit about some of the folks that the two of us were listening to in the early '60s, people like Woody Guthrie. And let's open, if we may, with a song you wrote about Woody Guthrie.

[*Dylan's "Song to Woody" plays.*]

Travers: And now let's play the real Woody Guthrie. Shall we?

[*Guthrie's "Pastures of Plenty" plays.*]

Travers: What about Guthrie? Did you ever meet him?

Bob Dylan: Yes, I did. I met him.

Travers: Was he very sick then?

Dylan: Well, I didn't meet him in his prime time, I guess. When I met him he was pretty laid up. But he was still alive and alert. I made many visits out to see him in the hospital.

Travers: Right, he had Huntington's chorea, which is—

Dylan: Kind of a shaky thing.

Travers: This is Mary Travers and I'll be right back after this message, with Bob Dylan.

[*Commercials air.*]

Travers: You've done an album that isn't released yet, called *Basement Tapes*. Want to tell me about that?

Dylan: That was recorded in '66, '67 up in Woodstock, before the big Woodstock festival, before Woodstock was discovered, exploited. We were just all up there sort of drying out.

Travers: You and the Band?

Dylan: Yeah. The members of the Band and various other people, up there making music and planting gardens and just watching time go by. So in the meantime we made this record. Actually, it wasn't a record, it was just songs which we'd come to this basement and record, out in the woods. That's basically it, really. The record's been exposed throughout the years so somebody mentioned it was a good idea to put it out as a record, so people could hear it in its entirety and just exactly what we were doing up there in those years, and it'll be out shortly.

Travers: Do you wanna play a track off of it?

Dylan: We can play all the tracks.

Travers: OK. Let's play one track now and play some more later.

[*Dylan and the Band's "Lo and Behold" plays.*]

Travers: Do you think that that period was a good period to hang out and kind of relax and get back to what music was about for you?

Dylan: For me? What do you mean?

Travers: I mean, I write poetry, I don't write songs, but I find it very difficult to write on the road, between getting on and off a plane and bad food—

Dylan: Right.

Travers: —and taking in a Holiday Inn ... It saps you of the kind of contemplative time you need to sit around and really think, and you also don't play so much together.

Dylan: Yeah, well, these songs basically on the tape, they were written in five, ten minutes. We'd just come off a ferocious tour of Australia, Europe, England.

Travers: These were more for fun.

Dylan: Yeah. Needed some time to let the—

Travers: —dust settle.

Dylan: Let the dust settle and the waves come in.

Travers: Well, I think a lot of people go through periods like that. If you forget how to have fun with music, you've just destroyed it for yourself, and I think, unfortunately, that's what heavy touring often does to us all. It becomes a job.

Dylan: It becomes a business.

Travers: And perhaps that's kind of the genesis of *The Basement Tapes*, is to go back and have fun with the music. Let's play another track from that.

[*"Yazoo Street Scandal" plays.*]

Travers: This is Mary Travers, and we'll be right back after this message.

[*Commercials air.*]

Travers: In a sense, this is a kind of a retrospective album for you, and you've had some funny albums in the sense that—well, I take that back, not funny albums, but most people do albums because the record company says you've got to do X number of albums a year. And then when you get tired or I get tired—and it's happened to me, too—you throw out a "Best Of" and kind of hang around and try to figure out what it is you really want to say musically.

Dylan: Musically? I play, and whatever comes out comes out. I don't plan albums. All that pressure's off. I don't have to go in and make an album every six months. I don't think of it that way. I just continue to play my guitar and if there's a song in my heart to do, I'll do.

[*Dylan's "Dirge" plays.*]

Travers: Let's maybe go back to Guthrie and see if we can't explore that a little bit more. He obviously had a great effect on your music and on a great many writers of that period, and you can see his influence even now. I mean, the talking blues form is a very viable, and will always be viable, form of saying something. And he wrote songs like "Pastures of Plenty" and "This Land Is Your Land"—those songs most people know and many songs that are not as familiar.

Dylan: Mm-hmm.

Travers: But he was also a very social writer and cared very much . . . and came from a time when many artists were very involved in caring about the country and what was happening to it, and I suppose Peter, Paul, and Mary and Pete Seeger and the Weavers and yourself even were caught up in that social commentary way of talking, of viewing the world as we saw it at that time. There were certainly a lot of your songs that were like that. Do you feel that that's not a reasonable position to take now or is it just that you're caring about other things?

Dylan: No, it's a very reasonable position to take now. It's just that it's hard to be specific about what we're even talking about here, let alone try to write a song or do a play or make some kind of art form out of these big situations which are happening in the world, which are changing so fast now. From day to day, it's like rolling over too fast to keep your eye on, whereas back then when Woody was doing all his writing, the media wasn't so powerful.

Travers: And it also took longer to get something changed.

Dylan: It took longer to get anywhere. It took longer to get from here to there.

Travers: I guess what you're saying, really, is that presents a special kind of problem for people who wanna write that kind of material.

Dylan: Well, it can be confusing if you wanna write what they call topical songs. It's hard to find the frontier.

Travers: You wrote a lot of good topical songs, of course.

Dylan: I wrote those songs, though, before it was happening and before everybody's on your case. Everybody gets on your case, you just don't wanna do it anymore. It's just like anything else—people tell you what to do, you don't wanna do what you're told to do. It's discouraging. Plus, you're just running over the same—

Travers: Same ground.

Dylan: Yeah.

Travers: Yeah. I mean, you have said it. I don't think you have to say times they are a-changing twice.

Dylan: Right. "Say it again! Say it again!" That's what they want.

Travers: Yeah. What they want. This is Mary Travers and I'll be right back after this message with Bob Dylan.

[*Commercials air.*]

Travers: Did you ever meet Nina Simone?

Dylan: I met her at a table once somewhere in a club.

Travers: She did a couple of your tunes.

Dylan: Yeah.

Travers: And well, I thought.

Dylan: Yeah.

Travers: I thought she brought something.

Dylan: Roberta Flack did "Just Like a Woman," but she got the words wrong.

Travers: She changed the words.

Dylan: I don't think she changed them. I think she just got 'em wrong.

Travers: I know Nina Simone did "Just Like a Woman" as well. I think she makes a lyric change there.

Dylan: Yeah. Personally, I don't understand why anybody would want to do that song, except me.

Travers: Richie Havens did it.

Dylan: Yeah, Richie. It made sense coming from Richie.

Travers: Let's play Richie.

Dylan: Yeah.

Travers: I like Richie. When you say, "I like Richie," that's not true—I love his work.

Dylan: That's an understatement, yeah.

Travers: Yeah. I love his work. I love him as a human being. I love him as a musician.

Dylan: He's like a king.

[*Havens's version of "Just Like a Woman" plays.*]

Travers: OK, let's talk about the present since we can't talk about the future, since it doesn't exist yet. In the future right now, is this—

Dylan: Oh, it all exists. The present exists, the past exists, and the future exists. It all exists.

Travers: How do you see the future as existing?

Dylan: It exists as part of the present, in Zen philosophy. You just live in the present, but that statement is more complicated than meets the eye, or really meets the ear. But it's all the same, the past, the present, and the future.

Travers: Historically, it would seem so.

Dylan: I think we might be crossing a line here . . .

Travers: OK. We'll drop that. That's fine. Those questions are philosophic questions and the program really isn't about philosophy per se.

Dylan: Right.

Travers: It's about music, although there's a lot of philosophy certainly in music, and a lot in yours, which is self-evident.

Dylan: That philosophy in my music, I have to admit, is accidental.

Travers: You really think so?

Dylan: Yeah. None of it is preconceived. I can tell you that much.

Travers: Well, when you say "preconceived" . . . when I write a poem, I don't sit around all day saying, "Gee, I'd like to write a poem about flowers," or children or caring about people. I don't think about what it is I'm going to write about. When you feel like writing, you sit down and out something pops. But it doesn't mean that you haven't been thinking about it.

Dylan: Yeah, that gets back to thinking again. My stuff has to do more with feeling than thinking.

Travers: OK.

Dylan: When I get to thinking, I'm usually in some kind of trouble.

Travers: Well, if you can trust your own feelings, you're probably in better shape. Is it more truthful?

Dylan: Oh, yeah. It comes down to mutual trust.

Travers: Always. On *Blood on the Tracks* . . . Needless to say, I loved the album, I really enjoyed the album, and it was funny because when we had talked before, we talked about recording processes and how when they get very complex, much of the truth of a piece of music is lost. It becomes something else. And one of the things I enjoyed about *Blood on the Tracks* was that it was very simple.

Dylan: That's the way things are, really. They are basically very simple. A lot of people tell me they enjoyed that album. It's hard for me to relate to that. I mean, people enjoying the type of pain.

Travers: It is a painful album. Well, perhaps maybe the word "enjoy" is the wrong word. Maybe a better word is to say that you're moved. I was moved by the album. There were things that I could relate to in that album—

Dylan: Mm-hmm.

Travers: —that made sense to me. You made sense to me. Let's play "If You See Her, Say Hello," 'cause I think that's a very beautiful song.

Dylan: Very pertinent.

[*Dylan's "If You See Her, Say Hello" plays.*]

Travers: For me, that is a very poignant song. And a very sad song. But together, one of the things I like about your work is that even when you're feeling bad, it isn't self-pity bad—it's just "I don't feel good."

Dylan: Mm-hmm. Even when you're feeling down you feel up.

Travers: Well, you're feeling something, and that's the positive as opposed to feeling destroyed by it.

Dylan: Do you write songs?

Travers: No. I'm writing a book.

Dylan: Mm-hmm.

Travers: I write a lot of poetry. But somehow I've never been able to figure out how to make poems into songs. It really seems to be a different way of writing.

Dylan: Yeah. It's confining.

Travers: What—songs?

Dylan: Mm-hmm.

Travers: Well, yeah. Poetry seems to give you a bigger canvas to play with, and you don't have to explain it the same way. Songs seem to have to be understandable. Somehow, in a poem you can ramble and deal with several thoughts and not have to necessarily connect the images. I know a song of yours that I think for me was most poem-like was "Hard Rain's Gonna Fall," 'cause it really wasn't a song, it was a series of images, and when you see it on a piece of paper it really looked like a poem.

Dylan: Play Leon [Russell]'s version. He did it, too.

[*Russell's version of "A Hard Rain's A-Gonna Fall" plays.*]

Travers: This is Mary Travers, and we'll be right back after this message.

[*Commercials air.*]

Travers: The in-concert album [*Before the Flood*] that you did with the Band on the last tour, which was an incredible piece of business for someone who doesn't do a lot of concerts . . . you sure made up for it with that tour.

Dylan: Mm.

Travers: I'd like to play something off of that album.

Dylan: Mm-hmm.

Travers: Was there something that you felt went well?

Dylan: Oh, you can play "All Along the Watchtower."

[*Dylan and the Band's concert version of "All Along the Watchtower" plays.*]

Travers: Let's finish off with a track from *The Basement Tapes*. Your choice.

Dylan: OK. Oh, "Apple Suckling Tree."

Travers: OK, we'll finish with that.

Dylan: Yeah.

Travers: And thank you.

[*Dylan and the Band's "Apple Suckling Tree" plays.*]

DYLAN ON

Whether He Was Living with His Wife

"When I have to, when I need to. I'm living with my wife in the same world . . . Do I know where she is most of the time? She doesn't have to answer to me . . . She has to answer to herself . . . Right now, things are changing in all our lives. We will always be together."

—from interview with Jim Jerome, *People*, November 10, 1975

BOB DYLAN: ". . . A SAILING SHIP TO THE MOON"

Neil Hickey | August 1976 (interview) | March 4, 2015 |
Adventures in the Scribblers Trade

This article appeared in 2015, in a book by Neil Hickey, but the fascinating Dylan encounter it describes dates from August 1976, when the New York–based journalist flew to California to interview the artist for a piece that ran in *TV Guide* in September of that year.

"The reason we did the article in *TV Guide*," Hickey told me, "was that Dylan had made a prime-time music special for NBC." *Hard Rain* aired September 14, 1976, and came out on LP that same week. "I contacted him and his people and said we might like to do a cover on the show," Hickey continued. "I think it's still the only such TV show he ever did.

"I got a phone call one Saturday at my house in [New York's] Putnam County saying, 'Can you be in Malibu on Tuesday?' So I went out there, and Dylan and I spent most of a day knocking around."

Hickey added that he'd been a fan "since Dylan's arrival in New York and his early appearances on MacDougal Street—my apartment was in the Village—and at the Newport Folk Festival, to which I traveled every year."

The interview took place a little more than six months after the release of *Desire*, the follow-up to *Blood on the Tracks*. The new album—which, like its predecessor, was a chart-topper—includes "Hurricane," Dylan's first overtly political song since "George Jackson," a 1971 single; and "Sara," one of his most openly personal records up to that time. —Ed.

He swung a sandaled foot over the roadside guardrail and slid down a sharp, 20-foot incline, then walked forward along Corral Beach and sat down in the sand. The whisper of surf mingled with the roar of traffic along Pacific Coast Highway. Bob Dylan wore jeans, a frayed lightweight black leather jacket, and a white burnoose over longish brown curls. The unshaved face enforced his resemblance to a hip shepherd from some biblical Brigadoon. As he popped a beer can, a teen-age girl approached, Frisbee in hand.

"Mister, is this yours?"

"No," said Dylan politely. The girl strolled off down the beach, unaware that she had addressed a legend.

The day had begun badly when I drove up to Dylan's house atop a Malibu hill and straight into a pocket of loose, deep sand near the front door. The car's wheels spun as I tried to burrow out, to no avail. Cracking the door and looking down, I saw that the car was up to its hubcaps in the sand. A gaggle of children and teen-agers trotted from the house to study my plight. I put the oldest of them in the driver's seat, motor running, and had the others join me at the rear bumper, rocking and rolling the vehicle vigorously to try to free it. Minutes elapsed without success in spite of my volunteers' enthusiasm for the task. Head down, I continued to shove hard. In the next moment I became aware of a figure next to me, his shoulder to the car's rear end and pushing vigorously with the rest of us. A minute later, the car rolled out of its sand trap onto firmer ground.

"Happens all the time," Bob Dylan said.

We mopped perspiration, strolling to undo the knots in leg muscles. I stared about at the Malibu hills.

"It's a long way from MacDougal Street," I said.

He nodded. "Want to take a drive?" He was hungry, he said.

In my newly-exhumed car, we drove down the winding path away from the house, then south, with the ocean on our right. The chat in the car, in that campaign summer, was about Jimmy Carter's race against President Gerald Ford. Carter had been quoting lines from Dylan songs in his stump speeches, and even in his acceptance speech at the Democratic convention.

"I don't know what to think of that," Dylan said. "People have told me that there's a man running for President and quoting me." He laughed.

"I don't know if that's good or bad." If his songs had meaning for Carter, that's OK with him, Dylan offered. "But he's just another guy trying to be President. I sometimes dream of running the country and putting all my friends in office. That's the way they do it now, anyway."

Sports cars bearing surfboards on their roofs streamed past. Dylan pointed to a roadside luncheonette rimmed with picnic tables and suggested we stop. ("The Bagelah Delicatessen: Established 1973") Getting out, he strode forward in a bent-kneed lope and ordered a pastrami sandwich and a can of beer.

Of all the major figures ever to populate the performing arts, Bob Dylan—he's in his seventies at this writing—has been among the most protective about his private life. It's still terra incognita to fans, journalists, and scholars who have tracked his career for more than half a century. "The press has always misrepresented me," he said, when we were settled. His eyes were pale blue, his fingernails long. "They refuse to accept what I am and what I do as just that. They always find something to carp about. They always sensationalize and blow things up. I know multitudes of people who feel that way." Instead of newspapers, he said, the country should get back to bulletins posted on walls. "I let them write whatever they want as long as I don't have to talk to them. They can see me anytime they want, doing what I do. I'm not in any popularity contest. It's best to keep your mouth shut and do your work." It suited him to talk to me on that summer day in 1976 because he'd recently finished the only TV concert special he'd ever done, called "Hard Rain," which would air soon on the NBC network.

I had first encountered Dylan in the dingy folk clubs that lined MacDougal Street in Greenwich Village during the "folk scare" of the 1960s when traditional and protest songs were about to dominate, ever so briefly, American popular music. I lived a block away on Sullivan Street and haunted Washington Square Park on Sunday afternoons for impromptu songfests. A ragamuffin Dylan showed up in New York in January, 1961, knowing nobody, having hitchhiked from northern Minnesota's Mesabi iron range, and having abandoned the name Robert Allen Zimmerman. (His grandparents were Lithuanian, Russian, and Ukranian Jewish immigrants.) As a teen-ager he'd been in thrall to rockers like Carl Perkins and Little Richard, and was a middling electric guitar player. After hearing Woody Guthrie's powerful prole anthems and his raw Oklahoma voice, Dylan abandoned the electric guitar (he'd famously reclaim it later) for a steel-strung acoustic model and a harmonica on a chest rack. For the first time, among many, he recreated himself.

Arriving in New York, he went looking for the singers whose recordings he'd heard back in Minnesota: Ed McCurdy, Josh White, Dave Van Ronk, Brownie McGhee and Sonny Terry, Pete Seeger, the New Lost City Ramblers, Reverend Gary Davis, and especially Woody Guthrie. The Village clubs were home to edgy comedians like Lenny Bruce, Mort Sahl, Shelly Berman, Woody Allen, and Richard Pryor.

A friend of my own, Israel "Izzy" Young, proprietor of a legendary, cluttered storefront at 110 MacDougal Street, took Dylan in and let him crash in the back room. The Folklore Center stocked musical instruments, along with books, vinyl records, and photographs. It was the first stop for every impoverished, traveling singer-songwriter with a cardboard guitar case. Izzy Young—exorbitantly generous and impractical—was kind to most of them, including the yearningly ambitious kid who claimed his name was Bob Dylan. The shop was "the citadel of Americana folk music," as Dylan later called it. In the back room was a potbelly, wood-burning stove and a phonograph, where he listened to folk music by the hour. In his 2004 book *Chronicles: Volume One*, he described Young:

> . . . an old-line folk enthusiast, very sardonic, wore heavy, horn-rimmed glasses, spoke in a thick Brooklyn dialect. . . . His voice was like a bulldozer and always seemed too loud for the little room. . . . To him, folk music glittered like a mound of gold. It did for me too . . . [He sold] extinct song folios of every type— sea shanties, Civil War songs, cowboy songs, songs of lament, church house songs, anti-Jim Crow songs, union songs—archaic books of folk tales, Wobbly journals, propaganda pamphlets. . . . People were always chasing him down for money, but it didn't seem to faze him.

At a picnic table outside the Bagelah Delicatessen, Dylan's attention strayed to the stream of traffic along Pacific Coast Highway. "Personally, I like sound effects records," he joked. "Sometimes late at night I get a mint julep and sit there and listen to sound effects. I'm surprised more of them aren't on the charts." He smiled, pleased with the idea. "If I had my own label, that's what I'd record." He once asked a sound effects expert how he produced the sound of a man being executed in the electric chair. Bacon sizzling, said the expert. The sound of breaking bones? Crunching a LifeSaver between the teeth.

I rehearsed for him some of the old history from his Village days. Remarkably, success in New York came almost instantly. Robert Shelton, the folk music critic of *The New York Times* (there *was* such a job then) wrote an admiring review in September 1961, barely 9 months after Dylan's arrival in the city. John Hammond, the buck-toothed, good-humored aristocrat (his mother was a Vanderbilt) at Columbia Records signed Dylan to a recording contract while the unkempt 20-year-old was still singing for tips in the clubs along MacDougal Street—Café Wha?, the Gaslight, and, nearby on 4th Street, Gerde's Folk City. The movie-makers Joel and Ethan Coen vividly dramatized that culture in their 2013 film *Inside Llewyn Davis*.

Hammond was the supernally acute talent scout and record producer who developed such talents as Billie Holiday, Bessie Smith, Teddy Wilson, Aretha Franklin, Cab Calloway, Lionel Hampton, Benny Goodman, Count Basie, and Bruce Springsteen. On November 20 and 22 in the very year of his arrival in New York, Dylan recorded his first album—traditional songs, plus a few of his own. ("Song to Woody," "Talkin' New York") and others credited to Blind Lemon Jefferson ("See That My Grave Is Kept Clean") and Jesse Fuller ("You're No Good"). The jacket photo showed a baby-faced youth in a fleece-lined jacket and a corduroy cap. The skinny kid who would become the reluctant "spokesman for a generation" and a powerful voice of protest and lamentation was off and running fast.

Dylan shrugged at the memory.

"The past—for me it doesn't exist. For me, there's the next song, the next poem, the next performance. The bunch of us who came through that time . . ." He paused. "A lot of people don't know how all this music got here. But the fifties and the sixties were a very high-energy period—right there in the middle of the century. It's an explosive time in every century. Eighteen-sixty was the Civil War. In seventeen-sixty you had the beginnings of the American Revolution. You might call it the mid-century energy explosion."

We talked about mutual friends and acquaintances—Johnny Cash, Alan Lomax, Robert Shelton, David Amram, Israel Young. "There was a lot of space to be born in then," he said. "The media was onto other things. The only scene was word-of-mouth. You could really breathe back then. You could develop whatever creative interests you had, without categories and definitions. That period lasted about three years. There's just as much creativity going on now," he added, but without the centrality and focus that the Village provided.

A lot of dangerous stuff was happening then as well, I reminded him: amphetamines, hallucinogens, mind-altering and recreational chemicals. When the Beatles and he met for the first time in 1964 at New York's Delmonico Hotel, Dylan introduced them to marijuana, which they embraced joyfully. Ringo spent part of the evening fearfully stuffing towels under the door lest the hotel staff get a whiff of that historic meeting, and summon the cops.

"A person's body chemistry changes every seven years," Dylan said. "No one on earth is the same now as they were seven years ago, or will be seven years from now. I could become you!" He laughed. "It's all intended growth. It doesn't take a whole lot of brains to know that if you don't grow you die. You have to burst out, you have to find the sunlight." He was silent for a moment. "I think of myself as more than a musician, more than a poet. That's just what I do. The real self is something more than that."

He looked toward the ocean. "My being a Gemini explains a lot," he said. "It forces me to extremes. I'm never really balanced in the middle. I go from one side to the other and pass through the middle. I'm happy, sad, up, down, in, out, over and under. Up in the sky and down in the depths of the earth."

Is it really such a roller-coaster ride, I wondered? If it is, how do you manage to turn out so prodigious a body of work amid such a hubbub of emotion?

"This is what I do, in this life and in this country. I could be happy being a blacksmith. I would still write and sing. I can't imagine not doing that. You do what you're geared for." He thought that over: "I don't care if I write. I can say that now. But as soon as the light changes, it'll be the thing I care about most in the world." When he's through with performing he'll continue to write, Dylan said: "Probably for other people." Traces of Minnesota remained in Dylan's speech, the voice well-modulated, the syntax perfect, none of the hobo patois and street vernacular that mark his lyrics. I'd often twinned Dylan and Bobby Fischer in my mind: a pair of reclusive, idiosyncratic Jewish striplings who evolved into genius by the extravagance of their natural powers.

Songs spewed from Dylan like lava. How many had he written? He had no idea. (*The Definitive Bob Dylan Songbook* published in 2004 contains 300, some of them forgettable, others classic bits of American pop culture.) He made it look easy, I offered.

"Are you kidding? Almost anything else is easy except writing songs." The hard part, he said, is when "the inspiration dies along the way. Then you spend all your time trying to recapture the inspiration." He shook his head. "You're talking to a total misfit here."

Somewhere along the line, the misfit learned to write lyrics that are taut, imagistic, and memorable.

> ... *take me disappearin' through the smoke rings of my mind,*
> *Down the foggy ruins of time, far past the frozen leaves,*
> *The haunted, frightened trees, out to the windy beach,*
> *Far from the twisted reach of crazy sorrow.*

Songwriters like George Gershwin and Irving Berlin "knew what they were doing," musically, Dylan said. "I write the only way I know how. It's the best I can do, that's all." He felt sure that some of his songs will be rediscovered and examined in the future the way ancient ruins are unearthed by archeologists, and found to have unrecognized historical importance. "Look at the castles and walls of the middle ages. Do you think anybody back then thought those structures were anything special?" The builders were too busy creating them, and using them in their quotidian lives, to care much if they'd endure for thousands of years.

Many of his idolaters expend talmudic scrutiny on teasing out meanings in his lyrics, I reminded him.

"If you define what something is, it's no longer that something," Dylan answered. "Definition destroys. When you see me performing, I often change the words of my songs because that's the way I feel at that moment. I have the license to do that. It's all temporary. There's nothing definite in this world. It changes too quickly. You're talking to somebody who doesn't comprehend the values most people operate under. Greed and lust I can understand. But I can't understand the values of definition and confinement."

He didn't spend his money the way the Beatles and other rock legends did—no baronial estates, fleets of autos, designer clothes, bodyguards, entourages, private jets. "It's the way I've been brought up," he answered. "My parents raised me right. I don't necessarily have a lot of money. I spend a lot of money."

He had married Sara Lownds in 1965 and they'd produced four children. He adopted one of hers by a previous marriage. In a hymn to her, he'd written: "Lovin' you is the one thing I'll never regret." His voice on the recording is full of stark yearning and dependency. He pronounces her name "Say-rah":

> Sara, oh Sara,
> Glamorous nymph with an arrow and bow,
> Sara, oh Sara,
> Don't ever leave me, don't ever go.

She did leave him. They divorced in 1977. What that rupture cost him emotionally and psychically we won't know precisely because he has never talked about it publicly, nor exploited their relationship for publicity in celebrity magazines. He made one brief allusion to it in a

2004 interview with *60 Minutes* while publicizing his book: "She was with me back then through thick and thin, you know? And it just wasn't the kind of life she had ever envisioned for herself, any more than the kind . . . that I had envisioned for mine." The clearest clues about his state of mind as the marriage ended are in his album, the angry, bitter, raging *Blood on the Tracks.*

> *I been double crossed now for the very last time and now I'm finally free,*
> *I kissed goodbye the howling beast on the borderline which separated you from me.*
> *You'll never know the hurt I suffered nor the pain I rise above . . .*

Where will he be ten years from today, I wondered.

"Maybe I'll be on a sailing ship to the moon." He laughed. "Write that down." Dylan had rarely appeared on television, but one live concert was taped and cobbled into a television special, called *Hard Rain*, for broadcast on NBC. Not until 2005—at the age of 64 and looking every day of it—did he sit for a substantial interview on television: the splendid 3½ hour public broadcasting documentary *No Direction Home*, directed by Martin Scorsese. By 2006 he had emerged sufficiently from his chrysalis to become a disc jockey on XM Satellite Radio, a career move that would have been unimaginable only a few years earlier. On the weekly show, called *Theme Time Radio Hour With Your Host Bob Dylan*, his musical catholicity was on full view: songs by Sinatra, Stevie Wonder, Jimi Hendrix, Judy Garland, Slim Harpo. (*The New York Times* described his commentary: "As DJ . . . he taps America's musical heritage with words that veer from the logically linear to the abstract.") Astonishingly, he did commercials for Apple Computer products and Victoria's Secret lingerie. Beyond that: he teamed up with the choreographer Twyla Tharp for the Broadway musical *Bringing It All Back Home*, a box-office dud. The prestigious Morgan Library in Manhattan mounted an exhibit in 2006 called "Bob Dylan's American Journey, 1956–1966," displaying his manuscripts, letters, handwritten lyrics, instruments, memorabilia, and photographs. Then came Todd

Haynes's fantastical, mythical meditation on Dylanology in the 2007 movie *I'm Not There*, in which a half-dozen actors (including Cate Blanchett, Richard Gere, and Heath Ledger) played Dylan in his varied aspects. A respected Manhattan art gallery mounted a collection of his paintings in 2011 (he's rather a good technical artist), which caused a mini-scandal when it turned out that many of the works were close copies of old photographs rather than (as the catalogue claimed) "first-hand depictions of people, street scenes, architecture and landscape" from his travels in Japan, China, Vietnam and Korea. Dylan never bothered to address the charge, and his defenders said it was just one more bit of Dylan whimsy.

There has been no end of tributes. In 2008, he won a Pulitzer Prize for his "profound impact on popular music and American culture, marked by lyrical compositions of extraordinary poetic power." After singing at the White House in 2010 to celebrate Black History Month, President Obama (a big fan) awarded Dylan the National Medal of Arts. In 2013: France's highest prize, the Legion of Honor. He turned 70 in May 2011, and a batch of new books about his life and his endlessly allegorical/metaphorical/enigmatic lyrics hit the bookstalls.

Dylan finished his sandwich and ordered another for the road.

"Want to go and sit on the beach for a while?" he asked.

I bought a six-pack of Coors and we headed back to the car. He slid into the driver's seat and wheeled out onto the highway. I reminisced about the Newport Folk Festivals of 1963 and 1964. Joan Baez, then a bigger star than Dylan, was his enthusiastic champion in those years, and later his lover. She had often brought him onstage during her own concerts. But in 1965—at the zenith of his popularity—the festival's most memorable, and now mythical, moment came when Dylan committed the sacrilege of playing electric guitar onstage, enraging the thousands of folk purists in that outdoor setting on the shores of Narragansett Bay. With members of the Paul Butterfield blues band playing behind him, Dylan "went electric," a sound never before heard at Newport. He screeched, loud and raucous, into the chill Rhode Island night air:

I ain't gonna work on Maggie's farm no more . . .
Well, I try my best
To be just like I am,
But everybody wants you
To be just like them . . .

The startled crowd emitted a torrent of boos and catcalls. I was sitting near the stage. To my left, Alan Lomax—the preeminent American archivist of traditional music—was on his feet shouting angrily and shaking his fist at Dylan. Pete Seeger was so chafed that he wanted to chop the microphone cables to end the ear-shattering din. Dylan, flustered by the crowd's outrage, fled into the wings. Peter Yarrow of Peter Paul and Mary, the evening's MC, took the microphone and tried vainly to placate the crowd. The jeers persisted for minutes. Dylan reappeared carrying his acoustic guitar. The crowd fell silent. Alone on stage, he sang "It's All Over Now, Baby Blue."

The lover who just walked out your door
Has taken all his blankets from the floor.
The carpet, too, is moving under you
And it's all over now, Baby Blue.

By the end of the song, the crowd's jeers had turned to wild cheering. But unbeknownst to most of the audience, Dylan was reinventing himself once again, right before their eyes. He was announcing that he wouldn't be hostage to their expectations, that he'd travel his own road and they could come along or not. The era of the Beatles had just dawned; they had made their celebrated appearance on the Ed Sullivan show more than a year earlier. It was time to move on.

In the car, Dylan said: "I wasn't hurt or offended by the audience's reaction. I had played electric guitar in the midwest before I ever went to New York. My mother will tell you that. I didn't do anything all that remarkable." If he hadn't introduced electric guitars at Newport, he said, somebody else would have. (Years later, in *Chronicles Volume One*, he would explain that "what I did to break away was to take simple folk chord changes and put new imagery and attitude to them, use catchphrases and metaphor combined with a new set of ordinances that evolved into something different that had not been heard before . . . I knew what I was doing . . . and wasn't going to take a step back or retreat for anybody.")

On a previous occasion in 1963 he had refused to compromise. Ed Sullivan invited him to appear on his popular Sunday night variety show. Dylan agreed and said he'd sing "Talkin' John Birch Society Blues," his satiric send-up of that radical right-wing guild of eccentrics. Sullivan said OK, but the CBS censors refused to let Dylan perform that song. Rather than knuckle under, he declined to appear and thus forsook television exposure that would have launched him nationwide.

A few skeptics have suggested that his protest songs of that period ("Masters of War," "With God on Your [sic] Side," "Blowin' in the Wind") were trendy, marketable tunes written in cold blood to feed the anti-war, pro-civil rights sentiments of the 1960s. (*Pravda*, the Russian newspaper, had once called him a money-hungry capitalist.)

Not true, Dylan insisted, navigating a bend in the Pacific Coast Highway. "I wrote them because that's what I was in the middle of. It swept me up. 'Blowin' in the Wind' holds up. I *felt* that song. Whenever Joan [Baez] and I do it, it really is just like an old folk song to me. It never occurs to me that I'm the person who wrote it." After a moment, he said, "Joan Baez means more to me than a hundred of these singers around today. She's more powerful. That's what we're looking for, that's what we respond to. She always did it and always will. Power for the species, not just for a select group." He paused, and then: "I've probably said too much about that."

But the characterization of himself that irks the most is being called the political and cultural leader, or "voice," of a generation of protestors and activists. In 1970, Princeton University awarded him an honorary Doctorate of Music; Dylan, still in his twenties, showed up on the campus to accept it. The speaker presenting the doctorate made the tone-deaf mistake of describing him as "the authentic expression of the disturbed and concerned conscience of young America." Dylan later wrote: "Oh, Sweet Jesus! It was like a jolt. I shuddered and trembled but remained expressionless . . . I was so mad I wanted to bite myself." Instead, he memorialized the occasion in the song "Day of the Locust":

> *I put down my robe, and picked up my diploma,*
> *Took hold of my sweetheart and away we did drive,*
> *Straight for the hills, the black hills of Dakota,*
> *Sure was glad to get out of there alive.*

Later, in 1997, he was one of five people on the Kennedy Center Honors list for "exemplary achievement in the performing arts." On the nationally televised show, he sat importantly and uneasily in the Presidential box alongside Lauren Bacall, Charlton Heston, Jessye Norman, and Edward Villella. The Center's publicity handout called him "the voice of a generation," "the sincerest social activist," and "perhaps the most influential figure in American popular music in our time." President Clinton in his remarks declared that Dylan had "captured the mood of a generation. Everything he saw—the pain, the promise, the yearning, the injustice—turned to song. He probably had more impact on people of my generation than any other creative artist. . . . He's disturbed the peace and discomforted the powerful. . . . Thank you Bob Dylan, for a lifetime of stirring the conscience of a nation." Those words seriously invaded Dylan's comfort zone. He squirmed visibly in his chair and looked unhappy. (He had performed at Clinton's first inauguration ball in 1993.) In May 2013, the illustrious American Academy of Arts and Letters inducted him into its ranks, noting that: "For more than 50 years, defying categorization . . . Bob Dylan has probed and prodded our psyches, recording and then changing our world and our lives through poetry made manifest in song." Dylan responded that he was "extremely honored and very lucky to be included in this great pantheon."

He has been nominated several times for the Nobel Prize in Music. In 2011, he was a 5-1 favorite to win the Nobel Prize in Literature, according to London bookies. (It went to a Swedish poet.) Writing in *The New Yorker* (Oct. 31, 2011), Dan Chiasson declared that, had Dylan won, ". . . I would have joined the worldwide chorus of hallelujahs, for Bob Dylan is a genius, and there is something undeniably literary about his genius, and those two facts together make him more deserving of this prize than countless pseudo-notables who have won it in the past."

One shudders, however, to imagine Dylan's conspicuous misery, seated onstage before the Swedish royal family, hearing himself described as a prophet and sachem of the benighted masses. "I had very little in common with and knew even less about a generation that I was supposed to be the voice of," he wrote in his memoir.

Dylan suffered a self-inflicted wound in April 2011 when he let the Chinese and Vietnamese governments censor concerts he gave in those countries. Gone from his set list were counterculture faves such as "Blowin' in the Wind" and "The Times They Are a-Changin'." "He sang his censored set, took his pile of Communist cash and left," Maureen Dowd grouchily wrote in her *New York Times* op-ed column.

At Corral Beach, Dylan parked the car on the highway's shoulder and slid down the embankment to the beach. I threw the six-pack of Coors down to him and followed. Once settled in the sand, I remarked on the catholicity of his musical tastes—as a teen-ager in Minnesota he'd sponged up the music of the 1950s rockers and rhythm and blues artists, then onward to Hank Williams, Roy Orbison, Josh White, Reverend Gary Davis, George Jones, Charlie Parker, Thelonious Monk, Dave Van Ronk, Robert Johnson. And Frank Sinatra. Listening to Sinatra sing "Ebb Tide," he later wrote, "I could hear everything in his voice—death, God and the universe, everything." (Uncharacteristically, Dylan performed on a nationally televised tribute to Sinatra in 1995. The aging crooner watched him, wide-eyed, clearly pleased and flattered that Dylan—who called him "Mr. Frank"—came to honor him. In May 1998, Dylan attended Sinatra's funeral at a Catholic church in Los Angeles.)

Dylan popped a can of beer as I mentioned the Beatles.

"They took all the music we'd been listening to and showed it to us again," he said. "They have everything in their music from Little Richard to the Everly Brothers. They helped give America's pride back to it. There ought to be statues to the Beatles."

What had he been reading lately?

He laughed. "You don't want to know. It would sound stupid. I'm open to everything. Whatever I have the stamina for. I have no information. I just have life—through these eyes and hands, what I've been given as I walk the earth." After a pause: "Rimbaud has been a big influence on me. When I'm on the road and want to read something that makes sense to me I go to a bookstore and read his words. Also Melville. He wrote *The Confidence Man*, didn't he, and *Moby-Dick*? He's someone I can identify with because of how he looked at life. Being in California, I've seen some whales." He grinned. "I'd like to see some more on my sailing trip to the moon."

Anybody else?

"Joseph Conrad. I also like him a lot."

Allen Ginsberg had accompanied Dylan the year before on the famous Rolling Thunder Revue tour, along with Joan Baez, Jack Elliott, Bob Neuwirth, Ronee Blakely, and others.

"Ginsberg is always a great inspiration," Dylan said. "I read *Howl* in Minnesota. That blew my mind. He's real balanced. A bit sentimental."

Had Ginsberg's immersion in Buddhism rubbed off on him?

"Just between you and me?" A long pause. "No, not at all."

Around his neck Dylan wore a lapis lazuli pendant with a star of David on one side and a bas relief lyre on the other.

"It's something from the earth," he explained. "It's energy. How do I know that? It's been written about in ancient books."

That opened the door a crack to Dylan's spiritual beliefs, a subject of tortuous speculation by his exegetes. After a serious motorcycle accident in 1966, he had disappeared from view, lived quietly in Woodstock, New York, and didn't return to touring for 8 years. But in 1967, Dylan released his *John Wesley Harding* album, which was rich with Old Testament allusions and imagery. One of the songs, "All Along the Watchtower," derived from the Book of Isaiah, 21:5–9

"That was the first biblical rock record," Dylan said, peering out to the ocean. "As opposed to spiritual rock. Biblical rock leans more toward what is tangible than what is spiritual. We take our symbols from the bible. The stories in the bible are stories we've all been through."

Then in 1971, he made a pilgrimage to Israel. "There was no great significance to that visit," he said. "It was part of the journey of life, but it wasn't really a spiritual occasion. There was an old rabbi there who kept trying to wrap the tallis around my arm and throw a yarmulke on my head. I had to deal with him. I wanted to experience the wall but the guy just wouldn't let it happen. I'm interested in what and who a Jew is. I'm interested in the fact that Jews are Semites the same as Babylonians, Hittites, Arabs, Syrians, Ethiopians." But Jews are different, said Dylan, and many people in the world perceive them differently. "People hate gypsies, too. Why? I don't know. Human beings are all the same behind the eyes."

All right then. Let's just cut to the meat-and-potatoes question: What is Bob Dylan's conception of God?

He laughed and leaned back in the sand. "How come nobody ever asks Kris Kristofferson questions like that? I should have read some books and studied up on this." And then: "God is a combination of man and woman and everything else. I can see God in a daisy. I can see God at night in the wind and the rain. I see creation just about everywhere. See that seagull? The highest form of song is prayer. King David's, Solomon's, the wailing of a coyote, the rumble of the earth. It must be wonderful to be God. There's so much going on out there that you can't get to it all. We're all mystical beings. There's a mystic in all of us. It's part of our nature. Some of us are shown more than others. Or maybe we're all shown the same but some of us make more use of it. I know taxi drivers who have it. It's not a continual feeling of ecstasy. Gurus tell you you can have ecstasy twenty-four hours a day. That means you have to give up everything else for that continual feeling. All the teachings of the gurus, like the Maharishi, are a way of quieting your mind so that you can be aware of the world."

In the late 1970's, Dylan's albums—*Slow Train Coming, Saved, Shot of Love*—began reflecting a deepening interest in Christianity; in live concerts he'd often deliver a brief sermonette. Then in the 1980s, he sported a renewed interest in Judaism, causing Jewish exegetes to redouble their ethnopaleontology to prove he is profoundly Semitic, and, indeed, a version of an Old Testament prophet. That scenario collapsed when—astonishingly—Dylan released an album in the winter of

2009 called "Christmas in the Heart," flaunting a Currier and Ives-style jacket and a medley of holiday chestnuts like "The First Noel," "O, Come All Ye Faithful," "Little Drummer Boy," and "Have Yourself a Merry Little Christmas." Once again, Dylan had confounded his acolytes. The royalties went to feed the homeless and the hungry.

Dylan adjusted his position in the sand and popped another can of beer. "I'm not really very articulate. I save what I have to say for what I do. Somebody said I'm the Ed Sullivan of rock 'n' roll." Laughter. "I don't know what that means but it sounds right."

So why hadn't he written an autobiography setting the record straight once and for all, thus confuting the Dylan obsessives, stalkers, and wackos who had spread rumors and often made his life miserable. Dylan had been the least reliable witness to the facts of his own life, improvising biography outrageously during unwelcome encounters with the press.

No chance, he replied. "I'd rather work on other things. I doubt I'll ever do one." Wrong again. *Chronicles, Volume One*, earned rave reviews, some of them overwrought and foolish: "... the greatest and most important Western writer since Shakespeare ..." (*Capital Times*, Madison, Wisc.); "... may be the most extraordinarily intimate autobiography by a 20th-century legend ever written ..." (*Daily Telegraph*, London); "... the most influential cultural figure alive ..." (*Newsweek*). The book is good sport for Dylan adepts, to be sure, in spite of its casual grip on chronology. If his habits in the early sixties, as related in the book, are to be believed, he has been a gluttonous reader: Thucydides, Machiavelli, Dante, Rousseau, Ovid, Sophocles, Simon Bolivar, Faulkner, Albertus Magnus, Byron, Shelley, Longfellow, Poe, Freud, Milton, Pushkin, Tolstoy, Dostoyevsky, Balzac, Edgar Rice Burroughs, Luke Short, Jules Verne, H.G. Wells, Clausewitz, Robert Graves, biographies of Thaddeus Stevens, Robert E. Lee, Frederick the Great.

"I can't tell you how Bob Dylan has lived his life," he was saying. "And it's far from over. If you play your cards right ..." His voice trailed off. I watched him as he fell silent. I thought of the many Dylan performances I'd seen. His guitar playing is rudimentary, the melodies often are borrowed or adapted, the lyrics sometimes forced and unpoetic. But the effect is one of unique power and range. Bob Dylan had invented an inimitable self. In 2014 at age 73, he was still touring the country and the world, playing 100 concerts a year.

An orange sun was dipping below the Pacific. It was time to go. Dylan hoisted himself upright.

"I hope there's not a snake in my beer," he said.

We returned to the car and I drove him to the foot of his driveway in Malibu. He wanted to walk the rest of the way, so we shook hands and he wandered off. After a minute, I noticed he'd left behind on the car seat the pastrami sandwich he'd bought at the roadside deli. I shouted after him, waving the sandwich above my head. He returned, nodded, smiled gratefully, retrieved the package, and strolled up the roadway.

I watched him go. Years later, in April 2012, it surprised me not at all—although it surely caused him to squirm—that he was awarded (along with John Glenn, Toni Morrison, Madeleine Albright, and Justice John Paul Stevens) the Presidential Medal of Freedom, the highest civilian honor given by the United States for being among "the most influential American musicians of the 20th century."

Yeah, we sort of know that. Let's just posit that there's never been anybody like Bobby Zimmerman of Hibbing, Minnesota, and there isn't going to be.

DYLAN ON

Drawing

"One time I was doing it all day for a couple of months in New York. This was a couple of years back; it was '74, '75. I did it every day from eight till four with a break or something, and it locked me into the present time more than anything else I ever did. More than any experiences I've ever had, any enlightenment I've ever had. Because I was constantly being intermingled with myself and all the different selves that were in there, until this one left, then that one left, and finally I got down to the one that I was familiar with."

—from interview with Karen Hughes, *Rock Express* (Australia), 1978

DYLAN ON

Filmmakers He Admires

"[Andy] Warhol did a lot for American cinema. He was before his time. But Warhol and [Alfred] Hitchcock and [Sam] Peckinpah and Tod Browning . . . they were important to me. I figured [Jean-Luc] Godard had the accessibility to make what he made, he broke new ground. I never saw any film like *Breathless*, but once you saw it, you said 'Yeah, man, why didn't I do that. I could have done that.' OK, he did it, but he couldn't have done it in America . . . I think American filmmakers are the best. But I also like [Akira] Kurosawa, and my favorite director is [Luis] Bunuel."

—from interview with Jonathan Cott, *Rolling Stone*, January 26, 1978

AN INTERVIEW WITH DYLAN

Randy Anderson | February 17, 1978 | *Minnesota Daily*

By the late 1970s, Dylan was granting interviews mostly just to major media outlets, but he spent a long time with Randy Anderson of the *Minnesota Daily*, the small, student-run campus newspaper at his alma mater, the University of Minnesota.

"Say, did you have any misgivings about granting us an interview?" asks Anderson at one point. "I mean . . . we're not exactly *Rolling Stone* or *Playboy*."

"No . . . not at all," answers Dylan, who seems to enjoy the opportunity to talk with someone who knows his old home turf.

The conversation took place shortly after the January 25, 1978, release of the singer's film *Renaldo and Clara*. It was also about seven months after Dylan's divorce. At the time, he had not issued any new music in about two years, just the live *Hard Rain*. But *Street-Legal* was only four months away. —Ed.

After spending half my life living closely with his words and music, I am now face to face with the most important artist of my generation. Bob Dylan shakes my hand weakly, puts down his coffee cup next to mine and bums a Marlboro.

———————

RA: Greetings from the Midwest—it's ten below there. Which coffee cup's mine?

BD: This one's mine, that must be yours.

RA: Mine's starting to curdle . . . I'm running out of cigarettes.

BD: I just got over the flu. Actually, I think I still got the flu.

RA: I heard that . . . Are you tired of doing this?

BD: Interviews?

RA: Yeah.

BD: (In an encouraging tone of voice.) No, not at all. (Strains of "Lay Lady Lay" in the background.)

RA: . . . Would you be interested in talking about your days at the University of Minnesota?

BD: Yeah, sure.

RA: When I talk about those days—and I don't even remember how long they were—what kind of feelings does that conjure up? Good times? Bad times?

BD: Well, I remember people more than events, you know. Ah, David Wicker, Hugh Brown, Ernie Washington—you know any of those people?

RA: No, I'm younger than you are—about six years.

BD: Ah, John Koerner—Dave Ray was just getting out of high school. [*A reference to the Minneapolis blues trio Koerner, Ray, and Glover. —Ed.*]

RA: . . . So how long were you in school at the U?

BD: (Taking a long drag on cigarette) I was registered there for about six months (1960). I never did get an academic rating. I registered there for six months and I was there beyond that time. I don't remember much about it—Scott Hall, Ford Hall.

RA: What classes did you take?

BD: I took, ah, . . . English. I remember an anthropology course I took, which took place in a big auditorium most of the time. Umm, I think those are the only classes I actually even attended. (smiles)

RA: Was there anything valuable about your academic experience? What turned you off or on?

BD: No, ah, nothing . . . I would hang around mostly at the café. What's the name of that place?

RA: The Scholar?

BD: No, no on campus there—

RA: Is it still there?

BD: Yeah, they turned it into an auditorium. I saw because I played there when I got back from New York the first time. You know the *Little Sandy Review* [*Influential folk-music journal published 1960-'68. —Ed.*] was published in Minneapolis?

RA: Yeah.

BD: And that was just starting up when I was there. So there was that type of general atmosphere and that was the atmosphere that I was only interested in. I didn't much get interested in any other activity school-wise. I figured after high school my schoolin' days were over.

RA: How was your high school experience?

BD: Ah well, I was playin' music in high school too and I was workin' in high school so (five second pause)—

RA: That must seem like light years away.

BD: (quickly) It does, it does now. (with an air of admission) My mind was always outside the classroom.

RA: Really?

BD: Yeah, I don't think I was compelled in any way in the classroom.

RA: Never any teachers or professors that meant anything to you?

BD: There were some good ones, some good teachers at Hibbing High. But I had teachers that my mother had so—

RA: They're probably still there! How important is Minnesota, Hibbing and Minneapolis to you?

BD: I feel very comfortable there. And I do get back every so often. I was up in Hibbing a few years ago. (six second pause)

RA: How was that?

BD: (quickly) Well it hasn't changed. I was glad to see that. (ten second pause) You know, like a lot of people go back to their hometown and they find their hometown's been replaced by a supermarket or something.

RA: When was the last time you saw the West Bank [*A Minneapolis neighborhood that borders the Mississippi River. —Ed.*]?

BD: Well the West Bank has changed since when I was there. The University has changed a lot, Minneapolis has changed a lot, but Hibbing hasn't.

RA: How has Minneapolis changed?

BD: All the recent development. I think that when I was goin' to school there, there was about 20,000 students, maybe 25,000. I don't know how many there are now but I think it's much more.

RA: Maybe 50,000.

BD: 50,000? So, there wasn't any development on the West Bank. There was that Seven Corners area where it was undeveloped. It was like London or New York or the Soho district. But I see they've taken all that and developed it and made it into dormitories or ah—

RA: Highrise apartments.

BD: Yes. There wasn't any of that there when I was there. It had a different look to it and a whole different feel. They didn't have any of that stuff when I was there, it was just old old houses.

RA: When you were there, were you already making plans to go to New York?

BD: Yeah, I had made plans to go to New York. Most of the people were leaving anyway. And I had done about as much as I could there in Minneapolis. I went to Chicago first and stayed there. Then I went up to Wisconsin, which was more or less the same general scene as it was at the school in Minnesota. And from there I went to New York. That was quite a trip . . . another guitar player and myself got a ride with a young couple from the campus whose parents were from Brooklyn. They were goin' there and wanted some more drivers, so we just drove.

RA: So what does it feel like when you go back to Minnesota and—

BD: Well, it feels the same. I relax more there than I do out here or anywhere else.

RA: Do you like LA—Malibu?

BD: I don't think in terms of liking it, I think of it in terms of a place I have to be. Now I have to be here because it is centrally located to what I'm doing.

———————

We are sitting in a stark room in a reconverted furniture factory that Dylan has rented as a rehearsal hall. He's working hard at whipping a new band into shape for his upcoming tour of Japan and Australia. Throughout the interview the band can be heard jamming upstairs.

It's a rainy day in Santa Monica, California. Earlier, I had rendez-voused with Paul Wasserman, Dylan's press agent, at his Beverly Hills offices. Together we drove down to the rehearsal hall, chatting amiably about—among other things—Dylan, the interview, the movie *Renaldo and Clara*. (It's been reported that after Dylan screened his long, cryptic movie for Wasserman—the man he had picked to launch the publicity campaign—Dylan said, "It's not *Star Wars*, is it Paul?").

During our engaging conversations, Wasserman tells me that Dylan felt he was burning himself out with these interviews, that he was having trouble coming up with new answers and that he was repeating himself.

"I told him not to worry about it, that it would add to the mystique," Wasserman says. "He didn't find that too humorous."

After the interview, as we walked toward his car in a torrential down-pour, Wasserman asks me, "Was he mystical?" I replied in the negative.

But that mystical stuff can get to you when you're sitting in this room alone for an hour and a half waiting for the man to appear. Was-serman, a very kind and considerate man (contrary to reports), keeps bringing me coffee and at one point apologizes for Dylan's lateness (it seems he's stopped off at the doctor's on the way in from his much-publicized, copper-domed Xanadu in Malibu). Band members, sound men and security guys come in and out, by and large a friendly bunch. One of them leans over to me and says, "This waiting—I think it's part of the technique."

The waiting does give me chance to drink in the environment, to get relaxed. I make a list of everything in the room: two non-descript beige couches; a big color TV; a grade school-level mural painting of a rainbow (red, yellow and green), some clouds and some birds; two huge speakers; two closed circuit TVs; a huge sound board behind me; and on top of a coffee table, a *TV Guide*, a white painter's hat, and a list of something. I lean over to check on the list—it's a list of songs: "Tambourine Man," "Like a Rolling Stone," "Positively 4th Street," "Ballad of a Thin Man" and on and on—I couldn't look anymore. It was the one thing in the room that seemed to be a grim reminder of the enormity of Dylan's contribution. I manage to avoid looking at it for the remainder of my wait, turning around to stare at the mixing board behind me and at a crazy drawing in orange, purple and green chalk on a blackboard behind that. I decide to kill time by sketching it.

I look closely at the smudged caption and it looks something like, "Another Self-Portrait." I chuckle to myself and hope that, yes indeed, there is some levity among these people.

I continue staring at the gray concrete floor and suddenly there's a noise, somebody walks in and plops down on the other couch. I look up and it's Dylan, unshaven and looking scruffy as usual (still "the unwashed phenomenon, the original vagabond," that strayed into Joan Baez' heart) with a Big Apple hat pulled over his riotous black locks. He's wearing a black leather jacket, an off-white collarless shirt, blue jeans and a pair of white, California penny loafers. We exchange nervous pleasantries and begin to talk about Minnesota.

As we talk, I notice that Dylan has many different rhythms to his speech—depending on how interested he is in the topic or how sure he is of what he's saying. Sometimes, he talks in a New York, street-jive style, sometimes in our bland Midwestern style and at other times, in a curious Southern drawl. He has a habit of taking long pauses when he's conversing with someone, something I'd luckily picked up beforehand in reading what others had said. Also, I knew he had once written: "experience teaches that silence terrifies people the most." I decide to gut those silences out, and soon I find he doesn't do it to offend anyone or to appear spacy, but to think, consider his words, or to show that he has nothing to say at the moment. He leans forward and talks faster when he's interested or has got something prefabricated to relate. And, he's obviously in shape to talk about *Renaldo and Clara*.

RA: How important is spontaneity to your art?

BD: Well, the movie wasn't spontaneous. It might seem that way cuz it was so natural. But it wasn't a spontaneous movie *at all*. People like to think it was because some of it's improvised. But not really, it wasn't a spontaneous movie in the sense that people go out and do anything they want to do and that will find its way into the movie. It was outlined by fact.

RA: You put things down on paper.

BD: Hmm—well, it seems so natural that people think that—well, it must be spontaneous.

RA: That's really hard to do, though.

BD: Yeah it is hard to do.

RA: What were some of your techniques?

BD: You just have to get that drama out of people. You have to have control and you have to know what it is you're doing, want to do and what the end result will be, and you can make it happen like that. Personally, I would rather see it happen like that. Your best actors are people who, when you're lookin' at 'em, you do think that they're acting spontaneously. (begins to slip into his street jive manner, sounding very sure and slightly defiant) You see Jack Nicholson in a movie—I mean you *never* think he's acting. You think he's thinkin' of them lines right at the time he's sayin' 'em.

RA: There were a lot of people who were not known as actors before who were able to pull that off.

BD: There were. Well, it's in everyone, everyone wants to act you know.

RA: How do you mean?

BD: Well, given the opportunity, people do want to act out a role other than themselves.

RA: Do you share that interest? Or, are you more interested in the directing end of it?

BD: To a certain degree, but I'm more related to the music.

RA: Do you find it's difficult to put words to a piece of art like the film? Would you rather have the music and visual images speak for themselves?

BD: Oh yeah, yeah, that's my preference. My preference isn't to talk about the film because it isn't explainable. Either it works for you or it doesn't work for you. And if it doesn't work for you, me explaining it isn't going to make it work for you.

RA: Exactly. Reading between the lines of some of the articles written about *Renaldo and Clara*, one gets the idea that the movie's inaccessible. But it's not—though it is inexplicable. Saying that it is can turn people off.

BD: It isn't an inaccessible movie, it isn't at all. It's a very simple movie to follow. It's inaccessible to people who are burdened down with their own logic, who have preconceived ideas. Those people aren't going to let themselves be affected by what they're seeing.

RA: Who do you think the audience is for the movie?

BD: Anybody who's been through any of those things at all is going to be a receptive audience for that movie. Anybody who's been through that struggle.

RA: What struggle?

BD: That alter-ego struggle against the subconscious which is always going through there. But we don't like to call it that or say that because it's an awful big undertaking. But that's exactly what is happening in that movie. It's the sub-conscious mind against the alter-ego in that movie. Something is wishing to become something else. Whether it's possible or whether it succeeds, we don't know that. The movie doesn't provide any answers. But nothing provides any answers—*War and Peace* doesn't provide any answers.

RA: But that's what people want, especially American moviegoers. They want simplicity, they want everything explained, they want that storyline.

BD: It doesn't have any of that.

RA: Europeans are more used to films as opposed to movies. Most Americans go to movies to be entertained. *Renaldo and Clara* is a film and you don't necessarily go to it to be entertained.

BD: Well, my songs aren't explainable, either. And there shouldn't be any reason why this movie or this *film* should be any different than a song I feel close to.

RA: Have you ever met Keith Jarrett?

BD: Yeah, I think so.

RA: I talked to him awhile back about popular music and he claimed that virtually all popular music is a waste of time, because if the words are good enough people aren't going to pay attention to the music, and if the music's good enough it doesn't need any words.

BD: I don't find that true.

RA: We went on about this, and he finally brought up your name, saying that you were the only person who is able to pull that off—mixing words and music. And of course, he has done some of your tunes on his early records.

BD: That's probably because subconsciously I'm aware of both as being equal. I'm always aware of that fact. I can't write something where the music is heavier or more loaded than the lyric or the lyric is more loaded than the music. It would just be something I couldn't do. That's why some of the tunes that have an emotional quality, an intense emotional quality, will have a very simple melody—a folk melody.

RA: Most of what happened to me as a moviegoer during *Renaldo and Clara* was in the realm of feeling. Sometimes I was depressed, sometimes I was exhilarated, at times my mind wandered—the times my mind wandered made the intense scenes that much more powerful by contrast—but comparing emotional notes with the person I saw the movie with, well, both of us felt very sad after the movie. Do you think that's a strange reaction?

Dylan: No, no, not at all. There's a lot of sadness that develops in that movie. A lot of dead ends. But the overall picture shouldn't be one of sadness, it should be one of—what's the word?—it should be one of resolve. It is resolved. But you're—there is a great deal of sadness in it, but it doesn't leave you sad—

RA: I don't follow you.

BD: —but it could, though. Well, it leaves you at the end with an out—because it is the morning of this man's life.

RA: Yeah.

BD: No matter what he's gone through, no matter who he knows, no matter what's been done to him, it still is the morning.

RA: Hope?

BD: Hope, yeah. So, although there is a great deal of sadness that develops, it is conceivable that the sadness will be broken after the movie ends.

RA: If I said there was a lack of humor and lightness in *Renaldo and Clara* would that strike you as wrong?

BD: No, no. Ummm . . .

RA: Every once in a while I wished for something to break the tension cuz I was concentrating so hard. Sometimes the music did that.

BD: Uh-huh. That's just the nature of the film to be that way. It is intense. There is no out.

RA: I think that's where the depression comes in, at least my feelings of it. I was very moved by parts of the film, but I'm wondering whether the mass audience will . . .

BD: Well, we don't know if the mass audiences will, but it's not really for a mass audience. The mass audience doesn't go for my music either. So there's no real reason why it should have to appeal to a mass audience to be successful.

RA: But you still have to sell a lot of tickets.

BD: You do have to sell tickets—

RA: And that's probably why we're doing the interview in the first place—to help out the film.

BD: I'm hopin' we would help out the film, so people know that there's a film to see. But we can't explain the film. There's no way we can do that.

RA: But do you see what I mean? There's a problem here. It's the old money and art problem I guess—a cliché but it's very real.

BD: It is, yeah. Well, we just do the best we can and that's all we can do, you know—we can try.

RA: Do you read any of the articles written about the film? You're old enough now, maybe that stuff doesn't affect you anymore.

BD: Personally, I don't believe that critical acclaim or denunciation is going to affect the movie one way or another. I think it's the people who see the movie which will decide for themselves whether they want their friends to see it.

RA: So the jury is still out as far as you're concerned?

BD: Well, there really isn't a *jury*—

RA: Well, there's a critical consensus from the masses or the people.

BD: (six second pause) Well, I think in 20 years we'll see. If that movie's still playin' in 20 years, well then I guess it'll have something to say that's speaking to the people. If it isn't, well then it just didn't reach enough people.

RA: I'm glad you brought that up, because another feeling I had was that the film had an aura of timeliness to it . . . Do you think in 20, 50 or 100 years, people will say *Renaldo and Clara* was "the '60s" or "the '70s"—like *Saturday Night Fever* is in the '70s—or will they say that it's a real timeless movie, that you just can't place it?

BD: Yeah, it's a timeless movie. There's nothing that locks that movie into any age.

RA: Except maybe the '60s a little bit.

BD: Well, there's a sign on a theater up in Harlem, showin' *Earthquake*—

RA: You mean the Apollo Theater scene.

BD: Yeah, so that'll date it if you want to get that specific.

RA: Speaking of the Apollo Theater, you once wrote: "the fact that the white house is filled with leaders that've never been to the apollo theater amazes me." (from the jacket notes to *Bringing It All Back Home*) Which made me think that this film has been simmering on your backburners for a few years and that you picked out scenes like the Apollo Theater that mean something to you.

BD: Yeah, this film—this is the right time for this film. I couldn't have made it before, but I've been thinkin' about it.

RA: For a long period of time?

BD: Off and on, yeah.

RA: . . . You've been up to the Apollo Theater in Harlem haven't you?

BD: Yeah, I used to go there on Monday nights a lot.

RA: You can't do that anymore, can you?

BD: Oh, well, I've never had any trouble walking around in neighborhoods.

RA: Think black people would be interested in the film?

BD: In this film?

RA: Yeah.

BD: (sincerely) I really don't know. It's a truthful film. And we're not lookin' at people as either black or white. It's an experience beneath the mind, it's—I don't think you have to be any certain color to relate to the film.

RA: But one of the things that you pick up in your film or your art is a great sensitivity and love for minorities and the disadvantaged.

BD: Well, it's not that so much as a love for truth. Ah, I don't love black or green or white or blue or whatever happens to be the color of different people. But in a search for truth you find different elements that happen to be involved with how certain people treat other people—economically, socially or personally.

RA: The quest for truth brings to mind *Moby Dick*—ever read it?

BD: Yeah.

RA: . . . Melville's book wasn't appreciated until long after he was dead—people never really read it until the 1920s.

BD: Right.

RA: Did you ever think *Renaldo and Clara* might be something like that?

BD: Probably. It probably is.

RA: You might not even be around to see it appreciated.

BD: I could believe that. Sure. Joseph Conrad wasn't appreciated either in his time. Look at Van Gogh, I mean he couldn't even sell a painting to eat.

RA: Does that bother you?

BD: Well, yeah, in a work like this it does. Because you know, you can't expect people to go out there and accept it the way they would the *Mona Lisa*. People lookin' at the *Mona Lisa*—they might just say, "Well, it's a picture of a woman with a *smile*." You know, that's all they might see. And in this movie too, they might go to it and say, "Well, it's a movie about Bob Dylan and Joan Baez." And that's all they might see. I understand that's where people are comin' from. But still I've got a belief that you have to do whatever it is that you're doing. You can't compromise with the fact that you must do what you must do.

RA: Compromise is an anathema to being an artist?

BD: Uh-huh. Yeah, the artists that are really successful, that make platinum records and that are makin' movies and all that—I mean, they're compromisin' a whole lot. I mean, they're just calculatin' what the audience will want.

RA: Is there any value at all in any of that stuff?

BD: I don't look at those people as true artists.

RA: Just production people—

BD: No, they're just intelligent people who can get it together to superficially satisfy a lot of people.

RA: That seems to be what a lot of Americans are after—fast food, McDonald's hamburgers—

BD: Yeah, yeah.

RA: —and a record is just like a hamburger, just consume it and it's over.

BD: Yeah.

RA: Do you find yourself alienated from the average, common person, leading the life that you do?

BD: Maybe so, maybe so. I don't know. I never eat in restaurants. I won't eat in one. Once in a while I will, but as a rule I won't eat in a restaurant. I don't go places most people go to ah—

RA: But as an artist don't we have to keep in touch with the people, the country, the earth—

BD: Sure, sure we do.

RA: So how do you do that? One has to, otherwise we become solipsistic—

BD: Otherwise we go into a monastery. No, I'm not livin' in a monastery. I'm out and about in the world, and I just come in contact with where people are and what their feelings are and from that I create the artistic experience—plus my own feelings and instinct that I have myself, I use that. But sometimes it seems like there isn't enough time to go and be where you wanna be.

RA: See, in other ages artists could walk among the people, and be of the people.

BD: Well, look at Baudelaire or Lord Byron. They could write a monumental work sittin' in a café, you know.

RA: Doesn't that bother you as a limitation—

BD: Yeah, but that's the environment in this country. You can't really do that. Your reality is broken up by plastic and it affects you. And if you don't want that plastic in your work you'll have to go elsewhere. So it's a continual search to find what's real. What's real and what's more organic in a way.

RA: One of my favorite poets is Walt Whitman and of course he was able to walk among the streets of Brooklyn and embrace the people.

BD: Allen Ginsberg does that to a certain degree.

RA: He can get away with that.

BD: Yeah, he can get away with that. Me, I'm not that type of poet, because I play music. And I have to play that on that stage. So when you're playin' on the stage it's a—you're of the people but you're not of the people.

RA: (making a gesture) There's a—

BD: No, there really isn't a wall there. It's all the same room. But, you really sometimes have to hole up to gain that inspiration.

———————

Only time will tell if *Renaldo and Clara* is Dylan's *Moby Dick* or a self-important, artistic white elephant. On a peaceful California evening, I saw the film at the Regent Theatre in Westwood near the UCLA campus. For four dollars you get four hours plus of film, one hour of which is devoted to concert footage from the Rolling Thunder tour of 1976. (Dylan edited down 100 hours of film to four hours—and I'm sure the A.J. Webermans [*a reference to the "Dylanologist." —Ed.*] of the world would kill to see the 96 hours that ended up on the cutting room floor.)

The musical interludes are arguably the best scenes in the film. Dylan's rendering of "Isis" is riveting (it drew a smattering of applause in Westwood)—as are "One More Cup of Coffee" and "Sara." The whole group of gypsies do righteous versions of Curtis Mayfield's "People Get Ready" (as Dylan's entourage tours an Indian gathering) and Dylan's "Knockin' on Heaven's Door."

As much as I dislike her, Joan Baez did raise goosebumps with "Diamonds and Rust," her transparent ode to Bob. But then she embarrasses herself with a non-seductive, flailing dance onstage while Roger McGuinn leads the band through "Eight Miles High." McGuinn follows that with a fine vocal on "Chestnut Mare." There are a lot of close-ups in the concert footage and all the performers come off as dedicated and intense throughout.

The three hours given over to improvised vignettes, broken and recurrent storylines and semi-documentary inserts would definitely make the movie tedious and cumbersome to a non-fan. Following Warhol's lead, Dylan lets the cameras roll on, waiting for special moments. The obligatory, Felliniesque bordello scenes which keep cropping up are questionable in their relevancy. So are the snippets of Ginsberg reading "Kaddish" to a confused bunch of Jewish matrons at some naugahyde nightclub. However, Sara Dylan is an interesting onscreen figure—still beautiful despite being in her upper thirties and having born five children and despite the fact she takes to wearing a hideous wig halfway through the movie.

Ronnie Hawkins, the big old rockabilly singer the Band backed up in their early days and who ostensibly plays "Bob Dylan" in the movie, does a good job in an improvised scene in which he tries to lure a farmer's daughter into joining him on the road—memorable quote: "Rock and roll's the answer—live fast, love hard and die young." The freeze-frame, street interviews with blacks on the Hurricane Carter issue are also affecting.

The film was shot down the line of the Rolling Thunder tour on the East Coast: New York, Cape Cod, Maine, with a sidetrip up to Quebec City. The film has an annoying randomness to it, with one attempt made at making it cohere: a sort of ad hoc, rambling narrative by [folksinger] David Blue who functions as Boswell to Dylan's Johnson, remembering things past as he plays a losing game of pinball poolside in some Cape Cod motel. Some of it's very funny.

Many of the characters (who seem to interchange roles as the movie rolls along) wear makeup. Dylan himself starts out the movie by singing "When I Paint My Masterpiece" onstage with a plastic, transparent mask on. Indeed, in watching the movie, it's confusing as to which was more important—the mask or what was behind the mask. *Renaldo and Clara* is also vaguely and hesitatingly autobiographical—the final scene of the Woman in White (Joan Baez) interrupting the love-making of Dylan and Sara is undeniably a contorted attempt to come to terms with the frighteningly fuzzy line between myth and reality that obtains in the movie. Still, it's a fascinating albeit somewhat false contretemps.

By the time I talked to Dylan, the critics had pretty much lambasted *Renaldo and Clara*. For most, figuratively and literally, it was a pain in the ass (with only a 100 millimeter cigarette intermission to ease the ache). It's not like eating at McDonald's. It's as if Dylan had made a huge, four-sided album that, condensed down, would have made a great double album. Still, for four dollars—if you can dismiss what critics have said about Dylan's self-indulgence and supposed Messianic complex—it's worth it. Just allow yourself to be dragged into the dreamy momentum of a long, late-night flight.

Sensing the non-commercial nature of *Renaldo and Clara*, Dylan had Wasserman (*the* publicity man in entertainment, he also has handled the likes of the Rolling Stones, Linda Ronstadt, Paul Simon and James Taylor) to set up interviews to plug the movie, in hopes of salvaging some of the 1.25 million dollars he sunk into it.

———

RA: . . . an interviewer sometimes feels like a thief when he interviews someone—

BD: Heh! Heh!

RA: It's like the old African tribesmen who feel like you're stealing part of their soul when you take a picture of them. Like I get people to talk and then I get it on tape and take it home and show it to the public. That make any sense to you?

BD: Oh yeah. I agree with that picture-taking thing. You gotta have a protective layer around ya to have your picture taken. And, I feel the same exact way as those old tribesmen, about havin' your picture taken. I don't believe it's really proper, to do that to somebody else.

RA: I really don't either and that's why sometimes I feel morally against interviews as verbal pictures—although it's my job. How do you approach an interview given that you feel like that?

BD: How do I do an interview?

RA: Yeah, you're obviously aware that that's my job.

BD: Yeah, I've just become accustomed to that. I used to do interviews in the old days so I know what they are. I haven't done 'em in a long time cuz I really had nuthin' to do an interview about. I didn't figger what I was doin' was that interesting. So now we're doin' interviews and *why*? I couldn't really say for sure. But it seemed like a good idea cuz of this movie, so whatever you wanna know I'm gonna try to tell ya.

RA: . . . I once saw the movie *Don't Look Back*. As an interviewer there's no way I can purge that from my mind when I come to talk with you and when I'm waiting here for you to come in. How you are now is totally different from the bullshit that's been passed down to us over the years.

BD: Yeah, a lot has changed though since those days. People in those days—that was the establishment press we were talking to. They didn't understand what was goin' on in the musical arena. But nowadays, I've found from doin' these interviews that there's a lot of people who do understand what I've been doin', so it isn't that difficult because people relate to me on that level where before people were relating to me—"What's this phenomenon that's being created?"; "What does that song mean?"—they would just coldly ask me these things. How was I to explain to them what the song meant? They should have asked the crowd. They should have asked the audience what the songs meant. And they never do. They never talk to my audience. They always wanna hear it from me or else they make up their own mind and they tend to disregard all the people that do find something worthwhile in my work.

RA: Have most of these interviews been enjoyable?

BD: I've found them to be interesting because I get a sense of what people are thinkin' of the movie when they see it. Some people say, "Gee, I saw it and I didn't understand it." Or some other people say, "I saw it and I understood a lot of it and didn't understand some of it." And some people say, "I thought it was—you know, brilliant." People react in different ways, and they usually say that right off.

RA: What's been the breakdown pro and con?

BD: Very mixed. Very, very mixed. If you really wanna know what the people are thinkin' you should just go to the movie theater and ask the people when they're comin' out. That's the way you're gonna find out what people are thinkin' of this movie cuz I can't tell you what anybody's thinkin' of this movie. And you can't tell me, you know.

RA: As a 36-year-old artist do you still suffer from insecurity in regard to your work? A lot of people think, "He's gone through it all, he probably doesn't care what we say about him anyway." Or, do you find that insecurity is a permanent part of existence no matter who you are.

BD: Yeah, insecurity in the area of being able to write and perform. (ten second pause) I had that for a while. . . . Yeah, around like '72, '73. I wasn't sure what I was gonna do and didn't really feel much like singin' and playin' or writing. But nowadays . . . if you have belief then you won't be insecure.

RA: Faith—in yourself and in your work?

BD: Yeah.

RA: Yet faith in yourself is something that goes up and down, isn't it?

BD: That's right . . . you want some more cigarettes?

RA: Yeah, I'd love some.

BD: Lemme go get some.

RA: How much more time we got, Bob?

BD: Well, let's just talk and see.

Tape off. Dylan returns; upstairs, the band plays on—sounds vaguely like the Allmans's "Mountain Jam."

RA: Say, did you have any misgivings about granting us an interview? I mean . . . we're not exactly *Rolling Stone* or *Playboy.*

BD: No I really didn't. Not at all.

———————

Dylan had talked to several people by the time *A&E* got an interview. In reading some of the interviews, I got the impression that he would be arrogant and unfriendly. (For *Playboy*, he didn't take his sunglasses off for days.) At the very least, I expected an encounter with the Jack of Hearts—that archetypal rascal, master of ambiguity. Yet already, one unforgettable thing about the interview is how friendly, how human he seems. Perhaps it's part of the demythologizing process. He isn't necessarily helpful to an interviewer (in fact he's a bit lazy in answering questions, and definitely considers interviews work) but he does, in subtle ways, make you feel relaxed. Invariably, a good stretch of music from his band upstairs distracts him a little, causing him to tap his feet. Essentially, though, he's a very restless person—like an energetic youth in a boring math class.

Nonetheless, he's undeniably charismatic. His eyes are most memorable—steel blue to some, "bluer than robins' eggs" to Joan Baez ("Diamonds and Rust"). They dart, dance and fix, attesting to an inner intensity when his voice falls silent. More than anything, they remind you that you're not talking to any "regular guy"—the man was not destined for anonymity.

RA: Did you ever read *The Great Gatsby*? (Young man leaves Minnesota, changes name and, answering the "drums of destiny," becomes a mysterious, famous figure in New York.)

BD: Yeah, I read it in high school, but I couldn't tell you anything about it, though.

RA: Did you have a dream you wanted to live out like Gatsby?

BD: No, not exactly that, because I always played the guitar. It was always directed toward the music I was playing.

RA: . . . Do you feel you have a public persona that functions as a mask for you that you can fall back on?

BD: No, I don't feel I have that persona to fall back on. I don't consider myself in the public eye. I'm in the public eye superficially but I don't consider myself being a public personality.

RA: I guess what I'm talking about is the Dylan myth, the one that you're making us confront somewhat in *Renaldo and Clara*.

BD: There's no myth for me to fall back on. It's ah . . . whoever said there was a myth? *Time* magazine or *Newsweek* magazine might have said there was a myth.

RA: Exactly. But that's something that you have to live with, that becomes part of your life that I don't have to live with . . .

BD: But I don't feel I'm in any danger because I've never believed it.

RA: But that's a struggle that you have that most people don't have. It's a struggle against what people are doing with your life.

BD: Yeah—

RA: What's that like?

BD: Well, sometimes, at different times you confront people who can't see you. I've met a lot of them. They can't see you. They're only seeing the myth, or whatever they're choosing to see.

RA: What do you do with a person like that?—give 'em the myth or say to hell with 'em and don't deal with 'em?

BD: Those incidents don't usually last a great deal of time—they don't usually last too long. But I know what you mean because I've experienced it.

RA: What I'm basically getting at is that those occurrences aren't everyday occurrences for everyday people. I would imagine the myth's a burden—maybe it isn't.

BD: Well, a myth is a story, a myth isn't a person necessarily. A myth is a happening. We think of things in mythological terms: the myth of the younger sister, the myth of the false bride, the myth of the two brothers, the myth of the king and queen. We think of those stories and involvements as myths. Singular people we can't really consider as being myths, although we can. We have the myth of Robin Hood—

RA: That's more like a legend.

BD: A legend, yeah. Legendary is for singular people. But mythological isn't. I think people have just got the wrong terminology when they think of me in terms of myth.

RA: But just because of the way the country is set up, it has a way of making living people seem larger than life. And maybe some people have an inner need to have heroes.

BD: Maybe so but ah . . . (ten second pause) legendary is something that happens after we die or after we're gone. So like if we experience a lot of different changes in this life you can become legendary, meaning that something you did yesterday you're not doing anymore.

RA: When the history of the 20th century is written, how would you like to be remembered? . . . The reason I bring it up is because of that scene in the movie when you and Ginsberg are standing by Kerouac's grave—or don't those things concern you?

BD: No, it doesn't really concern me—how I'm going to be remembered.

RA: But to get involved with art on such a grandiose scale there has to be an ego involved.

BD: You're concerned with being remembered by your children . . . and your neighbors. (ten second pause) In those terms, I'd like to be remembered as doing the best I could—for them and for myself.

RA: How important are your children in your life?—or is that an unfair question? (Dylan is recently divorced and for the past year has been playing a painful game of tug-o'-war with his wife over the children.)

BD: No, it's not an unfair question. (12 second pause)

RA: In other words, what fulfillment do they give you that art can't give you? Is it an extra dimension?

BD: (ten-second pause, and then he speaks softly and poignantly) Yeah, it's maybe the only dimension that really counts. We're all playin' games with this art business you know. But in reality it's a—we have to be able to, we have to be willing to be a fulfilled human being.

RA: Did you figure that out at an early age or was there a time when you thought of yourself as a permanent single person, traveling light and fast . . . or did you always want children?

BD: Well, that's just a belief in life. At a certain point, you must decide whether you want to sacrifice your ideas for something which may have more value. Sacrifice your ideas for something which has more value in terms of flesh and blood. You just are either orientated that way or you're not.

RA: You don't think all people are oriented that way?

BD: I don't think of all people as being fulfilled the same way.

RA: . . . I find I constantly change my attitude about something I've done. Do you have that problem with the film? The film is forever, a song you can redo onstage every time you sing it.

BD: No, the film's gotta stand because it's too involved, it's more involved than a song, it's gotta stand. Sure we coulda made it better, embellished it a bit. But I don't have any regrets about what it is.

RA: A favorite song of mine is Edith Piaf's "I Have No Regrets." Do you believe in regrets?

BD: No, regrets just keep you chained to the past. You gotta make peace with the past. There's no reason to regret it. You've done it, just make peace with it.

RA: Are you at peace with your past?

BD: I am, yeah. I try to be, yeah. I always try to keep my past and my present and my future all on the same level.

RA: What's next? You're obviously going on tour, you're rehearsing a new band—

BD: Yeah, that's basically, that's mainly what I do, write songs and tour and record. Making movies is somethin' which I'll be interested in doing and when we do it, if we can do it within the boundaries of the music . . .

RA: What do you do in your spare time?

BD: I don't have any spare time.

RA: What about in '72 and '73 when you said you weren't doin' anything?

BD: Yeah, when I have—in my spare time I probably like to go back to Minnesota . . . and just let everything else drift away.

RA: What do you do when you go back there?

BD: Ah . . .

RA: You gotta piece of land back home don't ya?

BD: Yeah, ah . . . (the music from upstairs is infectious)

RA: Do you just hang out, see friends and commune?

BD: Yeah, yeah. I just get to go for, you know, short periods of time.

RA: You can't tell me specifically what you do in that spare time?

BD: Well . . .

RA: Other interests besides writing or reading or playing music?

BD: Oh! Ah . . . you just mean what do I like to do?

RA: Yeah.

BD: I like to blast sculpture out of metal.

RA: Really?

BD: Yeah, and I also like to go roller skating or ice skating or go fishing or . . .

RA: You go fishing in Minnesota?

BD: Yeah, sometimes.

RA: I get the feeling you're ready to play.

BD: I think I am.

RA: I think you are.

BD: Yeah. Heh! heh!

RA: I really enjoyed it.

BD: OK. I hope you got somethin' you can use.

We shake hands and say goodbye. Waiting in the lobby for Wasserman, I spy a sopping wet figure hunched over in the rain outside. He looks very European in dress and has a guitar case, a tape recorder and some books. He keeps scribbling out notes, then tapping on the locked, glass door and giving the scraps of paper to Dylan's security man. It seems he wants to play with Dylan and has made a long pilgrimage in hopes of auditioning for his hero. The security guy tells me it happens a lot. I ask if that sort of thing depresses everybody and he says, "Yes, it does . . . if they only knew how it *really* is."

The hard rain keeps falling as Wasserman and I depart. For several hours I kept thinking of that forlorn musician. It just didn't seem fair.

DYLAN ON

Starving Artists

"The starving artist is a myth. The big bankers and prominent young ladies who buy art started it. They just want to keep the artist under their thumb. Who says an artist can't have any money? Look at Picasso. The starving artist is usually starving for those around him to starve. You don't have to starve to be a good artist. You just have to have love, insight, and a strong point of view. And you have to fight off depravity. Uncompromising, that's what makes a good artist. It doesn't matter if he has money or not. Look at Matisse; he was a banker. Anyway, there are other things that constitute wealth and poverty besides money."

—from interview with Ron Rosenbaum, *Playboy*, March 1978

DYLAN ON

Women and Relationships

"Women are sentimental. They get into that romantic thing more easily. But I see that as a prelude. Women use romance and passion to sweeten you up. A man is no more than a victim of that passion. You give me a woman who can cook and sew and I'll take that over passion any day. I'd like to find a mate. But I can't spend any time with a woman if we're not friends. If we're not friends I don't want to get involved on a personal level."

—from interview with Barbara Kerr, *Boston Herald*, March 1978

DYLAN ON

Playing Roles

"In any song I write or any movie I'm in, I always become the character in it. I play the character Renaldo in the movie [*Renaldo and Clara*]. When I sing 'It Ain't Me, Babe,' I'm another character. It's all a play. My songs are closer to theatre than to ordinary rock and roll."

—from interview with Philip Fleishman, *Maclean's* (Canada), March 20, 1978

DYLAN ON

His Personal Life

"Being in this kind of situation you meet a lot of people that are attracted to you, and also you become attracted to quite a few people, and you can't really be sure many times whether that's true or not, so you just have to let the situation run its course. I just kind of stay with my old friends, and my old loves and old mates, you know, and at least that allows me to work . . . I think ultimately man is better off if he can stay in one place and see the world revolve around him rather than have to be out there revolving. I try to stay put as much as I can, but I can't all the time, and I guess my personal life has suffered because of that."

—from interview with Craig McGregor, *New Musical Express* (UK), April 22, 1978

DYLAN ON

"So-Called Leaders from the '60s"

"What ever happened to them? There was Abbie Hoffman, who you never hear from any more. He could be sitting at the next table for all we know. There was Tom Hayden, who's running a children's camp. And Jerry Rubin, who is a sociologist or whatever. What did those 'leaders' really do? Maybe they did something then, but what are they doing now? That's the same thing a lot of people say about me . . . Well, I'm doing what I always did: I'm still playing my guitar and singing my songs."

—from interview with Robert Hilburn, *Los Angeles Times*, May 22, 1978

DYLAN ON

Taking His Songs Literally

"I've heard it said that Dylan was never as truthful as when he wrote *Blood on the Tracks*, but that wasn't necessarily *truth*, it was just *perceptive*. Or when people say 'Sara' was written for 'his wife Sara'—it doesn't necessarily have to be about her just because my wife's name happened to be Sara. Anyway, was it the real Sara or the Sara in the dream? I still don't know."

—from interview with Jonathan Cott, *Rolling Stone*, November 16, 1978

DYLAN ON

Hippies and Drugs

"I was always more tied up with the Beat movement. I don't know what the hippie movement was all about, that was a media thing, I think. . . . There was drugs but drugs were something that was just a playful thing or something which wasn't that romanticized. Drugs were always in the folk clubs and in the jazz clubs, but outside of those places I never really saw too many drugs. The drugs at the end of the '60s were artificial. They were those . . . L.S. . . . acid, all that stuff made in a laboratory. . . . I was never involved in the acid scene, either."

—from interview with Lynne Allen, *Trouser Press*, June 1979

DYLAN ON

His Religious Beliefs

"My ideology now would be coming out of the Scripture. You see, I didn't invent these things—these things have just been shown to me. I'll stand on that faith—that they are true. I believe they're true. I *know* they're true. . . . A religion which says you have to do certain things to get to God . . . that type of religion will not get you into the kingdom, that's true. However, there is a master creator, a supreme being in the universe."

—from interview with Bruce Heiman, KMEX (Tucson, Arizona), December 7, 1979

DYLAN ON

The Call of Jesus

"I guess He's always been calling me. Of course, how would I have ever known that? That it was Jesus calling me. I always thought it was some voice that would be more identifiable. But Christ is calling everybody; we just turn him off. We just don't want to hear. We think he's gonna make our lives miserable, you know what I mean? We think he's gonna make us do things we don't want to do. Or keep us from doing things we want to do. But God's got his own purpose and time for everything. He knew when I would respond to His call."

—from interview with Karen Hughes, *New Zealand Star*, July 10, 1980

RADIO INTERVIEW

Paul Vincent | November 19, 1980 | KMEL-FM (San Francisco)

Dylan released the underrated *Street-Legal* in June 1978 and the live *Bob Dylan at Budokan* the following April. Somewhere around that time, he turned to Christianity and, in August 1979, he issued *Slow Train Coming*, which includes such titles as "When He Returns" and "I Believe in You." The album was a hit, as was "Gotta Serve Somebody," a single culled from it that has since sparked numerous cover versions.

Ten months later, in June 1980, Dylan went further down the born-again road with *Saved*, an album that features a gospel backup and sold somewhat less well.

Five months after the LP's release, San Francisco radio personality and program director Paul Vincent met Dylan backstage at the Fox Warfield Theatre shortly before the artist began a show there. Vincent asked Dylan about his religious music and views, but the conversation touched on many other subjects as well. —Ed.

Paul Vincent: Over the past eighteen years or so, you've been written about and analyzed and criticized and second-guessed and worshipped and idolized by many. There was that fellow [*A. J. Weberman —Ed.*] back in Greenwich Village who went through your garbage. As time goes on, does it ever get easier being Bob Dylan?

Bob Dylan: [*Laughs.*] Well, it's easy being Bob Dylan. It's just trying to live up to what people would want Bob Dylan to do—that might be difficult, but it's not really that difficult.

Vincent: More than once you've been referred to as a legend—whatever that word may mean. People say that probably because they admire what you do. Is it difficult living up to those expectations? Is it something you've learned to live with, or is it a burden sometimes?

Dylan: Well, the things I've done in the past which would lead up to that—some of those things I still do. Some things I don't do. So as long as I keep it straight in my mind who I am and not get that confused with who I'm supposed to be, I think I'll be all right.

Vincent: You've said in the past that the songs were already there. I think Woody Guthrie may have said that, too, and that your job is to put them down on paper. Is that to say that writing your songs comes easily?

Dylan: Yeah, the best ones come real easy.

Vincent: Do you ever find yourself pondering the phrasing of a line for an hour or so?

Dylan: Um-hmm.

Vincent: There's been hundreds of analyses of your songs over the years. You're aware of that. Do any of your songs mean something totally different now than maybe they did when you wrote them originally? Or does the meaning remain just—

Dylan: The meaning stays the same. They don't change. Some bring out certain parts of 'em that may be not so evident years ago, and may be more evident to me now, but they don't change.

Vincent: Last night, for example, on "Simple Twist of Fate," you did some different lyrics. If you change lyrics in songs, is it spontaneous or is it planned out?

Dylan: Let me see. That particular song was recorded, I think, two times, and one time it had one set of lyrics, and another had another set of lyrics, but the difference wasn't that detrimental to the meaning of the song, on that particular song. I may sing some one night and another [on another] night depending what comes to my mind at the time.

Vincent: But the gist of the song is exactly the same. Does it bother you when people try to pick apart your lyrics? Should they be satisfied with it meaning to them whatever they would like it to mean to them as opposed to what it is you mean?

Dylan: Yeah, I think so. I think some place there's a road there that what I intend it to mean—and what they think it means—probably means something in the middle there.

Vincent: Doing the older songs that you do, do they mean something different in 1980? Does "Blowin' in the Wind" mean something different in 1980 than it meant in 1962?

Dylan: No, it's no different. I think it means the same thing.

[*Dylan's "Blowin' in the Wind" plays.*]

Vincent: Your career's been marked by many changes. How much do you concern yourself about how quickly people will accept your changes?

Dylan: Well, you just hope for the best. You just hope people will come and see you, and if they don't come and see you then I guess it's time to stop.

Vincent: Some critics have not been kind as a result of the past two albums, because of the religious content. Does that surprise you? For example, some have said that you're proselytizing. Is Jesus Christ the answer for all of us in your mind?

Dylan: Yeah, I would say that, uh-huh. What we're talking about is the nature of God and I think in order to go to God you have to go through Jesus, yeah. You have to understand that. You have to have an experience with that.

Vincent: Would you like to have us come away from your shows hopefully thinking more deeply in that direction?

Dylan: Oh, boy, I don't know. I don't get into what people feel as they leave the shows.

Vincent: You're not preaching to us?

Dylan: No, no. [*Pause.*] I could do a little bit of this and a little bit of that but right now I'm just content to play these shows. This is a stage show we're doing, it's not a salvation ceremony.

[*Dylan's "Saved" plays.*]

Vincent: I first saw you on *The Les Crane Show* . . . Back in, it must have been 1964 or so. [*Dylan's Crane show appearance aired February 17,*

1965. —Ed.] You did "[It's All Over Now,] Baby Blue" and "It's Alright, Ma [(I'm Only Bleeding)]." Since then you've only done TV a couple of times: Johnny Cash, the John Hammond PBS tribute, and one other. Do you have any interest in being exposed on the tube at all?

Dylan: No, I really don't. [*Laughs.*] It seems funny for me to say. I don't really care for the bright lights that much.

Vincent: As far as interviews, too, you haven't done that many interviews over the years. Is there a reason for that?

Dylan: No. No particular reason.

Vincent: When you listen to current music, are you influenced at all by what you hear? Do current trends concern you at all?

Dylan: Current trends not so much. There're songwriters that I admire, but . . .

Vincent: You've always done your own thing. Back when the Beatles did *Sgt. Pepper* and the Stones did *Satanic Majesties* you came out with *John Wesley Harding*, which was totally against the grain of the psychedelic—

Dylan: I wasn't going in the direction of that type of . . . never was, either. I've tried to keep my music simple.

Vincent: Your albums are a little more produced these days than they used to be.

Dylan: [*Laughs.*] If that's what you call it.

Vincent: Do you still use the same recording techniques?

Dylan: Oh, I'd say over the course of a year—maybe a period of six days in the studio. That's probably it. [*Laughs.*] If I can't make a record in six days I don't—

Vincent: That's the way it's always been, too, basically?

Dylan: Mm-hmm.

Vincent: How involved do you get personally with the day-to-day business activities of your records and concerts?

Dylan: Not too much. Not too deep.

Vincent: Are you aware of radio stations and whether they're playing—

Dylan: I listen to the radio, of course, and try to pick up different stations in different towns.

Vincent: We heard that you heard a cut from *Saved* on a Minnesota radio station and didn't—

Dylan: A St. Paul radio station— [*Laughs.*]

Vincent: —and didn't care for the mix and wanted to—

Dylan: It was mixed wrong or something. It didn't sound right to me. I must've told somebody at that time who was working on the album. I know I didn't say anything to the record company about it. But some people tell me that they saw it in the press that I'd said something about it, but I don't recall making too much of a fuss over it.

Vincent: You realize that almost anything you say will be made a fuss over because you're saying it.

Dylan: If you say it to the right people it will, yeah.

Vincent: Would you like to have a hit single on Top 40 radio?

Dylan: [*Laughs.*] Yeah, sure.

Vincent: Why not, right?

Dylan: [*Laughs.*] Yeah.

Vincent: When writing your songs, does that enter your mind at all, or is it just an interesting by-product?

Dylan: No, I don't really know what sells. Well, of course, we all do know what sells and what doesn't sell—what you need to make a hit record. I think most people in the business know that. But, I don't usually think of that being the end result because I'd rather keep my songs and make 'em happen so they last a while, rather than just be a hit record and gone.

Vincent: Your sets vary from night to night. How planned are your sets?

Dylan: They're not very well planned. [*Laughs.*]

Vincent: For example, I understand you did "We Just Disagree" [*a song recorded by English singer Dave Mason in 1977. —Ed.*]. And you've done

"Abraham, Martin, and John" [*the 1968 Dion hit —Ed.*] the opening night when I saw you and I guess you've done that since then.

Dylan: Yeah, well, we try stuff out to see what feels right and what doesn't. It's just trial and experiment.

Vincent: When you did "Abraham, Martin, and John" on opening night, you and Clydie [King], I believe, sat at the piano and, on the line, "Has anybody here seen our old friend, Bobby? / Do you wonder where he's gone?," the crowd reacted. Could they have been thinking, in this case, rather than Bobby Kennedy, could they have been thinking about where has our old Bobby Dylan gone?

Dylan: Sure, because they could think any Bobby. They don't necessarily have to relate it to me. It's just a name. When I first heard that song I didn't really know who the Bobby was in it. I didn't put that together for a while. I put together the rest of the names but for some reason I kinda was slow on that, for me.

Vincent: Going back to your Budokan [Japan] tour—that was a different feel, different look for you too, as far as the way you dressed on stage and the way you did the songs. In fact, I remember when you did it here at the Oakland Coliseum you made the statement, "You've been reading that this tour is show-bizzy and disco but we know better than that." In a way, I thought that you were maybe goofing on a bunch of us or maybe on the world with that tour.

Dylan: No. . . . It's always misinterpreted in some way, like the last show we had out [reporters said it] was like a gospel show. Well, it was because most all my stuff at that time was influenced or written right off the gospel, but that was no reason to say it wasn't a musical show. . . . A lotta people may read something like that and say, "Wow, I can read my own Bible. I don't have to get it preached at me." That's when they decide not to come. There's also a lot of people just turned off by the Bible, which is the case nowadays, too.

Vincent: Maybe it could be something as simple as people knowing and loving your older songs so much and they mean so much to them that they so much wanted to hear them.

Dylan: Yeah, that's true. But don't forget now, people say a lot of stuff they don't mean and there's different reasons for saying this and that. You may say one thing in a certain predicament and you find yourself in another predicament. You may find yourself saying the totally opposite thing. So when I hear that people expected me to sing the old songs, well, I was singing those old songs—we did a tour for it must've been nine months, singing them all over the world and there was a lot of complaints about that. In fact, that had more complaints than on the last tour we did because people said, "He doesn't sound like he used to sound and their arrangements are disco and they're slick." Well, that wasn't necessarily true. It wasn't disco, it wasn't slick, and people couldn't see beyond that. It's like when you have your hand up in front of your eye you can't see your hand.

Vincent: You've had those problems before—the Newport Folk Festival way, way back when you did the acoustic set and then came back with Mike Bloomfield and a bunch of people and did the electric.

Dylan: I don't know how I keep going. [*Laughs.*] I don't have any plan [*Laughs.*] I'll tell you that much. It's day by day. That's all I can think.

[*Dylan's "All Along the Watchtower" plays.*]

Vincent: You do some great new songs in the sets, here at the Warfield, too. Are you working currently on a new album?

Dylan: Umm . . .

Vincent: . . . 'Course you're performing now. What are your plans on the new—

Dylan: I don't know. Like I say, I may record an album when the time feels right. I'll take whatever I have into the studio and record it.

Vincent: Financially, you could have retired ten, fifteen years ago. [*Laughs.*]

Dylan: If you just think financially, I think you can retire when you're born really, but . . .

Vincent: What gives you a feeling of fulfillment now, at this point in your life?

Dylan: Just seeing growth in people, trying to love as much as I can.

Vincent: Your religious beliefs may stay the same. Do you foresee continuing recording songs of that nature for very much longer?

Dylan: Well, I don't know what's gonna change, which way it's gonna go. I'm sure it's gonna have some change. You can't record every album and have it be a *Saved*-type album, because you just don't get that many kinda songs all in a row like that. So I'm sure there'll be some difference but I couldn't say what it would be.

Vincent: You have a yacht now. Are you enjoying yachting?

Dylan: It's not a yacht, it's a sailing ship. It's like an old schooner. Me and this other guy have it. It took about three years to build it. It was built from the ground up.

Vincent: There was another story I remember reading in the press that when the yacht was unveiled you weren't there.

Dylan: I couldn't make it. I was on the road. We were playing in Cincinnati that night, I think.

Vincent: They expected you to be there, too. You can't please everybody, can you?

Dylan: You can't be in two places at the same time. [*Laughs.*]

Vincent: How is it to live with that all the time—everything you say being picked apart, knowing that the world is watching you at all times?

Dylan: I don't pay no mind to it. It just don't have any concern for me, really.

Vincent: What's in the future for you? That you can talk about?

Dylan: Well, we're just gonna play these shows and I'll be doing different things, probably go 'round the world one of these years again.

Vincent: Just for pleasure? Not performing?

Dylan: No, we'll probably be going to perform and for pleasure. I like to mix business with pleasure.

Vincent: You're on the road a lot, aren't you?

Dylan: Yeah. Well, half the year. Some people are on more, some people are on less. But about half the year.

Vincent: Bob, thank you very, very much. I've certainly appreciated it, and I've been looking forward to this for a long time.

DYLAN ON

His Born-Again Experience

"I truly had a born-again experience. If you want to call it that. It's an overused term, but it's something that people can relate to. It happened in 1978. I always knew there was a God or a creator of the universe and a creator of the mountains and the seas and all that kind of thing, but I wasn't conscious of Jesus and what that had to do with the supreme creator. . . . I was sleeping one day and I just sat up in bed at seven in the morning and I was compelled to get dressed and drive over to the Bible school. I couldn't believe I was there."

—from interview with Robert Hilburn, *Los Angeles Times*, November 23, 1980

DYLAN ON

European Audiences

"I think people in England react more spontaneously to the stuff that I do than the people here. You sit here for so long and they take you for granted, and anyway, I've taken a lot of my earlier songs from a lot of old English ballads and stuff like that, so people will probably relate to that a lot more over there than they do here. Here, I'm not really sure if people are aware of where songs like 'Masters of War' or 'Girl from the North Country' really originate."

—from telephone interview with Tim Blackmore,
Capital Radio (London), June 15, 1981

RADIO INTERVIEW

Paul Gambaccini | June 20, 1981 | *Rock On*, **BBC Radio 1 (UK)**

Seven months after he spoke with DJ Paul Vincent, Dylan was preparing for the release of *Shot of Love*, a motley collection that mingles more religious material with a few other tracks, including one that pays tribute to the late Lenny Bruce. He was also getting ready for a new European tour, which prompted this June 12, 1981, phone interview with the BBC's London-based Paul Gambaccini. Dylan—who was in Detroit, Michigan at the time of the call—sounds upbeat and more than a bit pleased about the forthcoming album. As it turned out, few critics shared his view of it.

Paul Gambaccini: Who's coming in the backing band this time? What's the music gonna be like?

Bob Dylan: I'm bringing the same band that I have been touring with for the last two years.

Gambaccini: You'd be at Earl's Court, which is where you were last time. Were you surprised last time by the friendly response?

Dylan: Ah, sometimes the response is less than friendly, and sometimes it's friendly, but over the years you just kind of get used to any kind of response.

Gambaccini: I know that recently in the States you've been performing a lot of your inspirational material. Will you be doing that in London?

Dylan: We'll be doing some of it. Most of the stuff comes from all the albums. And then we just finished an album, so we'll be including some new songs, too. The name of the new album is *Shot of Love*.

Gambaccini: Does that continue in the inspirational vein?

Dylan: Well, you kind of have to decide that for yourself. It's different than the last, it's different than *Saved*, and it's different than *Slow Train*, and it sounds old but it's new.

Gambaccini: Does it feature any of your recent players, like Barry Beckett?

Dylan: No, I didn't do this one down in Muscle Shoals. I did it in California. So Barry's not on this one. I did use my usual band. Actually, Ronnie Wood played on one song. So did Ringo.

Gambaccini: I've received some very exciting mail on the last couple of albums, because some people who shared your sense of what might be called ministry or message were very excited that you were with them on it and other people had thought, well, what is Bob doing now?

Dylan: Yeah, I don't know. Sometimes it takes . . . you know, the older albums don't really mean something to some people until they're hearing the new one and in retrospect they go back and hear something else from the past that'll seem like it takes the steps that lead up to the new one.

I think this new album we did, for mc, I think it's the most explosive album I've ever done. Even going back to *Blonde on Blonde* or *Freewheelin'* or any of those, *Bringing It All Back Home*, *Highway 61*, or whatever they were. I think this one, for its time right now, will be perceived in the same way and I may be totally wrong in saying that, but I feel that same way about this album as I did about when we recorded *Bringing It All Back Home*, that was like a breakthrough point.

It's the kind of music I've been striving to make, and I believe that in time people will see that. It's hard to explain it. It's that indefinable thing that people can write about, but they can only write about and around it, you can't really take charge over it, because it is what it is and you can't really expound on it. It itself is the beginning and the end of what it is.

Gambaccini: In *Blood on the Tracks*, which was another of my favorite albums, you were speaking right from the heart. Is that the kind of feeling you have lyrically on this album?

Dylan: Well, that was a different sort of thing. That was a breakthrough album for me, too, in another sense of lyrics. I've done things I've never done before. This is just a different sort of thing, it's like the thing I've always wanted to do. And, for one reason or another, I have always been bound in certain areas where I couldn't have the right structure around some kinds of things to make it come off, in a way, because mainly, when I don't do that much talking, so when I'm playing, you have to be able to communicate with the people around you in order to get your point of view across. And if you have to do too much of that communication it gets confusing and something is lost along the way. And this time that didn't happen. Everybody was pretty much together.

Gambaccini: Do you feel then, that you now have accomplished what you want to as an artist, or . . . ?

Dylan: I think so. I think I will do an instrumental album now.

Gambaccini: You think so?

Dylan: Yeah. I've come as far as there is to come and now I'm gonna start just doing instrumentals.

Gambaccini: Are you finding at the moment inspiration from any other artists, as I think you probably found from Dire Straits a couple of years ago?

Dylan: Oh, yeah, well, I just spoke with [Dire Straits'] Mark [Knopfler] recently. I've always liked Gordon Lightfoot . . .

Gambaccini: Recently here, Bruce Springsteen's gone down very well. Do you like him?

Dylan: Yeah, Bruce is a very, very talented guy.

Gambaccini: Did you know that Bruce has included "This Land Is Your Land" in his concert program?

Dylan: Oh, he has? That's amazing! That's good. Well, maybe he'll start doing "Blowin' in the Wind"! Maybe he'll do an album with Bob Dylan songs!

Gambaccini: Well, funnily enough, I heard on the radio recently, Manfred Mann's version of "With God on Our Side." And I thought that in this current atmosphere where there is so much talk about nuclear disarmament and the missile talks, particularly in Europe, where it is a great concern at the moment, that these songs of yours from the early albums about the nuclear disarmament situation take on a new timeliness. Do you ever think about that?

Dylan: No. Not really, but it doesn't surprise me. I thought they were timely then, and just as sure they're timely now.

DYLAN ON

How He Makes Records

"I learned how to make records when I started recording . . . which is, going into the studio and making a record, right then and there. I know the other way and I know a lot of people do it the other way and it's successful for them . . . but I'm not interested in that aspect of recording. Laying down tracks and then coming back and perfecting those tracks and then perfecting lyrics . . . I'm a live performer. I have to play songs which are gonna relate to the faces that I'm singing to. And I can't do that if I was spending a year in the studio, working on a track. It's not that important to me. No record is that important."

—from interview with Dave Herman,
WNEW-FM (New York), July 27, 1981

DYLAN ON

Working with Producer Daniel Lanois

"Lanois can get passionate about what he feels to be true. He's not above smashing guitars. I never care about that unless it was one of mine. Things got contentious once in the parking lot. He tried to convince me that the song ["Mississippi," from *Love and Theft*] had to be 'sexy, sexy and more sexy.' . . . I tried to explain that the song had more to do with the Declaration of Independence, the Constitution and the Bill of Rights than witch doctors, and just couldn't be thought of as some kind of ideological voodoo thing. But he had his own way of looking at things, and in the end I had to reject this because I thought too highly of the expressive meaning behind the lyrics to bury them in some steamy cauldron of drum theory."

—from interview with David Fricke, *Rolling Stone*, September 27, 1981

DYLAN ON

His Big California House

"I bought this house on about an acre of land, past Malibu. And my wife looked at it and said, 'Well it's OK, but it needs another bedroom.' . . . So we had architects come in and right away, they said, 'Oh, yeah, Bob Dylan, right. We'll really make something spectacular here.' . . . So I went out there one day to see how the room was progressing, and they'd knocked down the house! I asked the guys who were workin', 'Where's the house?' And they said they had to knock it down to restructure it for this bedroom upstairs. . . . So one thing led to another, and I said as long as they're knocking this place down, we're just gonna add more rooms to it. And anytime some craftsman came by . . . we'd say, 'Hey, you wanna do some work on this place?' And they'd do woodwork, tilework, all that kinda thing. And eventually it was built. But then they closed the school out there, and the kids moved away, and Sara moved away . . . So I was stuck with this place. As a matter of fact, I've never even put anything on the living room floor. It's just cement."

—from interview with Kurt Loder, *Rolling Stone*, June 21, 1984

"JESUS, WHO'S GOT TIME TO KEEP UP WITH THE TIMES?"

Mick Brown | July 1, 1984 | *Sunday Times* (UK)

"I'd been sent by the *Sunday Times* to Madrid, where Dylan was performing," music journalist Mick Brown told me, "in the wildly optimistic hope that I might be able to secure an interview with him prior to his arrival in Britain. The tour was being promoted by Bill Graham, whom I had met previously when he was managing Santana. I found out where Graham was staying and went to meet him. He was predictably pessimistic about the prospects of an interview, but said he'd try. After much to-ing and fro-ing, at the eleventh hour, I was told to wait in my hotel room and I might get a telephone call.

"At the moment when it finally seemed clear to me that I would not be interviewing Bob Dylan," Brown continued, "the telephone rang. I was told to be at the Cafe Alcazar at 7:30 PM [*on June 27, 1984 —Ed.*]. I arrived at 7:40. No sign. Obviously, I thought, he had come and gone. I have no idea what made me think that Dylan would be a fastidious timekeeper.

"Forty minutes late," Brown recalled, "he came through the door alone. He was wearing a Hawaiian shirt and a straw hat that looked like a disguise. It worked, at least for a while. Nobody seemed to notice him as he walked to the table. His manner was courteous and accommodating. Every question I asked he had heard before, but he treated them all with good grace."

When it was over, said Brown, "I seem to remember having about two hours to turn the piece around and was writing in a furious panic." —Ed.

This week Bob Dylan comes to Britain. The folksinger-cum-folk hero of the 1960s has not always had a good reception here. In 1965 purists attacked him for "going electric." In 1981 his new-found evangelism left many of his fans cold. What should they expect this time? Last week Mick Brown had an exclusive interview.

Bob Dylan tugged at a cigarette, stroked the beginnings of an untidy beard and gazed pensively at the stream of traffic passing down the Madrid street. "What you gotta understand," he said at length, "is that I do something because I feel like doing it. If people can relate to it, that's great; if they can't, that's fine too. But I don't think I'm gonna be really understood until maybe 100 years from now. What I've done, what I'm doing, nobody else does or has done."

THE MESSIANIC tone grew more intense. "When I'm dead and gone maybe people will realise that, and then figure it out. I don't think anything I've done has been even mildly hinted at. There's all these interpreters around, but they're not interpreting anything except their own ideas. Nobody's come close."

But a lot of people, it seems, still want to. Bob Dylan may no longer sell records in the consistently enormous quantities he once did—a fact to which he will allow a tinge of regret—but his capacity to hold his audience in thrall seems undiminished.

By the time Bob Dylan arrives in Britain this week for performances at St. James' Park, Newcastle, on Tuesday and Wembley Stadium on Saturday, he will already have performed to almost half a million people throughout Europe—half a million people singing the chorus of "Blowin' in the Wind," an esperanto that is as much a testament to Dylan's abiding influence and charisma as it is to the insatiable interest of the world's press in his activities.

This interest is equalled only by Dylan's determination to keep his own counsel whenever possible. As Bill Graham, the tour's garrulous American promoter and Dylan's closest adviser, keeps reminding you, Bob "is not your everyday folk singer."

All the German magazine *Stern* had wanted to do was touch base for five minutes in return for a front-cover. Dylan declined. The press conference that he had been persuaded to hold in Verona, attended by

150 excitable European journalists, had been a fiasco: photographers barred, and the first question from the floor—"What are your religious views nowadays?"—met by Dylan irritably brushing the table in front of him, as if to sweep aside that and all other questions to follow.

"I mean, nobody cares what Billy Joel's religious views are, right?" he tells me with a wry smile. "What does it matter to people what Bob Dylan is? But it seems to, right? I'd honestly like to know why it's important to them."

One expects many things of Bob Dylan, but such playful ingenuousness is not one of them.

DYLAN PROTECTS himself well, not with bodyguards but by a smokescreen of privacy and elusiveness of the sort that encourages speculation and myth. Meeting him involves penetrating a frustrating maze of "perhapses" and "maybes," of cautions and briefings—suggestive of dealing with fine porcelain—culminating in a telephone call summoning you to an anonymous cafeteria filled with Spanish families who give not a second glance to the figure in a Hawaiian shirt and straw hat who at last comes ambling through the door.

He is surprisingly genial, youthful for his 43 years, lean, interested and alert, who treats the business of being Bob Dylan with an engagingly aw-shucks kind of bemusement.

It was in striking contrast to the apparition Dylan had presented the previous night, on stage in front of 25,000 people in a Madrid football stadium, his black smock coat, high boots and hawkish profile suggesting some avenging backwoods preacher.

The emphasis in his performance has shifted from the overtly evangelical songs heard in Dylan's last visit to Britain three years ago. Now it spans every phase of his 21-year career. The themes of social protest, personal love and religious faith have never been more of a piece. Dylan remains what he has always been, an uncompromising moralist. And to hear songs such as "Masters of War," "A Hard Rain's A-Gonna Fall" (about nuclear war) and "Maggie's Farm" (about rebellious labor) invested with fresh nuances of meaning, not to say vitriol, is to realise that, while the sentiments may have become unfashionable in popular music, they are no less pertinent. Nobody else is writing songs like Bob Dylan. Nobody ever did.

"For me, none of the songs I've written has really dated," he says. "They capture something I've never been able to improve on, whatever their statement is. A song like 'Maggie's Farm'—I could feel like that just the other day, and I could feel the same tomorrow. People say they're 'nostalgia,' but I don't know what that means really. *A Tale of Two Cities* was written 100 years ago; is that nostalgia? This term 'nostalgic,' it's just another way people have of dealing with you and putting you some place they think they understand. It's just another label."

LABELS EXERCISE Bob Dylan greatly. People have been trying to put them on him since he started, he says, "and not one of them has ever made any sense."

The furor about his religious beliefs puzzled him most of all, "like I was running for Pope or something." When the word first spread that he had eschewed Judaism and embraced Christianity, and he toured America in 1979 singing overtly religious songs, the most hostile reception came not from rock audiences but when he played university campuses, "and the so-called intellectual students showed their true monstrous selves."

"Born-again Christians" is just another label, he says. He had attended Bible school in California for three months, and the book was never far from his side, but the idea that faith was a matter of passing through one swing door and back out of another struck him as ridiculous. "I live by a strict disciplinary code, you know, but I don't know how *moral* that is or even where it comes from, really. These things just become part of your skin after a while; you get to know what line not to step over—usually because you stepped over it before and were lucky to get back."

Was he an ascetic? Dylan lit another cigarette and asked what the word meant. "I don't think so. I still have desires, you know, that lead me around once in a while. I don't do things in excess, but everybody goes through those times. They either kill you, or make you a better person."

By this time in the conversation it did not seem awkward to ask: did he believe in evil?

"Sure I believe in it. I believe that ever since Adam and Eve got thrown out of the garden that the whole nature of the planet has been heading in one direction—towards apocalypse. It's all there in the Book of Revelations, but it's difficult talking about these things because most people don't know what you're talking about anyway, or don't want to listen.

"What it comes down to is that there's a lot of different gods in the world against *the* God—that's what it's all about. There's a lot of different gods that people are subjects of. There's the god of Mammon. Corporations are gods. Governments? No, governments don't have much to do with it anymore, I don't think. Politics is a hoax. The politicians don't have any *real* power. They feed you all this stuff in the newspapers about what's going on, but that's not what's *really* going on.

"But then again, I don't think that makes me a pessimistic person. I'm a realist. Or maybe a *sur*realist. But you can't beat your head against the wall forever."

He had never, he said, been a utopian: that was always a foreign term to him, something to do with moving to the country, living communally and growing rice and beans. "I mean, I wanted to grow my own rice and beans—still do—but I never felt part of that movement."

But he could still look back on the 1960s with something approaching affection. "I mean, the Kennedys were great-looking people, man; they had style," he smiles. "America is not like that any more. But what happened, happened so fast that people are still trying to figure it out. The TV media wasn't so big then. It's like the only thing people knew was what they knew; then suddenly people were being told what to think, how to behave. There's too much information.

"It just got suffocated. Like Woodstock—that wasn't about anything. It was just a whole new market for tie-dyed T-shirts. It was about clothes. All those people are in computers now."

This was beyond him. He had never been good with numbers, and had no desire to stare at a screen. "I don't feel obliged to keep up with the times. I'm not going to be here that long anyway. So I keep up with these times, then I gotta keep up with the '90s. Jesus, who's got time to keep up with the times?"

It is at moments such as this that Dylan—once, misleadingly perhaps, characterised as a radical—reveals himself as much of a traditionalist; an

adherent of biblical truths; a firm believer in the family and the institution of marriage—despite his own divorce from his wife, Sara; a man
disenchanted with many of the totems and values of modern life, mass
communications, the vulgarity of popular culture, the "sameness" of
everything. Did he read contemporary literature? "Oh yeah, I read a
detective story, but I can't remember what it was called.

"At least in the 1960s it seemed there was room to be different.
For me, my particular scene, I came along at just the right time, and I
understood the times I was in. If I was starting out right now I don't
know where I'd get the inspiration from, because you need to breathe
the right air to make that creative process work. I don't worry about it
so much for me. I've done it; I can't complain. But the people coming
up, the artists and writers, what are they gonna do, because these are
the people who change the world."

Nowadays, he admits, he finds songwriting harder than ever. A song
like "Masters of War" he would despatch in 15 minutes and move on to
the next one without a second thought. "If I wrote a song like that now
I wouldn't feel I'd have to write another one for two weeks. There's still
things I want to write about, but the process is harder. The old records
I used to make, by the time they came out I wouldn't even want them
released because I was already so far beyond them."

Much of his time nowadays is spent travelling. He was in Jerusalem
last autumn for his son Jesse's bar mitzvah—"his grandmother's idea,"
he smiles. Israel interests him from "a biblical point of view," but he had
never felt that atavistic Jewish sense of homecoming. In fact, he lives
principally on his farm in Minnesota, not far from the town of Hibbing where he spent his adolescence. Then there is the domed house in
Malibu, California, originally built to accommodate his five children—
good schools nearby, he says—but which he has seldom used since his
divorce, and a 63ft sailing boat with which he cruises the Caribbean
"when I can't think of anything else to do."

He had never contemplated retirement: the need to make money was
not a factor—he is a wealthy man—but the impulse to continue writing
was. "There's never really been any glory in it for me," he says. "Being
seen in the places and having everybody put their arm around you, I

never cared about any of that. I don't care what people think. For me, the fulfillment was always in just doing it. That's all that really matters."

As the conversation had progressed, more and more people had realised who the man in the straw hat was. A steady stream had made their way to his table, scraps of paper in hand. Dylan had signed them all, with a surprisingly careful deliberation—almost as if he was practising—but his discomfort at being on view was becoming more apparent. As peremptorily as he had arrived, Bob Dylan made his excuses and left.

DYLAN ON

Reaching a New Generation

"I don't reach anybody. They find me. It's not for me to go out and reach somebody. If they can find me, they find me, and if they don't, they don't. That's the way it's always been. I don't think it's gonna change now."

—from interview with Martha Quinn,
Wembley Stadium, London, MTV, July 7, 1984

DYLAN ON

Irish Music

"Irish music has always been a great part of my life because I used to hang out with the Clancy Brothers. They influenced me tremendously . . . Liam Clancy was always my favorite singer, as a ballad singer. I just never heard anyone as good, and that includes Barbra Streisand and Pearl Bailey."

—from interview with Bono, *Hot Press* (Ireland), August 26, 1984

RADIO INTERVIEW

Bert Kleinman and Artie Mogull | November 13, 1984 | Westwood One (US)

This extensive interview, which took place on July 30, 1984, at New York City's Ritz-Carlton Hotel, was conducted by radio programmer Bert Kleinman and Artie Mogull, the A&R man who in 1962 had signed Dylan to his first music-publishing contract. The conversation aired on stations belonging to the Westwood One radio network, beginning on November 13, 1984. —Ed.

Bert Kleinman: Is it true that you taught yourself guitar and harmonica?

Bob Dylan: Well, nobody really teaches themselves guitar and harmonica. When you don't know anything, first of all you get yourself a book or something. What I remember is learning a couple of chords from some books and then going out to watch people, to see how they're doing it. You don't go so much to hear 'em, you just go to see how they do what they do, get as close as you can, see what their fingers are doing.

In those early stages, it's more like a learning thing, and that can sometimes take many years. But I picked it up fairly quickly. I didn't really play with that much technique. And people really didn't take to me because of that, because I didn't go out of my way to learn as much technique as other people . . . I know people who spent their whole lives learning John Lee Hooker chords, just hammering on the E string, and that was all. But they could play it in such a beautiful way, it looked like a ballet dancer.

Everybody had a different style and techniques, especially in folk music. There was your Southern mountain banjo, then flat picking, then

271

your finger-picking techniques, and just all of these different runs, different styles of ballads. Folk music was a world that was very split up and there was a purist side to it. Folk people didn't want to hear it if you couldn't play the song exactly the way that Aunt Molly Jackson played it. And I just kind of blazed my way through all that stuff. [*Laughs.*] I would hear somebody do something and it would get to a certain point that you'd say, "What do you want from that?" You'd want to see what style they were playing . . . I just stayed up day and night, just barnstorming my way through all that stuff. And then I heard Woody Guthrie, and then it all came together for me.

Kleinman: Do you remember the first Woody Guthrie record you heard?

Dylan: Yeah, I think the first Woody Guthrie song I heard was "Pastures of Plenty." And "Pretty Boy Floyd" and another song . . . he used to write a lot of his songs from existing melodies. "Grand Coulee Dam." They just impressed me.

Kleinman: Got to you?

Dylan: Oh, yeah. Because they just had a mark of originality. Well, the lyrics did. I just heard all those songs and I learned them all off the records. All the songs of Woody Guthrie that I could find, anybody that had a Woody Guthrie record or that knew a Woody Guthrie song. And in St. Paul at the time, where I was, there were some people around who not only had his records but who knew his songs. So I just learned them all. Some of the best records that I heard him make were these records that he made on the Stinson label, with Cisco Houston and Sonny Terry.

I don't know if Leadbelly was on there, too. I learned a bunch of Leadbelly's stuff too and learned how to play like that. But one of the biggest thrills I ever actually had was when I reached New York, whenever it was, and I got to play with Cisco Houston. I think I got to play with him at a party someplace. But I used to watch him. He used to play at Folk City. He was an amazing-looking guy. He looked like Clark Gable, like a movie star.

Artie Mogull: He reminded me a little of Tennessee Ernie [Ford], actually.

Dylan: Yeah.

Mogull: Also very unheralded.

Dylan: Oh, completely. He was one of the great unsung heroes. One of the great American figures of all time, and nobody knows anything about him.

Kleinman: When do you think you started to develop something that was uniquely yours? You were talking about playing Woody Guthrie—

Dylan: Well, when I came to New York that's all I played—Woody Guthrie songs. Then about six months after that, I'd stopped playing all Woody Guthrie songs. I used to play in a place called Café Wha?, and it always used to open at noon and closed at six in the morning. It was just a nonstop flow of people. Usually they were tourists who were looking for beatniks in the Village. There'd be maybe five groups that played there.

I used to play with a guy called Fred Neil, who wrote the song "Everybody's Talkin'" that was in the film *Midnight Cowboy*. Fred was from Coconut Grove, Florida, I think, and he used to make that scene, from Coconut Grove to Nashville to New York. And he had a strong, powerful voice, almost a bass voice. And a powerful sense of rhythm. And he used to play mostly these types of songs that Josh White might sing. I would play harmonica for him, and then, once in a while, get to sing a song when he was taking a break or something. It was his show; he would be on for about half an hour.

Then a conga group would get on, called Los Congeros, with twenty conga drummers and bongos and steel drums. And they would sing and play maybe half an hour. And then this girl, I think she was called Judy Rainey, used to play sweet southern mountain Appalachian ballads, with electric guitar and a small amplifier. And then another guy named Hal Waters used to sing. He used to be a sort of crooner. Then there'd be a comedian, then an impersonator, and this whole unit would go around nonstop. And you'd get fed there, which was actually the best thing about the place.

Mogull: How long a set would you do?

Dylan: Oh, about half an hour. If they didn't like you back then you couldn't play. You'd get hooted off. If they liked you, you played more. If they didn't like you, you didn't play at all. You'd play one or two songs and people would just boo or hiss.

Kleinman: This wasn't your own stuff you were singing there?

Dylan: No, I didn't start playing my own stuff until much later.

Kleinman: When did you start to perform your own stuff?

Dylan: I just drifted into it. I just started writing. I'd always kinda written my own songs but I never played them. Nobody played their own songs then. The only person that did that was Woody Guthrie. And then one day I just wrote a song, and the first song I ever wrote that I performed in public was the song I wrote to Woody Guthrie. I just felt like playing it one night, and so I played it.

Kleinman: Was writing something that you'd always wanted to do?

Dylan: Not really. It wasn't a thing I wanted to do ever. I wanted just a song to sing, and there came a certain point where I couldn't sing anything. So I had to write what I wanted to sing 'cause nobody else was writing what I wanted to sing. I couldn't find it anywhere. If I could, I probably would have never started writing.

Kleinman: Was the writing something that came easy to you? Because it is a craft that you do very well and you talk about it so casually.

Dylan: Yeah, it does come easy. But then, after so many records sometimes you just don't know anymore: am I doing this because I want to do it or because you think it's expected of you? Do you know what I mean? So you'd start saying, well, it's time to write a song—I'll write a song. And you'll try to do something but sometimes it just won't come out right. At those kind of times it's best just to go sing somebody's songs.

Kleinman: Was it a lot of work writing? Was it a labor?

Dylan: No. It was just something I'd kinda do. You'd just sit up all night and write a song, or . . . in those days I used to write a lot of songs in cafés. Or at somebody's house with the typewriter. "A Hard Rain's A-Gonna Fall"—I wrote that in the basement of the Village Gate. All of it, at Chip Monck's [the rock lighting designer]. He used to have a place down in the boiler room, an apartment that he slept in, next to the Greenwich

Hotel. And I wrote "A Hard Rain's A-Gonna Fall" down there. I'd write songs in people's houses, people's apartments, wherever I was.

Kleinman: Were you much of a polisher? I mean, did you write it and then pore over it?

Dylan: Pretty much I'd just leave them the way they were.

[*Commercial break.*]

Dylan: Well, I don't know why I walked off that [Ed Sullivan] show [in 1963]. I could have done something else but we'd rehearsed the song so many times and everybody had heard it. They'd run through the show, and they'd put you on and you'd run through your number, and it always got a good response, and I was looking forward to singing it. Even Ed Sullivan seemed to really like it. I don't know who objected to it, but just before I was going to sing it they came in, and this was show time. There was this big huddle. I could see people talking about something. I was just getting ready to play, and then someone stepped up and said I couldn't sing that song. They wanted me to sing a Clancy Brothers song, and it just didn't make sense to me to sing a Clancy Brothers song on nationwide TV at that time. So I just left.

Mogull: Do you remember that time you were down in San Juan, Puerto Rico, at the CBS convention? And it was being held at the San Juan Hilton, I guess. This huge record convention, and it was just as Bob was beginning to hit. And the president of CBS at the time was a fabulous man named Goddard Lieberson. And they wouldn't let Bob in the hotel, because he was not wearing a tie or a jacket.

Dylan: Yeah, or a shirt.

Mogull: And Lieberson, to his credit, told the hotel manager, "Either he comes in the hotel or I'm pulling the whole convention out of here." Have I told the story right?

Dylan: Yeah, he was a big supporter of mine, Goddard Lieberson, as was John Hammond. Without those people like that, I don't think anything would have happened for me. If I was to come along now, in this day, with the kind of people that are running record companies now, they would bar the doors, I think. But you had people back then who were more entrenched in individuality.

Mogull: And also not as insecure in their jobs.

Dylan: No, they ran things—they made decisions and it stuck. Now, it seems like everybody chats with somebody else. It's like, "Well, I'll tell you tomorrow," "call me back later," "yeah, we almost got a deal," stuff like that.

Kleinman: Did you get along with Lieberson OK?

Dylan: Oh, yeah, he was great. He even used to come to some sessions of mine. He'd stop in and say hello.

Kleinman: Was there ever any pressure on you? I mean, some people considered your music almost subversive. Although I always considered it very American.

Dylan: I guess they did. I don't know. But like I said, they seemed to run things. Other people may have been talking under their breath or behind their back. But at this time their big acts were Mitch Miller, Andy Williams, Johnny Mathis. I didn't really begin to sell many records until the second record . . . and the "Subterranean Homesick Blues" that made the charts.

Kleinman: That was an amazing single when you think of what the singles were like at the time.

Dylan: They made some records then that were good pop records. Not on Columbia, though. Phil Spector was doing a lot of stuff at the time, and Jerry Leiber and Mike Stoller.

Kleinman: Were you listening to a lot of pop stuff at the time?

Dylan: Yeah, I listened to a lot of pop stuff, but it never influenced what I was doing. At least to any great degree. It had earlier, when rock 'n' roll came in after Elvis, Carl Perkins, Buddy Holly, those people. Chuck Berry, Little Richard.

You know, nostalgia to me isn't really rock 'n' roll, because when I was a youngster the music I heard was Frankie Laine, Rosemary Clooney, Dennis Day. And Dorothy Collins, the Mills Brothers, all that stuff. When I hear stuff like that, it always strikes a different chord than all the rock 'n' roll stuff. The rock 'n' roll stuff, I had a conscious mind at that time, but ten years before that, it was like "Mule Train" and . . . Johnnie Ray. Johnnie Ray was the first person to really knock me out.

Kleinman: What do you think it was about Johnnie Ray?

Dylan: Well, he was just so emotional, wasn't he? I ran into him in an elevator in Australia. He was one of my idols. I was speechless. There I was in an elevator with Johnnie Ray! I mean, what do you say?

Kleinman: When you started to move from the pure folk style into a more electric style, was that a tough one?

Dylan: We're getting into a touchy subject.

[*Laughter.*]

Kleinman: Well, I mean today you go on stage and both of those things coexist. Nobody thinks twice.

Dylan: Yeah, they always did coexist.

Kleinman: I'm not talking so much about that, but at least what it seemed like from the outside was that people were trying to tell you how to make your music.

Dylan: Oh, there's always people trying to tell you how to do everything in your life. If you really don't know what to do and you don't care what to do, then just ask somebody's opinion. You'll get a million opinions. If you don't want to do something, ask someone's opinion and they'll just verify it for you. The easiest way to do something is to just not ask anybody's opinion. I mean, if you really believe in what you're doing. I've asked people's opinion and it's been a great mistake, in different areas. In my personal life, I've asked people, "What do you think about doing this?" and they've said, "Oh, wow!," you know, and you end up not using it or else using it wrong.

Mogull: As a matter of fact, I think the artist has to make the innate decision about their—

Dylan: Yeah, you know what's right. A lot of times you might be farming around and not knowing what's right and you might do something dumb, but that's only because you don't know what to do in the first place. But if you know what's right and it strikes you at a certain time, then you can usually believe that instinct. And if you act on it, then you'll be successful at it. Whatever it is.

Kleinman: Recording is a whole other thing from being on stage. And you, from what I've read, try and record as spontaneously as possible.

Dylan: I have, yeah, but I don't do that so often anymore. I used to do that because recording a song bores me. It's like working in a coal mine. Well, it's not really as serious as that; you're not that far underground! Maybe not in a literal sense, but you could be indoors for months. And then what you think is real is just not anymore. You're just listening to sounds and your whole world is working with tapes and things. I've never liked that side of things.

Plus, I've never gotten into it on that level. When I first recorded I just went in and recorded the songs I had. That's the way people recorded then. But people don't record that way now, and I shouldn't record that way either, because they can't even get it down that way anymore. To do what I used to do, or to do what anybody used to do, you have to stay in the studio longer to get that right. Because you know technology has messed everything up so much.

Kleinman: It's messed it up?

Dylan: Yeah. Technology is giving a false picture. Like if you listen to any of the records that are done now, they're all done in a technology sort of way. Which is a conniving kind of way. You can dream up what you want to do and just go in and dream it up! But you go see some of that stuff live and you're gonna be very disappointed . . . I mean, if you want to see some of it live. You may not want to. Well, I think it's messed it up, but that's progress. You can't go back, the way it used to be. For a lot of people, it's messed things up, but then for a lot of other people it's a great advantage. In other words, you can get something right now; it doesn't have to be right but you can get it right. It can be totally wrong but you can get it right. And it can be done just with sound.

We were recording something the other night, and we were gonna put some handclaps on it. And the guy sitting behind the board was saying, "Well, do you guys wanna go out there and actually clap? I got a machine right here that can do that." And the name of this thing was Roland or something. [*Laughter.*] So we went out and clapped instead. It wasn't any big deal; we could have had some machine do it. But that's just a small example of how everything is just machine-oriented.

Kleinman: You talk almost like—I don't really know how to put it—like the world's gone here and you're old fashioned.

Dylan: Well, I feel I'm old fashioned, but I don't believe I'm old fashioned in the way that I'm not modern fashioned. On a certain level there is no old fashioned and there's no new fashioned. Really nothing has changed. I don't think I'm old fashioned in that I feel I'm a passé person that's sitting somewhere out in Montana, just watching it snow. But even if I was, I'm sure that would be OK.

Mogull: Yeah, Bob, but you can't go to a concert like Wembley and get that kind of—

Dylan: Yeah, OK. But life is like that. You don't get that many years to live, right? So how long can you manage to keep up with things? And when you're keeping up with things, what are you keeping up with? Who buys most of the records nowadays? Twelve-year-old kids? Who buys Michael Jackson's records? Twelve-year-olds. Fourteen-year-olds. Sixteen, twenty. I don't know who buys fifty million records of somebody. You can't compete with a market that's geared for twelve-year-olds. You have rock 'n' roll critics that are forty years old writing about records that are geared for people that are ten years old! And making an intellectual philosophy out of it.

Kleinman: But you don't listen to that stuff?

Dylan: No, and I don't listen to those critics. I've come up with a lot of people who should know a whole lot better, who have made a career about writing about rock 'n' roll. Writing about rock 'n' roll! I mean, how indecent can you be? Well, I'm not saying that it's all bad. People have to express themselves. So rock 'n' roll gives them a thrill, or did give them a thrill. Well, most of the people that I can think of as rock 'n' roll authorities are people who have documented what I remember growing up with as it started, right? So everybody knows where the roots of rock 'n' roll are. But to make such an intellectual game out of it is beside the point. It's not really going to add anything to the history of popular music. It's just going to feed a lot of cynical and self-righteous people who think they've got a claim on a rock 'n' roll gold mine or whatever. So I find that very distasteful.

Kleinman: Are there any things that you look back on and say, "Jesus, that was a good one."

Dylan: Oh, yeah. Some of the songs you're talking about, I can't write those songs today. No way. But I look at those songs, 'cause I sing 'em all the time. I wonder where they came from and how it's constructed. Even the simpler songs, I look at them that way. I couldn't do them now, and I'd be a fool to try. I think there are a lot of good songwriters, though. What I've done I've done all alone, but there's a lot of other good songwriters of my era.

Mogull: Like who, Bob?

Dylan: Randy Newman writes good songs. Paul Simon's written some good songs. I think "America" is a good song. "The Boxer" is a good song. "Bridge Over Troubled Water" is a good song. I mean, he's written a lot of bad songs, too, but everybody's done that. Let's see . . . some of the Nashville writers: Shel Silverstein writes great songs. Really. Like he's one of my favorite songwriters. You know, whatever you're expressing is out of the amount of knowledge and light and inspiration you're giving on it. If you're just given an inch . . . well, you've just got to make of that as much as you can.

Kleinman: Have you ever tried your hand at any of the other arts?

Dylan: Yeah, painting.

Kleinman: Really? Do you do much of it?

Dylan: Well, not so much in recent years, but it's something that I would like to do if I could. You've got to be in the right place to do it. You have to commit a lot of time, because one thing leads to another and you tend to discover new things as you go along. So it takes time to develop it, but I know how to do it fundamentally so once I get into the rhythm of it, and if I can hang with it long enough . . .

Kleinman: Do you take time for yourself?

Dylan: Oh, yeah. I don't have any public time. People think I do but that's my time.

Kleinman: That's a great place to be.

Dylan: Well, that's the place you were at when you were born. That's the place you should be. I mean, what's there to make you not be in that place? Do you have to be part of the machine? So what if you're not part of the machine?

[*Commercial break.*]

Dylan: I don't know if I've ever been happy if we're talking straight. I don't consider myself happy and I don't consider myself unhappy. I've just never thought of life in terms of happiness and unhappiness. It just never occurred to me.

Kleinman: Do you think of it in terms of growth?

Dylan: No! I tell you what I do think, though, that you never stop anywhere. There's no place to stop in. You know them places at the side of the road that you can stop? They're just an illusion.

Kleinman: The road goes on.

Dylan: Yeah, you've got to get back on the road. And you may want to stop but you can't stay there.

Kleinman: When you talk about getting back on the road, isn't that in a sense growth? Or at least it's movement. From point A to point B.

Dylan: Yeah, that's growth. But what's growth? I mean, everything grows, that's just the way life is—life just grows. It grows and it dies, it lives and it dies. Whenever you get to a plateau, that's not it, you got to go on to the next one. You can't stay nowhere, there's no place to stay, there's no place that will keep you.

Kleinman: Because of boredom or because that's the way it is?

Dylan: No, because that's just the nature of things.

Kleinman: So you see yourself just moving onward?

Dylan: I see everybody like that. I see the whole world that way. That which doesn't do that is stuff that's just dead.

Kleinman: Ha . . . what's that line? Those that are not busy being born are—

Dylan: Busy dying? What a line!

Kleinman: Didn't somebody write that?

Dylan: Classic line that. You know, people say, "Isn't it great to be able to do what you do?" Well, it is to a degree but they forget that anybody that is out touring, playing live from town to town night after night—they think that's easy. It's not easy. People think you're having a ball. They say, "How ya doin'?" I say, "I'm in Schenectady!" [*Laughter.*] And they say, "Oh, well, you're having a great time and I'm stuck here in Orlando."

When I get off the road, oh, man! For the first two or three weeks you can get up any time you want! You don't have to go to sleep at this hour and get up at that hour, and get yourself lined up to do this, and be there at that certain place, and go through this and go through that, and get back and get the proper amount of sleep. You know, eat right . . . in case you're afraid you'll get sick, or afraid you're gonna hurt yourself somewhere along the line. All those things, they just disappear on the last show. Then you can do anything you want. It's a high feeling.

Kleinman: You go sailing? [*Long silence.*] Yeah?

Dylan: Yeah.

Kleinman: Do you want to talk about anything you like to do other than—

Dylan: I like to do a lot of things, but I don't want to talk about the things I like to do.

Kleinman: OK.

Dylan: I'll talk about things I don't like to do!

Kleinman: You said that you consider yourself a pretty regular kind of a guy. Would you say you're just like anybody else?

Dylan: Sure. I breathe the same air as everybody else does. I have to do the same things most people do.

Kleinman: In a lot of the earlier songs there's a sense of separation.

Dylan: Oh, well, there's always a sense of separation, even in the later songs. There wouldn't be any point to it if there wasn't a sense of separation. If I didn't have anything different to say to people, then what would be the point of it? I could do a Ronettes album!

Mogull: I think the most interesting thing you've said so far, Bob—

Dylan: Have I said anything interesting?

Mogull: One thing that was exceedingly interesting to me was when you started writing because nobody was writing the songs you wanted to sing.

Dylan: Yeah, that's when I started writing, and that's why I'm still writing. I wish someone would give me some songs that I could do. It would be such a burden taken off my shoulder. It's heavy, man!

[*Laughter.*]

Kleinman: There's still a lot of expectation. Have you been able to get beyond that, to stop worrying about what people expect from you?

Dylan: Anybody that expects anything from me is just a borderline case. Nobody with any kind of reality is going to expect anything from me. I've already given them enough. What do they want from me? You can't keep on depending on one person to give you everything.

What I usually do is say, OK, I'm gonna write a song, whether it's a lyric or a rhythm, but I have to go out and play, and I'm not an admirer of stuff like videos. I don't mind making videos, but it's nothing for me to attempt to do because it's fake. It's all about how good it looks. Anybody can make a video. As long as you have a camera. Anybody can do it. And anybody can make a good one, and people will like it. Everything is done in a technological kind of way. You can dress it up in so many different ways. So people don't know what to think. Nobody's gonna sit there and say, "Oh, this is bullshit," or "This is awful . . . this don't make any sense." It's been a long time since I've even seen one of those things, but the last time I saw one, I was appalled. And then when you go see some of these groups, they aren't anything. That's because they go for the faking thing so much. And, in the other arena, you have to do it live or you just don't do it. I've always played live since I started, and that's where it's always counted for me. It don't count on a video or a movie. I don't care about being a movie star or a video star or any of that stuff.

[*Commercial break.*]

Dylan: I'm usually in a numb state of mind before my shows, and I have to kick in at some place along the line. Usually it takes me one or two songs, or sometimes now it takes much longer. Sometimes it takes me up to the encore! [*Laughs.*]

Kleinman: The band, I would imagine, has an effect on that.

Dylan: Oh, absolutely. I've played with some bands that have gotten in my way so much that it's just been a struggle to get through the show. At certain times it gets ridiculous.

Kleinman: I'd imagine the flip side, too. Have there been bands that turn you on?

Dylan: Yeah, this last band. I thought they were pretty good.

Kleinman: Rolling Thunder was an interesting tour. It wasn't just the performing but the whole idea of the thing. There was a spontaneity of a kind to it.

Dylan: Yeah, there was definitely a lot of spontaneity to that.

Kleinman: Was it scary or exciting?

Dylan: A little of both. We were doing double shows on the Rolling Thunder shows. We'd be in a hall, say, for fourteen hours. You know, Rolling Thunder shows were six hours long!

Kleinman: That had to be people loving making music.

Dylan: Well [*laughing*], there were so many people. You know, the people in the audience came and went. People would bring their lunch or dinner or something.

Mogull: Like a Grateful Dead concert?

Dylan: Yeah.

Kleinman: Was that your idea? Did it come from you?

Dylan: No, it just happened. We started out with a small show and it just evolved.

Kleinman: That's an amazing thing to me, that you're able to maintain that. A lot of people, when they get to a certain place in the business—

Dylan: I thought the Rolling Thunder shows were great. I think someday somebody should make a movie out of them!

Kleinman: And call it . . .

Dylan: Rolling Thunder!

Kleinman: [*Laughs.*] You've been smiling and laughing a lot here, but you don't do that much on stage. But you say you really enjoy yourself. You look so serious.

Dylan: Well, those songs take you through different trips. What's there to smile about in singing "A Hard Rain's A-Gonna Fall" or "Tangled Up in Blue" or "With God on Our Side" or "Mr. Tambourine Man" or "Like a Rolling Stone" or "License to Kill" or "Shot of Love" or "Poisoned Love"? Any of that. How can you sing that with a smile on your face? It'd be kind of hypocritical.

You'll do things on certain nights, which you know are just great, and you'll get no response. And then you'll go someplace else and you just don't have it that night, for a variety of reasons, and you're just trying to get through it. But you've got to get it to a place where it's consistent. Then it stays on that level. It can get great, which is really triple consistent. I've done things where I might have had a temperature of 104, or I might have been kicked in the side that day. I have done shows where I could hardly stand up.

And that's kind of humiliating in a way. Before it even starts, you know you're not gonna be as good not even as you wanna be but as you can be. There's only been one time when I've wanted to replay one show. We played a show in Montreal in 1978. I had a temperature of

104, couldn't even stand up. But the promotor said, "Well, you gotta play the show." And we played the show and I didn't have nothing—nothing! And the response, you'd think the pope was there! [*Laughter.*] And I've played other shows where I've had everything happening—I mean, I just rewrote the book. Nothing—no response.

When I do whatever it is I'm doing, there is rhythm involved and there is phrasing involved. And that's where it all balances out, in the rhythm and the phrasing. People think it's in the lyrics. Maybe on the records it's in the lyrics, but in a live show it's in the phrasing and the dynamics and the rhythm. It's got nothing whatsoever to do with the lyrics. The lyrics have to be there, sure they do. But . . . you know, there was this Egyptian singer Om Kalsoum. Have you ever heard of her? She was one of my favorite singers of all time, and I don't understand a word she sings! She'd sing one song—it might last forty minutes—and she'll sing the same phrase over and over and over again. But in a different way every time. I don't think there's any Western singer that's in that category . . . except possibly me! [*Laughter.*] But on another level, do you know what I mean?

[*Commercial break.*]

Dylan: To me, it's not a business, and to the people who have survived along with me, it's not a business. It's never been a business and never will be. It is just a way of surviving. It's just what you do. It's just like somebody who's trained to be a carpenter—that's what they do best. And that's how they make a living, I guess.

Kleinman: Were you ever going to be anything else? Were you ever going to be an insurance salesman?

Dylan: I was never gonna be anything else, never. I was playing when I was twelve years old, and that was all I wanted to do—play my guitar. I was always going to these parties where all these biggest guys were, and it was a way of getting attention. It starts out that way but I never really knew where it was going to lead. Now that it's led me here, I still don't know where it is.

Kleinman: You're older than you were in the '60s, but also you seem to have a degree of self-knowledge and certainty of where you're going as a person.

Dylan: I don't know where I'm going as a person.

Mogull: I hear contentment . . .

Dylan: Well, in certain areas, yeah, I hope so. I don't know what's gonna happen when I'm not around to sing anymore. I hope somebody comes along who could pick up on what I'm doing and learn exactly what it is that makes it quite different. I keep looking for that somebody, not necessarily to cover me, but to take it a step further. I've already taken it as far as I can take it. Maybe I won't see that person. I don't know. But somebody, sometime, will come along and take it that step further. But I haven't seen anyone. Now I don't want to say that in a bragging sort of way; it just hasn't gone any further.

Kleinman: But there is something . . . that's why you go back to the stage.

Dylan: Yeah, well, I'm just thankful I can play and people will come and see me. Because I couldn't make it otherwise. If I went out to play and nobody showed up, that would be the end of me. I wouldn't be making records, I'll tell you that. I only make records because people see me live. So as long as they're coming along to see me live I'll just make some more records.

RADIO INTERVIEW

Bob Coburn | June 17, 1985 | *Rockline*, **KLOS-FM (Los Angeles)**

By the time you finish this book, you'll have read lots of questions for Dylan from critics, radio personalities, and fellow musicians. But what would ordinary fans ask him if they had the chance? We got some strange answers to that question in Dylan's 1966 appearance on Bob Fass's overnight program on New York's WBAI. Here are some decidedly more straightforward ones, from fans who called in to a program hosted by Bob Coburn of Los Angeles–area station KLOS-FM. This was Dylan's first radio call-in show since the Fass appearance, and it aired live via satellite throughout the United States and Canada.

The conversation took place only a week after the release of *Empire Burlesque*, an album widely viewed as an attempt to update Dylan's sound. (As coproducer, he'd enlisted Arthur Baker, who was known for his work with hip-hop artists.) The CD reached only as high as number thirty-three on the American charts, perhaps partly because Dylan didn't support it with a tour. But it contains some strong material, including the catchy "Tight Connection to My Heart (Has Anybody Seen My Love)" and two of the artist's most effusive 1980s compositions, "Emotionally Yours" and "I'll Remember You." —Ed.

Bob Coburn: Hello, again. I'm Bob Coburn, your host for *Rockline*, brought to you by Budweiser, the king of beers. Tonight, *Rockline* has a very special evening with Bob Dylan. As always, we have plenty of phone lines but just one number to remember in the US: that number is toll-free, 1 (800) 222-ROCK, that's 1 (800) 222-7625. And one number for Canada too, toll-free as well: 1 (800) 344-ROCK. *Empire Burlesque*, the new release by Bob Dylan, rekindles the wit, spirit, and leadership that Dylan embodied in the '60s and early '70s. This album sizzles with emotions, stimulates with intellect, and satisfies musically. And *Rockline* welcomes Bob Dylan. Nice to have you here tonight.

Bob Dylan: Nice to be here.

Coburn: Now this is, amazingly, the first American release that you've given us with printed lyrics and the first one you've self-produced. Why did it take so long to get to that point?

Dylan: Well, I put the lyrics on so nobody would mistake the words, which so often they do, as you know.

Coburn: Aha, and why wait so long to self-produce? Did you finally feel that you could do it better than anybody else? The way that you want it this time?

Dylan: Yeah, I did.

Coburn: That's really it? Thirty releases, most of them have been really landmark releases. How do you feel about this current release? Is this one of your best, do you think?

Dylan: I like it.

Coburn: Well, we're going to hear a bunch of songs from it tonight. And we'll put you on the air with Bob Dylan, too. Right now, a song from *Empire Burlesque*, "Tight Connection to Your [*sic*] Heart."

[*"Tight Connection to My Heart (Has Anybody Seen My Love)" plays.*]

Coburn: It's an evening with Bob Dylan tonight on *Rockline*. I'm Bob Coburn and our first phone call for you, Bob, is from Chicago. Doug, this is Bob Dylan.

Caller: Hi, Bob, how are you?

Dylan: Oh, I'm doing all right.

Caller: Good. I've just got to say that I think your new album is fantastic, and I was just wondering if you're going to tour, and if so, who's going to be in your band?

Dylan: Oh, I don't know just yet. I might use some old people I've used and probably some new people.

Coburn: You are going to go on tour, though?

Dylan: Oh, yeah, I always do.

Coburn: Yeah, it seems like it. Well, there was a period quite a few years ago where sometimes you didn't, but that has changed. Any players on the album you think might be in there? You've got some big stars on the album, Mick Taylor and Ron Wood.

Dylan: Well, Mick was with me on the last tour I did, and there's always talk about Sly and Robbie.

Coburn: As the rhythm section. We'll wait and find out. Thanks for the call, Doug. Now we have a call from Knoxville, Tennessee. Alan, you're on the show.

Caller: Hi, Bob. I wanted to say thanks for the last twenty-three years of music, and I really do love your new album.

Dylan: Well, thank you.

Caller: I was wondering what poets you feel have had the most influence on your writing?

Dylan: Hmm, John Keats. I used to read him quite a bit. Now, let's see, the French poet Arthur Rimbaud and all those guys in the '50s—Ginsberg and Corso and those guys—

Coburn: Anything else, Alan?

Caller: No, I think that's it.

Coburn: All right. Thanks for the call. There's a joke that's been running around: Sylvester Stallone starring as Arthur Rimbaud.

Dylan: Oh, yeah.

Coburn: We'll talk to Ronald. He's in Carlisle, Ohio, in Dayton. Hi, there.

Caller: Hi there, Bob. I just want to say that it's a great honor for me to talk to one of the great Christian rock artists of the century. And was it a big inspiration for you to have Jimi Hendrix record your song "All Along the Watchtower"?

Coburn: Was that a big thrill for you or what were your feelings at the time?

Dylan: Oh, yeah, that was a big thrill. He recorded "All Along the Watchtower" and another song off *John Wesley Harding* called "Drifter's Escape," I think. And he recorded "Like a Rolling Stone." But he made "All Along the Watchtower" something different. When we play it now in person it's more like how Jimi would have played it.

Coburn: What were you going to say there, Ronald?

Caller: I thought it was really a great song.

Coburn: When that album came out, it wasn't received as one of your best records, but in retrospect, it appears to be one of your strongest albums—*John Wesley Harding*. What do you feel about that?

Dylan: I don't know if it really was one of the strongest albums. It was OK.

Coburn: You just think that is an OK record?

Dylan: I do, yeah.

Coburn: Huh, interesting. Thanks for the call, Ronald. We'll turn our view to Brooklyn now. Rich, you're on the *Rockline*.

Caller: Hello, I'll get right to my question. I'd like to know who are the women on the back of the *Infidels* album cover and the latest album cover?

Dylan: Hmm, let's see. The women?

Coburn: Well, there's one woman on the back.

Dylan: Oh, yeah, there's half a woman! That's a picture that was taken at a party somewhere. As you can see by my expression in the picture, I don't really know who she is even. [*Laughs.*]

Coburn: It's a drawing on *Infidels*.

Dylan: Oh, that picture. Who is that?

Coburn: Do you remember who those people are? This is just a drawing.

Dylan: Hmm, well, the woman is someone I knew. [*Laughs.*] The man I think I was wishing to be me, I guess.

Caller: The striking resemblance to Joan Baez, especially the sketch on the last album cover.

Dylan: Oh yeah! It does kind of look like her, but it's not her, though.

Coburn: It's not her. Good try, though, Rich.

Caller: Oh, by the way, I just had one more small question. What do you think of Joan Baez's imitation of you during her concerts?

Dylan: Well, I think Joan is fabulous. Anything she does usually sounds pretty good.

Caller: OK, thanks a lot. Nice talking to you, Bob.

Coburn: Thanks for the call, Rich. Our numbers are toll-free in Canada and the US. From the album *Infidels* that we were just kind of looking at the back of, this is "Neighborhood Bully," by Bob Dylan on *Rockline*.

[*"Neighborhood Bully" plays.*]

Coburn: *Infidels*, "Neighborhood Bully," by Bob Dylan, my guest tonight for the full ninety minutes tonight, on *Rockline*, and we wouldn't have it any other way. We have a call from Toronto. John, you're on the *Rockline*.

Caller: Hi, Bob. You worked with Mark Knopfler on a couple of albums. How did that come about?

Dylan: Well, I met Mark on the *Slow Train* album, and we just kept in touch over the years.

Coburn: Did you get in touch with him and say, "Hey, come play on my record?" Or did he call you? How did it happen?

Dylan: The first time it was [producer] Jerry Wexler who did that, and then the second time I ran into him in New York, and he had just released the previous album to his latest one.

Coburn: He certainly has his own style, but people in the beginning especially were saying he sounds a lot like Bob Dylan. Did somebody say that maybe you two should get together?

Dylan: No, not really. Jerry recommended him to play on that album, and I went down to see him and I thought he sounded sort of like me, not really but a little bit.

Coburn: Yeah, just a touch maybe. He's a great player. Thanks for the call, John.

Dylan: I don't play anything like guitar like he does, though.

Coburn: Yeah. He can really play some leads. We have another call from Chicago; they're cooking there tonight. And we'll talk to Rich. Hi, Rich.

Caller: Hi, Bob. Yeah. This is Rich Ingle from Chicago. How you doing?

Dylan: I'm doing all right.

Caller: Good. I'd like to ask you about a tape I've heard, which sounds like it comes off an acetate from the *Self Portrait* sessions, and on the tape you do the song "Yesterday." What I'd like to know is, was George Harrison at the session and did he play on that with you?

Dylan: Well, I don't remember that.

Caller: Maybe I can help refresh your memory. Also on that session you did the song "Da Doo Ron Ron."

Dylan: Hmm.

Caller: You don't remember it yet?

Dylan: Well, it must have been an old one. [*Laughs.*]

Caller: It sounds like it's from *Self Portrait*. It sounds like that period. You also did an electric version of "Song to Woody" and "Mama, You Been on My Mind."

Dylan: Oh! Well, maybe George was playing on that. We did do some sessions.

Caller: Did you do an album together that you didn't release or something?

Dylan: I don't think so.

Caller: No. How about that new song that he has out that you wrote—"I Don't Want to Do It."

Dylan: Oh, yeah, he dug that up somewhere.

Caller: Was that from around that time?

Dylan: Yes, it was.

Caller: OK, Bob. I just wanna tell you that I think that the new album is great and just keep up the great work.

Dylan: Well, thank you.

Coburn: Thanks for the call there, Rich. Do you have tons of material that's never been released? I know you recorded over twenty songs for *Empire Burlesque*. Is there a lot of backlog material?

Dylan: There's a lot of stuff that's laying around. Some are songs and some are just parts.

Coburn: I'd like to see some of that stuff. We'll talk to Michael now. He's in Norfolk, Virginia. You're on the show, Michael.

Caller: Good evening, Bob. How you doing?

Dylan: I'm doing fine.

Caller: What have you been listening to recently? Any good music?

Dylan: Hmm, you ever heard of a group called Fishbone? I thought they're pretty good.

Caller: You been listening to any jazz?

Dylan: Oh, yeah.

Caller: Tell me something. Did you ever record any tunes as Blind Boy Grunt?

Dylan: I'm sure I did. [*Laughs.*] That was a few years ago, I think.

Caller: OK, Bob. I just wanna say thanks for the thrill.

Coburn: Thanks for the call, Michael. We appreciate it. We'll talk to Peter now in Santa Monica. How you doing, Peter?

Caller: Oh, I'm doing great. I'm very excited to talk to Bob.

Coburn: Well, take advantage of it. You're on the air.

Caller: Oh, great. The question I wanted to ask is that I consider you one of the people who have proven that one person can change the world, make a difference in the world. First of all, I want to ask you if you agree with that and, if no, respond to that.

Dylan: Oh yeah, I do agree with that. I don't know if I've ever done anything like that but a lot of the great changes in the world were brought about by one person for sure.

Caller: Aha, do you think that in the '60s, there was that energy? Everybody was listening to your music and it promoted them to do things. Whereas here in the '80s there's more of a hope that one person can't do as much. Do you feel that that's what's happening?

Dylan: Well, maybe, but that'll probably change.

Caller: All right, I want to identify myself as Peter Landecker, the person who's doing this show about you. I've put together this show, which is a collection of your words and music. The thing I'm concerned about is when people see this show—a collection of your words and music—and they're going to leave the theater, what kind of a feeling would you want them to leave with?

Dylan: I don't really know, 'cause I do my own shows. So somebody else who's doing them, I don't know what they're doing.

Coburn: We'll take a time out and return with Bob Dylan, our guest for the full ninety minutes on *Rockline*.

[*Commercial break.*]

Coburn: We're gonna play a song now that was done by the Textones. It's on Bob's new album. He wrote it, of course. It's called "Clean Cut Kid."

[*"Clean Cut Kid" plays.*]

Coburn: Ron Wood of Stones fame on guitar on that track, sounding good. We're going to talk to somebody in Little Rock, Arkansas, right now, and this is Rust. Is that correct?

Caller: That's right. Hello there, Mr. Dylan. I want to say one thing first before I ask my question. I want to tell you that you're number one on the top of my list of musicians, for the simple reason that when I was twelve years old I listened to you, and I picked up the harmonica and I'm still playing, and I'm twenty-eight years old. Well, my question is, have you ever planned to take any of your private works and poetry and maybe simultaneously with autobiography write a book?

Dylan: No, I never did plan that. I haven't had time. I've been asked about it, though. Maybe one of these days.

Caller: Aha, and I think that producing your own LP there is a great accomplishment, and I hope to hear a lot from you in the future because I think that you're one of the best, sir.

Dylan: Well, thank you.

Coburn: All right. That's a from-the-heart call and we appreciate it. We'll talk to somebody in Milwaukee now. His name is Randy. Randy, meet Bob Dylan.

Caller: Hi, Bob. Listen, in 1976, I bought your album [*Desire*] and "Hurricane" struck me first, but "Isis" has always haunted me and I wanted to know what you meant by the song.

Dylan: Hmm . . . well, it's kind of like a journey. I wrote that with another person, and I think half the verses were mine and half the verses were his, and it just sort of ended up being what it was. I don't really know too much in depth what it would mean.

Coburn: Who did you cowrite that with?

Dylan: Jacques Levy.

Coburn: And the basis, I guess, is Egyptian mythology, Isis being a goddess. Is that what it stemmed from?

Dylan: [*Laughs.*] I guess so.

Coburn: You're not sure. Anything else on your mind there, Randy?

Caller: Well, "Like a Rolling Stone" is my favorite song and I appreciate him writing that. And I want to tell him that.

Coburn: Right. We appreciate that. We'll talk to Philip now. Where you calling from, Phil?

Caller: I'm calling from Indiana.

Coburn: OK. You're on the air.

Caller: Yeah. Hi, Bob. I was wondering how did you get involved in the USA for Africa [project]?

Dylan: Oh, Ken Cregan had called and asked me about it.

Coburn: And who is Ken Cregan? What does he do?

Dylan: Well, he put that together. He's the manager of Lionel Richie. That's how I got involved.

Coburn: Did you have any hesitation or say, "Yeah, I'll be there." What was your reaction?

Dylan: Oh, I said I'll be there.

Coburn: And you were. We're gonna listen to a song that's Randy's favorite cut. How can we not play "Like a Rolling Stone" by Bob Dylan on *Rockline*?

[*"Like a Rolling Stone" plays.*]

Coburn: A song that's burned into the mind of anyone who went through the '60s, "Like a Rolling Stone," originally on *Highway 61 Revisited.* So many of your songs, Bob, have been re-recorded by other people, yet I don't think I've ever heard another version of that. Have you? Is there another version of that?

Dylan: Yeah. Jimi Hendrix did it, and a couple of others did it.

Coburn: Oh, yeah, that's right. Boy, that's a song that you'd better do something really fine with, 'cause that one you don't mess with. That one's sacrosanct almost. We'll talk to Jeff now. He's in Knoxville, Tennessee. Jeff, you're on the *Rockline.*

Caller: Well, what I wanted to ask you, Bob, was what possessed you to change your name from Robert Zimmerman to Bob Dylan?

Dylan: Hmm, that's an interesting question. I really can't say. It's been so long. I think I was just playing somewhere one night and the club owner asked me what my name was, and that was the name that came into my mind. I don't think there was anything really profound about it.

Coburn: Are the stories that it was taken from the poet Dylan Thomas true?

Dylan: I think I'd heard that story [*laughs*] and I knew who Dylan Thomas was, but I'm not sure if I was familiar with his poetry or not.

Coburn: Yeah. Interesting, Jeff. Did you have another question?

Caller: Well, the second part of my question was, what's your favorite album and your favorite song? That's what I wanted to know.

Dylan: Favorite album? I think the Robert Johnson album. I listen to that quite a bit still.

Coburn: Some of that old blues stuff, huh? Do you have a favorite of any of your records? Is there one that stands out as your all-time album?

Dylan: Hmm, I like 'em all when I make 'em. And then I don't listen to them too often after they're released.

Coburn: Time to move on, I guess. Thanks for the call. We'll talk to Ken now. He's in Cleveland. Hi.

Caller: Hi, how you doing, Bob?

Dylan: I'm doing all right.

Caller: I'd just like to comment. The Young Rascals also did "Like a Rolling Stone." Also, my favorite song is your "[Bob Dylan's] 115th Dream" on *Bringing It All Back Home*. That brings me to my question. Right before the release of that album, there was a rumor [about] an album called *Bob Dylan in Concert*, and the rumors are that there was a disagreement between you and Columbia over what would be on the album and it was never released. Any chance of us hearing it ever?

Dylan: Hmm, that may have been the second album. They asked me to change a few songs, I think.

Caller: The "John Birch Society Blues" material?

Dylan: Yeah, I think they requested that I drop that from the record.

Caller: Do you think in these less prudent times that it could come out?

Dylan: [*Laughs.*] Yeah. It probably could now.

Caller: Well, you gonna shoot for it, maybe?

Coburn: [*Laughs.*] Definite ulterior motive there. Fire off a letter to the record company and see what you can get going there, Ken.

Dylan: They have the rights to that. They could release it.

Caller: Well, I'll bet you'll have a little more push in the matter than I would.

Coburn: You might have a point there. Thank you for the call, Ken. We appreciate it. It's Jim's turn. He's in Toronto. Hi, Jim.

Caller: Oh, hi. First of all, I've got to say that this is like talking on heaven's line. You're it to me, you're the end all. I guess what I want to ask you about is creative desire in general. But, to pose it, I'm an artist and I'm just starting out, and I want to know how you think your music has changed from the beginning when you had to give in to some kind of commercial ideas, compared to now where you're basically set and you can record whatever you want. Has that affected you?

Dylan: Well, I've just about all the time recorded whatever I want, but my music, my musicianship, is so limited that I just work within that sound. I stay pretty much to that so I can do most anything I wanna do within that small framework.

Caller: It hasn't really ever changed then, from when you first started out?

Dylan: No, I don't think so.

Caller: The other thing I wanted to ask you, and I've read an awful lot about you, and I've also read about other artists in general because I am an artist—a painter. You don't seem to have gone through, at least to my knowledge, any kind of really trying times that most of the other artists have that have reached the heights and success that you have. I'm talking artistically, not commercially. Is there anything I'm missing? Is there anything that sort of changed your direction in life, that gave you the creative desire that made you so prolific?

Dylan: No, I can't say what it is. A lot of times, I even think about stopping. But sometimes it just keeps coming, so as long as it does, I just keep bringing it out.

Coburn: Yeah, don't stop, please. Jim's hit on a really good point, in that in the early days you sounded like you had been around and really paid the dues, but were only eighteen years old, back in the early days when you left Minnesota and went to New York. You don't know what you had? That explains it all. Bob Dylan says, if you want somebody you can trust, "Trust Yourself."

[*"Trust Yourself" plays.*]

Coburn: A couple of Heartbreakers on that song, Mike Campbell and Benmont Tench. Bob Dylan's "Trust Yourself" from *Empire Burlesque*. . . . Still plenty more time for you to talk to Bob Dylan tonight on *Rockline*. I'm Bob Coburn. Marie called from Pittsburgh. Hi.

Caller: Hi. First, I'd like to wish you a happy birthday, a little belated.

Dylan: Well, thank you.

Caller: I was wondering, are you going to do any more movies, like *Don't Look Back* or *Pat Garrett* [*and Billy the Kid*]?

Dylan: Oh, I sure hope so. [*Laughs.*]

Coburn: A little tongue in cheek there. Do you seriously have any plans for doing anything, or are you going to avoid that?

Dylan: Well, somebody sent me a script the other day. I don't know what makes them think I could do it, but it's a fairly interesting script.

Coburn: Ha, so don't rule that out. Thanks for the call, Marie. We'll talk to Brian now. He's in Warren, Ohio. You're on the show, Brian.

Caller: Hi, how you doing, Bob?

Dylan: I'm doing all right.

Caller: I notice you've been touring a lot in Europe. What do you like better, the European audiences or the American, and why?

Dylan: Mostly they're all the same. Sometimes in a foreign country you wonder how people can understand what you're saying. But it seems like they can. Maybe when you go over to Europe and play, you've gone so far to do it, maybe people appreciate it differently.

Coburn: But there's really no discernible difference? The crowds are the crowds?

Dylan: Yeah, it's just whether you're playing in an indoor arena or outdoors. There's difference in those kind of different kinda places you play. There's a different kind of vibe in the air.

Coburn: We're gonna play another song from *Empire Burlesque*. This one is a bit lengthy but we wanted to get this on tonight. This is a song that's a tour de force from the latest LP, *Empire Burlesque*. Bob Dylan on *Rockline*, "When the Night Comes Falling from the Sky."

[*"When the Night Comes Falling from the Sky" plays.*]

Coburn: "When the Night Comes Falling from the Sky" is the name of that song. Bob Dylan reunited with Al Kooper, who worked on so many of the earlier Bob Dylan LPs. Nice to hear him back in the fold again. That's from *Empire Burlesque*. We'll take a brief time out and return with more.

[*Commercials air.*]

Coburn: It's a very special evening with Bob Dylan tonight on *Rockline*. I'm Bob Coburn. We're back on the phone lines. A call from Virginia . . .Tommy, you're on the air.

Caller: Yeah, Mr. Dylan, let me start by saying that I really enjoy your music, and your music is very deep and prophetic, very much like the late John Lennon. And I was just wondering what inspired you to write the song "Like a Rolling Stone."

[*Pause.*]

Coburn: Do you remember the inspiration for that?

Dylan: Well, it was just a riff, really. It was like the "La Bamba" riff.

Coburn: You mean Ritchie Valens.

Dylan: Yeah. I was just fooling with that, I think.

Coburn: What were you going to say there, Tommy?

Caller: I was thinking, was there any significance to the time period or anything? Did it tell a story?

Dylan: Well, yeah. It was so long ago I can't really remember the inspiration for it, but . . .

Caller: OK, I really appreciate talking to you. It's been a great honor.

Coburn: Thanks for the call, Tommy. You know, it's hard to say what a song means because it means what it means to the person that hears it. That's the beauty . . . that's called art.

Dylan: Yeah, it means what it means.

Coburn: Yeah. Let's talk to David. He's in Sierra Madre. David, how are you tonight?

Caller: I'm pretty good. Me and my buddy Pete would like to wish you a late happy birthday. And I was wondering, are you ever going to release the soundtrack to *Renaldo and Clara*?

Dylan: I think that is released. Well, maybe four songs from it. But that's a good idea. I'd like to release that, but the record company usually have their own idea what they like to release and what they don't.

Caller: Well, I watched the four-hour version a couple of times [*Dylan laughs*] and I wonder, was there any particular meaning behind that movie? I never really caught it. I just went to see the music.

Dylan: Well, there was, but it's hard to put it into words. I don't think I can put it into one line.

Caller: You probably can't explain it in the time that we've got.

Dylan: No.

Coburn: Well, thanks, David. Nice talking to you. OK, Bob, we'll talk to George now, in Detroit. George, meet Bob Dylan.

Caller: Hi, Bob, how you doing?

Dylan: I'm doing all right.

Caller: How are your kids?

Dylan: Fine.

Caller: That's good. A guy a couple before me already asked my question about what a song means to you. I was going to ask you about a personal favorite song of mine, an old one, "It's Alright, Ma (I'm Only Bleeding)." I was wondering if that was the situation in the '60s that caused you to write that or if you could view that as your own personal philosophy on life? I think that's a very strong song.

Dylan: Well, I still do that song. It's still very relevant to me.

Caller: Do you play it in concert?

Dylan: Yes, I do.

Caller: Oh, wow. I hope you come around soon to Detroit.

Dylan: Well, I hope I do, and I hope you come.

Caller: I'll be there, front row, me and all my friends. We're big fans of yours, Bob.

Coburn: That brings up a good point. How do you pick what you play live, out of thirty albums? Is it the closest to the heart, or new material? What do you do?

Dylan: Well, usually you just kind of go over the stuff that you can remember, and then once in a while somebody will suggest something else . . . I've had people in my bands say, "Let's do this song," and they've taught it back to me.

Coburn: Really! Interesting. Boy, you really do remove yourself from it when time goes by, don't you?

Dylan: Well, there's so many songs. Sometimes on the old records we used to make—I hate to think of them as what you call filler songs—but sometimes you'd do a song, just write it in five or ten minutes and do it, and not think much more of it. But it sticks in your mind after, and it sticks in other people's minds and you think, well, maybe we'll play it.

Coburn: Yeah. Let's take a Canadian call. We'll talk to Rick. He's in Kitchener. Hi, Rick.

Caller: Hi. How are you, Bob?

Dylan: I'm all right.

Caller: I'd just like to say that *John Wesley Harding* was a great album by you and that if I didn't happen to hear that song "Frankie Lee and Judas Priest," I probably wouldn't be calling you right now. It's a super album. Now, there's one other question I'd like to ask. In 1980, when you played Massey Hall [in Toronto] you did four concerts in a row and they were filming it every night. I was wondering, is there any sort of documentary or anything coming up on that?

Dylan: Hmm, well, they do a lot of filming at different shows sometimes. I don't remember that.

Caller: Well, we were there for four nights, and I've never seen you perform so great. It was just unbelievably super fantastic, as they say. And I just want to thank you. I really appreciate all you've done for the last twenty years of music, for me and other people in general.

Dylan: Well, thank you for saying that.

Coburn: Thanks, Rick, we appreciate it. We're gonna play a song now that . . . I'm glad that you mentioned this when we met before the program tonight, Bob, because *Blonde on Blonde* is, I guess, my favorite Bob Dylan album. Everybody's got their own favorite. You wanted us to play "Obviously Five Believers." Why do you still want us to play that song?

Dylan: I just like it.

Coburn: Here it is.

[*"Obviously Five Believers" plays.*]

Coburn: Some pretty nasty blues harmonica there, Bob Dylan.

Dylan: That's not me, though.

Coburn: That's not you, though? Who is it?

Dylan: That's Charlie McCoy.

Coburn: All right, good harmonica from McCoy there, the real McCoy. We'll take a brief time out and come back.

[*Commercial break.*]

Coburn: Now it's been quite a long time since there was a song on one of Bob's albums that just features Bob, his guitar, and his harmonica. There's one on this album, *Empire Burlesque*. It's called "Dark Eyes," and we'll listen to it now.

[*"Dark Eyes" plays.*]

Coburn: I listen to the words that you write, and it leaves me breathless. I know that you work hard on what you write, but does it come easy to you or do you really have to sit down and force yourself?

Dylan: That particular song just sort of came, well, I won't say easy, but it's all in one piece like that.

Coburn: Amazing. Let's talk to Mike. He's in Batesville. Mike, how are you tonight?

Caller: Pretty good. Bob, you're the greatest. OK, my question is, why was Carla Olson of the Textones chosen for the video of "Sweetheart Like You," instead of Mark Knopfler, who really played on it?

Dylan: Well, when we did the video, it was impossible to get Mark to play because he was on tour.

Coburn: Oh, so that answers that. You just couldn't get him. Thanks for the call, Mike. We'll talk to Carl now. We're about to run out of time, so I'm gonna move it up a little bit here. Carl's in Berlin, Connecticut. Carl, you're on.

Caller: Thank you. Oh, Bob, I was just wondering, between your first and second album, you seemed to go through a transition. Obviously, you got to write only two songs on your first album and then you wrote all of them on the second album, I believe. What was the story behind that?

Dylan: I don't think I was writing too many songs on the first album. If I did, I probably didn't think they were good enough to record. Then, by the second one, I think I'd been writing for a longer period of time.

Coburn: Thanks for the call, Carl. We have time for one more. It's Michael in California. Hi, Michael.

Caller: Hi, Bob. What have your feelings been lately on your influence on other musicians?

Dylan: Well, I don't have any feelings about it. It's nice to see that but I don't know. You don't really think about it too much. I don't.

Coburn: A lot of other people do, though, that's for sure. I want to say to everybody, thanks for the calls tonight. We really appreciate it. There's one thing that I want to say as we wrap up. First of all, thanks for being here. It's been a real thrill and a real pleasure.

Dylan: Oh, it's been real nice to be here.

Coburn: Thank you for coming. The way that I look at it, rock 'n' roll was really influenced by three people. Three people changed the way that rock was. That's Elvis Presley, the Beatles, and Bob Dylan. [*Actually, of course, that's six people. —Ed.*] Thank you for being here.

DYLAN ON

His Involvement in Farm Aid

"The idea came to me when all that money was being raised for the famine in Africa. I'd gotten a lot of letters from people who were having their farms repossessed. I think musicians have always responded to people in need. You see, musicians usually start out with nothing . . . so musicians always keep a tie to wherever they came from."

—from interview with Charles Young, MTV, September 1985

DYLAN ON

His Phrasing

"The phrasing I stumbled into. Some of the old folksingers used to phrase things in an interesting way, and then, I got my style from seeing a lot of outdoor-type poets, who would recite their poetry. When you don't have a guitar, you recite things differently, and there used to be quite a few poets in the jazz clubs, who would recite with a different type of attitude."

—from interview with Bob Brown, *20/20*, ABC-TV, October 10, 1985

BOB DYLAN—AFTER ALL THESE YEARS IN THE SPOTLIGHT, THE ELUSIVE STAR IS AT THE CROSSROADS AGAIN

Mikal Gilmore | October 13, 1985 | *Los Angeles Herald-Examiner*

Veteran rock critic Mikal Gilmore talked with Dylan in Los Angeles in late September 1985, which was a few months after the release of *Empire Burlesque* and about six weeks before the appearance of *Biograph*, a terrific, career-spanning anthology. Any other artist would be talking up such a set but not Dylan. He told Gilmore—who has since interviewed him several more times for *Rolling Stone*—that "I haven't been very excited about this thing."

Such comments are not the only reason this interview stands out. Another is that it finds Dylan complaining, after more than two decades of successes, that he still has relatively little control over his album releases. Yet another is that the conversation takes place not in a record company office, at a show, or in a hotel, but rather at the writer's home. Gilmore begins the piece by describing what it's like to have Dylan knock, knock, knockin' on his own door. —Ed.

The man who showed up at my door one afternoon a few weeks back looked exactly like I had hoped and feared he would: with his mazy brown hair and his taut smile and with smoky sunglasses masking his inscrutable stare, he looked just like Bob Dylan. Almost too much so. Dressed in a sleeveless torn T-shirt, weather-worn black jeans, and motorcycle boots and, at 44, looking far more fit than I had seen him in any recent photos or video appearances, he seemed remarkably like the image of the younger Bob Dylan that is burned into our collective memory; the keen fierce man who often tore apart known views of the world with his acerbic gestures and eloquent yowls.

What brought Dylan to my door was simply that we had an interview to do, and since he had come to Hollywood anyway that day, this was the easiest place for him to do it. While this certainly made the meeting a lot more thrilling for me, it also made it a bit scarier. More than 20 years of image preceded him. This was a man who could be tense, capricious and baffling, and who was capable of wielding his image at a whim's notice in a way that could stupefy and intimidate not only interviewers but sometimes friends as well.

What I found instead was a man who didn't seem too concerned with brandishing his image—even for a moment. He offered his hand, flashed a slightly bashful smile, then walked over to my stereo, kneeled down and started to flip through a stack of some unfiled records on the floor—mostly L.P.s by older jazz, pop and country singers. He commented on most of what he came across: "The Delmore Brothers—God, I really love them. I think they've influenced every harmony I've ever tried to sing . . . This Hank Williams thing with just him and his guitar—man, that's something, isn't it? I used to sing these songs way back, a long time ago, even before I played rock 'n' roll as a teenager . . . Sinatra, Peggy Lee, yeah, I love all these people, but I tell you who I've really been listening to a lot lately—in fact, I'm thinking about recording one of his earlier songs—is Bing Crosby, I don't think you can find better phrasing anywhere."

That's pretty much how he was that afternoon: good-humored and gracious, but also thoughtful and often elaborate in his answers. And sometimes—when he talks about his Minnesota youth, or his early days in the folk scene under the enthrallment of Woody Guthrie—his voice grew softer and more deliberate, as if he were striving to pick just the right words to convey the exact detail of his memory. During these moments he sometimes lapsed into silence, but behind his sunglasses his eyes stayed active with thought, flickering back and forth as if reading a distant memory.

For the most part, though, sipping a Corona beer and smoking cigarettes he seemed generous and relaxed, sometimes even surprisingly candid, as he ranged through a wide stretch of topics. He talked about his recent work in videos: "Making these things is like pulling teeth. For one thing, because of that movie *Renaldo and Clara* (Dylan's 1978 film of the Rolling Thunder Revue—widely viewed as a disaster), I haven't been in a place where I could ask for my own control over these things—plus, because my records aren't exactly selling like Cyndi Lauper's or Bruce's, I didn't feel I had the credibility to demand that control.

"But the company wanted me to try one more [to help boost *Empire Burlesque*'s sales] and I said I would, as long as I got to name Dave Stewart [of Eurythmics] as director. His stuff had a spontaneous look to it, and somehow I just figured he would understand what I was doing. And he did: He put together a great band for this lip-sync video and set us up with the equipment on this little stage in a church somewhere in West L.A. So between all the time they took setting up camera shots and lights and all that stuff, we could just play live for this little crowd that had gathered there.

"I can't even express how good that felt—in fact, I was trying to remember the last time I'd felt that kind of direct connection, and finally I realized it must have been back in the '50s, when I was 14 or 15 years old playing with four-piece rock 'n' roll bands back in Minnesota. Back in those days there weren't any sound systems or anything that you had to bother with. You'd set up your amplifiers and turn them up to where you wanted to turn them. That just doesn't happen anymore. Now there are just so many things that get in the way of that kind of feeling, that simple directness. For some reason, making this video just made me realize how far everything has come these last several years—and how far I'd come."

His reaction to pop's new social activism, and such efforts as Live Aid, U.S.A. for Africa and Farm Aid, is somewhat mixed. "While it's great that people are supporting U.S.A. for Africa and Farm Aid, what are they really doing to alleviate poverty? It's almost like guilt money.

Some guy halfway round the world is starving so O.K., put 10 bucks in the barrel, then you can feel you don't have to have a guilty conscience about it. Obviously, on some level it does help, but as far as any sweeping movement to destroy hunger and poverty, I don't see that happening.

"Still, Live Aid and Farm Aid are fantastic things, but then musicians have always done things like that. When people want a benefit, you don't see them calling dancers or architects or lawyers or even politicians—the power of music is that it has always drawn people together.

"But at the same time, while they're asking musicians to raise money, they're also trying to blacklist our records, trying to take somebody like Prince and Madonna off the radio—the same people that they ask to help raise funds. And it isn't just them: when they're talking about blacklisting records and giving them ratings, they're talking about everybody."

Dylan is pleased by Bruce Springsteen's growing popularity, but he has a warning too. "Bruce knows where he comes from—he has taken what everybody else has done and made his own thing of it—and that's great. But somebody'll come along after Bruce, say 10 or 20 years from now, and maybe they'll be looking to Bruce as their primary model and somehow miss the fact [that his music comes from Elvis Presley and Woody Guthrie]. In other words all they're going to get is Bruce, they're not gonna get what Bruce got.

"If you copy somebody—and there's nothing wrong with that—the top rule should be to go back and copy the guy that was there first. It's like all the people who copied me over the years, too many of them just got me, they didn't get what I got."

Dylan was a bit less expansive when it came to discussing his own historical presence in rock 'n' roll. He seemed more moved or involved when discussing the inspiration he felt during his early immersion in rock 'n' roll and the folk, beat and poetry scenes than in deliberating over any questions about his own triumphs—such as the seismic impact he had on international pop culture once he fused folk tradition, rock revolt, political insight and poetic ability into a personalized, myth-making style.

"There are certain things you can say you've done along the way that count," he said, "but in the end it's not really how many records you sell [Dylan has sold more than 35 million] or how big a show you play or even how many people end up imitating you. I know I've done a lot of things, but if I'm proud of anything, it's maybe that I helped bring somebody like Woody Guthrie—who was not a household name—to a little more attention, the same way that the Rolling Stones helped to bring Howling Wolf more recognition. It's because of Woody Guthrie and people like him that I originally set out to do what I've done. Stumbling onto Woody Guthrie just blew my mind.

"Then again, I never really dwell on myself too much in terms of what I've done. For one thing, so much of it went by in such a flash, it's hard for me to focus on. I was once offered a great deal of money for an autobiography, and I thought about it for a minute, then I decided I wasn't ready. I have to be sat down and have this stuff drawn out of me, because on my own I wouldn't think about these things. You just go ahead and you live your life and you move onto the next thing, and when it's all said and done, the historians can figure it out. That's the way I look at it."

Despite his reluctance, Dylan did look back recently at some length at the behest of Columbia Records, which has been trying for three years to elicit his cooperation and enthusiasm over *Biograph*, a five-L.P. retrospective of his career from 1962 to 1981. The package (which is due for release in early November) features 53 tracks, including 18 previously unreleased recordings and three scarce singles. Just as importantly, the set also includes a 36-page booklet by author-screenwriter Cameron Crowe (*Fast Times at Ridgemont High*) that features extensive commentary and reflections by Dylan. His own critiques of his political anthems, love songs, religious declarations, narrative epics, poetic fancies, rock inventions and long-buried gems are fascinating.

Except for Crowe's booklet, Dylan hasn't much use for the *Biograph* project. "I've never really known what this thing is supposed to be," he said, "There's more stuff that hasn't been heard before, but most of my stuff has already been bootlegged, so to anybody in the know, there's nothing on it they haven't heard before. I probably would've put different things on it that haven't been heard before, but I didn't pick the material. I didn't put it together and I haven't been very excited about this thing. All it is, really, is repackaging, and it'll just cost a lot of money. About the only thing that makes it special is Cameron's book."

Perhaps Dylan's objections to *Biograph* derive from an aversion to being consigned to any kind of definitive history when so much of his history remains to be written. Perhaps they also stem from an under-standing that no single collection could ever bind or explain a career as wide-ranging and restive as his, nor could it ever satisfy the critics, detractors, defenders and partisans who have scrutinized, acclaimed, assailed and debated his work with more fervor and attention than any other American post-war musician has received. Beginning with his ninth album, *John Wesley Harding* (1968), virtually every subsequent release has been greeted as either a comeback, a stinging disappointment or an out-and-out betrayal of his early promise and beliefs.

While this later work hasn't affected pop culture as much as his early songs did (but then, what could?), it's also true that much of it amounts to a resourceful body of music—often beautiful and daring, sometimes perturbing or confused, but always informed by an aspiring and uncompromising conscience.

Still, while *Empire Burlesque* sold respectably (around the half-million mark), it didn't attain the commercial prominence that was expected. Does that bother or disappoint Dylan?

"Yeah," he said without hesitation. "In fact, it concerns me to a point where I was thinking about regrouping my whole thought on making records. If the records I make are only going to sell a certain amount, then why do I have to spend a lot of time putting them together? You see, I haven't always been into recording all that much. It used to be that I would go in and try to get some kind of track which was magical, with a vocal on it, and just wait for those moments. I mean, talk about [Bruce Springsteen's] *Nebraska*. People say to me, 'When you gonna make a *Nebraska* album?' Well, I love that record, but I think I've made five or six *Nebraska* albums, you know."

Dylan stopped, shrugged and poured a little more beer into his glass. "You know," he said, "I can't release all the stuff I want to release.

I've got a lot of just melodic instrumentals laying around. I was think-ing the other day that maybe I should put them out, but I can't. I've also got a record of just me and Clydie King singing together and it's great, but it doesn't fall into any category that the record company knows how to deal with. It's like . . . well, something like the Delmore Brothers: It's very simple and the harmonies are great. If it was up to me I'd put that kind of stuff out, or I would've put some of it on *Biograph* but it's not up to me. Anyway, who's to know what people would make of it?"

I'd heard similar stories from various sources over the last few years—about whole projects that had been discouraged, if not altogether nixed by CBS. I'd even heard tapes of some of the unreleased works, and many of them are stunning. Such still-unreleased tracks as "Blind Willie McTell," "Death Is Not the End" and "Lord Protect My Child" are among the most stirring work he has done, providing sharp commentaries on physical and spiritual despair and hard-earned moral hope. Hearing these, as well as the better material on *Infidels* and *Empire Burlesque*, one real-izes that Dylan still has a great deal to say—that he is once again at a creative crossroads. At the same time, one fears that he may withhold such uncompromising work out of deference to the expectations of the marketplace.

That was a matter I didn't get to explore because, as quickly as Dylan can enter a room, he can also leave one. "It's late. I should go," he said, standing up, offering his hand and heading for the door. Looking out and realizing that night had fallen, he finally took off his sunglasses. It was nice to look, even if just for a moment, into those clear blue eyes.

In a way, I was glad that the question had gone unasked. How was I going to put it: Are you going to redeem every promise we've ever inferred from your work and legend? It was fitting to remember some-thing Sam Shepard once said of Dylan: "The repercussions of his art don't have to be answered by him at all. They fall on us as questions and that's where they belong." That his art still inspires such questions tells me everything I need to know about his remaining promise.

DYLAN ON

His Album Releases

"I really haven't had that much connection or conversation [over the years] with the people at Columbia [Records]. Usually I turn in my records, and they release them. But they really like this record [*Empire Burlesque*], so they asked me to do some videos and a few interviews to draw attention to it. But that doesn't mean I want to sit around and talk about the record. I haven't even listened to it since it came out. I'd rather spend my time working on new songs or listen to other people's records. Have you heard the new Hank Williams album, the collection of old demo tapes? It's great."

—from interview with Robert Hilburn,
Los Angeles Times, November 17, 1985

DYLAN ON

Psychiatry and Parents

"I don't think psychiatry can help or has helped anybody. I think it's a big fraud on the public. Billions of dollars have changed hands that could be used for far better purposes. A lot of people have trouble with their parents up until they're fifty, sixty, seventy years old. They can't get off their parents. I never had that kind of problem with my parents."

—from interview with Scott Cohen, *Spin*,
December 1985

DYLAN ON

The "Mass Monster"

"What I can see is the mass monster . . . in America, it's everywhere. It's invaded your home, your bed, it's in your closet. It's come real close to kicking over life itself. Unless you're able to go into the woods, the back country, and even there it reaches you. It seems to want to make everybody the same. People who are different are looked at as being a little bit crazy or a little bit odd. It's hard to stand outside of all that and remain sane."

—from telephone interview with Toby Creswell,
Rolling Stone (Australia), January 16, 1986

ASK HIM SOMETHING, AND A SINCERE DYLAN WILL TELL YOU THE TRUTH

Don McLeese | January 26, 1986 | *Chicago Sun-Times*

Dylan talked in Los Angeles with music writer Don McLeese about four months after he'd met with Gilmore. He seems to have been in a good mood, perhaps partly because of developments in his personal life that at the time were a well-guarded secret. On January 31, 1986, he became a father again when girlfriend Carolyn Dennis gave birth to a daughter, Desiree. (Dylan would marry Dennis in June, but they would divorce only a little more than six years later.) On the musical front, Dylan was working on *Knocked Out Loaded*, which would come out in July. —Ed.

LOS ANGELES "You got any questions for me? I love to talk," said Bob Dylan, as he motioned me toward the piano for a chat after rehearsal. He seemed sincere, even friendly, if a little guarded.

There was a time when hearing Dylan say he loved to talk would have been as surprising as hearing Mike Ditka say he loved to lose, or Elvis Presley confiding that he loved to diet. An interview with Bob Dylan offered the same prospects for congeniality as a Sean Penn photo session. Twenty years ago, Dylan's dealings with the press ranged from cryptic to combative. As the *"Don't Look Back"* documentary made plain, he didn't suffer fools gladly, and he seemed to find signs of foolishness everywhere. From behind his dark glasses, he preferred to let his lyrics—his parables and paradoxes, his amphetamine-fueled flights of surrealism—speak for themselves. He seemed like a hard man.

The Dylan that I encountered was far softer—a softer handshake, a softer demeanor—than I had expected. Maybe now that people aren't prying so much into his personal life—remember the self-proclaimed "Dylanologist" who dedicated himself to sifting through Dylan's garbage for revelations?—he can allow himself to be a little more open. Maybe religion or age or both have mellowed him a little. Maybe he tired of inventing and shedding new skins, new shields, new identities. Maybe he is simply more willing these days, in light of his declining commercial impact, to meet his audience halfway.

Whatever the case, Dylan's lyrical approach has become more straight-forward in recent years, and his personal manner seems more open as well. The man who once sang *"Don't ask me nothin' about nothin', I just might tell you the truth,"* had asked me if I had any questions. And he seemed to mean it. And, yeah, I had some.

Why New Zealand, Australia and Japan, rather than the long-awaited return to Stateside touring?

"I've never been offered that much here in the States," he said with a laugh. "There's really very little reason for most of the stuff I do. There's not very much logic behind it. I haven't been in Australia since '78 or so."

Why the Heartbreakers [Tom Petty's band, who played with Dylan on tour]?

"This just kinda fell into place for me," he said. "Mutual friends I know. It just happened. It wasn't like I woke up one morning and decided that I wanted to work with a particular band."

The band's guitar-and-keyboard sound reflects the enduring influence of Dylan's *"Highway 61 Revisited"/"Blonde on Blonde"* period, and the fact that the Heartbreakers would interrupt their own projects for a chance to tour with Dylan suggests that his stature in musical circles hasn't diminished with the passage of time. With the exception of Elvis Presley, it is hard to imagine another artist who has so completely reshaped the face of popular music in his own image.

When he turned to rock, his impact was so profound that it was impossible to ignore. Not only did he radically transform what was being sung, but he also revolutionized how it would be sung. Just listen to John Lennon singing *"Norwegian Wood"* or Mick Jagger singing *"She Smiled Sweetly,"* and you'll hear imitation Dylan. Just listen to the Four Tops' *"Reach Out (I'll Be There),"* and you'll hear Dylan in the way Levi Stubbs phrases the lyric.

A few years later, when glitter was the vogue in England, both David Bowie and Marc Bolan penned odes to the master. Bruce Springsteen reportedly drew the blueprint for his early career from a biography of Dylan, and took his music to the same man who had signed Dylan to Columbia Records.

Among the best of today's new bands, Dylan's influence stretches from Jason and the Scorchers to Mike Scott and the Waterboys. Few producers these days are hotter than the Eurythmics' Dave Stewart, who felt privileged to collaborate with Dylan on a recent video and tracks for his next album. And what are such socially conscious efforts as Live Aid, Farm Aid and *"Sun City,"* but the reflowering of the seeds sown by Dylan in the early '60s? Although the five-record *"Biograph"* set should reinforce the breadth and depth of Dylan's accomplishments for a new generation of listeners, there's no question that his commercial impact has diminished as the quality of his recorded work has become more erratic. Does it bother him to be away from the forefront of popular consciousness?

"Not really," Dylan said. "I mean, I've done what I wanted to do, and I really can't complain. Everybody gets their time to do whatever it is they're doing. You know what I mean: You gotta start out when you're young. Sometimes I forget I'm not that young."

How important are record sales to the 44-year-old Dylan?

"At this point really not that important, because of my contract. But in the future, it might be," he said. "There's more great records that don't sell, in a real crushing sort of way: Leonard Cohen's last record was a brilliant record. John Prine's last record I thought was incredible. Lou Reed always makes a great record.

"I've found, and I think it's true, that most people get their inspiration from records that they have to seek out, and really aren't that popular. I know that's the way it was with me. Whether it was folk music or rhythm and blues or rock 'n' roll, it wasn't that popular when we were growing up. You really had to be dedicated to seek that out, and make that a part of your life."

Of course, where the music that initially attracted Dylan represented an outsider's voice of expression—raw, vital, unpolished—much of what has passed for rock in recent years has been a triumph of mainstream merchandising. Little wonder that a man who never sang a song the same way twice has seemed increasingly uncomfortable in an era of rhythm-machine rigidity and frozen video images.

"I definitely think and believe that the popular music of today, it's not gonna work," Dylan said. "Because there's not really substance behind it. There's a lot of machines and a lot of riffs, and people are going to get tired of it, if they're not tired already."

When he's playing with people who once idolized him—or still do—is there any sense of intimidation that he has to dissolve?

"When they see what I'm about, you know it's all about being able to follow what I'm doing and stick with that," he said. "It really doesn't amount to any kind of intimidation. Maybe I might play with somebody who's really young, and they're kinda shaky, but then you have to encourage those people to play.

"When I play, people can play around what I play. I give people a lot of space."

Although Heartbreaker keyboardist Benmont Tench says that Dylan is an easy artist to work with, he remembered his initial experiences for the *"Shot of Love"* sessions.

"The first day that I worked with him, he didn't say a word the whole session, and I didn't know anybody at the session," he said. "At the end of the day, when I was leaving, he said, 'Can you come tomorrow?'"

At that point, Tench figured that he probably had done all right.

DYLAN ON

America

"To me, America means the Indians. They were here and this is their country, and all the white men are just trespassing. We've devastated the natural resources of this country, for no particular reason except to make money and buy houses and send our kids to college and shit like that. To me, America is the Indians, period. I just don't go for nothing more. Unions, movies, Greta Garbo, Wall Street, Tin Pan Alley, or Dodgers baseball games. It don't mean shit. What we did to the Indians is disgraceful. I think America, to get it right, has to start there first."

—from interview with Mikal Gilmore, *Rolling Stone*, July 17, 1986

THE INVISIBLE MAN

David Hepworth | October 1986 | *Q* magazine (UK)

Neither fans nor critics were knocked out by Dylan's *Knocked Out Loaded*, which hit stores on July 14, 1986, though the following article at least suggests that it received some good reviews. The album, which seems as cobbled together as *Self Portrait*, contains an ill-fitting batch of material, including a Junior Parker blues cover, a Kris Kristofferson track, and collaborations with Tom Petty and, of all people, mainstream pop songwriter Carole Bayer Sager. There is also one often-overlooked eleven-minute classic, the abstruse, sometimes funny, and consistently fascinating "Brownsville Girl," which Dylan coauthored with playwright Sam Shepard.

Maybe the artist wasn't too happy with the album himself because, as UK journalist David Hepworth reports in this piece, Dylan performed for three successive nights at New York's Madison Square Garden following *Knocked Out Loaded*'s release, and he failed to play anything from it.

Hepworth, who talked with Dylan during his three-night mid-July stand at the Garden, wrote this article for the debut issue of the now more than three-decades-old British rock magazine *Q*, which he cofounded. The piece contains fewer Dylan quotes than most of the features in this book, but it's at least as evocative as many of them. —Ed.

The man in the denim jacket hugs the battered guitar further into his chest and launches into the final verse of Shelter From The Storm, the backlighting picking out every starpoint of his tangled hair as he sings of beauty walking a razor's edge and pipes out a final solo on the harmonica attached around his neck. Awkwardly acknowledging the audience's applause he hops off the small, low stage. As he walks through the crowd people offer their muttered congratulations.

"Great, Bob."

"You did real good, Bob."

"Bob, thanks for everything."

The master of ceremonies takes the mike: "A big hand, ladies and gentlemen, for the legendary Bob Dylan."

Pause.

"And now, would you welcome to the stage, the one, the only . . . *Bob Dylan!*"

With a sweep of his arm he indicates a fair-haired man in glasses. This character is so small he's having trouble hoisting his backside on to the tall stool without dropping his guitar. The crowd stiffens. Bob Dylan is five feet, tops. And, yes, he's going to sing Just Like Tom Thumb's Blues . . .

THIS IS THE FIFTH annual Bob Dylan imitators contest, taking place in a Greenwich Village club called The Speakeasy. Entries are invited in six categories: folk-protest, amphetamine-rock, post-motorcycle accident, born again, freestyle and contemporary. Here on MacDougal Street they know their Dylan. When he first arrived in New York he headed like a homing pilgrim straight for the corner of Bleecker and MacDougal, making his reputation at The Gaslight, Café Rienzi, Gerde's Folk City and the other Village clubs and coffee houses, some of which still cluster around that holy intersection.

That was a quarter of a century ago. Tonight the "contemporary" Bob Dylan is midtown with Tom Petty And The Heartbreakers, playing the second of a three night engagement at Madison Square Garden, an ice-hockey facility that seats 22,000. Earlier that evening in his dressing room I'd mentioned the contest to him, saying I intended to drop by. He shook his head.

"It's crazy, isn't it? How would you feel if they were doing that about you?"

This is not something I often consider, Bob, but, well, flattered at first and then maybe a bit spooked. Don't you like the flattery?

"No, because you do get spooked by it and so you can't afford to get flattered by it. You can get trapped if you fall victim to flattery."

It would have been hard to persuade Bob Dylan that there was more affection for the spirit of his music in that cramped little alternative comedy joint than there had been in the gusty reaches of the Garden. The Speakeasy audience may have been traditionalists to the point of pedantry—applauding a particularly well-observed imitation of Dylan's harmonica work on Just Like A Woman and clicking their tongues in disapproval when a competitor tried to pass off Bringing It All Back Home material with Nashville Skyline intonation—but they were probably having a better time than those who'd paid twenty dollars and more to watch a distant silhouette act out the fiction of his rebirth for the umpteenth time.

Bob Dylan came off his motorbike the difficult way on July 29th 1966. That's twenty years ago. George Michael was in nappies. Every live performance he's undertaken since then has been greeted as the beginning of a Return to Form. The 1986 True Confessions tour of America and Australasia—for even Dylan tours have brand names these days—is no exception.

Critics claim that his alliance with The Heartbreakers has magically invoked what Dylan called that "wild mercury sound" of Blonde On Blonde. In actual fact they no more resemble the men who played on Obviously Five Believers than The Smiths do. Instead they sound like many of the line-ups Dylan has taken on the road since he ceased working with The Band—loud, approximate and confused.

This is not necessarily their fault. Dylan is notorious for refusing to articulate what he wants. The musicians who worked with him in Dave Stewart's North London studio late last year were amazed that anyone could spend two weeks leading a band without feeling the need to give instructions from time to time. Eric Clapton, an old friend, simply watches his hands for the changes and hopes for the best.

Ronnie Wood recalls the day before Live Aid when he and Keith Richards sat around with Dylan trying to familiarise themselves with his material. Dozens of songs were picked out and arranged. The next day, just a matter of minutes before they were due to follow

Mick Jagger and Tina Turner on stage in front of the world's largest television audience, Dylan announced that they would begin with the Ballad Of Hollis Brown. This was one of the few numbers they hadn't rehearsed.

Ronnie hadn't even *heard* it: "I thought, Hollis Brown? That's cough medicine, isn't it?" The rest you know.

IN STRICTLY COMMERCIAL TERMS Dylan had no more right to top that Philadelphia bill than The Hooters. Last year in New York CBS presented him with an award for lifetime's sales of 35,000,000 records. Respectable but no more. Michael Jackson has sold more copies of Thriller alone than Bob Dylan has of his thirty albums over twenty five years. And yet when Jack Nicholson used the adjective "transcendent" you know you weren't about to see Cyndi Lauper.

The three song shambles that followed would have finished most people's careers. Dylan claims never to have had one. Then he compounded the debacle by suggesting that some of the money raised by the event should be diverted to the over-mortgaged farmers of the mid-West. To the British artists sitting watching the American telecast on a large screen in a West End nightclub this seemed like typically tasteless isolationism. Picking his words carefully, Bob Geldof later commented: "I find it hard to get as concerned about people losing their livelihoods as I do about people losing their lives."

Nevertheless Dylan's remarks mustered the American musical community in a way that Band Aid and Live Aid had never quite managed. Headed up by Willie Nelson, Neil Young and John Cougar Mellencamp, Farm Aid was set to climax with a September concert in Champaign, Illinois. Obviously keen to avoid another Live Aid debacle, Dylan decided he needed a band, preferably a well-rehearsed one. He'd already worked with various Heartbreakers, notably keyboard player Benmont Tench, and the fact that his manager Elliott Roberts had recently gone into partnership with Tony Dimitriades, Petty's manager, made the liaison easier to contemplate. They rehearsed together for a week and successfully closed out Farm Aid. (The event raised barely enough money to pay off one day's interest on the debts accrued by American farmers; however, it was instrumental in drawing national attention to their plight.)

THE TRUE CONFESSIONS TOUR should not have been the box office hit it was. Dylan's last U.S. tour, undertaken in 1981, was not a great success. Eschewing all the old favorites, he stuck largely to songs that reflected his conversion to evangelical Christianity. Experience suggests that Your Average Rock Fan can put up with devil worship but tends to draw the line at the old rugged cross.

Dylan wasn't being coy about it either; he thumped that bible till the dust reached the rafters. He was shaken by how violently supposedly educated audiences reacted to songs which in his view were simply direct descendants of Masters Of War or I Shall Be Released, not to mention Father Of Night or Knockin' On Heaven's Door. What did these people think he'd been singing about all these years if it wasn't moral conflict and the prospect of salvation?

Dylan puts up a good show of not understanding the extent to which the music industry intercedes in his art. Ask him what draws a million people to buy tickets for this 40-date tour and he'll profess complete bewilderment. This pretense of ignorance is his strong shield against criticism and pressure. There he is, playing New York City on the very day his new record, Knocked Out Loaded, hits the stores. [*Actually, the day after. —Ed.*] There he is, playing for the best part of three hours in front of 22,000 people and the assembled brass of his record company and how many tunes does he play from this new release? Not one.

"Not even a mention," moans a CBS employee backstage.

Oh, he found room for Ricky Nelson's Lonesome Town and ancient gospel corn like That Lucky Old Sun but apparently wasn't ready to play Brownsville Girl or any of the other tracks that the American press were dutifully hailing as a Return To Form. (He'd probably read the CBS handout calling Brownsville Girl "a masterpiece"; all Bob Dylan songs of more than five minutes duration are "masterpieces".)

Bob Dylan has been signed to this record company for more than twenty five years. Twenty five years of advances, options, tour support and artwork approval. He's been with CBS longer than the vast majority of their employees. He may not sell the amount of product that Michael or Bruce or Barbra or even Journey shift but nevertheless the company President Walter Yetnikoff makes sure he's there at the Garden with his flexible friend, ready to take Dylan and a party of twenty to a swank East Side restaurant after the show.

I feel for Yetnikoff. He spends most of his time arguing over video production expenses and Japanese twelve inch single royalties with a succession of private plane-piloting, currency-dealing, Armani-wearing, aluminum briefcase-owning artists and their managers; then twice a year he has to sit down with this smoky old gipsy who isn't remotely interested in releasing singles, shrivels up at the thought of going on the radio or TV and only ever approves pictures of himself in which his eyes are closed. It can't be easy.

(Elliott Roberts discussing possible Italian TV interview with CBS person: "He doesn't want to do it sitting down with the camera pointing at him and he doesn't want to do it walking either." CBS person tries to look understanding.)

He's the only artist I've ever met who genuinely didn't seem to care what impression I took away. Mick Jagger wants to be feared, Bruce Springsteen wants to be loved and Sting badly wants to be admired.

Bob Dylan, ladies and gentlemen, doesn't give a shit.

EACH NIGHT AROUND SIX he is delivered into Madison Square Garden by camper van. The vehicle pulls up a few yards from his dressing room and out he swings looking like . . . well, rather like a middle-aged Bob Dylan imitator; mirror shades, black leather jacket with white buckskin fringes, black leather trousers, black fingerless gloves and black motorcycle boots. The expression on his face—what you can see of his face—defies you to recognise him. Consequently, all activity in the area freezes as he goes by.

This is the really poisonous thing about celebrity. When you're as famous as this every room is occupied by people discussing either your imminent arrival or your recent departure. Your reputation doesn't simply go before you; it clears the streets, checks the exits, halts the traffic, screams through a bullhorn. Everyone you're introduced to has read at least one book about you. It must be like being Adrian Mole. [*Mole is the fictitious protagonist in a series of books by British writer Sue Townsend. —Ed.*]

Dylan is followed down the corridor by three dark-haired, solemn-beyond-their-years teenagers. They are Jesse, Samuel and Jacob, the three Dylan sons. Jess, the oldest of them at 20, is being tugged along by an animal that appears to have been the product of a brief romance between a Labrador and a bus. "My God," someone hisses as the creature wheezes past, "the hound is a *horse!*" A bone is produced. It was probably donated by a camel. This snack is taken into Dylan's dressing room.

What's the dog called? I enquire, as the animal falls upon the bone. (It evidently hasn't eaten for quarter of an hour.)

"I'm sorry?" says Dylan.

"I said 'What's the dog's name?'."

"Could you repeat that?" he asks, cupping a hand to his ear.

"I just wonder whether the dog had a name . . ."

"Oh, the dog. No. (Pause as we both study the banqueting hound.) No, actually he's called 'Late For Dinner'."

"Sorry?"

"No, that dog has a name that is known only to me."

Oh. So far so good.

———————

COME INTO THIS DRESSING ROOM.

(Don't mind the middle-aged man fidgeting with the scratched acoustic guitar in the corner—he's just the spokesman for a generation.)

You know, if I was Bob Dylan I'd ask to be moved. This is neither a big nor a luxurious room. On a table in the corner there are ranks of half-bottles of Jim Beam whisky, one bottle of Stolichnaya vodka and various mixers. The low table in the middle bears a well-wisher's flowers and a book of Bible stories. The furniture is chipped and battered. A portable clothes rack is being stocked by a tall, red-haired girl called Susie.

Susie commutes between Dylan and the wider world outside the dressing room. She fetches fresh motorcycle boots from the giant flight case in the corridor, puts the booze on ice, informs him that Time Magazine have been waiting down the corridor for a couple of hours, even tells him what time it is.

"Is Bobby Womack out there?" he enquires suddenly.

She looks. Yes he is. (Course he is.)

"Oh. Listen . . . er . . . oh, forget it. I'm getting ahead of myself . . . er . . ."

He puts the guitar down, jumps up, disappears into the next door bathroom and expectorates noisily.

OUT IN THE CORRIDOR two men are waiting. They are Richard Marquand and Joe Eszterhas, respectively director and writer of Hearts Of Fire, the film that Dylan starts work on as soon as his tour finishes. [*Hepworth later discovered that the man he'd thought was Eszterhas was actually Iain Smith, one of the film's producers. —Ed.*] Marquand, who made Jagged Edge, is one of America's hottest directors. The film, which purports to be "about stardom and the relationship between Europe and America," also stars Rupert Everett and Fiona Flanagan, an MTV-bred ingenue who has already made two albums for Atlantic. It's Dylan's first acting role since Sam Peckinpah's Pat Garrett And Billy The Kid. Unless you count Renaldo And Clara. He doesn't.

"I don't know, man. Was that a film?"

We had Don't Look Back on British TV a couple of months ago.

Another grey smile: "I don't know, man. Half the stuff I do is someone else's idea."

(This is a stock Dylan posture. During our conversation he assures me that the collaboration with Petty, the release of Biograph, the composition of Knocked Out Loaded, his casting in Hearts Of Fire and numerous other ventures were all "someone else's idea.")

"Somebody called me from the William Morris Agency. I just read it and it seemed like I knew that character, whoever it was. It's a guy who plays oldies shows. I could relate to that. I've done all those things really."

The challenge of acting doesn't excite him so much as the prospect of getting to play music: "Marquand says that maybe one of the bands could be Woody and Steve Jordan and somebody that Woody knows. That'd be great."

Woody, who has joined Dylan on stage for the last half-dozen numbers throughout the New York engagement, is one of his firmest friends. Although one is known as one of the deeper thinkers of his generation while the other is regarded as a lairy connoisseur of the pleasures of the flesh, they appear to pal down famously, lurching around the dressing room in an unsteady embrace after the show as Ron listens back to his guitar work on the Knocked Out Loaded track Driftin'. Woody knows how to make Dylan laugh in a very elementary way.

The Stones guitarist is only marginally less puzzled about their friendship than anyone else: "I think we probably get on quite well because I'm quite happy if people don't particularly want to talk. I'll just carry on doing what I'm doing until he's ready."

IT'S RARE that a year goes by without another thick volume appearing in the tonier kind of bookshop, dedicated to documenting the life and anatomising the work of this obdurate individual. Within the last twelve months we've had Wilfrid Mellers' tortuous musicological analysis, A Darker Shade Of Pale, Jonathan Cott's seriously glossy picture book, Dylan, and already the presses are rolling out Robert Shelton's exhaustive memoir, No Direction Home. Bob Dylan gets his fan mail between hard covers.

All these books are alike in their failure to throw any light on his more oblique songs and their frenzied attempts to read major significance into his throwaways. Groaning with footnotes and thick with references to arcane Middle-Eastern works of philosophy they go in for a dismaying amount of "what Dylan is trying to say here is . . ." analysis. The day will doubtless arrive when we will read the words "what Muddy is trying to say here is that he has at last got his mojo working but can't *as yet* get it to work on the object of his desires."

The hero of all this literature claims not to be bothered by this scribbling industry: "I just don't pay any attention to it. Life's too short, man."

You must read the odd one.

"I try not to but every now and then I come across one of them at somebody's apartment or something. I was over at someone's place and there was a book there called Positively Main Street [by Toby Thompson]. I started reading it and it just made me crazed, you know, reading this stuff. On some level I was having a hard time separating me from the person I was reading about, you know what I mean?

"I was feeling pretty good when I got there and then I read part of it and I just felt like another person; it was like Doctor Jekyll and Mr Hyde."

What he would make of The Telegraph I can only guess. Here is a magazine devoted exclusively to documenting the life of Robert Allen Zimmerman, a singer from Hibbing, Minnesota.

This is no cut-and-paste fanzine bashed off on the photocopier while the Inspector Of Taxes is at lunch; this is a perfect-bound, colour-covered, ultra-devotional periodical published from Bury, Lancashire. If magazines are best run by obsessives, The Telegraph is the best. No minutiae is too minute for The Telegraph. Here you can find correspondence dealing with whether Al Kooper or Mike Bloomfield wore the spotted short at the infamous Newport concert and the exact circumstances of Dylan's meeting his former wife. Was it, as Tangled Up In Blue infers, in "a topless joint" or could that just have meant the Playboy Club? After all, she was married at the time to Victor Lownes . . . [*This is incorrect. Dylan's first wife had not been married to Victor Lownes, an executive at Playboy Enterprises. She had been married to magazine photographer Hans Lownds. —Ed.*] The only other place you find fact-fetishism taken to this pitch is among the pages of The Cricketer.

For the benefit of those who are either impervious to the appeal of Bob Dylan or too young to have known him as anything but the last act at Live Aid, it's useful to stand back and appreciate the strength of his hold on a lot of people. Bootleg recordings are the true measure of the constancy of an artist's following. Nobody ever sold Gerry And The Pacemakers bootlegs or Donovan bootlegs or Boomtown Rats bootlegs. Neither do they market illicit recordings of Michael Jackson so it's not a simple question of fame.

People buy bootlegs of artists they feel such kinship with that it's inconceivable that they could ever be disappointed with what they hear. If you were to produce a recording of Bob Dylan boiling a kettle I could find you a few buyers tomorrow. They would file it alongside the rest of their collection: the 1961 recordings of Dylan singing Pastures Of Plenty to Woody Guthrie's friend's daughter in a New Jersey motel room; the Washington Civil Rights rally of 1963; his interview with Studs Terkel in Chicago; his Woodstock duets with George Harrison from 1970; his 1975 ansaphone message; his ill-tempered telephone exchanges with A.J. Weberman ("Hey man, why don't you just get off my back?"); the video of his Isle of Wight press conference from 1969; a matchless, hovering blues called Blind Willie McTell that has become one of his most celebrated songs; the soundchecks from every date of his last world tour; the out-takes, false starts, rough drafts and abandoned masterpieces of half a lifetime.

No wonder he's careful about fans.

"Boy, coming out of the hotel tonight, it was a real zoo. I don't know who's a fan. It's a short word for fanaticism. I've always been uncomfortable in a crush of people who were fans of mine. I've always felt more comfortable with people who didn't know me. I can go really most places and nobody will recognise me except people who know who I am. I could just disappear into a crowd unless someone knows who I am and then they'll point me out to other people and then you suddenly find yourself the centre of all this attention."

LIKE SO MANY ROCK STARS Dylan is a shy man who's also an incorrigible show-off. On stage in New York he eschewed all frontal lighting in the sure knowledge that his silhouetted profile alone would be quite sufficient to divert attention from Tom Petty. He only spoke a couple of times, to enquire "anyone out there running for office? No? Good." before Ballad Of A Thin Man and [to] introduce In The Garden with the words "this is for all the people in gaol [British variant of jail —Ed.], not for doing evil things but for doing good things."

How he chooses twenty or so songs from such a repertoire is a mystery; some nights on this tour he's launched into forgotten favourites with the minimum of warning. But the sad truth is that the only artists who can win in venues like Madison are the people who can pump up their music way beyond life size. Springsteen can handle it. Dylan can't, shouldn't even be trying. It's an undignified way to carry on.

The audience, who divided equally between old fans along for the nostalgic ride and tanked-up teenagers waiting for that drug song about everybody getting stoned, didn't seem to be listening much. Petty's journeyman radio rock covered their needs adequately.

The star hits stride only intermittently; Hard Rain hammered out with a father's righteous indignation; In The Garden sufficiently deeply felt to slice its way through the band's vague shuffle. Positively Fourth Street on the other hand had only curiosity value. I confessed to not understanding why he still bothered with a song so specifically addressed to a person who's been out of his life for twenty years.

"Yes, but so are folk songs. Some of those are a hundred years old but so what?"

So Positively Fourth Street can bear the same degree of repetition as Wild Mountain Thyme?

"No . . . I don't know. On some level maybe. But Wild Mountain Thyme now . . ." He smiles and begins to pick a tune out on the guitar.

(It isn't Wild Mountain Thyme. It isn't anything much.)

"Do you know the McPeake Family?"

Afraid not . . .

"They're a group from Ireland."

So is that what he likes listening to?

"I like the Egyptian singer Om-Kalsoum. She passed away about fifteen years ago. I bought a record of hers when I was in Jerusalem in 1972. This guy was selling them on the street corner and they were obviously bootleg records." He laughs and then decides maybe we'd better not say they were bootlegs. (I presume he means pirates, anyway.) "I like Edith Piaf a lot."

In an attempt to gradually entice him into the present decade, I enquire about people like Boy George.

"I thought that was a nice record, that Do You Really Want To Hurt Me?. That and the Chameleon Song. I liked him when he wore that white coat and that black hat and the braids. I don't know why he ever changed."

He's been on a heroin charge in Britain.

"He has? Poor Boy George."

I FIRST HEARD BOB DYLAN'S MUSIC in a school room. Some powerful sophisticated 6th former descended from on high to play us young pups his precious copies of the first four Dylan albums. We'd seen the name as a songwriting credit, read about "protest music" in Disc but we'd no idea what to expect really. I thought you pronounced him Die-lunn.

I can clearly remember this callow 17-year-old playing Spanish Harlem Incident on the school's mahogany-panelled Ferguson gramophone and then telling us that with this album, Another Side Of Bob Dylan, the artist had moved on and matured, leaving protest music behind him for good. I felt vaguely cheated. So it had all scarpered already, before I'd even got my denim cap.

Nobody in popular music has been measured in such a relentlessly chronological fashion as Dylan. Every review harks back to the last album. Ever since 1964 somebody somewhere has been wistfully referring to the "Dylan of old." Some said it was all over before he'd made his first record. And still people are enquiring where he's been and where he's going as if Bob Dylan has a list of tasks to discharge in his lifetime and we're worried that he might not get them all done.

"I don't know if I'll still be doing this in twenty years' time. Twenty years ago I couldn't have imagined myself still doing it now. Actually I could if you don't think in terms of time. I try not to think in terms of time; years, minutes, hours and all that sort of thing. It's destructive for me to do that."

In actual fact, when people in the music business talk about time, what they're actually discussing is fashion. Pop stars aspire, above all things, to stay contemporary. It's this very prospect that Bob Dylan views with the most horror. Talking to him about the vicissitudes of the British music scene is like trying to explain the tax system of a distant planet. He doesn't understand and he doesn't care to either.

Bob Dylan reckons the proudest achievement of his entire career was to introduce the name of Woody Guthrie to a wider audience. He says, what the hell, if he *were* to remake Highway 61 tomorrow nobody would recognise it. And what if they did? What would they say then? What's a simple folk singer to do?

If there does need to be an argument for Bob Dylan it was provided last year by Biograph, an impeccably compiled and annotated five record box set that put All Along The Watchtower next to Solid Rock; Every Grain Of Sand next to Visions Of Johanna; and Caribbean Wind next to Can You Please Crawl Out Your Window?. It proved that this was a singer who'd always lived by his own lights, more concerned with the mystery of a moment than the need to make a statement; funnier, acuter, more spiritual and more musically sophisticated than most of us had ever guessed. And there wasn't a single song among the 52 recordings [*Actually, fifty-three. —Ed.*] that sounded even remotely dated. Needless to say Dylan denies having any part of it: "I didn't put it together and I haven't been very excited about it."

Instead he's spent the last year or so recording in studios all over the world with a bewildering variety of musicians and then shelving most of the results, boxing to keep fit and then smoking two packs of Kools a day to achieve the opposite effect, visiting Moscow at the invitation of the Soviet Writers' union and then professing to be perplexed with the experience: "To tell you the truth I didn't understand too much of it because I didn't understand the languages too well. The peculiar thing was there wasn't anybody at this particular poetry reading that I figured had even heard of me a little bit."

There was, however, an invitation to return with his guitar: "They said, don't do what Elton John did. He played 3,000-seat halls and the only people who got in to see him were bureaucratic people and there are a lot of bureaucrats there. It's really spooky."

What about the current squabbles between America and Russia?

"I don't know why America has got this problem with Russia because didn't the Russians finance the American Revolution? I'm sure they did. Who else would have? They finance revolutions all over the world, right? They did it then too. I think we ought to be grateful to them rather than trying to fucking blow them off the planet. But that's just my opinion and I'm not running for nothing."

Surely somebody ought to run for office?

"I don't know if there needs to be any office."

What about your fellow entertainer, the one in the White House?

"I don't know. I've seen a lot of Presidents come and go. I like the King and Queen idea. I like the idea of somebody . . ."

". . . somebody you can trust?"

"Yea," he laughs. "Somebody you can look up to."

A queue is building up in the corridor. There are familiar raddled Manhattan faces like Andy Warhol and Ric Ocasek alongside the newer Hollywood generation represented by Timothy Hutton, Debra Winger and Maria McKee. Judy Collins, who hit Greenwich Village at the same time as Dylan, is there, looking faintly matronly and talking about Farm Aid II and "the movement" as if it were still 1962. She is charming, well-mannered and completely lacking in the mystique that helped her old friend "Bobby" make it to where the air is rare. Everybody—Tom Petty, Ronnie Wood, even Dylan's girlfriend Carole Childs—*waits* to be admitted to the presence. [*Carole Childs was a Geffen Records executive with whom Dylan reportedly had a long affair; be that as it may, he had secretly married backup singer Carolyn Dennis only weeks before the concerts discussed here. —Ed.*] They all have one thing in common—they're all scared of him.

———————

BACK AT THE SPEAKEASY the party is in full swing. Some misguided soul has embarked on an ill-advised version of When The Ship Comes In and the crowd up by the bar at the back are making their own entertainment.

"Goddamn, you'll never guess who's in the bathroom!"

"The legendary Bob Dylan?"

"How'd you know?"

"Excuse me. I'd like three Heinekens and a gin and tonic for the Freewheelin' Bob Dylan . . ."

"Hey mister. Did anybody ever tell you you didn't look a bit like the enigmatic Bob Dylan?"

"Could you call a cab for the spokesman of a generation?"

DYLAN ON

Whether *Blood on the Tracks* Concerns His Divorce

"Yeah. Somewhat about that. But I'm not going to make an album and lean on a marriage relationship. There's no way I would do that, any more than I would write an album about some lawyers' battles that I had. There are certain subjects that don't interest me to exploit. . . . I've got to think I can do better than that. It's not going to positively help anybody to hear about my sadness. Just another hard-luck story."

—from interview with Bill Flanagan,
Written in My Soul, November 1986

DYLAN ON

Recovering from His July 1966 Motorcycle Accident

"Spent a week in the hospital, then they moved me to this doctor's house in town. In his attic. Had a bed up there in the attic with a window lookin' out. Sara stayed there with me. I just remember how bad I wanted to see my kids. I started thinkin' about the short life of trouble. How short life is. I'd just lay there listenin' to birds chirping. Kids playing in the neighbor's yard or rain falling by the window. I realized how much I'd missed. Then I'd hear the fire engine roar, and I could feel the steady thrust of death that had been constantly looking over its shoulder at me. [*Pause.*] Then I'd just go back to sleep."

—from interview with Sam Shepard, *Esquire*, July 1987

DYLAN ON

Mick Jagger

"I love Mick Jagger. I mean, I go back a long ways with him, and I always wish him the best. But to see him jumping around like he does—I don't give a shit in what age, from Altamont to RFK Stadium—you don't have to do that, man. It's still hipper and cooler to be Ray Charles, sittin' at the piano, not movin' shit. And still getting across, you know? Pushing rhythm and soul across. It's got nothin' to do with jumping around. I mean, what could it possibly have to do with jumping around? . . . Showbiz—well, I don't dig it. I don't go to see someone jump around."

—from interview with Kurt Loder, *Rolling Stone*, November 5, 1987

DYLAN ON

His Influences and What's Important

"I'd like to thank a couple of people who are here tonight who helped me a great deal coming up. Little Richard, who's sitting over there. I don't think I'd have even started out without listening to Little Richard. And Alan Lomax, who is over there somewhere, too. I spent many nights at his apartment house, visiting and meeting all kinds of folk music people which I never would have come in contact with. And I want to thank [the Beach Boys'] Mike Love for not mentioning me. [*Love had just made an acceptance speech during which he'd criticized various other musicians. —Ed.*] I play a lot of dates every year, too, and peace, love, and harmony is greatly important indeed, but so is forgiveness."

—from acceptance speech at Rock and Roll Hall of Fame induction ceremony,
Waldorf Astoria Hotel, New York, January 20, 1988

DYLAN ON

His Concert Tours

"I've always loved to travel and play my songs, meet new people and see different places. I love to roll into town in the early morning and walk the deserted streets before anybody gets up. Love to see the sun come up over the highway. Then of course, there's playing on the stage in front of live people, feeling hearts and minds moving. Everybody don't get to do that. Touring to me has never been any kind of hardship. It's a privilege."

—from interview with Edna Gundersen, *USA Today*, July 20, 1988

DYLAN ON

Why He Doesn't Talk Much in Concert

"It's not stand-up comedy or a stage play. Also, it breaks my concentration to have to think of things to say or to respond to the crowd. The songs themselves do the talking. My songs do, anyway."

—from interview with Edna Gundersen, *USA Today*, September 21, 1989

DYLAN ON

What His Father Taught Him

"Well, my daddy . . . he didn't leave me a lot, but what he told me was this. He did say, 'Son . . .' He said . . . [*Ten-second pause, a little nervous laughter.*] He said so many things, you know? [*Laughter.*] He said, 'You know, it's possible to become so defiled in this world that your own mother and father will abandon you. And if that happens, God will always believe in your own ability to mend your own ways.'"

—from acceptance speech for Grammy Lifetime Achievement Award,
Radio City Music Hall, New York, February 20, 1991

RADIO INTERVIEW

Elliot Mintz | May 1991| Westwood One (US)

Elliot Mintz, a DJ turned public relations man, was serving as Dylan's spokesman by the late 1980s. In early 1991, he interviewed Dylan in Los Angeles for a three-hour special that aired on the Westwood One radio network. The conversation was wide-ranging but the impetus for it was *The Bootleg Series, Vols. 1–3 (Rare and Unreleased), 1961–1991*, which hit the stores on March 26, 1991.

The Westwood One broadcast interspersed material from Mintz's 1991 interview not only with music but with clips from earlier conversations, including a 1987 Q&A with Mintz and the 1984 discussion with Bert Kleinman and Artie Mogull that appears earlier in this book. I've done my best to limit the transcript that follows to the 1991 interview but because the program was so heavily edited, I can offer no guarantees about exactly when or in what order the quotes originated. —Ed.

Elliot Mintz: A couple of weeks ago, on a rainy California night, I sat down with Bob at a Los Angeles hotel, where we embarked on an evening of conversation. It began like this.

Bob Dylan: When you did your first interview with John [Lennon], was it like this? You did interviews with him all over the world, correct?

Mintz: All over the world—

Dylan: You could have been in Osaka, Japan, at a hotel.

Mintz: And I was.

Dylan: Like this.

Mintz: And I interviewed him once in this hotel.

Dylan: In a bungalow?

Mintz: Yes.

Dylan: We got it, let's go. [*He strums guitar.*]

Mintz: When you listen to the *Bootleg* collection, you hear a demo for "Like a Rolling Stone." Not a demo but, obviously, you're playing it for other musicians in a studio and it's done as a waltz. The first and obvious question: when *Rolling Stone* did a list of the hundred best songs ever written, "Like a Rolling Stone" was way up there. You responded to a questionnaire of theirs where you talked about the song. Is it fair to say that you would consider that one of the best songs, if not the best song, you've ever written?

Dylan: Oh, to me it's not any better or any worse than any of the other songs I've written in that period. It just happened to be one of the ones that was on the Hit Parade and it's managed to survive because of that.

Mintz: But you don't have any particular affection for that song?

Dylan: Oh, yeah, to me it's alive.

Mintz: In the past twelve to eighteen months, the highest cultural award in France, the Rock and Roll Hall of Fame induction, Lifetime Achievement Award Grammy . . .

Dylan: Yeah, but you're not talking about Nobel Peace Prizes. Come on, really . . .

———————

Dylan: [*Regarding his Whitmark demos.*] You sit there in a room with a guitar or a piano, and there's a tape recorder and then you just sing your song into the recorder. In that particular room, they had photographs up, they had boxes stacked up at the sides of the wall, and mimeographed songs, and photographs of people with cigars in their mouth at parties. And formal photographs of earlier people who started these things.

Mintz: Tin Pan Alley.

Dylan: Well, no, it wasn't that. Tin Pan Alley, wasn't that that Brill Building thing at the front? It was in the same neighborhood. It seems like so long ago, don't it?

Mintz: It was thirty years.

Dylan: I had to write what I wanted to sing because what I wanted to sing nobody else was writing.

Mintz: "Who Killed Davey Moore," the song on the *Bootleg* collection, is played with a tremendous power, tremendous strength, tremendous indignation, and a bit of anger as well. Can you recall the circumstances under which you created that?

Dylan: No, but it was done at the same time as the "Hattie Carroll" song. It's like those two songs kinda went together. One got left off the record for some reason. Maybe those songs were done the same week, the same night even. They're very similar.

Mintz: Here are two songs where the question was always one of blame.

Dylan: Blame?

Mintz: Yeah, blame. "Hattie Carroll was just a maid in the kitchen."

Dylan: Well, but to me those songs were never about blame. They were more about justice than anything else.

Mintz: "Subterranean Homesick Blues." You know that there are an awful lot of people who spend a great deal of time looking for those Bob Dylan lines, just those great lines. Boom, boom, boom, boom.

Dylan: Like a treasure hunt or something, right?

Mintz: Like a treasure hunt.

Dylan: Yeah, like you get a map and go off and find the treasure somewhere.

Mintz: Or you hear things in your brain and it kinda goes back and forth.

Dylan: Exactly, yeah.

Mintz: And this particular tune has got a lot of those in 'em. I'm sure it must be very, very boring to you to hear your lines quoted back to you, but for the listeners . . . Does it, by the way? That's an assumption. Does it bore you to hear your own lines quoted back to you?

Dylan: Not really.

Mintz: "You don't need a weatherman to know which way the wind blows" or "twenty years of schooling and they put you on the day shift." "Subterranean Homesick Blues," how fast did it come to you? Do you have any recollection of where you were when you wrote that song? How it came down? If it was all done in one sitting? Any recall at all?

Dylan: No. Something like that, you can't be sure how much of it was made up beforehand, how much you made up right on the spot. A lot of it could have been made up right there.

Mintz: When you say "right there," do you mean at the recording studio?

Dylan: I mean right there, during it.

Mintz: Do you have any recollection about "Subterranean Homesick Blues," creating the song?

Dylan: Not really, just maybe the band that was playing the song, the atmosphere where it was done. It was just thrown out with a bunch of other stuff. It was kicked around.

Mintz: Do you ever just tire of having to be Dylan, of having to subject yourself to all the stuff that Bob Dylan has to be subjected to?

Dylan: Well, Bob Dylan doesn't really have to subject himself to anything more than me.

Mintz: Yes, he does.

Dylan: You mean like this interview?

Mintz: Yes, that would be one example.

Dylan: All right. Yeah, it's important to encourage me to do things, if that's the question. Everyone needs some encouragement to do something. It's hard for me to start my own motor, but outside of that, there's not really that much of a problem.

Mintz: I have a couple of Bob Dylan quotes that I would like to get your comments on, if anything comes through. First quote: "The closest

I ever got to the sound I hear in my mind was on individual bands on the *Blonde on Blonde* album. It's that thin, that wild, mercury sound. It's metallic, it's bright gold, with whatever that conjures up. That's my particular sound." First of all, did you say that?

Dylan: No, it doesn't sound like anything that would have come out of my mouth.

Mintz: I was quoting from *Playboy* magazine, the last interview that was done with you.

Dylan: Well, there you go. They could have just—

Mintz: So, first of all, you are not acknowledging that the quote is—

Dylan: Look, with me they do all kinds of things. If people can't have an interview—God knows why they would want one—but if they can't have one and they must have one, they'll write their own on me. They've done it. That's not a crime to do that. So when you say this was attributed to me, it may be or it may not be true.

Mintz: Well, you're saying it's not true.

Dylan: Just because it's got my name on it, to me doesn't mean that it was said by me. It could have been a misquote. It could have been pieced together. Well, let me take another tack at it. Let's say it is exactly what came out of my mouth, and there's really no reason to elaborate on it.

Mintz: Well, had you said yes, I was going to say what's intriguing to me is that on the *Bootleg* collection, we don't hear that sound. The sound that comes off the *Bootleg* is something very fundamental. It is not "a wild, mercury sound, metallic and bright gold."

Dylan: Yeah, you know why? Because that sound, that's unobtainable.

Mintz: "Farewell, Angelina" was popularized by Joan Baez. Did you like her version of it?

Dylan: Oh, it was wonderful.

Mintz: How come that at the time you created such a beautiful song, did you choose not to record it?

Dylan: Well, people have been asking me that for a long time. You can't use them all.

Mintz: So you're saying basically there was no specific reason, that there was just no space on the disc for it, that there were other songs that you thought were better?

Dylan: Well, on something like that, you're really asking the wrong person, because at that time nobody had really given me that much control over my records, and what was on and what was off.

Mintz: So somebody else, like a producer, maybe made the choices to what songs—

Dylan: Yeah. In those days you just went in and you played whatever you had and you never knew how it was going to be used.

Dylan: [*Referring to "Mama, You Been on My Mind."*] That was one of the California songs, Big Sur songs. There was a batch of them. Joan Baez could tell you probably more about that than me. She drove me once from the airport to her house, and that song might have been written during that trip in the backseat of her car.

Mintz: There was one other person who you've talked about in interviews who you really admired, really loved, really respected, and never met, but just ran into in an elevator once—Johnnie Ray. What was it about Johnnie Ray that touched you that way, that affected you that way?

Dylan: Do you remember Johnnie Ray?

Mintz: Very, very well.

Dylan: Well, yeah, he just had a lotta heart, didn't he? He was hard of hearing, too.

Mintz: Wore a hearing aid.

Dylan: Yeah. He was a stylist before there was such a thing. Well, but you could say everybody was a stylist. Except not like him. He kinda carried that pathos thing. Didn't he carry that thing kinda far? Just all of a sudden he'd break down and cry onstage.

Mintz: He would break down onstage. Seems like he'd cry, cry, and cry.

Dylan: How long's it been since you seen someone break down and cry singing a song? Well, in Mexico they do it every night, really. If you go to South America, you'll see it more often than you will in the States.

Mintz: And Judy Garland did that, and Edith Piaf did that, too, and James Brown I think did that too. And I think Joe Cocker did that once or twice.

Dylan: All right. Well, that's something to reach for. The perfect teardrop.

Dylan: My role as an artist would be to stay true to my art.

Mintz: I presume you would feel you have. If you were to listen to the *Bootleg* recordings around 1960–'61 through today, as we record this.

Dylan: Well, who says it's art, though? Who calls it art? Not me.

Mintz: You don't consider it art?

Dylan: No. My stuff? No. Why should it be? My stuff don't hang in museums.

Mintz: What is it?

Dylan: It's performance. It's like dance. It's like anything else you go to a stage and you see. You see movement on the stage; it's like a play. It's a dance. It's all that stuff that happens on the stage. That's what makes the records; it's not the other way around.

Mintz: Any thoughts about the song "Wallflower"?

Dylan: No. Really, it's just a sad song, sad experience, one of those pathetic situations in life that can be so overwhelming at times.

Mintz: [Regarding *Blood on the Tracks.*] An awful lot of people have commented on that album. I mean, that one seemed to stick with people for a very, very long time, and I think you once said that you were surprised about the number of people who were so moved and impressed and touched by that album, when for the most part, the album in many cases expresses such enormous sadness.

Dylan: Well, look, people write better from rejection than acceptance. Like people say you can't write good songs if you're happy. Who wants to hear a happy song? A lot of people do.

Mintz: "Tangled Up in Blue" and "If You See Her, Say Hello" from *Blood on the Tracks* . . . Did those songs represent a particular period for you?

Dylan: Yeah. That was my painting period. That was my excursion into the world of art, learning how to paint on canvas. It was almost like the medium is the message type trip. It's like they are paintings, those songs, or they appeared to be, or they seemed to try to be, or want to be. They have to be songs, anyway, so they have to be something, right. It's kinda hard to explain but they're more like a painter would paint a song as to compose it, more than a songwriter would write a song as to write it. It was like those songs were coming forth with just a burst of new insight.

Yeah, painting's cool. To see something, to be able to see it with your eye, to get it in your brain, to get it into your hands so you can transfer it from out there to over here, enjoy it.

Mintz: Painting songs. I never heard that expression.

Dylan: Painting, yeah. Well, maybe some other people have done it but that's really doing it. That's like taking a brush and painting those songs onto a canvas. They're all painted. That's what they are.

Dylan: "Foot of Pride," that's an outtake.

Mintz: Does anything come to your mind about composing it?

Dylan: Not about composing it. Composing it was all right. It had a bunch of extra verses that probably weren't necessary. They should have been combined. But the reason why it was never used was because the tempo speeded up, but there wasn't any drum machine used on that. The tempo just automatically took off, for some vague and curious reason.

Dylan: [*Regarding Blind Willie McTell.*] He was just a very smooth-operating bluesman. His songs always reminded me of trains, but that's just my hang-up, trains. And his vocal style and his sound seems to fit right in with that lonesome sound. His ragtime kinda thing on a twelve-string guitar made everything he did sound . . . give it a little higher pitch. You could probably say he was the Van Gogh of country blues.

Mintz: "When the Night Comes Falling from the Sky." Does anything come to your mind about the composition, about where you were at when you were recording it, when you were composing it?

Dylan: Composing it, yeah. It was bits and pieces of different places that went into writing that. Lines overheard here and there, strung together over a long period of time, resulted in that particular piece. It's not that uncommon for someone who writes a song to just go somewhere and sit around for a long time where you're going to throw yourself into the atmosphere of overhearing a lot of people talking to other people. If you're ever hung up for things to say, you can always use that old trick. It works better sometimes than sitting in a room, staring at the wall and trying to compose there.

Mintz: How concerned are you about the legacy you leave behind? I hope you live for another sixty to seventy years.

Dylan: Yeah, legacy?

Mintz: How history will remember you. Do you ever think about it?

Dylan: Yeah, definitely.

Mintz: Talk to us about it.

Dylan: Well, legacy . . . that word is very similar to the word "legend," which is also very similar to the word "legion." OK, and in the Bible, that's the Devil's name.

Mintz: Legion?

Dylan: So when you're asking me about leaving a legacy, there's nothing really that there'd be any great interest on my part in leaving because of the nature of the word itself.

Mintz: Being synonymous with the Devil?

Dylan: Yeah, to me that's a little too close to "legion," it's the same word.

Mintz: Let me find a different—

Dylan: "Legend" is the same thing. We might be getting too heavy for a Westwood One show. We're talking about the Devil.

Mintz: Well, it's a very heavy network.

Dylan: They may censor that, but—

Mintz: How would you like people to remember you a hundred years from now?

Dylan: If they remember me at all, it's devilish, because that means that there's been a legacy left, and you don't want to leave a legacy. If you try to attain some type of righteousness in this world, you don't want to leave a legacy. A legacy of what? It's all in the mind, anyway.

Mintz: So, as part of your overall musical contribution, the kind of music that you have made, that's an area that you own. Just nobody else messes with that. That's the Bob Dylan experience. You take no pride or satisfaction in the fact that you have to some degree preserved that form of the American musical experience?

Dylan: Yeah, it was mine to do, mine to give, mine to show up at the right time to do, and that's just the way it all happened.

Mintz: Was this a difficult experience? You have a history of resisting this kind of thing, the interview experience, taking about your songs—

Dylan: No, this is enjoyable for me.

Mintz: It is?

Dylan: Oh, yeah . . . this is OK for me.

Mintz: Some people upon hearing the past three hours that we've shared here together—and I thank you for your time and your honesty with all of this stuff—some of them might have come away saying, "Gosh, I don't know why he just isn't more proud of what he's done, what he's written, what he's contributed. I don't understand why he doesn't just give himself a little pat on the shoulder at the very least."

Dylan: Pride? No, pride goes before a big downfall. You've heard that, we've all heard that.

Mintz: Some degree of satisfaction?

Dylan: No, not unless you were expecting some kind of downfall. No, pride . . . what is there to be proud about? That we made another record? Is that something to be proud about? Is it something to be proud of that you built another building? That you built another highway? That you have a new automobile on the road? Is it something to be proud about that you've invented a new fertilizer?

Mintz: What about having created this enormous body of work that has touched, inspired, influenced so many millions of people all over the world? Does somebody not take some degree of joy in that?

Dylan: Not really. You can't do that. There's too many other people that have done far superior things than me, in the same field.

Mintz: Your overall relationship with the press, the *Bootleg* series covers a thirty-year period, thirty years of public awareness . . .

Dylan: Well, my struggle with the press isn't necessarily with the press. Certain publications at certain times tend to take liberties with you . . . by promising something they didn't deliver or having something come out in a way that the person who was involved never was told about. People don't like that kinda stuff. They don't mind being interviewed and having some kind of slant on whatever it is you're doing. You can let that wash off—that just rolls away. But the other stuff don't. But they are specific people that would do something like that. So there's no problem with the press for me. It's just liars and hypocritical people and ambitious people that wanna step over you.

Mintz: Do you ever view those [evangelical records] as being any different to the records that came before them or since them?

Dylan: Well, yeah, they're all different.

Mintz: How so?

Dylan: In many, many ways.

Mintz: Give me an example.

Dylan: Well, the content of the songs was much different, had a different vibe.

Mintz: The vibe could be called spiritual.

Dylan: Yeah, religious vibe.

Mintz: The song "Every Grain of Sand" seems to suggest, especially on the *Bootleg* collection, that you believe that this is a directed, purposeful universe where "every hair is numbered like every grain of sand." Am I reading too much into it?

Dylan: No!

Mintz: Or is that an honest depiction of how you see the world?

Dylan: Yeah. You can say that.

Mintz: There are no accidents?

Dylan: Accidents?

Mintz: No accidents in the world—that everything happens because it's supposed to happen.

Dylan: Yeah, but that's not what the song says. The song's talking about coincidences, not accidents.

Mintz: Coincidences?

Dylan: Yeah, yeah. Forget about accidents. Accidents can happen but coincidences are bound to happen.

Mintz: Do you believe literally that—taking your words again—"every hair is numbered like every grain of sand"? That someone, some entity, something has put all of this in order for some special—

Dylan: Yeah! Yeah! Yeah!

Mintz: You do?

Dylan: Oh, yeah, yeah.

Mintz: This song suggests that you wrestle with that one a little.

Dylan: Not really. Just because it's got an order and a purpose doesn't mean the way it's coming down is written in stone. Everything changes— have to leave room for something to change. I like to give things enough space so I can change when I feel.

Dylan: None of my songs are that good. It's the way they're performed, that's what it is. Hoagy Carmichael songs are much better than mine. So are George Gershwin's and Irving Berlin.

Mintz: You just said, "None of my songs are that good," and then you talked about the others.

Dylan: My songs are simple. They're very simple to do. That doesn't mean they're any better.

Mintz: You don't believe the statement that you just made that none of your songs are any good. That's not an accurate description.

Dylan: Hank Williams's songs are all better than mine.

Mintz: What makes you so special then? What is this whole experience thing if it's not the songwriting?

Dylan: It's the performing of that song. You're not going to get nowhere with just a good song. You've got to be able to perform it, too.

Mintz: And you would acknowledge that the way you perform your material is exceptional or unique?

Dylan: To the material itself, only to that. Nothing about me is exceptional.

Mintz: How has the imposition of success made it more difficult for you? I mean, presumably people think, well, his success made it easier for him, made it better for him, made it happier for him, made it more rewarding for him.

Dylan: Success! Well, it depends. Someone might look at my life and think of it as being a great success but maybe from my point of view, that wouldn't necessarily be true.

Mintz: Is it? Do you view yourself as a success?

Dylan: It's not for me to view myself. That's arrogant. It's arrogant for people to view themselves in any kind of way. It's a kind of arrogance. Where's arrogance going to get you, really?

Mintz: Let me phrase it differently. You've received so many public accolades over the years, and you've received obviously the approval not only of the public but of your peers, people who you respect, musicians who count.

Dylan: Very true.

Mintz: Do you view that as some kind of demarcation of success? Does that touch you in a way of saying, "I guess I did good, I guess I did right, I guess I made some kind of musical contribution"? Or do you say, "Well, none of that stuff has anything to do with me and I'm really indifferent to it"?

Dylan: Well, you say both things. There's no sense to limit yourself and put yourself in a box to say one thing and to be held account for that. A person can fall in a trap by doing that to himself. There's no reason to be extreme like that, especially if you're dealing with the limitations of success in America.

Mintz: Do you feel fulfilled with your work to date?

Dylan: Well, my work fulfills me, but that's all it has to do. That's not saying a lot.

Mintz: But the question is, you do feel that you're living up to your creative potential?

Dylan: Well . . . no . . . sometimes.

Mintz: There are, I think, about eleven million people listening to us tonight.

Dylan: There better be.

Mintz: There are a lot of people listening, and I assume that a number of them would have liked to have been in this chair, asking you these questions, and I'm sure that I overlooked a couple that they would like to have asked.

Dylan: They could be, someday.

Mintz: And I hope next time around it will be one of them. The thing that I would like to ask you: Is there anything that I have not asked you? Is there anything that you'd like to say to them? Just an open platform to the people who have been with you now on this odyssey for thirty years, the people who presumably are going to go out and buy this amazing collection of songs. You've been asked all the questions. Anything you just want to say to them about you or anything? Take the microphone, talk to them. Any thought you want to communicate to them?

Dylan: Well . . . don't forget to look over their shoulder, you know. Something might be coming.

Mintz: Like what, Bob?

Dylan: Like a train.

INTERVIEW

Paul Zollo | November 1991 | *SongTalk*

Paul Zollo first requested an interview with Dylan in 1987, when he became editor of *SongTalk*, the journal of the National Academy of Songwriters. About four years later, on May 8, 1991, he received a phone message from Dylan spokesman Elliot Mintz, whose own interview with the artist precedes this one in these pages. "Mr. Dylan appreciated your magazine," Mintz said. "He will be in touch."

Zollo phoned Mintz, who said that the interview could take place the following week, "somewhere in the middle of Los Angeles. We will let you know the date, time, and location that morning. Come alone."

"I loved the mystery of that," Zollo told me. "And 'come alone' I found funny, as if I might show up with all my friends."

When Zollo arrived for the May 16 interview at a bungalow in the back of the Beverly Hills Hotel, Mintz was there to greet him. Dylan emerged from a bedroom after about fifteen minutes.

"He was in a happy mood and we connected easily," Zollo recalled. "I began by paraphrasing something Arlo Guthrie had said about songwriting being like fishing, and he thought that was hilarious. He laughed even more when I asked, 'So, how'd you catch so many?'

"He said it was 'the bait'—a typically funny but cryptic Dylan answer, which most interviewers might let go," Zollo said. "But my whole mission was really to determine how this one man wrote so many amazing songs and changed the art form forever. So I asked him what kind of bait, and when I did his eyes lit up and he recognized I was going to follow him everywhere. And he liked that.

"He also liked that I was a musician and a songwriter myself, and he mentioned it," Zollo said. "Musicians talk differently to fellow musicians. So when I asked him about the key of A minor, for example, he knew where I was at. When I told him that to me 'One

More Cup of Coffee' was an ideal A minor song, he said I should try it in B minor. I asked why, and he said, 'It could be a hit for you.'

Zollo told me that at Mintz's request, he removed from the interview transcript a reference to the song "People," which Barbra Streisand had recorded. During the Q&A, Dylan had said, "You know that song [and he sort of sang], 'People, people who need people, are the luckiest people in the world.'" Then he asked, "Do you think that is true? Are people who need people really the luckiest people?"

Said Zollo: "That was golden, in that Dylan, like all serious songwriters, subscribes to the idea that any equation introduced into a song—like that one—should add up. And this does not. Because it is nothing more than a contrivance, an old-fashioned songwriting conceit that works OK in the song but is ultimately untrue. Phony. Not connected to real life. Whereas Dylan's songs do the very opposite, as was his intention.

"When he kept returning to the image of the 'yellow railroad' from 'Absolutely Sweet Marie,' he did so to make this very point," Zollo continued. "That these songs are not contrived. They are real. The equations in them—whether we like them or not—do add up.

"Dylan was also happy that I talked of some songs people rarely discuss," Zollo told me, "such as 'Joey' from *Desire*. But to my enormous dismay, when Dylan had not yet completed his thoughts about that song, Elliot reached over and turned off both of my tape recorders and said we were done.

"To this day," said Zollo, "I am not sure why that happened. Bob was on a roll and we were so connecting. I think I could have had another hour easy. But Elliot ensured it was over." —Ed.

> "I've made shoes for everyone, even you, while I still go barefoot."
> —from "I and I" by Bob Dylan

"Songwriting? What do I know about songwriting?" Bob Dylan asked, and then broke into laughter. He was wearing blue jeans and a white tank-top T-shirt, and drinking coffee out of a glass. "It tastes better out of a glass," he said grinning. His blonde acoustic guitar was leaning on a couch near where we sat. Bob Dylan's guitar. His influence is so vast that everything that surrounds him takes on enlarged significance: Bob Dylan's moccasins. Bob Dylan's coat.

Pete Seeger said, "All songwriters are links in a chain," yet there are few artists in this evolutionary arc whose influence is as profound as that of Bob Dylan. It's hard to imagine the art of songwriting as we know it without him. Though he insists in this interview that "somebody else would have done it," he was the instigator, the one who knew that songs could do more, that they could take on more. He knew that songs could contain a lyrical richness and meaning far beyond the scope of all previous pop songs, and they could possess as much beauty and power as the greatest poetry, and that by being written in rhythm and rhyme and merged with music, they could speak to our souls.

Starting with the models made by his predecessors, such as the talking blues, Dylan quickly discarded old forms and began to fashion new ones. He broke all the rules of songwriting without abandoning the craft and care that holds songs together. He brought the linguistic beauty of Shakespeare, Byron, and Dylan Thomas, and the expansiveness and beat experimentation of Ginsberg, Kerouac and Ferlinghetti, to the folk poetry of Woody Guthrie and Hank Williams. And when the world was still in the midst of accepting this new form, he brought music to a new place again, fusing it with the electricity of rock and roll. "Basically, he showed that anything goes," Robbie Robertson said. John Lennon said that it was hearing Dylan that allowed him to make the leap from writing empty pop songs to expressing the actuality of his life and the depths of his own soul. "Help" was a real call for help, he said, and prior to hearing Dylan it didn't occur to him that songs could contain such direct meaning. When he asked Paul Simon how he made the leap in his writing from fifties rock & roll songs like "Hey Schoolgirl" to writing "Sound of Silence" he said, "I really can't imagine it could have been anyone else besides Bob Dylan."

> *"Yes, to dance beneath the diamond sky*
> *with one hand waving free,*
> *silhouetted by the sea,*
> *circled by the circus sands,*
> *With all memory and fate*
> *driven deep beneath the waves,*
> *Let me forget about today until tomorrow."*
> —from "Mr. Tambourine Man"

There's an unmistakable elegance in Dylan's words, an almost biblical beauty that he has sustained in his songs throughout the years. He refers to it as a "gallantry" in the following, and pointed to it as the single thing that sets his songs apart from others. Though he's maybe more famous for the freedom and expansiveness of his lyrics, all of his songs possess this exquisite care and love for the language. As Shakespeare and Byron did in their times, Dylan has taken English, perhaps the world's plainest language, and instilled it with a timeless, mythic grace.

> "Ring them bells, sweet Martha, for the poor man's son
> Ring them bells so the world will know that God is one
> Oh, the shepherd is asleep
> where the willows weep
> and the mountains are filled with lost sheep"
> —from "Ring Them Bells"

As much as he has stretched, expanded and redefined the rules of songwriting, Dylan is a tremendously meticulous craftsman. A brutal critic of his own work, he works and reworks the words of his songs in the studio and even continues to rewrite certain ones even after they've been recorded and released. "They're not written in stone," he said. With such a wondrous wealth of language at his fingertips, he discards imagery and lines other songwriters would sell their souls to discover. *The Bootleg Series*, a recently released collection of previously unissued recordings, offers a rare opportunity to see the revisions and regrouping his songs go through.

"Idiot Wind" is one of his angriest songs ("You don't hear a song like that every day," he said), which he recorded on *Blood On The Tracks* in a way that reflects this anger, emphasizing lines of condemnation like "one day you'll be in the ditch, flies buzzin' around your eyes, blood on your saddle." On *The Bootleg Series*, we get an alternate approach to the song, a quiet, tender reading of the same lines that makes the inherent disquiet of the song even more disturbing, the tenderness of Dylan's delivery adding a new level of genuine sadness to lines like "people see me all the time and they just can't remember how to act." The peak moment of the song is the penultimate chorus when Dylan addresses America: "Idiot wind, blowing like a circle around my skull, from the Grand Coulee Dam to the Capitol." On the *Bootleg* version, this famous line is still in formation: "Idiot wind, blowing every time you move your jaw, from the Grand Coulee Dam to the Mardi Gras." His song "Jokerman" also went through a similar evolution, as a still unreleased bootleg of the song reveals. Like "Idiot Wind," the depth and intensity of the lyric is sustained over an extraordinary amount of verses, yet even more scenes were shot that wound up on the cutting room floor, evidence of an artist overflowing with the abundance of creation:

> *"It's a shadowy world*
> *skies are slippery gray*
> *A woman just gave birth to a prince today*
> *and dressed him in scarlet*
> *He'll put the priest in his pocket,*
> *put the blade to the heat*
> *Take the motherless children off the street*
> *And place them at the feet of a harlot"*
> —from "Jokerman" on *Infidels*

> *"It's a shadowy world*
> *skies are slippery gray*
> *A woman just gave birth to a prince today*
> *and she's dressed in scarlet*
> *He'll turn priests into pimps*
> *and make all men bark*
> *Take a woman who could have been Joan of Arc*
> *and turn her into a harlot"*
> —from "Jokerman" on *Outfidels*, a bootleg

Often Dylan lays abstraction aside and writes songs as clear and telling as any of Woody Guthrie's narrative ballads, finding heroes and antiheroes in our modern times as Woody found in his. Some of these subjects might be thought of as questionable choices for heroic treatment, such as underworld boss Joey Gallo, about whom he wrote the astounding song, "Joey." It's a song that is remarkable for its cinematic clarity; Dylan paints a picture of a life and death so explicit and exact that we can see every frame of it, and even experience Gallo's death as if we were sitting there watching it. And he does it with a rhyme scheme and a meter that makes the immediacy of the imagery even more striking:

> *"One day they blew him down*
> *in a clam bar in New York*
> *He could see it coming through the door*
> *as he lifted up his fork.*
> *He pushed the table over to protect his family*
> *Then he staggered out into the streets*
> *of Little Italy."*
> —from "Joey"

"Yes, well, what can you know about anybody?" Dylan asked, and it's a good question. He's been a mystery for years, "kind of impenetrable, really," Paul Simon said, and that mystery is not penetrated by this interview or any interview. Dylan's answers are often more enigmatic than the questions themselves, and like his songs, they give you a lot to think about while not necessarily revealing much about the man. In person, as others have noted, he is Chaplinesque. His body is smaller and his head bigger than one might expect, giving the effect of a kid wearing a Bob Dylan mask. He possesses one of the world's most striking faces; while certain stars might seem surprisingly normal and unimpressive in the flesh, Dylan is perhaps even more startling to confront than one might expect. Seeing those eyes, and that nose, it's clear it could be no one else than he, and to sit at a table with him and face those iconic features is no less impressive than suddenly finding yourself sitting face to face with William Shakespeare. It's a face we associate with an enormous, amazing body of work, work that has changed the world. But it's not really the kind of face one expects to encounter in everyday life.

Though Van Morrison and others have called him the world's greatest poet, he doesn't think of himself as a poet. "Poets drown in lakes," he said to us. Yet he's written some of the most beautiful poetry the world has known, poetry of love and outrage, of abstraction and clarity, of timelessness and relativity. Though he is faced with the evidence of a catalogue of songs that would contain the whole careers of a dozen fine songwriters, Dylan told us he doesn't consider himself to be a professional songwriter. "For me it's always been more con-fessional than pro-fessional," he said in distinctive Dylan cadence. "My songs aren't written on a schedule." Well, how are they written, we asked? This is the question at the heart of this interview, the main one that comes to mind when looking over all the albums, or witnessing the amazing array of moods, masks, styles and forms all represented on the recently released Bootleg Series. How has he done it? It was the first question asked, and though he deflected it at first with his customary humor, it's a question we returned to a few times. "Start me off somewhere," he said smiling, as if he might be left alone to divulge the secrets of his songwriting, and our talk began.

SongTalk: Okay, Arlo Guthrie recently said, "Songwriting is like fishing in a stream; you put in your line and hope you catch something. And I don't think anyone downstream from Bob Dylan ever caught anything."

Dylan: [*Much laughter*]

ST: Any idea how you've been able to catch so many?

Dylan: [*Laughs*] It's probably the bait. [*More laughter*]

ST: What kind of bait do you use?

Dylan: Uh . . . bait . . . You've got to use some bait. Otherwise you sit around and expect songs to come to you. Forcing it is using bait.

ST: Does that work for you?

Dylan: Well, no. Throwing yourself into a situation that would demand a response is like using bait. People who write about stuff that hasn't really happened to them are inclined to do that.

ST: When you write songs, do you try to consciously guide the meaning or do you try to follow subconscious directions?

Dylan: Well, you know, motivation is something you never know behind any song, really. Anybody's song, you never know what the motivation was. It's nice to be able to put yourself in an environment where you can completely accept all the unconscious stuff that comes to you from your inner workings of your mind. And block yourself off to where you can control it all, take it down. Edgar Allan Poe must have done that. People who are dedicated writers, of which there are some, but mostly people get their information today over a television set or some kind of a way that's hitting them on all their senses. It's not just a great novel anymore. You have to be able to get the thoughts out of your mind.

ST: How do you do that?

Dylan: Well, first of all, there's two kinds of thoughts in your mind: there's good thoughts and evil thoughts. Both come through your mind. Some people are more loaded down with one than another. Nevertheless, they come through. And you have to be able to sort them out, if you want to be a songwriter, if you want to be a good song singer. You must get rid of all that baggage. You ought to be able to sort out those thoughts, because they don't mean anything, they're just pulling you around, too. It's important to get rid of all them thoughts. Then you can do something from *some* kind of surveillance of the situation. You have some kind of place where you can see but it can't affect you. Where you can bring something to the matter, besides just take, take, take, take, take. As so many situations in life are today. Take, take, take, that's all that it is. What's in it for me? That syndrome which started in the Me Decade, whenever that was. We're still in that. It's still happening.

ST: Is songwriting for you more a sense of taking something from someplace else?

Dylan: Well, someplace else is always a heartbeat away. There's no rhyme or reason to it. There's no rule. That's what makes it so attractive. There isn't any rule. You can still have your wits about you and do something that gets you off in a multitude of ways. As you very well know, or else you yourself wouldn't be doing it.

ST: Your songs often bring us back to other times, and are filled with mythic, magical images. A song like "Changing of the Guard" seems to take place centuries ago, with lines like "They shaved her head / she was torn between Jupiter and Apollo / a messenger arrived with a black nightingale . . ." How do you connect with a song like that?

Dylan: [*Pause*] A song like that, there's no way of knowing, after the fact, unless somebody's there to take it down in chronological order, what the motivation was behind it. [*Pause*] But on one level, of course, it's no different from anything else of mine. It's the same amount of metric verses like a poem. To me, like a poem. The melodies in my mind are very simple, they're very simple, they're just based on music we've all heard growing up. And that and music which went beyond that, which went back further, Elizabethan ballads and whatnot . . . To me, it's old. [*Laughs*] It's old. It's not something, with my minimal amount of talent, if you could call it that, minimum amount . . . To me somebody coming along now would definitely read what's out there if they're seriously concerned with being an artist who's going to still be an artist when they get to be Picasso's age. You're better off learning some music theory. You're just better off, yeah, if you want to write songs. Rather than just take a hillbilly twang, you know, and try to base it all on that. Even country music is more orchestrated than it used to be. You're better off having some feel for music that you don't have to carry in your head, that you can write down. To me those are the people who . . . are serious about this craft. People who go about it that way. Not people who just want to pour out their insides and they got to get a big idea out and they want to tell the world about this, sure, you can do it through a song, you always could. You can use a song for anything, you know. The world don't need any more songs.

ST: You don't think so?

Dylan: No. They've got enough. They've got way too many. As a matter of fact, if nobody wrote any songs from this day on, the world ain't gonna suffer for it. Nobody cares. There's enough songs for people to listen to, if they want to listen to songs. For every man, woman and child on earth, they could be sent, probably, each of them, a hundred records, and never be repeated. There's enough songs. Unless someone's gonna come along with a pure heart and has something to say. That's a different story. But as far as songwriting, any idiot could do it. If you see me do it, any idiot could do it. [*Laughs*] It's just not that difficult of a thing. Everybody writes a song just like everybody's got that one great novel in them. There aren't a lot of people like me. You just had your interview with Neil [Young], John Mellencamp . . . Of course, most of my ilk that came along write their own songs and play them. It wouldn't matter if anybody ever made another record. They've got enough songs. To me, someone who writes really good songs is Randy Newman. There's a lot of people who write good songs. As songs. Now Randy might not go out on stage and knock you out, or knock your socks off. And he's not going to get people thrilled in the front row. He ain't gonna do that. But he's gonna write a better song than most people who can do it. You know, he's got that down to an art. Now Randy knows music. He knows music. But it doesn't get any better than "Louisiana" or "Cross Charleston Bay" ["Sail Away"]. It doesn't get any better than that. It's like a classically heroic anthem theme. He did it. There's quite a few people who did it. Not that many people in Randy's class. Brian Wilson. He can write melodies that will beat the band. Three people could combine on a song and make it a great song. If one person would have written the same song, maybe you would have never heard it. It might get buried on some . . . rap record. [*Laughs*]

ST: Still, when you've come out with some of your new albums of songs, those songs fit that specific time better than any songs that had already been written. Your new songs have always shown us new possibilities.

Dylan: It's not a good idea and it's bad luck to look for life's guidance to popular entertainers. It's bad luck to do that. No one should do that. Popular entertainers are fine, there's nothing the matter with that but as long as you know where you're standing and what ground you're on, many of them, they don't know what they're doing either.

ST: But your songs are more than pop entertainment . . .

Dylan: Some people say so. Not to me.

ST: No?

Dylan: Pop entertainment means nothing to me. Nothing. You know, Madonna's good. Madonna's good, she's talented, she puts all kind of stuff together, she's learned her thing . . . But it's the kind of thing which takes years and years out of your life to be able to do. You've got to sacrifice a whole lot to do that. Sacrifice. If you want to make it big, you've got to sacrifice a whole lot. It's all the same, it's all the same. [*Laughs*]

ST: Van Morrison said that you are our greatest living poet. Do you think of yourself in those terms?

Dylan: [*Pause*] Sometimes. It's within me. It's within me to put myself up and be a poet. But it's a dedication. [*Softly*] It's a big dedication. [*Pause*] Poets don't drive cars. [*Laughs*] Poets don't go to the supermarket. Poets don't empty the garbage. Poets aren't on the PTA. Poets, you know, they don't go picket the Better Housing Bureau, or whatever. Poets don't . . . Poets don't even speak on the telephone. Poets don't even talk to anybody. Poets do a lot of listening and . . . and usually they know why they're poets! [*Laughs*] Yeah, there are . . . what can you say? The world don't need any more poems, it's got Shakespeare. There's enough of everything. You name it, there's enough of it. There was too much of it with electricity, maybe, some people said that. Some people said the lightbulb was going too far. Poets live on the land. They behave in a gentlemanly way. And live by their own gentlemanly code. [*Pause*] And die broke. Or drown in lakes. Poets usually have very unhappy endings. Look at Keats' life. Look at Jim Morrison, if you want to call him a poet. Look at him. Although some people say that he is really in the Andes.

ST: Do you think so?

Dylan: Well, it never crossed my mind to think one way or the other about it, but you do hear that talk. Piggyback in the Andes. Riding a donkey.

ST: People have a hard time believing that Shakespeare really wrote all of his work because there is so much of it. Do you have a hard time accepting that?

Dylan: People have a hard time accepting anything that overwhelms them.

ST: Might they think that of you, years from now, that no one man could have produced so much incredible work?

Dylan: They could. They could look back and think nobody produced it. [*Softly*] It's not to anybody's best interest to think about how they will be perceived tomorrow. It hurts you in the long run.

ST: But aren't there songs of your own that you know will always be around?

Dylan: Who's gonna sing them? My songs really aren't meant to be covered. No, not really. Can you think of . . . Well, they do get covered, but it's covered. They're not intentionally written to be covered, but okay, they do.

ST: Your songs are much more enjoyable to sing and play than most songs . . .

Dylan: Do you play them on piano or guitar?

ST: Both.

Dylan: Acoustic guitar?

ST: Mostly.

Dylan: Do you play jazz? It never hurts to learn as many chords as you can. All kinds. Sometimes it will change the inflection of a whole song, a straight chord, or, say, an augmented seventh chord.

ST: Do you have favorite keys to work in?

Dylan: On the piano, my favorite keys are the black keys. And they sound better on guitar, too. Sometimes when a song's in a flat key, say B flat, bring it to the guitar, you might want to put it in A. But . . . that's an interesting thing you just said. It changes the reflection. Mainly in mine the songs sound different. They sound . . . when you take a black key song and put it on the guitar, which means you're playing in A flat, not too many people like to play in those keys. To me it doesn't matter. [*Laughs*] It doesn't matter because my fingering is the same anyway.

So there are songs that, even without the piano, which is the dominant sound if you're playing in the black keys—why else would you play in that key except to have that dominant piano sound?— the songs that go into those keys right from the piano, they sound different. They sound deeper. Yeah. They sound deeper. Everything sounds deeper in those black keys. They're not guitar keys, though. Guitar bands don't usually like to play in those keys, which kind of gives me an idea, actually, of a couple of songs that could actually sound better in black keys.

ST: Do keys have different colors for you?

Dylan: Sure. Sure. [*Softly*] Sure.

ST: You've written some great A minor songs. I think of "One More Cup of Coffee"—

Dylan: Right. B minor might sound even better.

ST: How come?

Dylan: Well, it might sound better because you're playing a lot of open chords if you're playing in A minor. If you play in B minor, it will force you to play higher. And the chords . . . you're bound, someplace along the line, because there are so many chords in that song, or seem to be anyway, you're bound someplace along the line to come down to an open chord on the bottom. From B. You would hit E someplace along the line. Try it in B minor. [*Laughs*] Maybe it will be a hit for you. A hit is a number one song, isn't it? Yeah.

ST: When you sit down to write a song, do you pick a key first that will fit a song? Or do you change keys while you're writing?

Dylan: Yeah. Yeah. Maybe like in the middle of the thing. There are ways you can get out of whatever you've gotten into. You want to get out of it. It's bad enough getting into it. But the thing to do as soon as you get into it is realize you must get out of it. And unless you get out of it quickly and effortlessly, there's no use staying in it. It will just drag you down. You could be spending years writing the same song, telling the same story, doing the same thing. So once you involve yourself in it, once you accidentally have slipped into it, the thing is to get out. So your primary impulse is going to take you so far. But then you might think, well, you know, is this one of these things where it's all just going to come? And then all of a sudden you start thinking. And when my mind starts thinking, "What's happening now? Oh, there's a story here," and my mind starts to get into it, that's trouble right away. That's usually big trouble. And as far as never seeing this thing again. There's a bunch of ways you can get out of that. You can make yourself get out of it by changing key. That's one way. Just take the whole thing and change key, keeping the same melody. And see if that brings you any place. More times than not, that will take you down the road. You don't want to be on a collision course. But that will take you down the road. Somewhere. And then if that fails, and that will run out, too, then you can always go back to where you were to start. It won't work twice, it only works once. Then you go back to where you started. Yeah, because anything you do in A, it's going to be a different song in G. While you're writing it, anyway. There's too many wide passing notes in G [on the guitar] not to influence your writing, unless you're playing barre chords.

ST: Do you ever switch instruments, like from guitar to piano, while writing?

Dylan: Not so much that way. Although when it's time to record something, for me, sometimes a song that has been written on piano with just lyrics here in my hand, it'll be time to play it now on guitar. So it will come out differently. But it wouldn't have influenced the writing of the song at all. Changing keys influences the writing of the song. Changing keys on the same instrument. For me, that works. I think for somebody else, the other thing works. Everything is different.

ST: I interviewed Pete Seeger recently—

Dylan: He's a great man, Pete Seeger.

ST: I agree. He said, "All songwriters are links in a chain." Without your link in that chain, all of songwriting would have evolved much differently. You said how you brought folk music to rock music. Do you think that would have happened without you?

Dylan: Somebody else would have done it in some other kind of way. But, hey, so what? So what? You can lead people astray awfully easily. Would people have been better off? Sure. They would have found somebody else. Maybe different people would have found different people, and would have been influenced by different people.

ST: You brought the song to a new place. Is there still a new place to bring songs? Will they continue to evolve?

Dylan: [*Pause*] The evolution of song is like a snake with its tail in its mouth. That's evolution. That's what it is. As soon as you're there, you find your tail.

ST: Would it be okay with you if I mentioned some lines from your songs out of context to see what response you might have to them?

Dylan: Sure. You can name anything you want to name, man.

ST: "I stand here looking at your yellow railroad / in the ruins of your balcony . . . [from "Absolutely Sweet Marie"]

Dylan: [*Pause*] Okay. That's an old song. No, let's say not even old. How old? Too old. It's matured well. It's like wine. Now, you know, look, that's as complete as you can be. Every single letter in that line. It's all true. On a literal and on an escapist level.

ST: And is it truth that adds so much resonance to it?

Dylan: Oh yeah, exactly. See, you can pull it apart and it's like, "Yellow railroad?" Well, yeah. Yeah, yeah. All of it.

ST: "I was lying down in the reeds without any oxygen / I saw you in the wilderness among the men / I saw you drift into infinity and come back again . . ." [from "True Love Tends to Forget"]

Dylan: Those are probably lyrics left over from my songwriting days with Jacques Levy. To me, that's what they sound like. Getting back to the yellow railroad, that could be from looking some place. Being a performer you travel the world. You're not just looking off the same window every day. You're not just walking down the same old street. So you must make yourself observe whatever. But most of the time it hits you. You don't have to observe. It hits you. Like "yellow railroad" could have been a blinding day when the sun was bright on a railroad someplace and it stayed on my mind. These aren't contrived images. These are images which are just in there and have got to come out. You know, if it's in there it's got to come out.

ST: "And the chains of the sea will be busted in the night . . ." [from "When the Ship Comes In"].

Dylan: To me, that song says a whole lot. Patti Labelle should do that. You know? You know, there again, that comes from hanging out at a lot of poetry gatherings. Those kind of images are very romantic. They're very gothic and romantic at the same time. And they have a sweetness to it, also. So it's a combination of a lot of different elements at the time. That's not a contrived line. That's not sitting down and writing a song. Those kind of songs, they just come out. They're in you so they've got to come out.

ST: "Standing on the water casting your bread / while the eyes of the idol with the iron head are glowing . . ." [from "Jokerman"]

Dylan: [*Blows small Peruvian flute*] Which one is that again?

ST: That's from "Jokerman."

Dylan: That's a song that got away from me. Lots of songs on that album [*Infidels*] got away from me. They just did.

ST: You mean in the writing?

Dylan: Yeah. They hung around too long. They were better before they were tampered with. Of course, it was me tampering with them. [*Laughs*] Yeah. That could have been a good song. It could've been.

ST: I think it's tremendous.

Dylan: Oh, you do? It probably didn't hold up for me because in my mind it had been written and rewritten and written again. One of those kinds of things.

ST: "But the enemy I see wears a cloak of decency . . ." [from "Slow Train"]

Dylan: Now don't tell me . . . wait . . . Is that "When You Gonna Wake Up"?

ST: No, that's from "Slow Train."

Dylan: Oh, wow. Oh, yeah. Wow. There again. That's a song that you could write a song to every line in the song. You could.

ST: Many of your songs are like that.

Dylan: Well, you know, that's not good either. Not really. In the long run, it could have stood up better by maybe doing just that, maybe taking every line and making a song out of it. If somebody had the will power. But that line, there again, is an intellectual line. It's a line, "Well, the enemy I see wears a cloak of decency," that could be a lie. It just could be. Whereas "Standing under your yellow railroad," that's not a lie. To Woody Guthrie, see, the airwaves were sacred. And when he'd hear something false, it was on airwaves that were sacred to him. His songs weren't false. Now we know the airwaves aren't sacred but to him they were. So that influenced a lot of people with me coming up. Like, "You know, all those songs on the Hit Parade are just a bunch of shit, anyway." It influenced me in the beginning when nobody had heard that. Nobody had heard that. You know, "If I give my heart to you, will you handle it with care?" Or "I'm getting sentimental over you." Who gives a shit! It could be said in a grand way, and the performer could put the song across, but come on, that's because he's a great performer, not because it's a great song. Woody was also a performer and songwriter. So a lot of us got caught up in that. There ain't anything good on the radio. It doesn't happen. Then, of course, the Beatles came along and kind of grabbed everybody by the throat. You were for them or against them. You were for them or you joined them, or whatever. Then everybody said, Oh, popular song ain't so bad, and then everyone wanted to get on the radio. [*Laughs*] Before that it didn't matter. My first records were never played on the radio. It was unheard of! Folk records weren't played on the radio. You never heard them on the radio and nobody cared if they were on the radio. Going on into it further, after the Beatles came out and everybody from England, rock and roll still is an American thing. Folk music is not. Rock and roll is an American thing, it's just all kind of twisted. But the English kind of threw it back, didn't they? And they made everybody respect it once more. So everybody wanted to get on the radio. Now nobody even knows what radio is anymore. Nobody likes it that you talk to. Nobody listens to it. But, then again, it's bigger than it ever was. But nobody knows how to really respond to it. Nobody can shut it off. [*Laughs*] You know? And people really aren't sure whether they want to be on the radio or whether they don't want to be on the radio. They might want to sell a lot of records, but people always did that. But being a folk performer, having hits, it wasn't important. Whatever that has to do with anything . . . [*Laughs*]

ST: Your songs, like Woody's, always have defied being pop entertainment. In your songs, like his, we know a real person is talking, with lines like "You've got a lot of nerve to say you are my friend."

Dylan: That's another way of writing a song, of course. Just talking to somebody that ain't there. That's the best way. That's the truest way. Then it just becomes a question of how heroic your speech is. To me, it's something to strive after.

ST: Until you record a song, no matter how heroic it is, it doesn't really exist. Do you ever feel that?

Dylan: No. If it's there, it exists.

ST: You once said that you only write about what's true, what's been proven to you, that you write about dreams but not fantasies.

Dylan: My songs really aren't dreams. They're more of a responsive nature. Waking up from a dream is . . . when you write a dream, it's something you try to recollect and you're never quite sure if you're getting it right or not.

ST: You said your songs are responsive. Does life have to be in turmoil for songs to come?

Dylan: Well, to me, when you need them, they appear. Your life doesn't have to be in turmoil to write a song like that but you need to be outside of it. That's why a lot of people, me myself included, write songs when one form or another of society has rejected you. So that you can truly write about it from the outside. Someone who's never been out there can only imagine it as anything, really.

ST: Outside of life itself?

Dylan: No. Outside of the situation you find yourself in. There are different types of songs and they're all called songs. But there are different types of songs just like there are different types of people, you know? There's an infinite amount of different kinds, stemming from a common folk ballad verse to people who have classical training. And with classical training, of course, then you can just apply lyrics to classical training and get things going on in positions where you've never been in before. Modern twentieth century ears are the first ears to hear these kind of Broadway songs. There wasn't anything like this. These are musical songs. These are done by people who know music first. And then lyrics. To me, Hank Williams is still the best songwriter.

ST: Hank? Better than Woody Guthrie?

Dylan: That's a good question. Hank Williams never wrote "This Land Is Your Land." But it's not that shocking for me to think of Hank Williams singing "Pastures of Plenty" or Woody Guthrie singing "Cheatin' Heart." So in a lot of ways those two writers are similar. As writers. But you mustn't forget that both of these people were performers, too. And that's another thing which separates a person who just writes a song . . . People who don't perform but who are so locked into other people who do that, they can sort of feel what that other person would like to say, in a song and be able to write those lyrics. Which is a different thing from a performer who needs a song to play on stage year after year.

ST: And you always wrote your songs for yourself to sing—

Dylan: My songs were written with me in mind. In those situations, several people might say, "Do you have a song laying around?" The best songs to me—my best songs—are songs which were written very quickly. Yeah, very, very quickly. Just about as much time as it takes to write it down is about as long as it takes to write it. Other than that, there have been a lot of ones that haven't made it. They haven't survived. They could need to be dragged out, you know, and looked at again, maybe.

ST: You said once that the saddest thing about songwriting is trying to reconnect with an idea you started before, and how hard that is to do.

Dylan: To me it can't be done. To me, unless I have another writer around who might want to finish it . . . outside of writing with the Traveling Wilburys, my shared experience writing a song with other songwriters is not that great. Of course, unless you find the right person to write with as a partner . . . [*Laughs*] . . . you're awfully lucky if you do, but if you don't, it's really more trouble than it's worth, trying to write something with somebody.

ST: Your collaborations with Jacques Levy came out pretty great.

Dylan: We both were pretty much lyricists. Yeah, very panoramic songs because, you know, after one of my lines, one of his lines would come out. Writing with Jacques wasn't difficult. It was trying to just get it down. It just didn't stop. Lyrically. Of course, my melodies are very simple anyway so they're very easy to remember.

ST: With a song like "Isis" that the two of you wrote together, did you plot that story out prior to writing the verses?

Dylan: That was a story that [*Laughs*] meant something to him. Yeah. It just seemed to take on a life of its own, [*Laughs*] as another view of history. [*Laughs*] Which there are so many views that don't get told. Oh history, anyway. That wasn't one of them. Ancient history but history nonetheless.

ST: Was that a story you had in mind before the song was written?

Dylan: No. With this "Isis" thing, it was "Isis" . . . you know, the name sort of rang a bell but not in any kind of vigorous way. So therefore, it was name-that-tune time. It was anything. The name was familiar. Most people would think they knew it from somewhere. But it seemed like just about any way it wanted to go would have been okay, just as long as it didn't get too close. [*Laughs*]

ST: Too close to what?

Dylan: [*Laughs*] Too close to me or him.

ST: People have an idea of your songs freely flowing out from you, but that song and many others of yours are so well-crafted; it has an ABAB rhyme scheme which is like something Byron would do, interlocking every line—

Dylan: Oh, yeah. Oh, yeah. Oh, sure. If you've heard a lot of free verse, if you've been raised on free verse, William Carlos Williams, e.e. cummings, those kind of people who wrote free verse, your ear is not going to be trained for things to sound that way. Of course, for me it's no secret that all my stuff is rhythmically oriented that way. Like a Byron line would be something as simple as "What is it you buy so dear / with your pain and with your fear?" Now that's a Byron line, but that could have been one of my lines. Up until a certain time, maybe in the twenties, that's the way poetry was. It was that way. It was . . . simple and easy to remember. And always in rhythm. It had a rhythm whether the music was there or not.

ST: Is rhyming fun for you?

Dylan: Well, it can be, but, you know, it's a game. You know, you sit around . . . you know, it's more like it's mentally . . . mentally . . . it gives you a thrill. It gives you a thrill to rhyme something you might think, "Well, that's never been rhymed before." But then again, people have taken rhyming now, it doesn't have to be exact anymore. Nobody's going to care if you rhyme "represent" with "ferment," you know. Nobody's gonna care.

ST: That was a result of a lot of people of your generation for whom the craft elements of songwriting didn't seem to matter as much. But in your songs the craft is always there, along with the poetry and the energy—

Dylan: My sense of rhyme used to be more involved in my songwriting than it is . . . Still staying in the unconscious frame of mind, you can pull yourself out and throw up two rhymes first and work it back. You get the rhymes first and work it back and then see if you can make it make sense in another kind of way. You can still stay in the unconscious frame of mind to pull it off, which is the state of mind you have to be in anyway.

ST: So sometimes you will work backwards, like that?

Dylan: Oh, yeah. Yeah, a lot of times. That's the only way you're going to finish something. That's not uncommon, though.

ST: Do you finish songs even when you feel that maybe they're not keepers?

Dylan: Keepers or not keepers . . . you keep songs if you think they're any good, and if you don't . . . you can always give them to somebody else. If you've got songs that you're not going to do and you just don't like them . . . show them to other people, if you want. Then again, it all gets back to the motivation. Why you're doing what you're doing. That's what it is. [*Laughs*] It's confrontation with that . . . goddess of the self. God of the self or goddess of the self? Somebody told me that the goddess rules over the self. Gods don't concern themselves with such earthly matters. Only goddesses . . . would stoop so low. Or bend down so low.

ST: You mentioned that when you were writing "Every Grain of Sand" that you felt you were in an area where no one had ever been before—

Dylan: Yeah. In that area where Keats is. Yeah. That's a good poem set to music.

ST: A beautiful melody.

Dylan: It's a beautiful melody, too, isn't it? It's a folk derivative melody. It's nothing you can put your finger on, but, you know, yeah, those melodies are great. There ain't enough of them, really. Even a song like that, the simplicity of it can be . . . deceiving. As far as . . . a song like that just may have been written in great turmoil, although you would never sense that. Written but not delivered. Some songs are better written in peace and quiet and delivered in turmoil. Others are best written in turmoil and delivered in a peaceful, quiet way. It's a magical thing, popular song. Trying to press it down into everyday numbers doesn't quite work. It's not a puzzle. There aren't pieces that fit. It doesn't make a complete picture that's ever been seen. But, you know, as they say, thank God for songwriters.

ST: Randy Newman said that he writes his songs by going to it every day, like a job—

Dylan: Tom Paxton told me the same thing. He goes back with me, way back. He told me the same thing. Every day he gets up and he writes a song. Well, that's great, you know, you write the song and then take your kids to school? Come home, have some lunch with the wife, you know, maybe go write another song. Then Tom said for recreation, to get himself loose, he rode his horse. And then pick up his child from school, and then go to bed with the wife. Now to me that sounds like the ideal way to write songs. To me, it couldn't be any better than that.

ST: How do you do it?

Dylan: Well, my songs aren't written on a schedule like that. In my mind it's never really been seriously a profession . . . It's been more confessional than professional. Then again, everybody's in it for a different reason.

ST: Do you ever sit down with the intention of writing a song, or do you wait for songs to come to you?

Dylan: Either or. Both ways. It can come . . . some people are . . . It's possible now for a songwriter to have a recording studio in his house and record a song and make a demo and do a thing. It's like the roles have changed on all that stuff. Now for me, the environment to write the song is extremely important. The environment has to bring something out in me that wants to be brought out. It's a contemplative, reflective thing. Feelings really aren't my thing. See, I don't write lies. It's a proven fact: Most people who say I love you don't mean it. Doctors have proved that. So love generates a lot of songs. Probably more so than a lot. Now it's not my intention to have love influence my songs. Any more than it influenced Chuck Berry's songs or Woody Guthrie's or Hank Williams'. Hank Williams, they're not love songs. You're degrading them songs calling them love songs. Those are songs from the Tree of Life. There's no love on the Tree of Life. Love is on the Tree of Knowledge, the Tree of Good and Evil. So we have a lot of songs in popular music about love. Who needs them? Not you, not me. You can use love in a lot of ways in which it will come back to hurt you. Love is a democratic principle. It's a Greek thing. A college professor told me that if you read about Greece in the history books, you'll know all about America. Nothing that happens will puzzle you ever again. You read the history of Ancient Greece and when the Romans came in, and nothing will ever bother you about America again. You'll see what America is. Now, maybe, but there are a lot of other countries in the world besides America . . . [*Laughs*] Two. You can't forget about them. [*Laughter*]

ST: Have you found there are better places in the world than others to write songs?

Dylan: It's not necessary to take a trip to write a song. What a long, strange trip it's been, however. But that part of it's true, too. Environment is very important. People need peaceful, invigorating environments. Stimulating environments. In America there's a lot of repression. A lot of people who are repressed. They'd like to get out of town, they just don't know how to do it. And so, it holds back creativity. It's like you go somewhere and you can't help but feel it. Or people even tell it to you, you know? What got me into the whole thing in the beginning wasn't songwriting. That's not what got me into it. When "Hound Dog" came across the radio, there was nothing in my mind that said, "Wow, what a great song, I wonder who wrote that?" It didn't really concern me who wrote it. It didn't matter who wrote it. It was just . . . it was just there. Same way with me now. You hear a good song. Now you think to yourself, maybe, "Who wrote it?" Why? Because the performer's not as good as the song, maybe. The performer's got to transcend that song. At least come up to it. A good performer can always make a bad song sound good. Record albums are filled with good performers singing filler stuff. Everybody can say they've done that. Whether you wrote it or whether somebody else wrote it, it doesn't matter. What interested me was being a musician. The singer was important and so was the song. But being a musician was always first and foremost in the back of my mind. That's why, while other people were learning . . . whatever they were learning. What were they learning way back then?

ST: "Ride, Sally, Ride"?

Dylan: Something like that. Or "Run, Rudolph, Run." When the others were doing "Run, Rudolph, Run," my interests were going more to Leadbelly kind of stuff, when he was playing a Stella 12-string guitar. Like, how does the guy do that? Where can one of these be found, a 12-string guitar? They didn't have any in my town. My intellect always felt that way. Of the music. Like Paul Whiteman. Paul Whiteman creates a mood. Bing Crosby's early records. They created a mood, like that Cab Calloway, kind of spooky horn kind of stuff. Violins, when big bands had a sound to them, without the Broadway glitz. Once that Broadway trip got into it, it became all sparkly and Las Vegas, really. But it wasn't always so. Music created an environment. It doesn't happen anymore. Why? Maybe technology has just booted it out and there's no need for it. Because we have a screen which supposedly is three-dimensional. Or comes across as three-dimensional. It would like you to believe it's three-dimensional. Well, you know, like old movies and stuff like that that's influenced so many of us who grew up on that stuff. [*Picks up Peruvian flute*] Like this old thing, here, it's nothing, it's some kind of, what is it? . . . Listen: [*Plays a slow tune on the flute*] Here, listen to this song. [*Plays more*] Okay. That's a song. It don't have any words. Why do songs need words? They don't. Songs don't need words. They don't.

ST: Do you feel satisfied with your body of work?

Dylan: Most everything, yeah.

ST: Do you spend a lot of time writing songs?

Dylan: Well, did you hear that record that Columbia released last year, *Down in the Groove*? Those songs, they came in pretty easy.

ST: I'd like to mention some of your songs, and see what response you have to them.

Dylan: Okay.

ST: "One More Cup of Coffee" [from *Desire*]

Dylan: [*Pause*] Was that for a coffee commercial? No . . . It's a gypsy song. That song was written during a gypsy festival in the south of France one summer. Somebody took me there to the gypsy high holy days which coincide with my own particular birthday. So somebody took me to a birthday party there once, and hanging out there for a week probably influenced the writing of that song. But the "valley below" probably came from someplace else. My feeling about the song was that the verses came from someplace else. It wasn't about anything, so this "valley below" thing became the fixture to hang it on. But "valley below" could mean anything.

ST: "Precious Angel" [from *Slow Train Comin'*]

Dylan: Yeah. That's another one, it could go on forever. There's too many verses and there's not enough. You know? When people ask me, "How come you don't sing that song anymore?" It's like it's another one of those songs: it's just too much and not enough. A lot of my songs strike me that way. That's the natural thing about them to me. It's too hard to wonder why about them. To me, they're not worthy of wondering why about them. They're songs. They're not written in stone. They're on plastic.

ST: To us, though, they are written in stone, because Bob Dylan wrote them. I've been amazed by the way you've changed some of your great songs—

Dylan: Right. Somebody told me that Tennyson often wanted to rewrite his poems when he saw them in print.

ST: "I and I" [*from "Infidels"*]

Dylan: [*Pause*] That was one of them Caribbean songs. One year a bunch of songs just came to me hanging around down in the islands, and that was one of them.

ST: "Joey" [*from "Desire"*].

Dylan: To me, that's a great song. Yeah. And it never loses its appeal.

ST: And it has one of the greatest visual endings of any song.

Dylan: That's a tremendous song. And you'd only know that singing it night after night. You know who got me singing that song? [Jerry] Garcia. Yeah. He got me singing that song again. He said that's one of the best songs ever written. Coming from him, it was hard to know which way to take that. [*Laughs*] He got me singing that song again with them [The Grateful Dead]. It was amazing how it would, right from the get go, it had a life of its own, it just ran out of the gate and it just kept on getting better and better and better and better and it keeps on getting better. It's in its infant stages, as a performance thing. Of course, it's a long song. But, to me, not to blow my own horn, but to me the song is like a Homer ballad. Much more so than "A Hard Rain," which is a long song, too. But, to me, "Joey" has a Homeric quality to it that you don't hear every day. Especially in popular music.

ST: "Ring Them Bells" [*from "Oh Mercy"*]

Dylan: It stands up when you hear it played by me. But if another performer did it, you might find that it probably wouldn't have as much to do with bells as what the title proclaims. Somebody once came and sang it in my dressing room. To me. [*Laughs*] To try to influence me to sing it that night. [*Laughter*] It could have gone either way, you know.

Elliot Mintz: Which way did it go?

Dylan: It went right out the door. [*Laughter*] It went out the door and didn't come back. Listening to this song that was on my record, sung by someone who wanted me to sing it . . . There was no way he was going to get me to sing it like that. A great performer, too.

ST: "Idiot Wind" [*from "Blood on the Tracks"*]

Dylan: "Idiot Wind." Yeah, you know, obviously, if you've heard both versions you realize, of course, that there could be a myriad of verses for the thing. It doesn't stop. It wouldn't stop. Where do you end? You could still be writing it, really. It's something that could be a work continually in progress. Although, on saying that, let me say that my lyrics, to my way of thinking, are better for my songs than anybody else's. People have felt about my songs sometimes the same way as me. And they say to me, your songs are so opaque that, people tell me, they have feelings they'd like to express within the same framework. My response, always, is go ahead, do it, if you feel like it. But it never comes off. They're not as good as my lyrics. There's just something about my lyrics that just have a gallantry to them. And that might be all they have going for them. [*Laughs*] However, it's no small thing.

DYLAN: JOKES, LAUGHTER, AND A SERIES OF DREAMS

Peter Wilmoth | April 3, 1992 | *The Age* (Australia)

About a year after Dylan talked with Paul Zollo, he met with Australian journalist Peter Wilmoth in his dressing room after an April 1, 1992, concert in Melbourne.

"I had rung promoter Michael Gudinski and let him know how much I wanted an interview with the man," Wilmoth told me. "I was about to sit down at the Palais Theatre for the show when I got a tap on the shoulder from Gudinski. 'Bob Dylan will see you after the show.'

"I had no tape recorder (this was well before smartphones), no questions, no notice. I was bundled into a Terago [Australian Toyota model] and driven to my nearby apartment to get the recorder. I sat in the dark for two hours writing out my questions. Not easy. What hasn't Bob Dylan been asked?"

Wilmoth wound up getting thirty minutes with the artist. "It went OK," he recalled.

"And twenty-five years later, I still feel blessed that I had the chance to spend even a little time with the man who so profoundly shaped contemporary music and culture." —Ed.

Bob Dylan is considering the symbolism of the '60s voice of youth turning 50 last year. "Well, Rod's around," he says. "He must be close to me or even above me. [Rod Stewart is 47.] A couple of 'em are around. The Stones." What does he think of the Stones 30 years later? Dylan breaks up laughing. "If you like that sort of thing."

Bob Dylan: sit-down-comic? The man who has been called one of this country's most influential—and possibly earnest—figures is not

381

expansive, but he's not walking out of the interview after seven minutes either, as he did to one journalist. This is a kinder, gentler Dylan, cooling off after his first Melbourne show on Wednesday night. Dylan is a small man, almost curled up in his chair. His shoulders are hunched against intrusion. He offers a limp hand and a grunt in greeting. This is Dylan in a good mood. Why Dylan has agreed to meet a journalist after refusing 300 requests for interviews when he turned 50 in May last year is unclear. But *The Age* is the beneficiary of half an hour of sometimes incomprehensible, sometimes lucid thoughts, punctuated by three or four belly laughs. America's greatest living poet is actually being charming.

Since he became famous in the coffee shops of New York's Greenwich Village in 1961, Dylan has embodied other people's dreams and ideals of the '60s. "People seem now to have forgotten about it," he says. "People are now more or less interested in the '90s. Sixties memories are fading a little." There seems to be a '60s revival every few months. Dylan smiles. "There were '60s revivals in the '60s."

When journalists are finally allowed to touch the hem, they are usually forewarned not to get personal. "There's nothing that is really very interesting about me," Dylan protests, laughing. "Talking about me doesn't make a conversation more interesting. It doesn't interest me to talk about me. It's my least favorite subject [*laughs again*]."

But Dylan seems happy enough when asked about his children Anna, 25, and Jacob, 21, who with Sara Dylan, were immortalized in the song *Sara* from his acclaimed 1975 album *Desire*. "They're just around. I have an extended family, this, that and the other. We get on well, for the most part."

After 30 years of singing *Blowin' in the Wind*, does he perform the early songs under sufferance? "I do those songs because they feel right to sing," he says. "Even if they weren't my songs, they're my style of song, and they are oriented to what I am doing today."

He is tired of interpreting his early songs too literally. "Some of my records I've been overloaded with, some parts and arrangements," he admits. "Whereas the song itself still has its strength for me. With some of the older songs, the vision is still quite focused."

Strangely he admits to changing the list of songs he performs to keep certain fans happy. "There are a lot of people that come to our shows lots of times, so just for them, it's a good idea to do different things. It's not like they come and see me once."

Dylan has recently been the subject of a biography, Clinton Heylin's _Behind the Shades,_ and there are several retrospectives, including a three-CD boxed set of "bootlegged" versions of his earliest songs. "Well, you know, people bootleg concerts, they might as well be out legally. Nobody would ever have thought that was that big a business. They sell quite a bit."

Was there any music Dylan admires today? "No. Nothing." He believes music lost the plot. "There was a cut-off point sometime." The early 70's? "Maybe. When the machines got into making music, you could turn it off more. It seemed to take a different turn at that point and the purpose got kind of lost."

The audience at Dylan's shows consists largely of people who were in nappies when he released "All Along the Watchtower" in 1968. "I'm lucky to have any audience," Dylan says. "A lot of my contemporaries really don't have any."

His views on Australia are a little disjointed, but he claims to be fascinated by a country so different from his own. "To me Australia is ancient ground broken off from Africa, and that's why there are different animals here. Someone told me kangaroos are prehistoric. The people who are indigenous are prehistoric, too. Just looking at the ground . . . it doesn't look this way in America or Europe. This is ancient territory. For that reason alone, it's worth spending time here."

Dylan said recently that he'd written enough songs. "My songs aren't written like they used to be, which was all the time. They come slower now [_laughs_]." Dylan ties a towel around his head and walks out of the dressing room and disappears into his tour bus. To rejuvenate himself, he sometimes decides to escape from the circus. "Oh, I get away to the boondocks somewhere."

DYLAN ON

His Life in Woodstock

"It was like a wave of insanity breakin' loose around the house *day* and *night*. You'd come in the house and find people there, people comin' through the *woods*, at all hours of the day and night, knockin' on your door. It was really dark and depressing. And there was no way to *respond* to all this, you know? It was as if they were suckin' your very *blood* out. I said: 'Now, wait, these people can't be my *fans*. They just *can't* be.' And they kept comin' We *had* to get out of there. This was just about the time of that Woodstock Festival, which was the sum total of all this bullshit. And it seemed to have something to do with *me*, this Woodstock Nation and everything it represented. So we couldn't *breathe*. I couldn't get any space for myself and my family, and there was no help, nowhere. I got very resentful about the whole thing, and we got outta there."

—from interview with Kurt Loder, *Rolling Stone*, October 15, 1992

DYLAN ON

Recording Technology

"Modern recording technology never endeared itself to me. My kind of sound is very simple, with a little bit of echo, and that's about all that's required to record it. . . . The way most records sound these days, everything is equalized. My kind of music is based on non-equalized parts, where one sound isn't necessarily sup-posed to be as loud as another. When producers try to equal everything out, it's to dismal effect on my records."

—from interview with Greg Kot, *Chicago Tribune*, August 1993

DYLAN ON

Nostalgia

"I'd rather live in the moment than some kind of nostalgia trip, which I feel is a drug, a real drug that people are mainlining. It's outrageous. People are mainlining nostalgia like it was morphine. I don't want to be a drug dealer."

—from interview with Malcolm Jones Jr., *Newsweek*, March 20, 1995

A MIDNIGHT CHAT WITH DYLAN

John Dolen | September 28, 1995 | *SunSentinel* **(Fort Lauderdale, Florida)**

Dylan experienced eventful times shortly after his April 1992 meeting with Peter Wilmoth—especially in October of that year. That's when he issued *Good As I Been to You*, the first of two acclaimed albums of blues and folk covers. It's also the month when he obtained a divorce from Carolyn Dennis. Finally, it's the month when New York's Madison Square Garden hosted an all-star concert that marked the thirtieth anniversary of Dylan's debut album release. Performers at the show—which subsequently became available on CD and in video formats—included George Harrison, Neil Young, Stevie Wonder, Eric Clapton, Tom Petty, and, in the finale, the man himself.

The next few years were less momentous, though Dylan released a second album of blues/folk covers, *World Gone Wrong*, in October 1993, and a live set from *MTV Unplugged* in April 1995. He toured extensively in North America and Europe during these years, however.

On September 25, 1995, he had just ended a two-month break after a summer spent performing in Germany, Spain, France, Switzerland, and England. And he had arrived in Florida, where he would begin a North American tour. That's where he spoke with newspaper journalist John Dolen.

The interview, Dolen told me, took place only after three days of delays. It finally happened, he said, "late in the evening when I had almost given up, sitting nearly alone in the newsroom. Dylan had just returned to his hotel. I thought he would be tired. But it sounded as if he'd just had a pot of coffee.

"The quality of his voice surprised me, too," Dolen added. "Not soft, not loud, and not the slightest bit hoarse or raspy.

"Another thing that struck me was a bit of a revelation," Dolen continued. "Dylan does not come off as an intellectual, although he's read very widely. He is wise, of course, but it is more folksy than cerebral. In other words, he talks like a musician, which shouldn't be surprising because that's what he is. On the bookish side myself, I realized that all these years I had put my own trappings on who he is—just as others have."

The scope and tone of the conversation surprised Dolen as well. "He ranged far beyond [the focus of] your typical musician, speaking at times like a poet or even a prophet, with that elliptical logic reminiscent of the biblical teachers, cutting to the very core of things. He did all this without pretense, without affectation, and with professional respect for where I was coming from.

"It was an unforgettable experience," Dolen concluded. —Ed.

When Bob Dylan calls, it's nearly midnight. When he speaks it is with a clear, distinctive voice. Even though he's at the end of his day, having just returned to a Fort Lauderdale hotel after a band rehearsal, he is contemplative, enigmatic, even poetic.

The Southern leg of his current tour cranks into high gear tonight with the first of two concerts at the Sunrise Musical Theatre. The tour, which has been in progress for more than a year, has earned rave reviews from critics in New York, San Francisco, Dublin. In a nearly hour-long interview with Arts & Features Editor John Dolen, the first in-depth interview he has given to a newspaper this year, Dylan talks about his songs, the creative process and the free gig at the Edge in Fort Lauderdale last Saturday.

Like many others over the years I've spent thousands of hours listening to your albums. Even now, not a month goes by without me reaching for *Blonde on Blonde, Highway 61 Revisited, Slow Train Coming, Street-Legal, Oh Mercy.* **Do you ever just sit back and look at all these albums and say, hey, that's pretty good?**

You know, it's ironic, I never listen to those records. I really don't notice them anymore except to pick songs off of them here and there to play. Maybe I should listen to them.

As a body of work, there could always be more. But it depends. Robert Johnson only made one record—his body of work was just one record. Yet there's no praise or esteem high enough for the body of work he represents. He's influenced hundreds of artists. There are people who put out 40 or 50 records and don't do what he did.

What was the record?

He made a record called *King of the Delta Blues Singers.* In '60 or '62. He was brilliant.

Your performance at the Rock and Roll Hall of Fame concert in Cleveland earlier this month drew a lot of great notices. Is that important to you? What's your feeling about that institution?

I never visited the actual building, I was just over at the concert, which was pretty long. So I have no comment on the interior or any of the exhibits inside.

But how do you feel about the idea of a rock hall of fame itself?

Nothing surprises me anymore. It's a perfect time for anything to happen.

At the Edge show Saturday, you did a lot of covers, including some old stuff like *Confidential.* Was that a Johnnie Ray song?

It's by Sonny Knight. You won't hear that again.

Oh, was that the reason for your "trying to turn bull— into gold" comment at the show?

(Laugh) Something like that.

Were these covers just something for folks at the Edge? Does that mean you aren't going to be doing more material like that on your tour, including the Sunrise shows?

It will be the usual show we're used to doing on this tour now, songs most people will have heard already.

In the vein of non-Dylan music, what does Bob Dylan toss on the CD or cassette player these days?

Ever heard of John Trudell? He talks his songs instead of singing them and has a real good band. There's a lot of tradition to what he is doing. I also like Kevin Lynch. And Steve Forbert.

Are there new bands you think are worth bringing to our attention?

I hear people here and there and I think they're all great. In most cases I never hear of them again. I saw some groups in London this summer. Don't know their names.

At this stage of your career, when you've earned every kind of honor and accolade that a person can get, what motivates you?

I've had it both ways. I have had good and bad accolades. If you pay any attention to them at all, it makes you pathological. It makes us pathological, to read about ourselves. You try not to pay attention or you try to discard it as soon as possible.

For some writers the motivation is that *burden*, that you have to get what's inside of you out and down on paper. How is it with you?

Like that, exactly. But if I can't make it happen, when it comes—you know, when other things intrude—I usually don't make it happen. I don't go to a certain place at a certain time every day to build it. In my case, a lot of these songs, they lay around imperfectly . . .

As a songwriter, what's the creative process? How does a song like *All Along the Watchtower* come about?

There's three kinds of ways. You write lyrics and try to find a melody. Or, if you come up with a melody, then you have to stuff the lyrics in there some kinda way.

And then the third kind of a way is when they both come at the same time. Where it all comes in a blur: The words are the melody and the melody is the words. And that's the ideal way for somebody like myself to get going with something.

All Along the Watchtower was that way. It leaped out in a very short time. I don't like songs that make you feel feeble or indifferent. That lets a whole lot of things out of the picture for me.

How did you feel when you first heard Jimi Hendrix's version of *All Along the Watchtower*?

It overwhelmed me, really. He had such talent—he could find things inside a song and vigorously develop them. He found things that other people wouldn't think of finding in there. He probably improved upon it by the spaces he was using. I took license with the song from his version, actually, and continue to do it to this day.

Angelina, off the *Bootleg Series*, is such a great song, but no matter how hard I try I can't figure out the words; any clues for me?

I never try to figure out what they're about. If you have to think about it, then it's not there.

A song that always haunted me was *Señor* [(Tales of Yankee Power)], from *Street Legal*. Have you played that at all in the last few years?

We play that maybe once every third, fourth or fifth show.

In the '70s after years abroad, I remember the incredible elation I felt coming back to the States and hearing your Christian songs—a validation of experiences I had been through in Spain. I remember the lines, "You talk about Buddha / You talk about Muhammad / But you never said a word about / The one who came to die for us instead . . ." Those were fearless words. How do you feel about those words and the songs you wrote during that period now?

Just writing a song like that probably emancipated me from other kinds of illusions. I've written so many songs and so many records that I can't address them all. I can't say that I would disagree with that line. On its own level it was some kind of turning point for me, writing that.

With the great catalog you have and with the success this year with the *MTV Unplugged* disc, why does this concert tour have such a heavy guitar and drums thing going?

It's not the kind of music that will put anybody to sleep.

The other night at the Edge you left the harmonicas on the stand without touching them—any reason for that?

They are such a dynamo unto themselves. I pick them up when I feel like it.

You've made several passes through here in the past 10 years. Your thoughts on South Florida?

I like it a lot, who wouldn't? There's a lot to like.

Now there is Bob Dylan on CD-ROM, Bob Dylan on the Internet and all that stuff. Are some people taking you too seriously?

It's not for me to say. People take everything seriously. You can get too altruistic on your own self because of the brain energy of other people.

Across the Atlantic is a fellow named Elvis Costello, who, after you, takes a lot of shelf space by my stereo. Both of you are prolific, turn out distinctive albums each time, have great imagery, have a lot to say and so on. Is there any reason that in all the years I've never seen your names or faces together?

It's funny you should mention that. He just played four or five shows with me in London and Paris. He was doing a lot of new songs, playing them by himself. He was doing his thing. You sorta had to be there.

Is America better or worse than, say, in the days of *The Times They Are A-Changin'*?

I see pictures of the '50s, the '60s and the '70s and I see there was a difference. But I don't think the human mind can comprehend the past and the future. They are both just illusions that can manipulate you into thinking there's some kind of change. But after you've been around awhile, they both seem unnatural.

It seems like we're going in a straight line, but then you start seeing things that you've seen before. Haven't you experienced that?

It seems we're going around in circles.

When you look ahead now, do you still see a Slow Train Comin'?

When I look ahead now, it's picked up quite a bit of speed. In fact, it's going like a freight train now.

DYLAN ON

Time Out of Mind

"Some people, when it comes to me, extrapolate only the lyrics from the music. But, in this case, the music itself has just a far-reaching effect, and it was meant to be that way. It's definitely a performance record instead of a poetic literary type of thing. You can feel it rather than think about."

—from Columbia Records press release, July 10, 1997

DYLAN ON

Jimmie Rodgers

"When I was growing up, I had a record called *Hank Snow Sings Jimmie Rodgers*, and that's the first clue I had that Jimmie was unique. The songs were different than the norm. They had more of an individual nature and an elevated conscience, and I could tell that these songs were from a different period of time. I was drawn to their power. I like his songs, anyway, because on the surface their lyrics seem really funny and bright, but underneath, they could be alarmingly dark and dreary."

—from interview with Nick Krewen, *Toronto Star*, September 8, 1997

DYLAN ON

Performing in Concert

"A lot of people don't like the road, but it's as natural to me as breathing. I do it because I'm driven to do it, and I either hate it or love it. I'm mortified to be on the stage, but then again, it's the only place where I'm happy. It's the only place you can be who you want to be. You can't be who you want to be in daily life. I don't care who you are, you're going to be disappointed in daily life. But the cure-all for all that is to get on the stage, and that's why performers do it."

—from interview with Jon Pareles, *New York Times*, September 28, 1997

DYLAN ON

The Life-Threatening Fungal Infection He Suffered in 1997

"It was intolerable pain, where it affects your breathing every waking moment. I didn't have any philosophical profound thoughts. The pain stopped me in my tracks and fried my mind. I was so sick my mind just blanked out. I'm getting better; that's all I can say right now."

—from interview with Edna Gundersen, *USA Today*, September 28, 1997

DYLAN ON

Growing Up in Minnesota in the 1950s

"Knife sharpeners would come down the street, and the coal man, too, and every once in a while a wagon would come through town with a gorilla in a cage or, I remember, a mummy under glass. People sold food off of carts, and it was a very itinerant place—no interstate highways yet, just country roads everywhere. There was an innocence about it all, and I don't recall anything bad ever happening. That was the '50s, the last period of time I remember as being idyllic."

—from interview with Alan Jackson,
Times on Saturday (London), November 15, 1997

DYLAN ON

His Youthful Ambitions

"I knew growing up that I wanted to do something different than anybody else. I wanted to do something that no one else did or could do, and I wanted to do it better than anyone else had. I didn't know where that was going to lead me, but where it did lead me was to folk music at a time when it was totally off the radar screen. Maybe there were 12 people in all of America who even heard of Woody Guthrie, Roscoe Holcomb, the Carter Family, Lead Belly—at least 12 people my age. They were free spirits who took chances, and I never wished to annul any of that spirit."

—from interview with Robert Hilburn, *Los Angeles Times*, December 14, 1997

DYLAN ON

Buddy Holly

"When I was about sixteen or seventeen years old, I went to see Buddy Holly play at Duluth National Guard Armory and I was three feet away from him and he looked at me. And I just have some kind of feeling that he was . . . I don't know how or why but I know he was with us all the time we were making this record in some kind of way."

—from acceptance speech for Album of the Year Grammy for *Time Out of Mind*, Radio City Music Hall, New York, February 25, 1998

DYLAN ON

His Earlier Albums

"Records that were made in that day and age were all good. They all had some magic to them because the technology didn't go beyond what the artist was doing. It was a lot easier to get excellence back in those days on a record than it is now. . . Those records seem to cast a long shadow. But how much of it is the technology and how much of it is the talent and influence, I really don't know."

—from interview with Murray Engleheart, *Guitar World*, March 1999

NO DIRECTION HOME OUTTAKES

2000 (interview) | Broadcast Date Unknown | WBAI-FM (New York)

Some excellent interview material, including much about Dylan's early years in Minnesota, wound up on the cutting-room floor during the making of Martin Scorsese's fine 2005 Dylan biopic, *No Direction Home*. The following are Dylan's answers to questions posed sometime in 2000 by his manager, Jeff Rosen. (WBAI's recording of this conversation does not include the questions.) —Ed.

I was playing guitar pretty early on, actually. Maybe when I was about ten or eleven. Had a guitar in the house that my father bought. And I found something else in there that had kind of mystical overtones. The people who had lived in the house previous to that time, they had left some of their furniture, and among the furniture was a great big mahogany radio. It was like a jukebox. And it had a 78 turntable when you opened up the top. And I opened it up one day and there was a record on there, a country record. It was a song called "Drifting Too Far from Shore," but I think it was the Stanley Brothers; if not, Bill Monroe. I played the record, and it just brought me into a different world.

And when I began listening to the radio, I began to get bored being there. But up until I heard stuff coming over the radio, I don't remember really being bored. I don't remember the name of the station that came out of Mexico. There was some station that came out of Mexico, and then there was one that came out of some place in Louisiana. I don't remember the call letters, but those stations would come on toward the later part of the evening. And the earlier part of the evening would be the radio shows like *Fibber McGee and Molly* and *Inner Sanctum* and *FBI* and those kind of things. I don't ever remember being entranced by anything on the radio really, except maybe when Grand Ol' Opry came on.

OK, so what was the entertainment around town? Well, I'll tell you who the heroes were. Gorgeous George, the wrestler, he'd come through maybe three, four times a year with his troupe. There'd be boxing shows. The Flanagan Brothers [professional boxers from Minnesota] were top draws; we always watched them. Bobo Olson, a middleweight champ, came through. And then there were country western shows, somebody like Slim Whitman or Hank Snow, a lot of those guys. Ferlin Huskey, he'd be in 'em. A lot of spangled suits. And then the carny shows would come through, and there'd be the stock-car races and bands playing in the park in the summertime. And small Big Bands kinda music, pop music from the '40s and '50s, dance bands playing stuff like "Begin the Beguine," and then I started listening to the radio and hearing songs which were different, like "Mule Train" and "(Ghost) Riders in the Sky." Songs in a minor key. And when rock and roll came in, it seemed to be a kind of an extension of all that and it was accessible to me so I kind of jumped on that bandwagon and rolled on down the road.

At that time, my favorite rock and roll performer was the inimitable Little Richard. And I played all of his songs. They were easy enough to play and I could scream them out. Eddie Cochran songs, Gene Vincent stuff, we played just about all those songs that we heard, that'd come across on the pop radio stations. But then I was also listening to the more deeper stations that came across late in the evening.

The circuses came through. There were tent shows and carny midways. There was an awful lot of stock-car races, like the old cars with the country stock-car races—those were popular. I think it was the last days of carny shows. We'd see anything from the snake woman to pygmies to, God, the fat man, the snake woman, and some pretty risqué shows. Oh, risqué'd be hard-core burlesque. And guys in blackface. You'd see that, too. George Washington in blackface. And Napoleon wearing blackface. Weird Shakespearean things. People playing stuff that didn't even make any sense at the time. But actually it did. I probably retained a lot of it because when I started writing songs, I started subliminally writing a lot of songs which I probably wouldn't have even attempted to even think about unless I had some concept of that type of reality of mixing genres and ages and different historical figures.

As far as being bad, it was so cold that law and order prevailed. But there was very little law and order. I think our town had maybe three policemen.

I did get to see Woody [Guthrie]. I got the impression I was one of the few people if not the only person that came to visit him. I visited him at the Morristown [New Jersey] hospital. I think it was an insane asylum. Maybe he was misdiagnosed at that time. I don't know. But it was obvious to me that he was in control of his mind. He asked me to bring him things. I was young and impressionable and I think I must have been shocked in some kind of way to find him where I found him.

I heard Lead Belly singing some "Becky Deem" or "Walk from East St. Louis" [*Probably a reference to Jimmie Rodgers's "Out on the Road."* —*Ed.*] with only "One Thin Dime." I thought, *I want to sing that. I don't want to sing "Hound Dog" or whatever.* I wanted to sing like Blind Lemon [Jefferson] song, like, "She's got eyes like diamonds, hair like an Indian squaw." [I thought], *That's what I want to sing. I want to sing that. I don't want to listen to the popular radio anymore.*

Folk music was delivering me something which was the way I always felt about life. And people. And institutions. And ideology. And it was just uncovering it all. And finding it all there.

Lonnie [Johnson, the blues and jazz artist] was playing at Folk City and I thought he was just great. He could play rings around anybody and he sang fantastic. One night he showed me something on the guitar that didn't make any sense to me at the time. But it was a style of playing that was mathematically different than any other kind of way to play. This was just one of the ways that he knew how to play. He could play very intricately also. But he showed me this mathematical formula that worked anywhere on the scale. It didn't mean anything to me at the time, and I never got to develop it until many, many years later. That's about the only thing anybody ever taught me that was profound on the guitar, which I've been able to use in my songs.

You would have to make an impression on somebody. I picked that up from [Dave] Van Ronk. There was many, many singers who were good but they couldn't focus their attention on anybody. So they couldn't really get inside somebody's head. So that person would be ambivalent towards them and not really care if they pass 'em by. But I learned you gotta be able to pin somebody down like where they couldn't get away so easy. You have to make yourself memorable in some kinda way.

Café Wha. The place opened about noon and it would be nonstop enter-tainers, if you want to call them that, from noon until eight. Everyone played I think twenty minutes. I played with Freddy Neil, a guy who later wrote "Everyone's Talkin'." [*Actually, "Everybody's Talkin'." —Ed.*] He was a big star down there. He would play mostly chain-gang songs and popular blues-based ballads and maybe some calypso-type folk songs. And he was the ringmaster besides, so I played in his band all day, played the harmonica for him, and I fit in. I didn't really learn much. I did that until about eight and they got fed and he would give me what he could. And the place was usually packed from twelve to eight with sailors or tourists and lunch-hour secretaries and people like that.

And then at eight, all the rest of the houses would open, like where you'd pass the basket and play. You had to be somewhat good to even play at those places. They had auditions but they didn't pay you any-thing and you made what you could. But the place that did pay was the Gaslight. That was a tough place to get into for someone without a reputation. And the guy down there that was the star of the street at the time was Dave Van Ronk. I'd heard his records when I was in Twin

Cities. I'd heard some compilation records that he was on, and I thought he was really great.

Folklore Center was where all the folk music in the world was happening. It was all going on there. Records and books and there weren't any tapes then but instruments, dulcimers, and banjos, and autoharps and harmonica racks. I'd never seen a harmonica rack before, a real one. I was makin' 'em out of a coat hanger. And records, of course. So it was a place to stay warm in the winter and just listen to records and learn stuff and meet all the folksingers that were coming in and out of town.

All these people were monumental performers. John Jacob Niles was just incredible. He sounded like an old woman, but like an old, scary woman out of a Shakespeare play with a high, piercing, eerie, wailing voice, and he had long, white hair and he played a strange instrument that I don't think anybody'd ever seen. Something that maybe only came over from the old country and didn't have many of them. That's where I got the song "It Ain't Me, Babe," from listening to him play. He used to sing a song called "Go Away from My Window." He used to play a bunch of eerie, spooky ballads and I only saw him a few times but he was highly impressive, left a lasting memory. Van Ronk himself was a colossal performer. He drove people crazy.

The New Lost City Ramblers played at schoolhouses and churches. They were never on the scene but I always made an attempt to see them. And I'd see the gospel shows. I'd go see Sister Rosetta Tharpe and Dixie Hummingbirds and Swan Silvertones, I heard a lot of Blind Willie Johnson in Sister Rosetta Tharpe and I thought if she wasn't singing gospel, she would be a great blues singer. She was singing gospel blues. And she played electric hollow-body guitar. I just loved the way she sounded and with a driving rhythm.

But I'd never really seen who I'd wanted to see. I would have wanted to see Blind Willie Johnson a lot. Like, "The Holy Ghost is a mystery" [*A line from Johnson's "I'm Gonna Run to the City of Refuge." —Ed.*], that kind of thing. I thought he was the deepest singer but I'd only heard him on records. The Robert Johnson record at that time was astounding. I played it for Van Ronk, and Van Ronk was like, "Who's this guy?" No one had heard of him before. That was an astounding record. What was astounding was just the sheer songwriting. I hadn't heard that before. I hadn't heard twelve-bar songs which could be each one identifiable in its own genre. And so many different rhythms that he'd set up just with his one guitar. I was pretty overwhelmed, actually.

I never listened to any of the records I made. Once we completed the record and it was released, I didn't have any real reason to listen to them again and I never did. I never really thought they were perfect records in any kind of way. They weren't well-produced. You can say what you will about pop music; all the pop records were extremely well-produced and my records weren't well-produced. A lot of the sound on them was distorted. I always wanted to make the song come through in the best way possible. That's all I was concerned with. So, therefore, the performances weren't ideal on *any* of the records that I made.

John Hammond. Yeah, he was [*laughs*] . . . John Hammond. He was kind of like a Damon Runyon character. [*Runyon, a journalist, was also known for his short stories about the world of Broadway. —Ed.*] One of these old Broadway guys. Buzz-cut haircut. Conservative dress, little narrow tie, well-schooled in all the music that we all loved. Before I left that day, he gave me some records . . . he gave me the Robert Johnson record. At the time, Columbia was putting it out and no one had ever heard any Robert Johnson songs. Maybe they were on a few of the reissue things here and there but they had 'em all in the vaults and they issued that record called *King of the Delta Blues*. He gave me one of the first copies of it. So that was early 1961 probably. And he gave me Bessie Smith records and Charlie Christian and a lot of stuff that he thought would interest me and then he told me, come back at a certain time to record.

It came to me that a producer really didn't do that much—Hammond didn't, the one that followed him didn't, the one after that didn't. After a certain period of time, the producer, whoever they were, assumed that I would bring in a preconceived song, which meant that they didn't have to do that. Usually a producer in charge of a session is in charge of everything, including the song. Well, if an artist is writing his own song, he doesn't have to do that. So what does the producer do? Beats me. On my records, it was more important to have a good engineer, I would think.

I wrote a lot of songs in a quick amount of time. I could do that then, because the process was new to me. I felt like I'd discovered something no one else had ever discovered, and I was in a certain arena artistically that no one else had ever been in before, ever. Although I might have been wrong about that, considering some of the old troubadours who were in the days before recording but I thought that I needed to press on and get as far into it as I could.

"Subterranean Homesick Blues" . . . I don't think I'd have wanted to do it all by myself. I could get more power out of it with a small group in back of me. Well, there wasn't any negative response to people who hadn't heard it before. I didn't understand what the gripe was all about. I'm a musician first and I can't self-analyze my own work, and I wasn't gonna cater to a crowd because I knew certain people would like it and certain people didn't like it. I mean, there's many of us who could've probably gone into this field or that field because of guaranteed success one way or another. But I never was interested in that. Negative response to me would be somebody stops coming to see you play or they flat-out don't want to deal with your recording. The negative response had nothing to do with me. I've read that Stravinsky had negative response, Coltrane, many negative responses. Charlie Parker had lots of negative responses. People are always emotionally charged up when they feel some artist is not doing what they used to do.

The British audiences were the first audiences that really accepted what I was doing at face value. To that crowd, it wasn't different at all. It was right in line with everything that they'd read about in school—the Shakespearean tradition, Byron, and Shelley.

Mary Martin is this woman . . . she worked at [Dylan manager Albert] Grossman's office, and I had many shows coming up and it was obvious that I needed a band to play them. Putting together a band can be tedious, and I was hoping that there was some existing band that I could just use. [Paul] Butterfield was doing his thing. So who I really wanted was Al Kooper, who I thought was a perfectly complementary keyboard guy and he had a bass player named Harvey [Brooks] and there were a bunch of other people around.

But Mary said that she knew of a band out of Canada that were working out in Jersey. And in the past, I'd played with Ronnie Hawkins, who had made some records for Roulette, and I knew who Ronnie Hawkins was. And she said this band had been with him a long time and they knew this kind of music, and I should use them. And she knew them personally and a couple of 'em came up to New York. And we talked a while. I said I needed a band.

But I was just looking for a couple of guys, 'cause I wanted to put 'em with Kooper and the other guy, the bass player. But I ended up taking the guitar player and the drummer . . . Later, they became the group known as the Band but at that time I think they were called Ronnie Hawkins or the Hawks. Or something like that. They were working just rhythm and blues clubs. And the kind of music they were playing was cover tunes by Bobby Blue Bland and Junior Parker songs. And they did it quite well. But that wasn't what was happening at the time.

Well, Mike Bloomfield, I always thought he should've stayed with me instead of going with Butterfield but that was his life to lead. I first heard him when Grossman had me come out to play at a club they had started in Chicago, and I think the name of the club was The Bear. He just introduced himself and said he'd heard my first record and he wanted to show me how the blues were played [*laughs*]. And I didn't feel much competitive with him. He could outplay anybody even at that point. Well, when it was time to bring in a guitar player to play on my record, I couldn't think of anybody but him. I mean, he was the best guitar player I ever heard on any level. He could flatpick and he could fingerpick, and it looked like he'd been just born to play guitar. And he came into the session once more carrying his guitar in a paper bag.

You can be famous on the street where you live and that's one type of fame. You can be famous in your town, another kind of fame, you can be famous in a county. Or you can be famous and known only to a few people who are in a similar field. I mean, certain doctors are famous to other doctors, certain lawyers are famous to other lawyers, but the common man wouldn't really know who they were. The kind of fame that musicians seem to get is the kind of fame where everybody, whether they want to know who you are or not, your whole personal condition is just forced on them. And that becomes tricky, when people who don't know what you're really about suddenly know who you are.

DYLAN ON
Love and Theft

"All the songs are variations on the twelve-bar theme and blues-based melodies. The music here is an electronic grid, the lyrics being the substructure that holds it all together. The songs themselves don't have any genetic history. Is it like *Time Out of Mind*, or *Oh Mercy*, or *Blood on the Tracks*, or whatever? Probably not."
—from Columbia Records press release, June 2001

PRESS CONFERENCE

July 23, 2001 | Rome

Thirteen journalists from twelve countries participated in this press conference at Rome's Hotel de la Ville Inter-Continental. The Q&A took place two months prior to the release of *Love and Theft*, a Top 10 album that is widely viewed as a continuation of a comeback that began with 1997's *Time Out of Mind*.

Dylan sounds much more accommodating and respectful of the reporters than he did in his early press conferences, but he makes some puzzling statements. Though he has now been one of the world's most admired artists for more than thirty-five years, for example, he claims to have no "hard-core" fans. And though he has long expressed great admiration for artists like Woody Guthrie, Robert Johnson, and Buddy Holly, he says, "I don't really look up to entertainers at all. They don't have any meaning for me." —Ed.

Reporter: *Love and Theft* sounds like a return to the allegorical [*inaudible*] of *Time Out of Mind*. I haven't seen the lyric sheets but do you see that's a fair assumption?

Bob Dylan: Pretty fair.

Reporter: Could you explain the title of the album *Love and Theft*? Does it refer to one of the songs or to the general atmosphere?

Dylan: Probably. Yeah.

Reporter: Can I rephrase it?

Dylan: Sure.

Reporter: Love and theft are synonymous or opposite concepts?

Dylan: [*Laughs.*] Are they what?

Reporter: Synonymous or opposite concepts? Is it the same or the opposite?

Dylan: No. I don't think of them as contrary, no.

Reporter: Love and theft are the same?

Dylan: I don't think they're at opposite ends of the line, no. Do you?

Reporter: For me, they are the same.

Dylan: Yeah, exactly.

Reporter: Someone steals something for something.

Dylan: Yeah, exactly. Exactly! That's just what I said. [*Laughs.*]

Reporter: Would you say they go hand in hand?

Dylan: Exactly! Like fingers in a glove.

Reporter: Do you enjoy to be in Rome?

Dylan: Oh, yeah.

Reporter: You write songs about—

Dylan: Quite a few.

Reporter: "[When] I Paint My Masterpiece."

Dylan: Exactly.

Reporter: You speak exactly of this place. [*The song refers to the "streets of Rome" and also to the "Spanish Stairs," an apparent reference to the famous Spanish Steps, which are outside the hotel where this press conference took place. —Ed.*]

Dylan: This is it. Spanish Steps.

Reporter: Would you say this is the first record of yours that people can dance to? We've listened to it now all morning and—

Dylan: You been dancing all morning?

[*Laughter.*]

Reporter: Was it one of the intentions, to make it swinging and—

Dylan: I can't say that, no.

Reporter: But you seem to have returned to the music of your youth, the '40s and the '50s, the Western swing, the rockabilly, and these things, and those are forms that Bob Dylan has not utilized before. Was this a conscious intention?

Dylan: No. Most of the songs have some traditional roots to them. If not all of them.

Reporter: Since there's no producer credit, was it an album you produced with the band in the studio or are you the producer de facto?

Dylan: Well, exactly, yeah.

Reporter: The song "High Water" is for Charley Patton. I think it's a reference to [Patton's 1929 blues number] "High Water Everywhere."

Dylan: Exactly.

Reporter: What is your relationship to the music of Charles Patton?

Dylan: Oh, he's one of my favorite performers.

Reporter: Did the songs of Charley Patton or Robert Johnson or the old blues players . . . do you think that these guys have too little respect in American cultural—

Dylan: Maybe thirty years ago. But wasn't there a Robert Johnson record come out a few years ago that displayed his music to quite a few people who maybe weren't aware of it? When I first heard him, I was given that record before it was even released by the man who kind of discovered me at the record company, John Hammond. No one had heard of Robert Johnson then outside of maybe a dozen people in all of America.

Reporter: When was this?

Dylan: About 1961. They were about to release it.

Reporter: Was it a shock to hear that voice?

Dylan: No one had heard him. People had only heard the records that were reissued on rural labels at that time, and you could find a song by this person or that person on all the different records, which actually weren't that many. But I think this was the first record where everything was by one singular performer, which had taken years and years to put that together.

Reporter: It seems to be a very happy record.

Dylan: The Robert Johnson?

Reporter: No. [*Laughter.*] Your record.

Dylan: Oh, *Love and Theft*.

Reporter: A lot of the music seems like good-time music. Three or four tunes are like swing. But the lyrics are very harsh and rough, I think.

Dylan: Yeah. When you're working with a producer, they can take you this way or that way on a particular song if you're not determined that it should go a certain way. And in many cases, a lot of my records have been compromised in that way.

Reporter: Which ones do you think?

Dylan: Most of them. When we play live on the stage, people would say, "Oh, this song doesn't sound like it did on the record or it doesn't go that particular way." Well, of course not, because that way was never the way it should be really perceived, anyway.

Reporter: Is it hard to be a Dylan record then without any—

Dylan: Oh, no. I wouldn't call myself a record producer but if you have a singular vision, there's nothing really a producer can do to help you.

Reporter: Did it come out on record like you wanted it to sound?

Dylan: Well, I don't know about the audio part of it, but as far as all the arrangements go, yeah.

Reporter: Did you catch the songs at a certain point in their history? And do the arrangements still vary and evolve? And does this record document a certain moment in these songs and their life?

Dylan: No, no. These songs really weren't written when we recorded them. They were written earlier. So I had the idea in my mind for months and months before everything was pretty set.

Reporter: I noticed your voice sounds much darker than on the last one.

Dylan: Well, I've never been recorded that properly—

Reporter: What was wrong?

Dylan: Well, usually, when it comes to me, whoever is operating the controls is just thinking, *Well, this is a Bob Dylan record. This is a Bob Dylan song.* So they're not really thinking about what I particularly sound like. One person who was working with me earlier on did a whole entire record with me and then realized that he used the wrong mikes on me and for a variety of reasons, my vocal range would fall into the exact line of another instrument that would be playing on every song and so there's a presence tug-of-war there.

Reporter: But you think it's hard to record your voice?

Dylan: I don't think so. On this particular record, we had a young guy who understood how to do it. I don't think anybody really has understood how to record me, which is no fault of theirs. But what was the last record we put out? [*Time Out of Mind.* —Ed.] I think that my vocal track was tricked up with effects put on after to make it sound like I actually did sound.

Reporter: Would you say that it's different?

Dylan: They take highs off and they take lows off, and my particular vocal range just subverts the system. It always has, actually. I don't know why.

Reporter: Do you think the producers who are working for you are also kind of prisoners of the Bob Dylan myth?

Dylan: Exactly, yeah. I find that to be an unbearable problem. Sometimes people . . . you can feel they're uncomfortable.

Reporter: Do you think there's a standard preconception about what voices should sound like?

Dylan: Sure.

Reporter: Your voice and Leonard Cohen's voice and Lou Reed's voice are not the way voices should be—

Dylan: Well, I don't know about Lou's and Leonard's, but I think Leonard's would be a little bit more understandable to somebody because of where his vocal range is—so down that you can only do so much with it, anyway. Lou sort of talks and sings at the same time, and I don't really think that would present a problem for anybody who's recording.

Reporter: But it's not what you would you consider a normally good singer a crooner or something like that? The three of you?

Dylan: Well, I really don't know but I've said it before—that the best way to record me or even deal with what I do is the more antiquated system. I was better served by that system rather than whether it's analog or stereophonic or whatever. I'm served the simpler way better.

Reporter: You certainly seem to stretch yourself on "Po' Boy" where you go to those high notes and it's kind of unexpected of you . . . on that chorus where you go really high, sort of jazz inflection. Do you know what I'm talking about?

Dylan: I do know what you're talking about. But that song sort of plays itself. I have to sing that way on that particular song. Because that's a song that can exist without any lyric. It exists just on chord structures with no instrumentation except maybe a minimalistic acoustic guitar playing and the lyrics are just trying to stay in the path and not lay too much emotional rhetoric here or there. But as far as how to sing that, you have to sing it that way. It's just not gonna come off [otherwise].

Reporter: Do you think the success of the *Time Out of Mind* album reflected the way you did this album?

Dylan: I haven't listened to that *Time Out of Mind* album for a long, long time. I very rarely listen to the records that I make.

Reporter: You said around that time that you'd gotten used to being slagged off your records—

Dylan: I don't know what I said at that time but don't really pay any attention. Why would you? Something you wrote five years ago? Should we pay attention to that?

Reporter: To have a success like that, does it change your sense of confidence in what you do or do you just keep on doing what you would have done anyway?

Dylan: I would just do it, yeah. I mean, I'm fortunate that I have an audience. I don't know if I'd do it if I didn't have an audience.

Reporter: Your audience is growing, it seems. After all these years, there's still young people—

Dylan: Well, people of my age . . . they either die or they fade away or they get—

Reporter: They don't stay with you?

Dylan: Well, some do but not very many because at a certain time in a person's life, they start to have families and different priorities than light entertainment—

Reporter: Listening to the record, the impression is this is a very fresh sound, like you were playing for the public. This was intentional?

Dylan: Yeah. This is not a record for me. If I wanted to make a record for me, I'd record Charlie Patton songs.

Reporter: Is this the Dylan version of the blues albums that you originally liked?

Dylan: No, I just use blues formats or twelve-bar formats that are altered somewhat or Elizabethan ballads that are deconstructed. I just use those as forms.

Reporter: It's a record that has influences from all the American roots music—Western swing, jazz, blues, but the smallest part of influence for roots music is folk music. It seems to me like it's the opposite of *World Gone Wrong* and *Good as I Been to You*, which were the deepest folk records you've done since '62.

Dylan: Well, what you call folk music is fundamentally there on the ground level.

Reporter: I'm talking more about the arrangements.

Dylan: The arrangements are as tight as can be. And that was all done intentionally. There really isn't any superfluous playing on it. Actually, I wanted to accomplish that.

Reporter: Who else is on this record apart from your live band?

Dylan: I'd have to look at the labels to tell ya. My memory gets a little froggy. Am I an idiot? Am I not understanding? [*Chatter and laughter*] I mean, I'm trying here. Is this something I should concentrate on?

Reporter: My point is, from what I've heard of the record it seems the images associate with one another and flow in a natural way, rather than the songs being about something specifically and describing a feeling.

Dylan: My avenue of approach on all of it is to just allow it to happen and reject what doesn't seem to fit, if that makes sense to you.

Reporter: Is the songwriting process . . .

Dylan: The songwriting process is a small process of performing. As it happens to be, I write the songs—

Reporter: The process of live concerts . . . how has that changed over the years? I'm told that you only recently started to use set lists, for instance.

Dylan: You mean a list of songs? [*Laughs.*] Well, we can use a set list or . . . we don't need one, I guess.

Reporter: The process of how you go about concerts . . . has that changed over the years?

Dylan: I don't think so.

Reporter: When you go onstage, how much do you know is going to happen?

Dylan: Pretty much all of it. I usually play to the people in the back. I disregard the people in the front because usually these people have come to quite a few shows. They're gonna be there anyway, and they're gonna like what they hear one way or another. So we're not trying to reach them. We're trying to reach the people in the back who might not have been there ever before.

Reporter: You don't think about the people who are at each and every show?

Dylan: No, we don't think about those people. Because they're always there. We think about the people we've never seen.

Reporter: Do you feel annoyed by those who come for every show?

Dylan: No, no.

Reporter: They're just there.

Dylan: Yeah.

Reporter: Bob, you play a lot of live gigs and probably a lot more than you used to. Between '66 and '70 you hardly played any at all. Are you happier onstage now than you were back then? Do you like the audience more now than you liked the audience back then?

Dylan: Well, "back then" . . . I assume you're talking about when people were either reacting in a kind of a negative way to either playing electric or—

Reporter: No, I don't mean that necessarily. But quite the opposite. They were acting messianic in a way. What I'm saying now is they go to see Bob and see some music and you get up there and go on the same way.

Dylan: Oh, I wouldn't know. People are people, really.

Reporter: But do you prefer the audiences now to the audiences you used to play—

Dylan: I don't know. It's really all the same.

Reporter: What's the reason why you play live so much these days?

Dylan: I may play more than someone you're accustomed to seeing and hearing who might release a record every certain amount of time and then do a big tour. Maybe when you add it all up we play more shows than that. But I'm sure there's people in Europe and in England—I know there are in America—who play far more than me.

Reporter: You wrote these liner notes in *World Gone Wrong* about being fooled by this never-ending tour business.

Dylan: Oh, sure. I think titles belittle whatever it is a person is trying to do. And that kind of irritated me, hearing what I do referred to as that. I mean, of course everything's gonna end. . . . Why would people think I'd be doing a never-ending tour? It's undoubtedly gonna end. What ties us all together, really, the one basic characteristic of all of us, is mortality. Nothing else makes us so married to each other.

Reporter: Do you reflect upon mortality a lot?

Dylan: I wouldn't say a lot, but when people close to ya get put in the ground, you kind of—

Reporter: What about your own mortality?

Dylan: Well, I can see myself in others, so that's the way I would think about it. I wouldn't think about it any more than you would think about yours. I mean, as soon as a person enters the world, they're old enough to leave it.

Reporter: What I mean is the fact that people you like and are friends of yours are going to die hurts you and your own mortality hurts the others.

Dylan: Exactly.

Reporter: I don't mean to pry but there's two songs in which the narrator refers to . . . there's "Lonesome Day Blues," when the character says, "I wish my mother was still alive" and there's "Po' Boy" where the character goes, "When my mother died . . ." Was that inspired by your personal—

Dylan: Probably. I don't see how it couldn't be.

Reporter: You didn't block it or you didn't consciously put it in—

Dylan: Some of these lyrics are written within a stream-of-consciousness kind of thing. I don't sit there and dwell or meditate on each line.

Reporter: Do you fear analysis from other people? Is that something that you sort of dread?

Dylan: No. I don't know what anybody can find in any of my stuff. Freudian analysis, you mean? Or German idealism? Or maybe a Freudian Marxist? I don't know.

Reporter: Portuguese implication.

Dylan: Portuguese implication. [*Laughs.*] I like that.

Reporter: When you say, "The future for me is already a thing of the past" [in *Love and Theft*'s "Bye and Bye"]—

Dylan: I say that for everyone. I'm a spokesman for our generation. [*Laughter.*] I say that for us all.

Reporter: Are you comfortable as a spokesmodel, which you have been in the '60s and which you still are? When people look up to you and they want to know what you think about general topics and stuff like that?

Dylan: Every so often.

Reporter: When you are on the stage and play really old songs, like "Song to Woody," is that more an abstract relationship to your own songs, like written by someone else?

Dylan: Well, I'm glad I wrote that. I'm glad I have that song to sing because he's still a phenomenal performer. There is some kind of movie footage of him singing and it stands up there with Charlie Parker, Hank Williams, or anybody of that high altitude.

Reporter: Your older songs . . . it's so far away, it's more a playground?

Dylan: No. My songs are all singable. They're current. Something doesn't have to drop out of the sky yesterday to be current. We're living in the Iron Age. But what was the last age? The Age of Bronze or something? We can still feel that age. If you walk around in this city, people today can't build what you see out there. But at least when you walk around a town like this, you know that people were here before you, and they were probably on a much higher, grander level than any of us are. I mean, we couldn't conceive of building these kind of things. America doesn't really have stuff like this.

Reporter: Do you read books about history? Are you interested in that?

Dylan: Not any more than would just be natural to do.

Reporter: . . . In an old song of yours, you have a line in which you said, "Inside the museums, history goes up on trial." [*The reporter is thinking of the song "Visions of Johanna," but the correct line is "Inside the museums, infinity goes up on trial." —Ed.*] How does it feel to be here—

Dylan: "Inside the museums . . ." Is it history?

Reporter: History. [*Laughs.*] You don't remember.

Dylan: I sing that song. It doesn't sound right.

Reporter: "Inside the museums, history goes up on trial."

Dylan: *No.*

Reporter: No? So correct me.

Dylan: I'm trying to.

[*Laughter.*]

Reporter: It's your song.

Dylan: "Inside the museums—"

Reporter: "—history goes up on trial."

Dylan: I don't think that's right.

Reporter: So what is it?

Dylan: I'm trying to think. "Inside the museums—"

Reporter: It's from—

Dylan: Yeah, I know where it's from. "Inside the museums . . ." No, it's not. Is it? Well, where's the salvation line?

Reporter: Even if that's not the right quotation—

Dylan: "Inside the museums" doesn't sound right when you say it. Is it right? It could be. But I'm not willing to say you are. [*Laughter.*] Not quite yet.

Reporter: "Salvation goes up on trial," isn't it?

Dylan: I think so! [*Actually, the next line is, "Voices echo this is what salvation must be like after a while." —Ed.*]

Reporter: "Salvation goes up on trial."

Dylan: No, no, no.

Aide to Dylan: I'll tell you what, why don't we take a break for a few minutes? Everyone can debate.

Dylan: And let me go look in the book. All right, gentlemen.

[*After a break, the press conference resumes. —Ed.*]

Reporter: It was "infinity goes up on trial."

Dylan: Yes! Yes!

Reporter: But isn't it the same?

[*Laughter.*]

Dylan: Similar, yeah.

Reporter: I was wondering if in the last few years that I've seen you play the look of the band has evolved. I don't know if it's Daniel Lanois's influence. You've become this sort of drifting cowboy: sort of Bob Wills and the Texas Playboys outfits, the hats, and the suits and the mustaches. Was it just a gradual common choice or did you say, "Hey, boys, let's dress up now."

Dylan: Well, we kinda dress like people where we're from. It's not a fashionable statement of any kind. I'm not aware that it is.

Reporter: You had your sixtieth birthday recently and all the magazines celebrated it.

Dylan: Yes!

Reporter: Did you celebrate it?

Dylan: Just in the usual way. Blew out some candles and that's about it.

Reporter: Invited some friends?

Dylan: Yeah, mostly just family people.

Reporter: Are you "younger than that now"?

Dylan: Sure hope so. [*Laughter.*] Yeah. That's the song. *That's* correct. You got that right.

Reporter: Does the amount of celebration around such an event bother you? Does it please you?

Dylan: No.

Reporter: All these prizes . . . you never win before and now—

Dylan: I know, I'm winning a lot of stuff. Yeah, it's funny, isn't it?

Reporter: Are they catching up on wasted time? "We didn't give him anything for all these years. Let's just dump all these—"

Dylan: Maybe there's an element of that in it. I wouldn't know.

Reporter: You mentioned about being nominated for the Nobel Prize.

Dylan: Yeah, I hear about that but who would that put me in the company of? I'm not sure.

Reporter: Hemingway.

Dylan: Oh, Hemingway. I think all those guys like Hemingway write for *Time* magazine, don't they?

Reporter: Steinbeck is an old favorite of yours.

Dylan: Steinbeck? I'm not sure that I really belong in that category of people because I play—

Reporter: Is that a question of higher or lower?

Dylan: That's difficult to say. It's all really pretty relative.

Reporter: You mentioned that the producers are kind of prisoners of Bob Dylan. How about yourself, having done so many things, being a legend, how does it affect your—

Dylan: Well, 95 percent of the time it doesn't affect my life whatsoever.

Reporter: How about the other 5?

Dylan: The other part, we who get involved in fame, we just have to learn to deal with it any kind of way we can.

Reporter: What kind of strategies are there?

Dylan: I don't have any strategy for it. I usually try to be as polite as possible.

Reporter: Do you sometimes wonder, "Why me?"

Dylan: Not at this point. I know what it is I've done to be so famous so . . .

Reporter: In one of your last conversations with Allen Ginsberg, you said fame had no redeeming qualities whatsoever. My question is, what would you substitute your fame for?

Dylan: Huh?

Reporter: I mean, if you weren't that famous you couldn't do the Never Ending Tour and do the albums you wanted to the way you wanted to. Fame must have some advantages.

Dylan: It probably has quite a few. I really don't travel in that world of the rich and famous, though, so I don't really feel I'm part of that culture in any way.

Reporter: Do you find it hard to go to places where you're not being recognized everywhere?

Dylan: Well, at this point I'm recognized just about everywhere.

Reporter: When was the last time you went out unrecognized?

Dylan: I don't even remember.

Reporter: Do you feel that the work you've done, the poetry or singing or the combination of both . . . that you've arrived at a certain time in American history perhaps where you've been allowed to achieve great fame and a certain degree of fortune? Would you consider this lucky compared to doing the same work but maybe thirty years before you'd have been an obscure artist? Do you think that the same work that you do is gaining great exposure through the time that you write in? Is it a benediction? Is it good that your work was exposed so broadly? Do you understand what I'm saying?

Dylan: Sort of. I didn't really choose to do what it is you see me doing. I mean, it chose me. If I had anything to do with it, I'd have been something different. A scientist or engineer or doctor. Those are the people I look up to. I don't really look up to entertainers at all. They don't have any meaning for me one way or another.

Reporter: You must have had ambition in the beginning to do something. You said music chose you. You also chose music in that way.

Dylan: Mmm . . . maybe. Yeah.

Reporter: Saying that it chose me. That's interesting.

Dylan: I said it. That's what I did.

Reporter: In one of the lines [in *Time Out of Mind*'s "Mississippi"], you say, "I been in trouble ever since I set my suitcase down." Is that the theme for you still?

Dylan: That's the only line that you remember? [*Laughter.*] That's it?

Reporter: I'm wondering—

Dylan: Well, anybody want to know what was in the suitcase? [*Laughter.*] I don't know. Or where I set it down? I don't know.

Reporter: Or why you did.

Dylan: Yeah.

Reporter: Do you feel good in the present time or you miss something from the past?

Dylan: Oh, there must be something. I think I miss plenty, but I'm not a very nostalgic person so I don't really yearn for things like that from the past.

Reporter: Do you have fun?

Dylan: Am I having fun? What is fun?

Reporter: Enjoy life.

Dylan: Like kick a football or . . . what is fun? Drink—

Reporter: Do you enjoy life?

Dylan: I'm here. I mean . . . is there any choice?

[*Laughter.*]

Reporter: People have killed themselves.

Dylan: Sure. But not on their own accord.

Reporter: That may be up to discussion. Did you enjoy the Oscar celebration?

Dylan: Wasn't that something? I wasn't there. I don't know.

Reporter: Do you agree that at some point you reflected your times?

Dylan: I think I always do. I don't think I could reflect any other time than the time I find myself in.

Reporter: Do you try to reflect or react upon the time that you're in?

Dylan: Probably the latter. Maybe a bit of both.

Reporter: Can you imagine yourself being a newcomer nowadays? Would you have any chance in the business?

Dylan: Me? As a newcomer? I think so, because if you have the ability and the knowledge and the strength to do it, that's all you really need. And I think I know more about what I'm doing now. I know I could find a place if that's what I wanted to do. But I don't think I'd want to do it if I came out now. I'd do something else.

Reporter: Do you keep in contact with George Harrison?

Dylan: I do.

Reporter: Will the [Traveling] Wilburys travel again?

Dylan: It's hard to say.

Reporter: What was that period like for you?

Dylan: The Wilburys? Well, we made a few records, didn't we? [*Laughter.*] It was a time of great undertaking.

Reporter: It was a surprise to people to see you as part of the band like that.

Dylan: Really? It surprised me, too. [*Laughs.*]

Reporter: Do you feel that you're part of a band now, the whole crowd of guys that you play with? It seems there's a good unity, at least when I saw you onstage. There's a good sort of band atmosphere rather than Bob Dylan with his backup musicians.

Dylan: Well, I always try to have current performers with the ability to play this music. You never know how long you can keep a band together or when a band will change, one individual to another. Those things are unforeseen. But this particular group is pretty competent and can go a lot of different ways musically.

Reporter: How long can you see yourself doing this?

Dylan: I don't really know. Until one day I just might've had it. I can't say "when the crowds dwindle down" because the crowds aren't dwindling down but I may just one day have had enough.

Reporter: What keeps up the energy?

Dylan: Well, it's fictitious, the energy. . . . There are certain strategies or stratagems, codes, techniques, that play in a certain way. So once you can set these things up and you know how to do them, then the energy and emotion and whatever it seems like is happening, it's just a combination that happens in a kind of combustible way. But as far as energy goes, it doesn't take the type of energy you're talking about. It's not that kind of energy that's being used.

Reporter: Do you feel like you're still getting better?

Dylan: I feel I could get better if I really put my mind to it.

Reporter: Your singing on the new record might be the best I've heard from you.

Dylan: Well, it may be. But I don't think I'm singing any better on it than I have in the past. I may be perceived or recorded in a better way.

Reporter: Bob, there's well-documented changes in your life, perceived or otherwise. One for a lot of people was after a lot of time onstage and after *Bringing It All Back Home* and *Highway 61* [*Revisited*] and *Blonde on Blonde*, you had a motorbike accident. Whether it was exaggerated or real, did that allow you to change and be different, be yourself and not be on the treadmill?

Dylan: What was the question?

Reporter: The question was basically, when *John Wesley Harding* came out a few years later, people said this is a different Dylan. It was a time of love and peace, et cetera. Did the motorbike accident allow you to change? Or did *it* change you? Like around the same time, George Harrison was flying back from [San Francisco's] Candlestick Park, he said, "I'm never playing for these people again. This is just madness. You can't hear anything onstage." And they never did play again. Got him off the treadmill. Was that a conscious decision? You kind of used the motorbike accident and it really wasn't as bad as—

Dylan: Well, it's difficult for me to pinpoint any time where I made any conscious decision to do this or that. But obviously, that period of time you're talking about, I just didn't feel like going out and play. I didn't feel I was part of that culture.

Reporter: When you said earlier that you don't necessarily look up to celebrities or people who are currently in the business or whatever, you did get on very well with Bono in the early 1980s. Did you tell him that because of what you knew in Greenwich Village, say from [*unintelligible*] Tommy Maken [*unintelligible*], maybe he should be looking back at [*unintelligible*] music because it's obviously in his blood.

Dylan: I could've. I don't remember verbatim or time and place. If I'm being held responsible for telling him that, I don't really know that I could deny that.

Reporter: Are you still eagerly looking for poets that you may not have heard of or read yet? Or do you go back to the ones that have interested you? Like maybe Rimbaud or somebody?

Dylan: [*Pause.*] I don't really study poetry—

Reporter: I didn't mean that. Are you still searching for new writers to—

Dylan: Well, yeah, but I just don't think there are any. Because we're living in a different time. The media is all-pervasive. What can a writer think of to write that you don't see every day in a newspaper or on television?

Reporter: There are emotions that need to be expressed.

Dylan: Yeah, but the media's moving people's emotions anyway. When Rimbaud was writing, or William Blake or Shelley or Byron or any of those people, there probably wasn't any media. Just bulletins. And you could feel free to put down anything that came into your mind.

Reporter: Bob, do you feel free when you are writing? You are writing in this time.

Dylan: Well, like I say, I don't particularly sit down and write. My lines go into songs and they have a certain structure and they have to conform to a certain idiom and they're not free-form, and there's no point to trying to throw in some ideological type of thing . . . well, you can't do it in a song.

Reporter: You've done it.

Dylan: If I've done it, I did it de facto. But I've never intentionally started out with that in mind. Maybe some others have, but I haven't.

Reporter: But you think that TV and the media have killed poetry and literature—

Dylan: Oh, absolutely. Because even literature is written for an audience. Everybody's not Kafka—sit down and write something that you don't want anybody to see. Most people want people to read it. They want a person's reaction. They want some type of acceptance.

Reporter: All writers have wanted that?

Dylan: Yeah, of course. But the media is doing that for everybody now. And movies and TV. You can't see any more horrific things than you see on the media. Especially in the news, which is showing people absolutely everything they've ever even dreamed about. Even thoughts that they might think and suppress forever. They'll see it in the media so you can't suppress those things anymore. What's a writer to do if every idea is exposed in the media before he can get to it or let it evolve? What's a writer gonna write about?

Reporter: How do you react to that?

Dylan: Well, it's a science-fiction world. We're living in a world that Disney has conquered. Disney is science fiction. Theme parks. Trendy streets. It's all science fiction. So I would say if a writer has got something to say, he would have to do it in that—

Reporter: Outside of the real world?

Dylan: That is the real world. Science fiction has become the real world. Whether we've realized it or not, it has.

Reporter: In the liner notes to *World Gone Wrong*, you were talking about I'll show you the real alternative lifestyle, the agrarian one. Do you think that's one of the solutions, perhaps?

Dylan: I think so, but it's quite difficult with corporate entities paying farmers not to grow things. It becomes a problem.

Reporter: Is that one of the issues that still moves you enough to—

Dylan: Well, yeah. I'm partial to the land, so . . .

Reporter: In the same liner notes he's referring to in *World Gone Wrong*, you talk about the new Dark Ages in the contemporary world.

Dylan: Well, the Stone Age, maybe I put it that way. We talked about the ages before, the Golden Age, which was I guess the Age of Homer. And then we got the Silver Age. And you got the Bronze Age. You have the Heroic Age someplace in there. And then we're living in what people call the Iron Age. But we could be living in the Stone Ages.

Reporter: Living in the Silicon Age.

Dylan: Exactly. [*Laughter.*] Silicon Valley.

Reporter: Do you go on the Internet?

Dylan: I'm afraid to go on the Internet. I'm afraid some pervert's gonna lure me somewhere.

[*Laughter.*]

Reporter: Don't you think that the emotions and the fears, and love and religion and the basic emotional feelings that humans have, are the same since the Romans or the Egyptians? Pretty much people look for the same thing. People look for a connection to another human being and connection to a higher being.

Dylan: Probably, but everybody knew their role and their place. Their class system was different in the Roman Age—

Reporter: Was that good?

Dylan: I don't know; I wasn't there. [*Laughter.*] You know it. You especially. 'Cause you weren't there with me. [*Laughter.*]

Reporter: And I am Roman.

Dylan: Exactly.

Reporter: There seems to be an apocalyptic dimension to your work. The end is nigh. You sing, "If the Bible is right, the world will explode" in "Things Have Changed" [*A song from the film* Wonder Boys. —*Ed.*] and "People are crazy and times are strange." Is this a particularly bad time we're living in, beside it being the Stone Age?

Dylan: I don't know. I mean, who knows?

Reporter: Do you go to religion for comfort? Do you go to some meditative state?

Dylan: Well, I try. [*Laughter.*] I mean, who would I be if I didn't try?

Reporter: Do you read the Bible?

Dylan: Of course. Who doesn't?

Reporter: Do you read Shakespeare?

Dylan: I do. Yeah.

Reporter: Your records are referring a lot to old lines from old movies. *Empire Burlesque.* Did you read those writers? [Dashiell] Hammett? [Raymond] Chandler?

Dylan: Did I read them? I don't remember. I know what you mean but I think I just saw the movies.

Reporter: Do you listen to a lot of music now?

Dylan: Some. Yeah. Not any more than I ever did.

Reporter: Do you listen to any new music or is it all—

Dylan: I don't know. Like who's new?

Reporter: You did Stanley Brothers covers in your shows when I saw you in Horsens Theatre [in Denmark] last year. You played "I'm Ready to Go"—

Dylan: Me? Oh, yeah, but those aren't new songs.

Reporter: I know. Those are old songs. But what is so special about the Stanley Brothers—

Dylan: It's like the old thing, if somebody has to tell you then you'd never know.

Reporter: Talking about new music: Eminem . . . people tend to call him a poet. Do you think about this?

Dylan: I wouldn't know anything about that.

Reporter: You don't pay attention to hip-hop and soul? Do you recognize maybe a sort of folk quality to the storytelling? In the storytelling sense—Eminem is a good example. Some of the people will actually tell their life stories or reflect. Chuck D said that hip-hop is the CNN of music.

Dylan: Beats me. It never really occurred to me to pay attention to whatever is supposed to be going on.

Reporter: Sometimes when you're standing with your guitar onstage it reminds me of somebody old: Elvis Presley poses from 1955, '56. How do you react to that?

Dylan: No. Is that a compliment or—

Reporter: Yeah, it's a compliment. But Elvis had a strong influence on you—

Dylan: He did. Growing up he did.

Reporter: He had a beautiful recording of your song "Tomorrow Is a Long Time." Do you remember how you reacted to that?

Dylan: Oh, well, what can you say? When somebody like that records a song I'm sure any songwriter would feel intensely gratified.

Reporter: Would you say that there's a lineage? Somebody said that Elvis freed the body, Bob Dylan freed the mind.

Reporter: Bruce Springsteen [said that].

Dylan: Freed the mind? Well, it's good to be liberated from whatever. [*Laughs.*] We should all feel that way.

Reporter: Did you play this record to your son Jacob?

Dylan: I think he got it maybe from one of his brothers but I'm not sure. I've been traveling for a while.

Reporter: One more Elvis question. Did you meet Elvis?

Dylan: I never did meet him. That's what I'm supposed to say.

[*Laughter.*]

Reporter: Why aren't you playing any new songs from *Love and Theft* live yet?

Dylan: Well, there's no point to it because—

Reporter: Not tomorrow?

Dylan: No way. You won't hear any of those songs.

Reporter: There'll be twelve people in the audience who know those songs.

Dylan: Exactly.

[*Laughter.*]

Reporter: But some of the old folk songs that you played probably not more than twelve people in the audience have heard.

Dylan: That's true.

Reporter: So what's the difference?

Dylan: There is a difference. I'm not really free to say it right now but if you know the songs on this record and you know the songs that nobody's heard before, then you would know how to tell the difference.

Reporter: There's almost a religious feeling within your hard-core fans about you. How do you feel about that?

Dylan: I don't really feel like I have any hard-core fans. I mean, I just don't. There's some people that do. I really just don't. We have a few people who see an abundance of my shows but we don't think of them as hard-core fans.

Reporter: But the religious feeling?

Dylan: Well, what religion are they? If they are, what sacrifices do they make and to who? Do they sacrifice, these hard-core religious fans? If they do, then we have hard-core religious fans. And I would like to know where and when they do make their sacrifices 'cause I want to be there.

[*Laughter.*]

Reporter: Somebody once told me that your collected work is like the Bible, because everything is in there somewhere.

Dylan: Well, that goes without saying.

[*Laughter.*]

Reporter: A short while ago, I had an interview with Leonard Cohen in which he told me that claiming to himself the fact of being a poet was too much of a burden and too much responsibility. Do you agree with that in your case?

Dylan: I know what he was trying to say, and he's right.

Reporter: There are quite a few books published about you. Do you read biographies about you?

Dylan: I haven't read any since that Bob Shelton book [*No Direction Home: The Life and Music of Bob Dylan*] . . . and I knew him. I don't know these other people.

Reporter: Did you like the Shelton book?

Dylan: It's difficult reading about oneself because in your own mind things really didn't go that way, they don't appear that way . . . it seems like you're reading about other people. If it's going to be fictitious, well, then where is all the good stuff?

Reporter: Have you had any temptation to write about—

Dylan: Me? Yeah, I have. And I will.

Reporter: Are you in the process of doing that?

Dylan: Mm-hmm.

Reporter: They just translated *Tarantula* [Dylan's prose poetry collection, written in 1965 and 1966] in French, which is a scary concept.

Dylan: Mm-hmm.

Reporter: The ambition of being a poet that writes as opposed to a song-and-dance man . . . did you get it out of the way with *Tarantula*? Was that something that you sort of said, "I've done that"?

Dylan: Oh . . . things were running wild at that point and it never was my intention to write a book. . . . I had a manager who, when asked, "Well, he writes all these songs. What else does he write?" might've said, "What do you got?" And they said, "Well, does he write books?" And he might've said, "Of course he does." And they said, "Well, we would like to publish one." I think it was one of those kind of things where he arranged the whole thing and then it was up to me to write the book. It was never anything that I consciously set out to do. But he did that on different occasions. He had me on a television show being an actor whereas I didn't know anything about it until the day I appeared. I thought I was gonna sing. These things would happen back in the early part of the last century.

[*Laughter.*]

Reporter: It's a long time ago, isn't it?

Dylan: Ages ago.

Reporter: You just did a TV sitcom in America. *Dharma & Greg*, I think. [*"Play Lady Play," first broadcast October 12, 1999. —Ed.*]

Dylan: I did.

Reporter: Why?

Dylan: I don't know. I wasn't doing anything and I knew the guy who was writing it.

Reporter: Was it fun?

Dylan: Yeah. Why wouldn't it have been?

Reporter: There was a rumor about you doing a variety show on television.

Dylan: Just a rumor.

Reporter: 'Cause that seemed like the craziest thing.

Dylan: I know.

[*Laughter.*]

Reporter: The thing that you're writing now—is that a sort of a memoir?

Dylan: It is.

Reporter: Are you having any plans for publication of that?

Dylan: Mm-hmm.

Reporter: Is it coming quite soon?

Dylan: I think it will be published as I'm told in an article form but as a book. But articles because they're ongoing and that's about as much as—

Reporter About your own life.

Dylan: Yeah.

Reporter: Is that the only thing you're writing now? Are you thinking of writing any fiction?

Dylan: No. I'm not writing any fiction.

Reporter: To come back to George Harrison, now that you're here in Europe, are you gonna visit him?

Dylan: I don't think I'm gonna have time but I probably will be eventually trying to see him when he gets back home or something.

Reporter: Does the fact that you wrote your own memoirs have an influence on the songs you play onstage?

Dylan: Well, that's interesting that you say that because a lot of the memoirs, they use as a starting point certain songs. I find that that's a good way to unlock a lot of memories.

Reporter: Are you writing on the road?

Dylan: I'll write ideas but I won't really develop 'em on the road. But I'll write big blocks of where I want to get to.

Reporter: But you have not read any of the biographies after Robert Shelton?

Dylan: Well, I don't know. Have there been any?

Reporter: Oh, yes.

Dylan: I'll have to see. I'm not aware there were any.

Reporter: Why do you feel the time is right now for you to reflect on your past? Or were you preparing this years ago?

Dylan: You know, in this kind of stuff that I'm writing, I think it was just finding the right way to get into it rather than make it some kind of self-serving story of my particular past. It doesn't come off that way. Well, it comes off that way but it's dissimilar in a lot of ways. I can do it because I'm a famous person. So I use that fame. Because a lot of the things I write about other people know about, anyway. So, with a person like myself, the process of doing it this way works.

Reporter: Do you find it exhilarating, this writing, as opposed to the more deconstructed way of writing songs that you were describing?

Dylan: No, I don't really think about it one way or another. I'm not making a real attempt to do this. I just do it almost in spare time.

Reporter: Is there any phase in your life that you see as a very difficult phase?

Dylan: I'm sure there've been many but—

Reporter: The most difficult?

Dylan: Oh, man. [*Long pause.*] There have been a lot of tricky parts where you have to assume another character in order to survive.

Reporter: What part are you thinking of? What years?

Dylan: Well, basically you have to surrender your ambitions at a certain point in order to get to where you need to be.

Aide to Dylan: We're going to have time for just a few more questions.

Dylan: That was a good one.

[*Laughter.*]

Reporter: What kind of ambition did you have to surrender?

Dylan: [*Laughs.*] Now that's what you're gonna have to find out.

[*Laughter.*]

Reporter: In one of those books or articles, it said that you are probably happier in the tour bus than in any of your seventeen homes. Is that correct?

Dylan: Well, the buses . . . yeah, they're becoming quite luxurious now. I'm pretty happy anywhere. As far as happy goes, as far as feeling at home goes, I can't say I don't feel at home most anywhere. I feel at home at home and I feel it when I'm not there. It's not like I'm longing for anything that's not presently where I'm at.

Reporter: What's it like being Bob Dylan nowadays? Is it easier than it was before?

Dylan: I'm not the one to ask. That's a philosophical question for philosophical matters.

Reporter: Ever try being someone else?

Dylan: I'm sure. But we all try to be someone else when we're starting from point zero.

Reporter: Bob, you mentioned earlier on that some of the stuff from the past you don't really want to listen to that much. You don't go back and listen to your old albums. Yet this autobiographical stuff you're writing, the journals or whatever, you say the entry is the sounds, in which case you're being forced to go back. It's like somebody getting their greatest hits together.

Dylan: Well, I'm only looking at it from an angle that maybe it's never occurred to me before to look at it. A lot of the things that happen to us, we just seem to go through without ever wondering if there's a purpose to go from this to that. Or why did this happen? Could this have happened if that didn't happen? And if this seemed so bad at the time, why it led to something so beneficial in the long run. So it's written from a variety of angles, really. And it interests me to write it. But I'm not painstakingly doing it, no.

Reporter: When you're looking back on your poetry, which ones do you think are the most successful at expressing Bob Dylan's point of view?

Dylan: You know, I never listen to them. I'm sure they're all successful in their way and I'm sure they all have failures in their own way.

Reporter: But you expressed great discontent with producers and when we talked about *Love and Theft* you expressed discontent with the way it was produced but some of them must hold up better than others in your own opinion even though you don't listen to them that much.

Dylan: I don't listen to them because I never feel the songs have been perfected. I used to have a problem—I don't anymore—with working on some record album where a song might have been recorded but I didn't particularly think it had been recorded very well or the right way or the way I hear it in my mind or . . . for myriad reasons. And then the song as it exists gets out. People you trust make copies and they put it out for the public to hear, and I feel like that's happened too much in my case with people we have no reason to distrust at the time. I've been asked, "How come you're such a bad judge of your material? You don't put the best stuff on your record." Well, I don't know who judges what the best stuff is, but I'm not judging the material. I would love to put certain things on. I just don't think they were recorded right. And then once it gets out, I'm not really that keen on going in and rerecording it—except on this record that you all just heard.

Reporter: "Mississippi."

Dylan: Yeah, we had that on the *Time Out of Mind* record but it wasn't recorded particularly well, and thank God it never got out. [*Alternate versions of "Mississippi" from the* Time Out of Mind *sessions did ultimately surface on* The Bootleg Series, Vol. 8: Tell Tale Signs. *—Ed.*] So we went and rerecorded it again but something like that would never have happened ten years ago. You'd have probably all heard the trash version of it. And I never would have rerecorded it.

Reporter: You mean you take more care in—

Dylan: Well, you just don't trust anybody. It's that simple.

Reporter: Do you think sometimes a record needs a second chance? There was a remixed version of *Street-Legal* that came out two years ago. Do you think some of these albums were overlooked because they came out at a time when people were interested in something else than Bob Dylan?

Dylan: Well, I don't know about *Street-Legal*. There were probably other artists who were being featured in the media, and the cultural landscape was a little different back then, probably. I know that I've always been with the same record company. [*Actually, Dylan left Columbia Records briefly; in 1974, the Asylum label released* Planet Waves *and* Before the Flood. *—Ed.*] They tried everything to sell it; it probably wasn't what people wanted to hear at that time.

Reporter: You said about this [*Love and Theft*] record: it's a greatest-hits album without the greatest hits.

[*Laughter.*]

Dylan: Yeah—yet. Well, you're all gonna have to really even see about this particular album. It just might be a landmark album. I mean, we never know these things until much later than the event itself, even though it might be an invisible event that we're talking about. However, you all in this room have the responsibility of saying what this record is and knowing that in ten years' time, people are still gonna be writing about it. And not commenting on the record because the record will be set in stone at that time. But everything you all say, that's what everybody'll be commenting on.

Reporter: It's a great album, and I think most of the people here are enjoying listening.

Dylan: Well, you're gonna have to listen a whole lot more. Like you do those early albums.

Reporter: You're playing your songs onstage year after year. Do you feel that they change? That they are different each time you sing them?

Dylan: Well, that goes back to what I said earlier. My records are undeveloped from day one. Basically, I sing a song and I strum it on the guitar. In recording technology, that's called making demos. It's no accident that other singers have had better hits with my songs than I have. Because they've sensed there's a structure to them. But I have never been allowed to develop that structure working with slipshod producers or fakes or a bunch of non-entities. And so be it. But I was willing to allow that to happen because I was always able to go on stage and rectify it.

Reporter: So the songs are getting better—

Dylan: No, what I'm saying is that songs need structure, stratagems, codes, and stability. And then you can hang lyrics on . . . I mean, I'm speaking here as someone who sings a song that's written. And when we transfer these songs to the stage, that's where all that comes into play. They don't come into play on a record because my cohorts at the time never really sought to develop any of that stuff. And I can't do it at the time of recording because the song at the time is new to me. I'm more concerned with getting this lyric to fit into this frame. And does this line work here and can we change the key to make it work better or can we change the tempo? Can we change the dynamic of a tune? Can we use different syncopation? I'm more concerned with those things. I'm not concerned with what exactly is the structure and I've been disappointed because no one outside of myself has ever come in and given me one. All these people who claim to know my music and songs so well, they don't have a clue.

Aide to Dylan: We have time for one more question.

Reporter: On this record, it seems like you have a real cohesive sound, a sort of Bob Wills or Spade Cooley type thing—

Dylan: Let's stop talking about Bob Wills! And Spade Cooley. Let's put them on the pedestal where they belong and let's stop.

Reporter: I just mean there's a lot of music going on. It feels very cohesive. It doesn't feel collected.

Dylan: You know what my comment is on that? It should. It should sound that way. It was intentionally delivered that way.

Reporter: Is *Love and Theft* the best album you ever made?

Dylan: I'll tell you one thing: it's the most current album I've ever made.

[*Laughter.*]

Aide to Dylan: Thank you all. [*Applause.*]

Dylan: Now I'm gonna go see the Coliseum . . . Gentlemen, pleased to have met ya. Pleasure always.

DYLAN ON

His Marriages

"I've been married a bunch of times. [*Only two marriages are publicly known. —Ed.*] I mean, I've never tried to hide that. I just don't advertise my life. I write songs, I play on stage, and I make records. That's it. The rest is not anybody's business."

—from interview with Edna Gundersen, *USA Today*, September 10, 2001

DYLAN ON

His Destiny

"I've had a God-given sense of destiny. This is what I was put on earth to do. Just like Shakespeare was gonna write his plays, the Wright Brothers were gonna invent an airplane, like Edison was gonna invent a telephone, I was put here to do this. I knew I was gonna do it better than anybody ever did it."

—from interview with Christopher John Farley, *Time*, September 17, 2001

DYLAN ON

Receiving His Grammy Lifetime Achievement Award

"The only thing I remember about that whole episode, as long as you bring it up, was that I had a fever—like 104. I was extremely sick that night. Not only that, but I was disillusioned with the entire musical community and environment. If I remember correctly, the Grammy people called me months before then and said that they wanted to give me this Lifetime Achievement honor. Well, we all know that they give those things out when you're old—when you're nothing, a has-been. Everybody knows that, right? So I wasn't sure whether it was a compliment or an insult."

—from interview with Mikal Gilmore, *Rolling Stone*, November 22, 2001

DYLAN ON

Johnny Cash

"Johnny was and is the North Star; you could guide your ship by him . . . There wasn't much music media in the early Sixties, and *Sing Out!* was the magazine covering all things folk in character. The editors had published a letter chastising me for the direction my music was going. Johnny wrote the magazine back an open letter telling the editors to shut up and let me sing, that I knew what I was doing. . . . the letter meant the world to me. I've kept the magazine to this day."

—statement on the death of Johnny Cash, September 2003

DYLAN ON

Songwriting

"There are so many ways you can go at something in a song. One thing is to give life to inanimate objects. Johnny Cash is good at that. He's got the line that goes, 'A freighter said . . . "She's been here, but she's gone, boy, she's gone."' That's great. 'A freighter says, "She's been here."' That's high art. If you do that once in a song, you usually turn it on its head right then and there."

—from interview with Robert Hilburn, *Los Angeles Times*, August 4, 2004

DYLAN ON

Writing Songs and Books

"I'm used to writing songs, and songs—I can fill 'em up with symbolism and metaphors. When you write a book like this [his autobiographical *Chronicles, Volume One*], you gotta tell the truth, and it can't be misinterpreted. Lest we forget, while you're writing, you're not living. What do they call it? Splendid isolation. I don't find it that splendid."

—from interview with David Gates, *Newsweek*, October 4, 2004

DYLAN ON

What Mattered to Him

"My family was my light and I was going to protect that light at all cost. That was where my dedication was, first, last and everything in-between. What did I owe the rest of the world? Nothing. Not a damn thing. The press? I figured you lie to it. For the public eye, I went into the bucolic and mundane as far as possible. In my real life I got to do the things that I loved the best and that was all that mattered—the Little League games, birthday parties, taking my kids to school, camping trips, boating, rafting, canoeing, fishing."

—from *Chronicles, Volume One*, October 5, 2004

DYLAN ON

Why He Continues Performing

"Well, because I don't really feel like anybody else's doing what I do. That's probably the long and short of it right there."

—from interview with Steve Inskeep,
National Public Radio (US), October 12, 2004

TV INTERVIEW

Ed Bradley | December 5, 2004 | *60 Minutes*, CBS (US)

Dylan's first television interview in almost two decades—undoubtedly prompted by the recent release of his memoir, *Chronicles, Volume One*—is among the conversations I most wanted to include in this anthology. Journalist Ed Bradley, who met with the artist on November 19, 2004, in Northampton, Massachusetts, covers wide-ranging topics, including how Dylan managed to write his early masterpieces, his parents, why he changed his name, and why he continues to work. And the artist's answers are uniformly memorable, albeit sometimes strange. While he laughs often during many interviews, incidentally, he almost never even hints at a smile in this one—at least not until the end, when questions about his "destiny" twice bring hearty laughs. —Ed.

Ed Bradley: [*In studio.*] For as long as I have been here with *60 Minutes*, I've wanted to interview Bob Dylan. Over his forty-three-year career, there is no musician alive who has been more influential. His distinctive twang and poetic lyrics have produced some of the most memorable songs ever written. In the '60s, his songs of protest and turmoil spoke to an entire generation. While his life has been the subject of endless interpretation, he has been largely silent. Now, at age sixty-three, he's written a memoir called *Chronicles, Volume One*. I finally got to sit down with him in his first television interview in nearly twenty years. What you will see is pure Dylan—mysterious, elusive, fascinating—just like his music.

[*Video of Dylan performing "Blowin' in the Wind" plays.*]

439

Bradley: I read somewhere that you wrote "Blowin' in the Wind" in ten minutes. Is that right?

Bob Dylan: [*Nods.*] Probably.

Bradley: Just like that?

Dylan: Yeah.

Bradley: Where did it come from?

Dylan: It just came. It came from . . . right out of that wellspring of creativity, I would think.

Bradley: [*Voiceover, with snippets from "Mr. Tambourine Man," "Positively Fourth Street," and "Like a Rolling Stone" playing.*] That wellspring of creativity has sustained Bob Dylan for more than four decades, and produced five hundred songs and more than forty albums.

Bradley: Do you ever look at music that you've written and look back at it and say, "Whoa! That surprised me!"?

Dylan: I used to. I don't do that anymore. I don't know how I got to write those songs.

Bradley: What do you mean you "don't know how"?

Dylan: Well, those early songs were almost magically written. "Darkness at the break of noon / Shadows, even the silver spoon / A handmade blade, a child's balloon..." [*Video of Dylan performing "It's Alright, Ma (I'm Only Bleeding)," the song Dylan is quoting, plays.*]

Bradley: [*Voiceover.*] This Dylan classic, "It's Alright, Ma," was written in 1964.

Dylan: Well, try to sit down and write something like that. There's a magic to that, and it's not Siegfried and Roy kind of magic, you know? It's a different kind of a penetrating magic. And I did it. I did it at one time.

Bradley: You don't think you can do it today?

Dylan: Uh-uh.

Bradley: Does that disappoint you?

Dylan: Well, you can't do something forever. And I did it once, and I can do other things now. But I can't do that.

Bradley: [*Voiceover.*] Dylan has been writing music since he was a teenager in the remote town of Hibbing, Minnesota. The eldest of two sons of Abraham and Beatty Zimmerman.

Bradley: Did you have a good life—a good, happy childhood growing up?

Dylan: I really didn't consider myself happy or unhappy. I always knew that there was something out there that I needed to get to. And it wasn't where I was at that particular moment.

Bradley: It wasn't in Minnesota.

Dylan: No.

Bradley: [*Voiceover.*] It was in New York City. As he writes in his book, he came alive when at age nineteen, he moved to Greenwich Village, which at the time was the frenetic center of the '60s counterculture. Within months, he had signed a recording contract with Columbia Records.

Bradley: You refer to New York as the capital of the world. But when you told your father that, he thought that it was a joke. Did your parents approve of you being a singer/songwriter? Going to New York?

Dylan: No. They wouldn't have wanted that for me. But my parents never went anywhere. My father probably thought the capital of the world was wherever he was at the time. It couldn't possibly be anyplace else. Where he and his wife were in their own home, that, to them, was the capital of the world.

Bradley: What made you different? What pushed you out of there?

Dylan: Well, I listened to the radio a lot. I hung out in record stores. And I slam-banged around on a guitar and played the piano and learned songs from a world which didn't exist around me.

Bradley: [*Voiceover.*] He says even then he knew he was destined to become a music legend. "I was heading for the fantastic lights," he writes. "Destiny was looking right at me and nobody else."

Bradley: You use the word "destiny" over and over throughout the book. What does that mean to you?

Dylan: It's a feeling you have that you know something about yourself nobody else does—the picture you have in your mind of what you're about will come true. It's kind of a thing you kind of have to keep to your own self, because it's a fragile feeling. And you put it out there, somebody will kill it. So it's best to keep that all inside.

Bradley: [*Voiceover.*] When we asked him why he changed his name, he said that was destiny, too.

Bradley: So you didn't see yourself as Robert Zimmerman?

Dylan: No, for some reason I never did.

Bradley: Even before you started performing?

Dylan: Nah, even then. Some people get born with the wrong names, wrong parents. I mean, that happens.

Bradley: Tell me how you decided on Bob Dylan?

Dylan: You call yourself what you want to call yourself. This is the land of the free.

Bradley: [*Voiceover.*] Bob Dylan created a world inspired by old folk music, with piercing and poetic lyrics, as in songs like "A Hard Rain's A-Gonna Fall." [*Video of Dylan performing that song plays.*] Songs that reflected the tension and unrest of the civil rights and antiwar movements of the '60s. It was an explosive mixture that turned Dylan, by age twenty-five, into a cultural and political icon—playing to sold-out concert halls around the world, and followed by people wherever he went. He was called the voice of his generation—and was actually referred to as a prophet, a messiah. Yet he saw himself simply as a musician.

Dylan: You feel like an impostor when someone thinks you're something and you're not.

Bradley: What was the image that people had of you and what was the reality?

Dylan: The image of me was certainly not a songwriter or a singer. It was more like some kind of a threat to society in some kind of way.

Bradley: What was the toughest part for you, personally?

Dylan: It was like being in an Edgar Allan Poe story. And you're just not that person everybody thinks you are, though they call you that all the time. "You're the prophet." "You're the savior." I never wanted to be a prophet or savior. Elvis maybe. I could easily see myself becoming him. But prophet? No.

Bradley: I know that, and I accept, you don't see yourself as the voice of that generation, but some of your songs did stop people cold. [*Dylan nods.*] And they saw them as anthems, and they saw them as protest songs. It was important in their lives. It sparked a movement. [*Clip of Dylan performing "The Times They Are A-Changin'" plays.*] I mean, you may not have seen it that way, but that's the way it was for them. [*Dylan nods.*] How do you reconcile those two things?

Dylan: My stuff were songs, you know? They weren't sermons. If you examine the songs, I don't believe you're gonna find anything in there that says that I'm a spokesman for anybody or anything, really.

Bradley: But they saw it.

Dylan: Yeah, but they must not have heard the songs.

Bradley: It's ironic that the way that people viewed you was just the polar opposite of the way you viewed yourself.

Dylan: Isn't that something?

Bradley: [*Voiceover.*] Dylan did almost anything to shatter the lofty image many people had of him. He writes that he intentionally made bad records; once poured whiskey over his head in public; and as a stunt, he went to Israel and made a point of having his picture taken at the Wailing Wall wearing a skullcap.

Bradley: When you went to Israel, you wrote that "the newspapers changed me overnight into a Zionist and this helped a little." How did it help?

Dylan: Look, if the common perception of me out there in the public was that I was either a drunk, or I was a sicko, or a Zionist, or a Buddhist, or a Catholic, or a Mormon—all of this was better than Archbishop of Anarchy.

Bradley: . . . and Spokesman for the Generation . . .

Dylan: Yeah.

Bradley: . . . opposed everything.

Dylan: Mm-hmm.

Bradley: [*Voiceover.*] He was especially opposed to the media, which he says was always trying to pin him down. [*Video clip from 1965 San Francisco press conference airs. A reporter asks, "Do you think of yourself primarily as a singer or as a poet?" and Dylan answers, "I think of myself more as a song-and-dance man."*]

Bradley: Let me talk a little bit about your relationship with the media. You wrote, "The press, I figured, you lied to it." Why?

Dylan: I realized at the time that the press, the media, they're not the judge—God's the judge. The only person you have to think about lying twice to is either yourself or to God. The press isn't either of them. And I just figured they're irrelevant.

Bradley: [*Voiceover.*] Bob Dylan tried to run away from all of that in the mid '60s. He retreated with his wife and three young children to Woodstock, New York. But even there, he couldn't escape the legions of fans who descended on his home, begging for an audience with the legend himself.

Bradley: So people would actually come to the house?

Dylan: Mm-hmm.

Bradley: And do what?

Dylan: They wanted to discuss things with me—politics and philosophy and organic farming and things.

Bradley: What did you know about organic farming?

Dylan: Nothing. Not a thing.

Bradley: What did you mean when you wrote that "the funny thing about fame is that nobody believes it's you"?

Dylan: People, they'll say, "Are you who I think you are?" And you'll say, "I don't know." Then, they'll say, "You're him." And you'll say, "OK, yes." And then, the next thing they'll say, "Well, no." Like "Are you really him? You're not him." And that can go on and on.

Bradley: Do you go out to restaurants now?

Dylan: I don't like to eat in restaurants.

Bradley: Because people come up and say, "Are you him?"

Dylan: That's always gonna happen, yeah.

Bradley: Do you ever get used to it?

Dylan: [*Pause.*] No.

Bradley: [*Voiceover.*] At his peak, fame was taking its toll on Bob Dylan. He was heading towards a divorce from his wife, Sara. In concerts, he wore white makeup to mask himself. But his songs revealed the pain. [*Video of Dylan performing "Tangled Up in Blue" airs.*]

Bradley: You said, "My wife, when she married me, had no idea of what she was getting into."

Dylan: Well, she was with me back then through thick and thin, you know? It just wasn't the kind of life that she had ever envisioned for herself, any more than the kind of life that I was living, that I had envisioned for mine.

Bradley: [*Voiceover.*] By the mid-1980s, he felt he was burned out and over the hill.

Bradley: You also wrote that: "I'm a '60s troubadour, a folk-rock relic. A wordsmith from bygone days. I'm in the bottomless pit of cultural oblivion." Those are pretty harsh words.

Dylan: Well, I'd seen all these titles written about me.

Bradley: And you started to believe it?

Dylan: Well, I believed it, anyway. I wasn't getting any thrill out of performing. I thought it might be time to close it up.

Bradley: You really thought about quitting, folding up the tent?

Dylan: I had thought I'd just put it away for a while. But then I started thinking, "That's enough."

Bradley: [*Voiceover.*] But within a few years, Dylan told us, he recaptured his creative spark, and he went back on the road. [*Video of Dylan performing "Knockin' on Heaven's Door" plays.*] Performing more than one hundred concerts a year. In 1998, he won three Grammy awards. [*Clip from Grammies ceremony airs.*] At age sixty-three, Bob Dylan remains a voice as unique and powerful as any there has ever been in American music. His fellow musicians paid tribute to him when he was inducted into the Rock and Roll Hall of Fame, joining him in a rousing rendition of his most famous song. [*Clip from that performance of "Like a Rolling Stone" airs.*]

Bradley: As you probably know, *Rolling Stone* magazine just named your song, "Like a Rolling Stone," the number-one song of all time. Twelve of your songs are in their list of the Top 500. That must be good to have as part of your legacy.

Dylan: Oh, maybe this week. But you know, the lists, they change names, and quite frequently, really. I don't really pay much attention to that.

Bradley: But it's a pat on the back, Bob.

Dylan: This week it is. But who's to say how long that's gonna last?

Bradley: Well, it's lasted a long time for you. I mean, you're still out here doing these songs, you know. You're still on tour.

Dylan: I do, but I don't take it for granted.

Bradley: Why do you still do it? Why are you still out here?

Dylan: Well, it goes back to that destiny thing. I made a bargain with it, long time ago. And I'm holding up my end.

Bradley: What was your bargain?

Dylan: To get where I am now.

Bradley: Should I ask who you made the bargain with?

Dylan: [*Laughs.*] You know, with the chief commander.

Bradley: On this earth?

Dylan: [*Laughs.*] In this earth and then in the world we can't see.

Bradley: [*Back in studio.*] Bob Dylan has been nominated this year for the Nobel Prize in Literature for his songwriting. His new book has been a bestseller for the past seven weeks. It was published by Simon and Schuster, which is owned by Viacom, the parent company of CBS. Dylan is planning to write two more volumes of his memoirs.

DYLAN ON

Street-Legal, Slow Train Coming, and Infidels

"I was just being swept along with the current when I was making those records. I don't think my talent was under control. But there's probably good stuff on all of them. Shelley said the point was to make unpremeditated art. I don't think those records fall into that category."

—from interview with Austin Scaggs,
Rolling Stone, December 9, 2004

DYLAN ON

What He Did After High School

". . . Left the very next day. I'd gone as far as I could in my particular environment. . . . I was a musical expeditionary. I had no past to speak of, nothing to go back to, nobody to lean on. I came down to Minneapolis. I didn't go to classes. I was enrolled but I didn't go to classes. I just didn't feel like it. We were singing and playing all night. Sleeping most of the morning. I didn't really have any time for studying."

—from interview with Jeff Rosen, *No Direction Home*, 2005

THE GENIUS AND MODERN TIMES OF BOB DYLAN

Jonathan Lethem | September 7, 2006 | *Rolling Stone*

Dylan had a busy and productive year in 2006. In May, he debuted his engrossing *Theme Time Radio Hour*, a weekly program for XM Satellite Radio (which became Sirius XM Radio after a merger) that demonstrated his encyclopedic musical knowledge. And on August 29, he released *Modern Times*, the third in a series of comeback albums, following 1997's *Time Out of Mind* and 2001's *Love and Theft*. Unlike those two predecessors, *Modern Times* made it all the way to the top of the charts in the United States.

Shortly before the album's release, Dylan met with novelist and essayist Jonathan Lethem, a longtime fan. Dylan talks about the record, as well as file-sharing, the '60s, and his so-called Never Ending Tour. He also concedes that he has never been quite as inaccessible to the media as his reputation—and sometimes he himself—have suggested. —Ed.

"I don't really have a herd of astrologers telling me what's going to happen. I just make one move after the other, this leads to that." Is the voice familiar? I'm sitting in a Santa Monica seaside hotel suite, ignoring a tray of sliced pineapple and sugar-dusty cookies, while Bob Dylan sits across from my tape recorder, giving his best to my questions. The man before me is fitful in his chair, not impatient, but keenly alive to the moment, and ready on a dime to make me laugh and to laugh himself. The expressions on Dylan's face, in person, seem to compress and encompass versions of his persona across time, a sixty-five-year-old with a nineteen-year-old cavorting somewhere inside. Above all, though, it is the tones of his speaking voice that seem to kaleidoscope through time: here the yelp of the folk pup or the sarcastic rimshot timing of the hounded hipster-idol, there the beguilement of the Seventies sex symbol, then again—and always—the gravel of the elder statesman, that antediluvian bluesman's voice the young aspirant so legendarily invoked at the very outset of his work and then ever so gradually aged into.

It's that voice, the voice of a rogue ageless in decrepitude, that grounds the paradox of the achievement of *Modern Times*, his thirty-first studio album. Are these our "modern tunes," or some ancient, silent-movie dream, a fugue in black-and-white? *Modern Times*, like *Love and Theft* and *Time Out of Mind* before it, seems to survey a broken world through the prism of a heart that's worn and worldly, yet decidedly unbroken itself. "I been sitting down studying the art of love / I think it will fit me like a glove," he states in "Thunder on the Mountain," the opening song, a rollicking blues you've heard a million times before and yet which magically seems to announce yet another "new" Dylan. "I feel like my soul is beginning to expand," the song declares. "Look into my heart and you will sort of understand."

What we do understand, if we're listening, is that we're three albums into a Dylan renaissance that's sounding more and more like a period to put beside any in his work. If, beginning with *Bringing It All Back Home*, Dylan garbed his amphetamine visions in the gloriously grungy clothes of the electric blues and early rock & roll, the musical glories of these three records are grounded in a knowledge of the blues built from the inside out—a knowledge that includes the fact that the early blues and its players were stranger than any purist would have you know, hardly restricting themselves to twelve-bar laments but featuring narrative recitations, spirituals, X-rated ditties, popular ballads and more. Dylan offers us nourishment from the root cellar of American cultural life. For an amnesiac society, that's arguably as mind-expanding an offering as anything in his Sixties work. And with each succeeding record, Dylan's convergence with his muses grows more effortlessly natural.

How does he summon such an eternal authority? "I'd make this record no matter what was going on in the world," Dylan tells me. "I wrote these songs in not a meditative state at all, but more like in a trancelike, hypnotic state. This is how I feel? Why do I feel like that? And who's the me that feels this way? I couldn't tell you that, either. But I know that those songs are just in my genes and I couldn't stop them comin' out." This isn't to say *Modern Times*, or Dylan, seems oblivious to the present moment. The record is littered—or should I say baited?—with glinting references to world events like 9/11 and Hurricane Katrina, though anyone seeking a moral, to paraphrase Mark Twain, should be shot. And, as if to startle the contemporary listener out of any delusion that Dylan's musical drift into pre-rock forms—blues, ragtime, rockabilly—is the mark of a nostalgist, "Thunder on the Mountain" also name-checks a certain contemporary singer: "I was thinking 'bout Alicia Keys, I couldn't keep from crying / While she was born in Hell's Kitchen, I was livin' down the line." When I ask Dylan what Keys did "to get into your pantheon," he only chuckles at my precious question. "I remember seeing her on the Grammys. I think I was on the show with her, I didn't meet her or anything. But I said to myself, 'There's nothing about that girl I don't like.'"

Rather than analyzing lyrics, Dylan prefers to linger over the songs as artifacts of music and describes the process of their making. As in other instances, stretching back to 1974's *Planet Waves*, 1978's *Street-Legal* and 2001's *Love and Theft*, the singer and performer known for his love-hate affair with the recording studio—"I don't like to make records," he tells me simply. "I do it reluctantly"—has cut his new album with his touring band. And Dylan himself is the record's producer, credited under the nom-de-studio Jack Frost. "I didn't feel like I wanted to be overproduced anymore," he tells me. "I felt like I've always produced my own records anyway, except I just had someone there in the way. I feel like nobody's gonna know how I should sound except me anyway, nobody knows what they want out of players except me, nobody can tell a player what he's doing wrong, nobody can find a player who can play but he's not playing, like I can. I can do that in my sleep."

As ever, Dylan is circling, defining what he is first by what he isn't, by what he doesn't want, doesn't like, doesn't need, locating meaning by a process of elimination. This rhetorical strategy goes back at least as far as "It Ain't Me, Babe" and "All I Really Want to Do" ("I ain't looking to compete with you," etc.), and it still has plenty of real juice in it. When Dylan arrives at a positive assertion out of the wilderness of so much doubt, it takes on the force of a jubilant boast. "This is the best band I've ever been in, I've ever had, man for man. When you play with guys a hundred times a year, you know what you can and can't do, what they're good at, whether you want 'em there. It takes a long time to find a band of individual players. Most bands are gangs. Whether it's a metal group or pop rock, whatever, you get that gang mentality. But for those of us who went back further, gangs were the mob. The gang was not what anybody aspired to. On this record I didn't have anybody to teach. I got guys now in my band, they can whip up anything, they surprise even me." Dylan's cadences take on the quality of an impromptu recitation, replete with internal rhyme schemes, such that when I later transcribe this tape I'll find myself tempted to set the words on the page in the form of a lyric. "I knew this time it wouldn't be futile writing something I really love and thought dearly of, and then gettin' in the studio and having it be beaten up and whacked around and come out with some kind of incoherent thing which didn't have any resonance. With that, I was awake. I felt freed up to do just about anything I pleased."

But getting the band of his dreams into the studio was only half the battle. "The records I used to listen to and still love, you can't make a record that sounds that way," he explains. It is as if having taken his new material down to the crossroads of the recording studio Dylan isn't wholly sure the deal struck with the devil there was worth it. "Brian Wilson, he made all his records with four tracks, but you couldn't make his records if you had a hundred tracks today. We all like records that are played on record players, but let's face it, those days are gon-n-n-e. You do the best you can, you fight that technology in all kinds of ways, but I don't know anybody who's made a record that sounds decent in the past twenty years, really. You listen to these modern records, they're atrocious, they have sound all over them. There's no definition of nothing, no vocal, no nothing, just like—static. Even these songs probably sounded ten times better in the studio when we recorded 'em. CDs are small. There's no stature to it. I remember when that Napster guy came up across, it was like, 'Everybody's gettin' music for free.' I was like, 'Well, why not? It ain't worth nothing anyway.'"

Hearing the word "Napster" come from Bob Dylan's mouth, I venture a question about bootleg recordings. In my own wishful thinking, *The Bootleg Series*, a sequence of superb archival retrospectives, sanctioned by Dylan and released by Columbia, represents a kind of unspoken consent to the tradition of pirate scholarship—an acknowledgment that Dylan's outtakes, alternate takes, rejected album tracks and live performances are themselves a towering body of work that faithful listeners deserve to hear. As Michael Gray says in *The Bob Dylan Encyclopedia*, the first three-disc release of outtakes "could, of itself, establish Dylan's place as the pre-eminent songwriter and performer of the age and as one of the great artists of the twentieth century." On *Love and Theft*'s "Sugar Baby," the line "Some of these bootleggers, they make pretty good stuff" was taken by some as a shout-out to this viewpoint. Today, at least, that line seems to have had only moonshine whiskey as its subject. "I still don't like bootleg records. There was a period of time when people were just bootlegging anything on me, because there was nobody ever in charge of the recording sessions. All my stuff was being bootlegged high and low, far and wide. They were never intended to be released, but everybody was buying them. So my record company said, 'Well, everybody else is buying these records, we might as well put them out.'" But Dylan can't possibly be sorry that the world has had the benefit of hearing, for instance, "Blind Willie McTell"—an outtake from 1983's *Infidels* that has subsequently risen as high in most people's Dylan pantheon as a song can rise, and that he himself has played live since. Can he? "I started playing it live because I heard the Band doing it. Most likely it was a demo, probably showing the musicians how it should go. It was never developed fully, I never got around to completing it. There wouldn't have been any other reason for leaving it off the record. It's like taking a painting by Manet or Picasso—goin' to his house and lookin' at a half-finished painting and grabbing it and selling it to people who are 'Picasso fans.' The only fans I know I have are the people who I'm looking at when I play, night after night."

Dylan and his favorite-band-ever are just a few days from undertaking another tour, one that will be well under way by the time *Modern Times* is released in late August. I've always wanted to ask: When a song suddenly appears on a given evening's set list, retrieved from among the hundreds in his back catalog, is it because Dylan's been listening to his old records? "I don't listen to any of my records. When you're inside of it, all you're listening to is a replica. I don't know why somebody would look at the movies they make—you don't read your books, do you?" Point taken. He expands on the explanation he offered for "Blind Willie McTell": "Strangely enough, sometimes we'll hear a cover of a song and figure we can do it just as well. If somebody else thought so highly of it, why don't I? Some of these arrangements I just take. The Dead did a lot of my songs, and we'd just take the whole arrangement, because they did it better than me. Jerry Garcia could hear the song in all my bad recordings, the song that was buried there. So if I want to sing something different, I just bring out one of them Dead records and see which one I wanna do. I never do that with my records." Speaking of which: "I've heard it said, you've probably heard it said, that all the arrangements change night after night. Well, that's a bunch of bullshit, they don't know what they're talkin' about. The arrangements don't change night after night. The rhythmic structures are different, that's all. You can't change the arrangement night after night—it's impossible."

Dylan points out that whether a song comes across for a given listener on a given night depends on where exactly they're sitting. "I can't stand to play arenas, but I do play 'em. But I know that's not where music's supposed to be. It's not meant to be heard in football stadiums, it's not 'Hey, how are you doin' tonight, Cleveland?' Nobody gives a shit how you're doin' tonight in Cleveland." He grins and rolls his eyes, to let me know he knows he's teasing at *Spinal Tap* heresy. Then he plunges deeper. "They say, 'Dylan never talks'. What the hell is there to say! That's not the reason an artist is in front of people." The words seem brash, but his tone is nearly pleading. "An artist has come for a different purpose. Maybe a self-help group—maybe a Dr. Phil—would say, 'How you doin'?' I don't want to get harsh and say I don't care. You do care, you care in a big way, otherwise you wouldn't be there. But it's a different kind of connection. It's not a light thing." He considers further. "It's alive every night, or it feels alive every night." Pause. "It becomes risky. I mean, you risk your life to play music, if you're doing it in the right way." I ask about the minor-league baseball* stadiums he's playing in the new tour's first swing: Do they provide the sound he's looking for? "Not really, not in the open air. The best sound you can get is an intimate club room, where you've got four walls and the sound just bounces. That's the way this music is meant to be heard." Then Dylan turns comedian again, the guy newly familiar to listeners of his XM satellite radio show, whose casual verbal riffs culminate in vaudeville one-liners. "I wouldn't want to play a really small room, like ten people. Unless it was, you know, $50,000 a ticket or something."

Let me take a moment and reintroduce myself, your interviewer and guide here. I'm a forty-two-year-old moonlighting novelist, and a life-long Dylan fan, but one who, it must be emphasized, doesn't remember the Sixties. I'm no longer a young man, but I am young for the job I'm doing here. My parents were Dylan fans, and my first taste of his music came through their LPs—I settled on *Nashville Skyline*, because it looked friendly. The first Dylan record I was able to respond to as new—to witness its arrival in stores and reception in magazines, and therefore to make my own—was 1979's *Slow Train Coming*. As a fan in my early twenties, I digested Dylan's catalog to that point and concluded that its panoply of styles and stances was itself the truest measure of his genius—call us the *Biograph* generation, if you like. In other words, the struggle to capture Dylan and his art like smoke in one particular bottle or another seemed laughable to me, a mistaken skirmish fought before it had become clear that mercurial responsiveness—anchored only by the

---

*So what's Bob Dylan's favorite baseball team, anyway? "The problem with baseball teams is all the players get traded, and what your favorite team used to be—a couple of guys you really liked on the team, they're not on the team now—and you can't possibly make that team your favorite team. It's like your favorite uniform. I mean . . . yeah . . . I like Detroit. Though I like Ozzie [Guillen] as a manager. And I don't know how anybody can't like Derek [Jeter]. I'd rather have him on my team than anybody."

existential commitment to the act of connection in the present moment—was the gift of freedom his songs had promised all along. To deny it to the man himself would be absurd. By the time I required anything of Bob Dylan, it was the mid-Eighties, and I merely required him to be good. Which, in the mid-Eighties, Dylan kind of wasn't. I recall taking home *Empire Burlesque* and struggling to discern songwriting greatness under the glittery murk of Arthur Baker's production, a struggle I lost. The first time I saw Dylan in concert, it was, yes, in a football stadium in Oakland, with the Grateful Dead. By the time of 1988's *Down in the Groove*, the album's worst song might have seemed to describe my plight as fan; I was in love with the ugliest girl in the world.

Nevertheless, Eighties Dylan was my Dylan, and I bore down hard on what was there. Contrary to what you may have heard (in *Chronicles, Volume One*, among other detractors), there was water in that desert. From scattered tracks like "Rank Strangers to Me," "The Groom's Still Waiting at the Altar" and "Brownsville Girl," to cassette-tape miracles like "Lord Protect My Child" and "Foot of Pride" (both later to surface on *The Bootleg Series*), to a version of "San Francisco Bay Blues" I was lucky enough to catch live in Berkeley, to a blistering take on Sonny Boy Williamson's "Don't Start Me to Talkin'" on *Late Night With David Letterman*, the irony is not only that "bad" Dylan was often astonishingly good. It is that his then-seemingly-rudderless exploration of roots-music sources can now be seen to point unerringly to the triumphs to come—I mean the triumphs of now. Not that Dylan himself would care to retrace those steps. When I gushed about the Sonny Boy Williamson moment on *Letterman*, he gaped, plainly amazed, and said, "I played that?"

So, the drama of my projected relationship to my hero, thin as it may seem to those steeped in the Sixties or Seventies listeners' sense of multiple betrayals—*he's gone Electric! Country-Domestic-Unavailable! Christian!*—was the one Dylan described to David Gates of *Newsweek* in 1997, and in the "Oh Mercy" chapter of his memoir, *Chronicles*—the relocation and repossession of his voice and of his will to compose and perform, as enacted gradually through the Nineties. Early in that decade it might have seemed he'd quit, or at least taken refuge or solace in the solo acoustic folk records he'd begun making in his garage: *Good As I Been to You* and *World Gone Wrong*. Live shows in what had become "The Never Ending Tour" were stronger and stronger in those years, but new songs were scarce. Then came *Time Out of Mind*, an album as cohesive—and ample—as any he'd ever recorded. When that was followed by *Love and Theft*, and then *Chronicles*, a reasonable Dylan fan might conclude he was living in the best of all possible worlds. In fact, with the satellite radio show beaming into our homes—Dylan's promised to do fifty of the things!—Dylan can be said to have delivered more of his voice and his heart to his audience in the past decade than ever before, and more than anyone might have reasonably dared to hope. "Well, isn't that funny," Dylan snorts when I mention "the myth of inaccessibility." "I've just seen that Wenner Books published a book of interviews with me that's that big." He stretches out his hands to show me. "What happened to this inaccessibility? Isn't there a dichotomy there?" Yet it's awfully easy, taking the role of Dylan's interviewer, to feel oneself playing surrogate for an audience that has never quit holding its hero to an impossible standard: The more he offers, the more we want. The greatest artist of my lifetime has given me anything I could ever have thought to ask, and yet here I sit, somehow brokering between him and the expectations neither of us can pretend don't exist. "If I've got any kind of attitude about me—or about what I do, what I perform, what I sing, on any level, my attitude is, compare it to somebody else! Don't compare it to me. Are you going to compare Neil Young to Neil Young? Compare it to somebody else, compare it to Beck—which I like—or whoever else is on his level. This record should be compared to the artists who are working on the same ground. I'll take it any way it comes, but compare it to that. That's what everybody's record should be, if they're really serious about what they're doing. Let's face it, you're either serious about what you're doing or you're not serious about what you're doing. And you can't mix the two. And life is short."

I can't help but wonder if he's lately been reconditioned by the success of the Martin Scorsese *No Direction Home* documentary, to feel again the vivid discomfort of his unwanted savior's role. "You know, everybody makes a big deal about the Sixties. The Sixties, it's like the Civil War days. But, I mean, you're talking to a person who owns the Sixties. Did I ever want to acquire the Sixties? No. But I own the Sixties—who's going to argue with me?" He charms me with another joke: "I'll give 'em to you if you want 'em. You can have 'em." For Dylan, as ever, what matters is the work, not in some archival sense, but in its present life. "My old songs, they've got something—I agree, they've got something! I think my songs have been covered—maybe not as much as 'White Christmas' or 'Stardust,' but there's a list of over 5,000 recordings. That's a lot of people covering your songs, they must have something. If I was me, I'd cover my songs too. A lot of these songs I wrote in 1961 and '62 and '64, and 1973, and 1985, I can still play a lot of those songs—well, how many other artists made songs during that time? How many do you hear today? I love Marvin Gaye, I love all that stuff. But how often are you gonna hear 'What's Going On'? I mean, who sings it? Who sings 'Tracks of My Tears'? Where is that being sung tonight?" He's still working to plumb the fullest truth in the matter of his adventures in the recording studio. "I've had a rough time recording. I've managed to come up with songs, but I've had a rough time recording. But maybe it should be that way. Because other stuff which sounds incredible, that can move you to tears—for all those who were knocked off our feet by listening to music from yesteryear, how many of those songs are really good? Or was it just the record that was great? Well, the record was great. The record was an art form. And you know, when all's said and done, maybe I was never part of that art form, because my records really weren't artistic at all. They were just documentation. Maybe bad players playing bad changes, but still something coming through. And the something that's coming through, for me today, was to make it just as real. To show you how it's real." Dylan muses on the fate of art in posterity. "How many people can look at the *Mona Lisa*? You ever been there? I mean, maybe, like, three people can see it at once. And yet, how long has that painting been around? More people have seen that painting than have ever listened to, let's name somebody—I don't want to say Alicia Keys—say, Michael Jackson. More people have ever seen the *Mona Lisa* than ever listened to Michael Jackson. And only three people can see it at once. Talk about impact."

Conversation about painting leads to conversation about other forms. "That's what I like about books, there's no noise in it. Whatever you put on the page, it's like making a painting. Nobody can change it. Writing a book is the same way, it's written in stone—it might as well be! It's never gonna change. One's not gonna be different in tone than another, you're not gonna have to turn this one up louder to read it." Dylan savored the reception of *Chronicles*. "Most people who write about music, they have no idea what it feels like to play it. But with the book I wrote, I thought, 'The people who are writing reviews of this book, man, they know what the hell they're talking about.' It spoils you. They know how to write a book, they know more about it than me. The reviews of this book, some of 'em almost made me cry—in a good way. I'd never felt that from a music critic, ever."

While my private guess would have been that Dylan had satisfied the scribbling impulse (or as he says on *Modern Times*, "I've already confessed / No need to confess again"), in fact he seems to be deep into planning for a Chronicles, Volume Two. "I think I can go back to the *Blonde on Blonde* album–that's probably about as far back as I can go on the next book. Then I'll probably go forward. I thought of an interesting time. I made this record, *Under the Red Sky*, with Don Was, but at the same time I was also doing the Wilburys record. I don't know how it happened that I got into both albums at the same time. I worked with George [Harrison] and Jeff [Lynne] during the day—everything had to be done in one day, the track and the song had to be written in one day, and then I'd go down and see Don Was, and I felt like I was walking into a wall. He'd have a different band for me to play with every day, a lot of all-stars, for no particular purpose. Back then I wasn't bringing anything at all into the studio, I was completely disillusioned. I'd let someone else take control of it all and just come up with lyrics to the melody of the song. He'd say, 'What do you want to cut?'—well, I wouldn't have anything to cut, but I'd be so beat down from being up with the Wilburys that I'd just come up with some track, and everybody would fall in behind that track, oh, my God." He laughs. "It was sort of contrary to the Wilburys scene, which was being done in a mansion up in the hills. Then I'd go down to these other sessions, and they were in this cavelike studio down in Hollywood, where I'd spend the rest of the night, and then try to get some sleep. Both projects suffered some. Too many people in the room, too many musicians, too many egos, ego-driven musicians that just wanted to play their thing, and it definitely wasn't my cup of tea, but that's the record I'm going to feature."

Now, this may be the place for me to mention that I find Side Two of *Under the Red Sky* one of the hidden treasures of Dylan's catalog. The album's closer, a garrulous but mysterious jump-blues called "Cat's in the Well," in particular, wouldn't be at all out of place on *Love and Theft* or *Modern Times*. But as he's told me, Dylan doesn't listen to the records. And unlike me, he claims no familiarity with *The Bob Dylan Encyclopedia*. ("Those are not the circles I really move around in," he chuckles when I ask. "That's not something that would overlap with my life.") But just as when he praises his current band as his absolute best—an evaluation supporters of Mike Bloomfield and Al Kooper, not to mention Garth Hudson and Rick Danko, et al., might take issue with—I've come to feel that Dylan's sweeping simplifications of his own journey's story are outstandingly healthy ones. Puncturing myths, boycotting analysis and ignoring chronology are likely part of a long and lately quite successful campaign not to be incarcerated within his own legend. Dylan's greatest accomplishment since his Sixties apotheosis may simply be that he has claimed his story as his own. (Think of him howling the first line of "Most Likely You'll Go Your Way and I'll Go Mine" upon his return to the stage during the 1974 tour: "You say you love me and you're thinkin' of me / But you know you could be wroooonnggg!"). I take our conversation today the way I took *Chronicles*, and the long journal-song "Highlands": as vivid and generous reports on the state of Bob Dylan and his feelings in the present moment.

In other words, never mind that I think *Under the Red Sky* is pretty good. After that early-Nineties disillusionment, how did he decide to record *Time Out of Mind*? "They gave me another contract, which I didn't really want. I didn't want to record anymore, I didn't see any point to it, but lo and behold they made me an offer and it was hard to refuse. I'd worked with [Daniel] Lanois before, and I thought he might be able to bring that magic to this record. I thought, 'Well, I'll give it a try.' There must have been twelve, fifteen musicians in that room—four drummers notwithstanding. I really don't know how we got anything out of that." He pauses to consider the record's reception. Released just after a much-publicized health scare, the album's doomy lyrics were widely taken as a musical wrestling match with the angel of death. "I mean, it was perceived as me being some chronic invalid, or crawling on bleeding knees. But that was never the case." I mention that some are already describing the new album as the third in a trilogy, beginning with *Time Out of Mind*. Dylan demurs: "*Time Out of Mind* was me getting back in and fighting my way out of the corner. But by the time I made *Love and Theft*, I was out of the corner. On this record, I ain't nowhere, you can't find me anywhere, because I'm way gone from the corner." He still toys with the notion I've put before him. "I would think more of *Love and Theft* as the beginning of a trilogy, if there's going to be a trilogy." Then swiftly gives himself an out: "If I decide I want to go back into the studio."

In a day of circular talk we've circled back to the new record, and I venture to ask him again about certain motifs. *Modern Times* shades *Love and Theft*'s jocular, affectionate vibe into more ominous territory, the language of murder ballads and Edgar Allan Poe: foes and slaughter, haunted gardens and ghosts. Old blues and ballads are quoted liberally, like second nature. "I didn't feel limited this time, or I felt limited in the way that you want to narrow your scope down, you don't want to muddle things up, you want every line to be clear and every line to be purposeful. This is the way I feel someplace in me, in my genealogy—a lot of us don't have the murderous instinct, but we wouldn't mind having the license to kill. I just let the lyrics go, and when I was singing them, they seemed to have an ancient presence." Dylan seems to feel he dwells in a body haunted like a house by his bardlike musical precursors. "Those songs are just in my genes, and I couldn't stop them comin' out. In a reincarnative kind of way, maybe. The songs have got some kind of a pedigree to them. But that pedigree stuff, that only works so far. You can go back to the ten-hundreds, and people only had one name. Nobody's gonna tell you they're going to go back further than when people had one name." This reply puts an effective end to my connect-the-dots queries about his musical influences. I tell him that despite the talk of enemies, I found in the new record a generosity of spirit, even a sense of acceptance. He consents, barely. "Yeah. You got to accept it yourself before you can expect anybody else to accept it. And in the long run, it's merely a record. Lyrics go by quick."

When all is said and done, Bob Dylan is keen that I understand where he's coming from, and for me to understand that, I have to grasp what he saw in the artists who went before him. "If you think about all the artists that recorded in the Forties and the Thirties, and in the Fifties, you had big bands, sure, but they were the vision of one man—I mean, the Duke Ellington band was the vision of one man, the Louis Armstrong band, it was the individual voice of Louis Armstrong. And going into all the rhythm & blues stuff, and the rockabilly stuff, the stuff that trained me to do what I do, that was all individually based. That was what you heard—the individual crying in the wilderness. So that's kind of lost too. I mean, who's the last individual performer that you can think of—Elton John, maybe? I'm talking about artists with the willpower not to conform to anybody's reality but their own. Patsy Cline and Billy Lee Riley. Plato and Socrates, Whitman and Emerson. Slim Harpo and Donald Trump. It's a lost art form. I don't know who else does it beside myself, to tell you the truth." Is he satisfied? "I always wanted to stop when I was on top. I didn't want to fade away. I didn't want to be a has-been, I wanted to be somebody who'd never be forgotten. I feel that, one way or another, it's OK now, I've done what I wanted for myself." These remarks, it should be noted, are yet another occasion for laughter. "I see that I could stop touring at any time, but then, I don't really feel like it right now." Short of promising the third part of the trilogy-in-progress, this is good-enough news for me. May the Never Ending Tour never end. "I think I'm in my middle years now," Bob Dylan tells me. "I've got no retirement plans."

DYLAN ON

Not Feeling the Urge to Write

"If you don't have to write songs, why write them? Especially if you've got so many you could never play—there wouldn't be enough time to play them all, anyway. I've got enough where I don't really feel the urge to write anything additional."

—from interview with Jann S. Wenner, *Rolling Stone*, May 3, 2007

DYLAN ON

How the Music World Compares with the Book and Art Worlds

"The music world's a made-up bunch of hypocritical rubbish. I know from publishing a memoir that the book people are a whole lot saner. And the art world? From the small steps I've taken in it, I'd say, yeah, the people are honest, upfront and deliver what they say. Basically, they are who they say they are. They don't pretend. And having been in the music world most of my life [*laughs*], I can tell you it's not that way. Let's just say it's less . . . dignified."

—from interview with Alan Jackson, *Times* (UK), June 2008

DYLAN ON

Hitler

"How you take a failed landscape painter and turn him into a fanatical madman who controls millions—that's some trick. . . . In hindsight, you can see that someone would have to take control. But still, it's so perplexing. Look at the faces of the millions who worshipped him and you see that he inspired love. It's scary and sad. The torch of the spoken word. They were glad to follow him anywhere, loyal to the bone. Then of course, he filled up the cemeteries with them."

—from interview with Bill Flanagan, *Telegraph* (UK), April 13, 2009

BOB DYLAN'S LATE-ERA, OLD-STYLE AMERICAN INDIVIDUALISM

Douglas Brinkley | May 14, 2009 | *Rolling Stone*

On April 7 and 9, 2009, a few weeks before the release of Dylan's superb *Together Through Life*, he spent hours talking with author and university professor Douglas Brinkley in Paris and in Amsterdam, Holland.

"He's very old-fashioned," Brinkley later told radio personality Don Imus. "He's really a 1950s kind of guy, when America was in black and white, not the psychedelic '60s that's in Technicolor. And he champions American poetry, novelists . . . There's a touch of nationalism in him, which is I think surprising to some people."

What was it like to interview Dylan? "He couldn't have been warmer and more of a gentleman," Brinkley said on MSNBC-TV. "We had a great time talking. . . . And I went to areas he likes to talk about. Y'know, he's an expert on Civil War songs, both from the South and the North. We talked about that. We talked about Walt Whitman. He misses the kind of poetic vision of Whitman's America, when everything was very big. We talked about John Ford, the movie director. He loved those old westerns and in some ways it [those films] informs this new ten songs that he's just written." —Ed.

On April 7th, French president Nicolas Sarkozy and his wife, Carla Bruni-Sarkozy, stroll into the Palais des Congrès in Paris. Nobody in the sold-out auditorium, however, pays the First Couple much attention. Bob Dylan, who in 1990 was named a Commandeur dans l'Ordre des Art et des Lettres, the highest cultural award France can bestow, is about to take the stage for an evening of *nostalgie* (as the tickets read). After an old-style-vaudevillian introduction, out walks Dylan with his five-member band, all sharply dressed in Pretty Boy Floyd suits and fedoras. As Dylan launches into a hard-rock version of "Cat's in the Well," from his *Under the Red Sky* album, the cheering crowd holds up cellphones, trying to film the enigmatic legend, who immediately ensconces himself behind an electric piano. Dylan plays guitar on only a single song—as is usually the case—but throughout the night his harmonica riffs soar through the cavernous hall. Everyone feels energized by his charismatic presence. After about two and a half hours, he ends the performance with a defiant version of the crowd-pleasing "Blowin' in the Wind."

After the show, the Sarkozys wander backstage, anxious to meet Dylan. The French president is attired in a black turtleneck and jeans. In a single swooping motion, Sarkozy seizes Dylan's hand, welcoming him to France. "It was like looking at my mirror image," Dylan tells me later, about the encounter. "I can see why he's the head of France. He's genuine and warm and extremely likable. I asked Sarkozy, 'Do you think the whole global thing is over?' I knew they just had a big G-20 meeting and they maybe were discussing that. I didn't think he'd tell me, but I asked him anyway."

While Dylan—who will be playing around 30 concerts in minor-league baseball stadiums this summer along with Willie Nelson and John Mellencamp—is celebrated in America, he is lionized in Europe. The French periodicals were all abuzz that Dylan had just collaborated with the popular 41-year-old film director Olivier Dahan on a new movie soundtrack. The following evening, at Dylan's second sold-out Paris show, I chatted with the genial Dahan, a scruffy-looking guy straight from the pages of *Oliver Twist*. In 2007, Dahan directed *La Vie en Rose*, the celebrated biopic of Edith Piaf that won two Academy Awards. Last year, he brazenly solicited a handful of songs from Dylan, via a letter, for his new road movie, *My Own Love Song*. Starring Forest Whitaker and Renée Zellweger, *My Own Love Song* is the tale of an infirm female singer who journeys across America, from Kansas to Louisiana. "I wanted the songs to feel Southern," Dahan says. "Real songs of the American spirit. What that meant for me, like millions of others worldwide, is Bob Dylan's songs."

"At first this was unthinkable," Dylan recounts. "I mean, I didn't know what [Dahan] was actually saying. [*In faux French accent*] 'Could you write uh, 10, 12 songs?' Ya know? I said, 'Yeah, really? Is this guy serious?' But he was so audacious! Usually you get asked to do, like, one song, and it's at the end of the movie. But 10 songs?" Dylan continues, "Dahan wanted to put these songs throughout the movie and find different reasons for them. I just kind of gave the guy the benefit of the doubt that he knew what he was doing. I always liked those movies, ya know, those black-and-white movies where, like, Veronica Lake all of a sudden out of nowhere is singing in a nightclub. Or Diahann Carroll is singing in a cafe. All those movies where the action stops and the heroes are represented as walking past a barn dance where the Sons of the Pioneers are playing on a truck. It's so musical. They don't put that kind of thing in movies anymore. Now it's come down to just an end-title song—which has nothing to do with the movie, and basically people are walking out."

The audiences at the Palais des Congrès were cross-generational: The gray-hairs and the body-pierced youths sat side by side. At this juncture Dylan's audience is . . . well, everybody. The French troubadour Charles Aznavour attended that second Paris show with one of his sons. Dylan, in homage to Aznavour, played the Frenchman's melancholic composition "The Times We Have Known" with sublime grace. After the show, the 84-year-old Aznavour joined Dylan backstage for a bit of banter. Wearing a suede coat with a sky-blue scarf around his neck, the deeply tanned Aznavour epitomized to Dylan how a popular musician can comport himself with dignity in the fourth quarter of life. "I finally caught up with you," Dylan tells him. "I saw you in 1963 at Carnegie Hall. It was filled with French people and me. I was the only American there, really."

After a round of Obama fist bumps, Dylan heads down a flight of stairs and onto his touring bus for the five-hour drive to Amsterdam, where he will be playing three more shows. For Dylan, it seems, life is always the next gig. Changing pace and location are essential to his survival as an artist. Contrary to reputation, however, he is no recluse.

People populate his waking hours (although they're primarily of the worker-bee kind). "You're always aware of what town you're in," Dylan says of the millions of miles logged. "But in another sense, touring is like being on a freighter out on the open sea. You're really out there for days and months."

Critics have claimed that since 1988 Dylan has been on a Never Ending Tour, playing more than 100 concerts a year. The aggrieved Dylan bristles at the term. "Critics should know that there's no such thing as forever," he says. "So that speaks more about them who would use that phrase as if there's some important meaning in it. You never heard about Oral Roberts and Billy Graham being on some Never Ending Preacher Tour. Does anybody ever call Henry Ford a Never Ending Car Builder? Is Rupert Murdoch a Never Ending Media Tycoon? What about Donald Trump? Does anybody say he has a Never Ending Quest to build buildings? Picasso painted well into his 90s. And Paul Newman raced cars in his 70s. Anybody ever say that Duke Ellington was on a Never Ending Bandstand Tour? But critics apply a different standard to me for some reason. But we're living in an age of breaking everything down into simplistic terms, aren't we? These days, people are lucky to have a job. Any job. So critics might be uncomfortable with me [working so much]. Maybe they can't figure it out. But nobody in my particular audience feels that way about what I do. Anybody with a trade can work as long as they want. A welder, a carpenter, an electrician. They don't necessarily need to retire. People who have jobs on an assembly line, or are doing some kind of drudgery work, they might be thinking of retiring every day. Every man should learn a trade. It's different than a job. My music wasn't made to take me from one place to another so I can retire early."

Dylan has spent a lifetime dodging people's attempts to define him. He scorns "newsy people" who constantly try to pin him down about his personal life. Random strangers sometimes come up to him asking for a critique of Martin Scorsese's *No Direction Home* documentary about his life. "I've never seen it," he tells me. "Well, a lot of that footage was gathered up from the Sixties. So I'd seen that, and I thought that was like looking at a different character. But it certainly was powerful. And I don't, or can't, do that anymore."

Dylan's principal frustration, however, is that he feels misunderstood as an artist: "Popular music has no, whatever you call them, critics, that understand popular music in all of its dynamic fundamentalism. The consensus on me is that I'm a songwriter. And that I was influenced by Woody Guthrie and sang protest songs. Then rock & roll songs. Then religious songs for a period of time. But it's a stereotype. A media creation. Which is impossible to avoid if you're any type of public figure at all." Where critics think he's deconstructing old songs, he instead sees himself as an old-time musical arranger. "My band plays a different type of music than anybody else plays," Dylan says. "We play distinctive rhythms that no other band can play. There are so many of my songs that have been rearranged at this point that I've lost track of them myself. We do keep the structures intact to some degree. But the dynamics of the song itself might change from one given night to another because the mathematical process we use allows that. As far as I know, no one else out there plays like this. Today, yesterday and probably tomorrow. I don't think you'll hear what I do ever again. It took a while to find this thing. But then again, I believe that things are handed to you when you're ready to make use of them. You wouldn't recognize them unless you'd come through certain experiences. I'm a strong believer that each man has a destiny."

These days, Dylan has largely decommissioned the electric guitar in favor of an electric keyboard. Does he have arthritis? Or was he sick of jamming on "Leopard-Skin Pill-Box Hat" for the thousandth time? The answer is neither. "I was looking for a keyboard player to play triplet forms for a long period of time," he explains. "I tried different musicians for it, and we couldn't find anybody who understood the style of what we were doing and to stay within the boundaries. And, finally, you've just got to do it on your own. As far as guitar, I was looking for a guitar player who could play exactly like me, only better. I can't find that person either. The same thing applies to keyboards. I'm looking for a piano player who can play just like me, only better. If I could find him or her, I would hire that person. So far it hasn't happened. I wish it would. We could do more if I was freed up there."

I ask whether, as bandleader, Dylan had ever played a set with the perfect guitarist. Dylan jumps at the opportunity to answer rather reminiscently. "The guy that I always miss, and I think he'd still be around if he stayed with me, actually, was Mike Bloomfield," Dylan says of his collaborator on *Highway 61 Revisited* (who also famously played electric guitar with him at the Newport Folk Festival in 1965). "He could just flat-out play. He had so much soul. And he knew all the styles, and he could play them so incredibly well. He was an expert player and a real prodigy, too. Started playing early. But then again a lot of good guitarists have played with me. Freddy Tackett, Steve Ripley—Mick Taylor played with me for a minute."

Full of memory lane, Dylan goes on to tell a story about first meeting Bloomfield in Chicago at a headhunt on the South Side. A social misfit, Bloomfield was the rare white guitarist who had recorded with the likes of Sleepy John Estes and Big Joe Williams. "He could play like Willie Brown or Charlie Patton," Dylan says. "He could play like Robert Johnson way back then in the Sixties. The only other guy who could do that in those days was Brian Jones, who played in the Rolling Stones. He could also do the same thing. Fingerpicking rhythms that hardly anyone could do. Those are the only two guys I've ever met who could . . . from back then . . . the only two guys who could play the pure style of country blues authentically."

Dylan, who is about to turn 68, continues to be a force of nature, a veritable one-man Johnstown Flood. It's impossible to categorize or comprehend his confounding output of new songs. His youthful rebelliousness has now matured into an old-style American individualism. As a composer, Dylan now fits comfortably alongside George Gershwin or Irving Berlin, though he grumpily refuses to wear any man's collar. Casually dressed in jeans and a sweater vest, Dylan offers me coffee for our interview in a second-floor suite at Amsterdam's Intercontinental Hotel along the Amstel River. Dylan's curly hair is still tousled, his deeply creased face full of mischief. He has a razor-sharp memory. For two evenings, he proves to be a lucid, if circumspect, conversationalist.

Like the dour-faced farmer in Grant Wood's "American Gothic," Dylan seems to have the American Songbook in one hand and a raised pitchfork in the other, aimed at rock critics, politicians, Wall Street financiers, back-alley thieves, the World Wide Web—anything that cheapens the spirit of the individual. His nostalgia is more for the Chess Records Fifties than the psychedelic Sixties. He believes that Europe should lose the euro and go back to its old currencies ("I miss the pictures on the old money," he says). If Dylan had his way, there'd be Sousa bands on Main Street and vinyl albums instead of CDs. Teenagers would go on nature hikes instead of watching YouTube. "It's peculiar and unnerving in a way to see so many young people walking around with cellphones and iPods in their ears and so wrapped up in media and video games," he says. "It robs them of their self-identity. It's a shame to see them so tuned out to real life. Of course they are free to do that, as if that's got anything to do with freedom. The cost of liberty is high, and young people should understand that before they start spending their life with all those gadgets."

Ever since 2001's *Love and Theft,* Dylan has been producing his own albums under the pseudonym Jack Frost. "It's better that I produce," he says. "It saves a lot of time. A lot of rigmarole. A lot of communication, ya know? It's just easier for me to make records. Translating my own ideas directly rather than having them go through somebody else. I know my form of music better than anyone else would."

Right now, Dylan is focused on *Together Through Life,* the new studio album he recorded last fall. The album's genesis was the song "Life Is Hard," his first gift to Dahan. With a pocket full of lyrics and melodies, Dylan booked a studio to lay down nine other new tracks. To help capture the Texas-Mexico-escapism aura, Dylan hired Grateful Dead lyricist Robert Hunter to work with him. The 68-year-old Hunter had previously written two songs with Dylan, for *Down in the Groove* in 1988: "Silvio" and "Ugliest Girl in the World." It's rare, but not unprecedented, for Dylan to collaborate on songs. Over the years, he's shared songwriting credits with the likes of Tom Petty, Willie Nelson, the late Rick Danko of the Band—even Michael Bolton. (When he was in the Traveling Wilburys, Dylan wrote numerous songs with George Harrison. He hopes one day to sit down and work with Paul McCartney: "That'd be exciting to do something with Paul! But, ya know, your paths have to cross for something like that to make sense.")

Dylan and Hunter view the world through a similar lens. "Hunter is an old buddy," Dylan says. "We could probably write a hundred songs together if we thought it was important or the right reasons were there. He's got a way with words, and I do too. We both write a different type of song than what passes today for songwriting. I think we'll be writing a couple of other songs too, for some off-Broadway play." For guitar, Dylan brought in Mike Campbell (on loan from Tom Petty and the Heartbreakers). "Mike and I played before lots of times when I was on tour with Tom," Dylan says. "There was always some part of the show where Mike and myself and [organist] Benmont Tench would play two or three ballads. On my new record I didn't think he'd have any problem."

On *Together Through Life*, Dylan's mystic-drifter persona of his recent records has moved from the Mississippi Delta to Houston and the U.S.-Mexico borderland. Brownsville. McAllen. Laredo. El Paso. "You feel things, and you're not quite sure what you feel," Dylan says about the region. "But it follows your every move, and you don't know why. You can't get out of it. It's the pressure that's imposed on us." The album bottles the feeling of King Ranch country along Highway 77—down toward San Benito, where the water tower reads "Hometown of Freddy Fender." "Spirited guys from down there," Dylan believes. "Independent-thinking guys. Texas might have more independent-thinking people than any other state in the country. And it shows in the music. Realistically speaking, that is the same type of music that I heard growing up most nights in Minnesota. The languages were just different. It was sung in Spanish there. But where I came from, it was sung in Polish."

The first track of *Together Through Life*—"Beyond Here Lies Nothin'"—is pure Tex-Mex torque. Already getting a lot of radio play, the song conjures up shiny automobiles rumbling across "boulevards of broken cars" through the vast Rio Grande Valley night. No grapefruit trees or warm salt breezes or beef-jerky stands here. You imagine forlorn bank buildings and tiny grain elevators and faded billboard advertise-ments. The last-chance gas is behind you a good 20 miles. By the second track, "Life Is Hard," Dylan is wandering past the old schoolyard, looking for strength to fight back the grim tide of old age. A red-brick afterglow lingers in the ballad like in an Edward Hopper painting. A Broadway singer has already recorded a demo of the song; it would be perfect for Dianne Reeves or Norah Jones.

The third track, "My Wife's Home Town," a gloss on the old blues standard "I Just Want to Make Love to You," echoes the haunting Tom Waits vibe of *Mule Variations.* Dylan sounds like a phlegmatic Cab Calloway scatting and coughing before the coffin closes. Everything feels condemned. The fiendish specter of suicide is omnipresent: "State gone broke / The county's dry / Don't be looking at me with that evil eye." Dylan even menacingly cackles "*a-hah-heh-heh*" on the track. "The song is a tribute, not a death chant," he says. "Deep down, I think that everybody thinks like me sooner or later. They just might not be able to express it."

The sense of dislocation continues in the more upbeat "If You Ever Go to Houston." The long-shot chance of redemption (or at least a good night of fun) is palatable. Dylan and Hunter are tapping into the rootlessness of Houston, which is about to supplant Chicago as the third-largest city in the United States. There is a feeling of operating on the undetected margins of the sprawl. The Dylan-Hunter lyric noticeably references the Mexican-American War of 1846 to 1848 as a remembrance of survival against adversity.

I ask Dylan about the wave of recent violence reaching up from Mexico into the Southwest borderlands, an area that the Grateful Dead had once happily celebrated in "Mexicali Blues" and other songs. "That's always been dangerous ground," he says. "It has a different kind of population than Austin or Dallas or other big cities. Texas is so big. It's a republic; it's its own country. The Texas borderlands are like a buffer zone for Mexico and the rest of the States. You get that leftover vibe from northern Mexico, central Mexico, where you have that legacy of Aztec brutality. That's where they used to slash the hearts out of people, captives and thousands of slaves offered up on bloody altars. On the other hand, you have Cortés and all those conquistadors who were coming out of the Spanish Inquisition-type scene. So I can imagine it got pretty brutal. And

I think it's got a lot of spillover from that time, in our times. I see the violence as some kind of epidemic that has lasted until this day maybe."

Not that Dylan isn't having fun in *Together Through Life*. In "I Feel a Change Comin' On," the wayward stranger gets a little oomph in his stride. Surveying the crazy world, Dylan is hopeful that a new love will fall into his arms. Dreams come and go, Dylan sings, but love is eternal. Every good Dylan album has a first-person line, one that his fans gravitate toward with wild enthusiasm. The winner in *Together Through Life* is the quip "I'm listening to Billy Joe Shaver / And I'm reading James Joyce / Some people they tell me / I've got the blood of the land in my voice." Dylanologists will probably have a field day analyzing why he chose to call out Shaver (a hand-maimed Texas guitar-picker who wrote many of Waylon Jennings' best songs). And why James Joyce? "Waylon played me [Shaver's] 'Ain't No God in Mexico,' and I don't know, it was quite good," Dylan says. "Shaver and David Allen Coe became my favorite guys in that [outlaw] genre. The verse came out of nowhere. No . . . you know something? Subliminally, I can't say that this is actually true. But I think it was more of a Celtic thing. Tying Billy Joe with James Joyce. I think subliminally or astrologically those two names just wanted to be combined. Those two personalities." (Maybe it's just that "Joyce" rhymes with "voice"?)

Something about the Old West mythologies of gunslinger John Wesley Hardin, political maverick Sam Houston and short-story writer O. Henry appeals to Dylan's imagination. Like a Western hero, he has given up the sedentary life and chosen the difficult path of his own ideals, made real by noble isolation. "I think you really have to be a Texan to appreciate the vastness of it and the emptiness of it," Dylan says. "But I'm an honorary Texan."

"What do you mean?" I ask.

"Well," he says, "George Bush, when he was governor, gave me a proclamation that says I'm an honorary Texan [*holds hand up in pledge, laughs*]. As if anybody needed proof. It's no small thing. I take it as a high honor."

While Dylan has praised Obama and rhapsodized about Obama's memoir, *Dreams From My Father*, he's been uncritical of the Bush administration. Almost every American artist has taken a piñata swipe at Bush's legacy, but Dylan refuses. He instead looks at the Bush years as just another unsurprising incident of dawn-of-man folly. "I read history books just like you do," Dylan says. "None of those guys are immune to the laws of history. They're going to go up or down, and they're going to take their people with them. None of us really knew what was happening in the economy. It changed so quickly into a true nightmare of horror. In another day and age, heads would roll. That's what would happen. The rot would be cut out. As far as blaming everything on the last president, think of it this way: The same folks who had held him in such high regard came to despise him. Isn't it funny that they're the very same people who once loved him? People are fickle. Their loyalty can turn at the drop of a hat."

At heart Dylan is an old-fashioned moralist like Shane, who believes in the basic lessons taught by *McGuffey's Readers* and the power of a six-shooter. A cowboy-movie aficionado, Dylan considers director John Ford a great American artist. "I like his old films," Dylan says. "He was a man's man, and he thought that way. He never had his guard down. Put courage and bravery, redemption and a peculiar mix of agony and ecstasy on the screen in a brilliant dramatic manner. His movies were easy to understand. I like that period of time in American films. I think America has produced the greatest films ever. No other country has ever come close. The great movies that came out of America in the studio system, which a lot of people say is the slavery system, were heroic and visionary, and inspired people in a way that no other country has ever done. If film is the ultimate art form, then you'll need to look no further than those films. Art has the ability to transform people's lives, and they did just that."

The word "caustic" takes on a whole new meaning in *Together Through Life*'s final cut, the sure-to-be-canonical "It's All Good." Dylan belittles all those arrogant narcissists who constantly say it's all good, even when the world crumbles around them. Drums and guitar rumble in a mad-attic rush of grunge blues while Dylan spits out sarcasm with such lines as "Big politicians telling lies / Restaurant kitchen all full of flies / Don't make a bit of difference / Don't see why it should . . . it's all good." It's a raucous affair. I ask Dylan if he has ever uttered the slang expression "It's all good," even once, himself. "I might have, who knows?" he says with a sidelong, savvy smile. "Maybe if I was joking or something, just like in the song."

If there is a guiding spirit to *Together Through Life*—Dylan's 33rd studio album—it's the ghost of Doug Sahm. At age 11, Sahm, a San Antonio native, had already recorded his first song, "A Real American Joe." By the time he was 13, the Grand Ole Opry offered him a regular gig; his mother disapproved. Eventually, Sahm's band—the Sir Douglas Quintet—became the Lone Star answer to the Beatles. The cosmic-cowboy sound was born. An impressed Dylan volunteered to sing harmony and play guitar on Sahm's 1973 *Doug Sahm and Band* as a sign of outsider solidarity; the album remains a weird, loose-grooving and quirky rock & roll classic. Dylan even wrote the lighthearted song "Wallflower" for it. Bootleg tapes of the Sahm-Dylan sessions now float around the black market. Tejano accordionist Flaco Jiménez anchored that band, Doug Sahm and Friends, back in 1973, just as David Hidalgo is doing with *Together Through Life*. As late as 1995, Sahm had joined Dylan onstage, in Austin, to play electric guitar on six numbers, including a version of the Grateful Dead's "Alabama Getaway." Sahm told the Texas audience that Dylan was a "beautiful friend" whom he loved dearly.

"Doug was like me, maybe the only figure from that old period of time that I connected with," Dylan explains. "His was a big soul. He had a hit record, 'She's About a Mover,' and I had a hit record ["Like a Rolling Stone"] at the same time. So we became buddies back then, and we played the same kind of music. We never really broke apart. We always hooked up at certain intervals in our lives . . . here and there from time to time. Like Bloomfield, Doug was once a child prodigy too. He was playing fiddle, steel guitar and maybe even saxophone before he was in his teens. I'd never met anybody that had played onstage with Hank Williams before, let alone someone my own age. Doug had a heavy frequency, and it was in his nerves. It's like what Charlie Patton says, 'My God, what solid power.' I miss Doug. He got caught in the grind. He should still be here."

In the pecking order of rock & roll survivors, Dylan sees himself as number two, behind only Chuck Berry. Two songs from the new album—"Jolene" and "Shake Shake Mama"—sound like cuts from Berry's *After School Session*. (Another new Dylan song is "Forgetful Heart," which lyrically touches upon Berry's "Drifting Heart" off that 1958 album.) A friendship has developed between Dylan and Berry over the years. "Chuck said to me, 'By God, I hope you live to be 100, and I hope I live forever,'" Dylan says with a laugh. "He said that to me a couple of years ago. In my universe, Chuck is irreplaceable. . . . All that brilliance is still there, and he's still a force of nature. As long as Chuck Berry's around, everything's as it should be. This is a man who has been through it all. The world treated him so nasty. But in the end, it was the world that got beat."

When I ask Dylan if he'd ever thought of collaborating on a project with Berry, he laughs. "Chuck Berry?" he says. "The thought is preposterous. Chuck doesn't need anybody to do anything with or for him. You got to say that at this point in history he's probably the man. His presence is everywhere, but you never know it. I love Little Richard, but I don't think he performs as much as Chuck. And he's certainly not as spontaneous as Chuck. Chuck can perform at the drop of a hat. Well, Little Richard, he can too, actually, but he doesn't."

After a little more talk on Berry, I shift gears to Elvis Presley, who inspired Dylan as a young man. Dylan has quipped that when he first encountered Elvis' voice as a teenager, it was like "busting out of jail." For Dylan, the very fact that Elvis had recorded versions of "Don't Think Twice, It's All Right," "Tomorrow Is a Long Time" and "Blowin' in the Wind" remains mind-boggling. Dutifully, as if returning a favor, Dylan recorded Elvis' hit "(Now and Then There's) A Fool Such As I" during both the *Basement Tapes* and *Self-Portrait* sessions.

But that was about as close as they ever got. "I never met Elvis," Dylan says. "I never met Elvis, because I didn't want to meet Elvis. Elvis was in his Sixties movie period, and he was just crankin' 'em out and knockin' 'em off, one after another. And Elvis had kind of fallen out of favor in the Sixties. He didn't really come back until, whatever was it, '68? I know the Beatles went to see him, and he just played with their heads. 'Cause George [Harrison] told me about the scene. And Derek

[Taylor], one of the guys who used to work for him. Elvis was truly some sort of American king. His face is even on the Statue of Liberty. And, well, like I said, I wouldn't quite say he was ridiculed, but close. You see, the music scene had gone past him, and nobody bought his records. Nobody young wanted to listen to him or be like him. Nobody went to see his movies, as far as I know. He just wasn't in anybody's mind. Two or three times we were up in Hollywood, and he had sent some of the Memphis Mafia down to where we were to bring us up to see Elvis. But none of us went. Because it seemed like a sorry thing to do. I don't know if I would have wanted to see Elvis like that. I wanted to see the powerful, mystical Elvis that had crash-landed from a burning star onto American soil. The Elvis that was bursting with life. That's the Elvis that inspired us to all the possibilities of life. And that Elvis was gone, had left the building."

Clearly, Dylan wants to make sure he doesn't flame out like Elvis. Not a minute of his Paris or Amsterdam shows were golden-oldie dial-ins. "All these shows I play are in the zone," he says. Touring helps Dylan stay focused and fit as a fiddle. Not only are concerts workouts, but all the hustle and bustle of travel keeps him taut and thin. In movement, Dylan believes, man has a chance. Even on the road, boxing remains his primary training exercise. For years, in fact, he had a "professional opponent," Mouse Strauss, who would ferociously spar with him. "Mouse could walk on his hands across a football field," Dylan says. "He taught me the pugilistic rudiments back a while ago, maybe 20 or 30 years. That's not when I started, though. Boxing was a part of the curriculum when I went to high school. Then it was taken out of the school system, I think maybe in '58. But it was always good for me because it was kind of an individualist thing. You didn't need to be part of a team. And I liked that."

I tell Dylan about a bootleg CD producer Bob Johnston once sent me of him sounding drunk crooning "Yesterday" with Johnny Cash. His eyes open wide. "Me and Johnny would sit around hotel rooms in London and sing all kinds of stuff into a tape recorder," he says. "As far as I know those tapes have never surfaced anywhere. But they've been in a few films here and there. I don't really remember 'Yesterday.'" When

I ask him if he thinks much about Cash, who died in September 2003, he turns somber.

"Yeah, I do. I do miss him. But I started missing him 10 years before he actually kicked the bucket."

"What does that mean?" I ask.

"You know," he says, "it's hard to talk about. I tell people if they are interested that they should listen to Johnny on his Sun records and reject all that notorious low-grade stuff he did in his later years. It can't hold a candlelight to the frightening depth of the man that you hear on his early records. That's the only way he should be remembered."

Dylan has become our great American poet of drifting, inheriting a baton that was passed from Walt Whitman to Vachel Lindsay to Carl Sandburg to Allen Ginsberg. It was Sandburg, in fact, who captured Dylan's imagination. The Illinois populist represented the poetic flip side of his endless fascination with Woody Guthrie. Just as Dylan famously sat at Guthrie's sickbed in Greystone Hospital in New Jersey, he spontaneously drove with friends from New York to Hendersonville, North Carolina, simply to bang on the screened-in door of his all-seasons hero. It was in early February 1964. Mrs. Sandburg greeted the stoned-out New Yorkers with Appalachian warmth. "I am a poet," is how Dylan introduced himself to her. "My name is Robert Dylan, and I would like to see Mr. Sandburg." The 86-year-old Sandburg had collected more than 280 ballads in *The American Songbag*, and Dylan wanted to discuss them. "I had three records out at the time," Dylan says, laughing at his youthful temerity. "The *Times They Are a-Changin'* record was the one I gave him a copy of. Of course he had never heard of me." After just 20 minutes, Sandburg excused himself. While Dylan felt it was a pleasant exchange, he didn't get to discuss "I'm a-Ridin' Old Paint" or "Frankie & Albert" with the bard. I ask Dylan whether it was worth the drive to North Carolina. "Oh, yeah," Dylan says. "It was worth meeting him. He was the Grand Ol' Man at the time. I always liked his poetry because it was so simple and poignant. You didn't need reference books to read him."

More famously, around this time Dylan forged a bond with Ginsberg, whose poem "Howl" Dylan had practically memorized line by line. "I like Ginsberg when he invented his own language," Dylan says. "When he put his—nobody I don't think did that before—language down on paper. There's definitely a Ginsberg-ian language. And I don't think anybody uses it, because nobody has ever caught on to it. But it's powerful, confident language. All that neon jukebox and lonesome farms and grandfather night stuff. The way he puts words together. The ways that, you know, he used the English vocabulary, sharp words that seem to sweat as you read them."

Ginsberg once told me a story about a night in the 1980s when Dylan raced over to his East Village apartment, hungry for a title to what eventually became the album *Empire Burlesque.* I ask Dylan whether he recalls the incident. "Yeah, of course!" he says. "I went over to see Allen. I think I played [the songs] to him over at his place at 5th Street and Avenue B. I played it for him because I thought he would like it. I never dreamed that Ginsberg would latch on to the pop-music world. I always thought they were jazz guys. I asked Allen what he would think a good title for this record was. And he listened. And he thought for a moment. And he said, 'Razzmatazz.'" Dylan laughs and says, "I was kind of speechless. It was not the kind of title that I was expecting. I wasn't sure about that idea. Later on, though, I realized that he might be right. I probably should have called it that."

When tabulating literary influences, Dylan summons the name Walt Whitman, for *Leaves of Grass* continues to inspire him. Toward the end of his life, Whitman was preparing a "Death-Bed" edition of *Leaves of Grass,* reflecting on the indignities and ragged joys of growing old. "I don't think the dream of Whitman has ever been fulfilled," Dylan says. "I don't know if Whitman's spirit is still here. It's hard to say if it holds up except maybe in a nostalgic sense. That westward-expansion thing has been dead for a while now. When Whitman started out, he had such great faith in humankind. His mind must have been destroyed when the War between the States fell at his front door. His vision, which was so massively phallic, suddenly must have become plundered, ruined and emasculated when he saw all that indescribable destruction."

We talk about Whitman serving as a nurse in a Washington, D.C., hospital during the Civil War, draining gangrene from a wounded soldier's limbs. "I think you can see the change in Whitman," Dylan says.

"Before that and after that. He had the most grand view of America. Almost like he's America himself. He's just so big, and he's all that there is. The Greek Empire. The Roman Empire. The British Empire. All of European history gone. Whitman is the New World. That's what Whitman is all about. But it isn't the New World anymore. Poor man. He was hounded and mistreated, too, in his lifetime. And ridiculed. Emerson, Thoreau, all those guys, you don't know what they really thought of him."

If any American personifies life on what Whitman called the "open road," it's Bob Dylan. Traveling allows Dylan's aloofness to ferment into clarity. Woody Guthrie, Blind Willie McTell and Jack Kerouac treasured this rootless way too. "*On the Road* speeds by like a freight train," Dylan tells me. "It's all movement and words and lusty instincts that come alive like you're riding on a train. Kerouac moves so fast with his words. No ambiguity. It was very emblematic of the time. You grabbed a hold of the train, hopped on and went along with him, hanging on for dear life. I think that's what affected me more than whatever he was writing about. It was his style of writing that affected us in such a virile way. I tried reading some of his books later, but I never felt that movement again."

Sometimes on the road Dylan stops by the homes or graves of musicians he admires. He once went to Tupelo, Mississippi, to soak in the essence of Elvis. He's made pilgrimages in Texas to search out Buddy Holly and Roy Orbison. I ask Dylan if he minds people visiting Hibbing or Duluth or Minneapolis searching for the root of his talent. "Not at all," he surprisingly says. "That town where I grew up hasn't really changed that much, so whatever was in the air before is probably still there. I go through once in a while coming down from Canada. I'll stop there and wander around." As for Duluth, where his grandparents lived, he thinks it's one of the country's forgotten gems. "You'll never see another town like Duluth," he says. "It's not a tourist destination, but it probably should be. Depends what season you're in there, though. There are only two seasons: damp and cold. I like the way the hills tumble to the waterfront and the way the wind blows around the grain elevators. The train yards go on forever too. It's old-age industrial, that's what it is. You'll see it from the top of the hill for miles and miles before you get there. You won't believe your eyes. I'll give you a medal if you get out alive."

Dylan then recounts a recent side excursion he made from Minnesota to Manitoba. "I went to see Neil Young's house in Winnipeg," he says. "I just felt compelled. I wanted to see his bedroom. Where he looked out of the windows. Where he dreamed. Where he walked out of the door every day. Wanted to see what's around his neighborhood in Winnipeg. And I did just that."

"How did you do that?"

"I don't know," he answers. "Somebody found out for me where he used to live. I mean, there's no marker or anything. And some people were living in his house. He lived in an upstairs duplex with his mother. I wanted to walk the steps that Neil walked every day."

"Does he know you did that?" I ask.

"I don't think so," Dylan says with a grin. "I was meaning to send him a card afterward and tell him that. That I'd been there. Where he used to hang out and where he started out. Neil, I respect him so much."

Long a master of disguise, Dylan can slip into truck stops or taprooms with relative ease. He's learned the art of blending in. If necessary, there is always a sweatshirt hood. Irregular in his daily routine, mainly a night owl, Dylan sometimes draws sketches for his paintings. For years, Dylan's artwork was mostly monochromatic, but recently, in his Drawn Blank series, he has added bursts of color to his drawings. He likes dazzling purples, pinks and sunflower yellow. For all of his bouts of lyrical darkness, Dylan, like Van Gogh, relishes color, and he lets it show; even when the subject matter is a dismal rail yard or a ramshackle house.

When I question Dylan about his genius for disconnecting from the rat race, he quotes Scipio. "Scipio, the great conqueror of Hannibal, who says, 'I'm never in such good company as when I'm alone.'" To Dylan, this is ancient folk wisdom to live by. Wisdom that Hank Williams understood. Later in our conversation, he quotes Scipio again. "'I'm never so busy,'" he says, "'as when I've got nothing to do.'" (I get the weird feeling that this maxim will soon show up in a new Dylan lyric.) "A person's solitude is important," Dylan tells me in teacher mode. "You have to learn about yourself and figure things out, and that's a good way to do it. Obviously, though, too much of it is no good. You can abuse anything."

Dylan has become habituated to eminence. Wherever he goes, people treat him like a king. A cross eye from Dylan can have a devastating effect on a roadie or band member's psyche. Deeply idiosyncratic, mood changing by the minute, Dylan has an unerring ability to make anyone in the room feel they're not equal to the talent present. But he also plays shaman and sprinkles your life with magic dust. When a musician friend turns ill, Dylan plays one of that musician's songs in concert as a personal tribute. Months before Mike Bloomfield died of a drug overdose, Dylan, learning he was struggling, reunited with him in San Francisco to play "Like a Rolling Stone" one last triumphant time. Playing the role of passing angel, Dylan has sung the songs of Jerry Garcia, Warren Zevon, Frank Sinatra, George Harrison and Waylon Jennings, to name just a few, soon after they died, as a spontaneous tribute to their artistry.

Dylan spends most of the afternoon of April 9th at the Rijksmuseum in Amsterdam. I am not allowed to come along. But later he recaps to me what crossed his mind, like who his favorite artists are. "Well, of course, Jackson Pollock and Mark Rothko are good as far as Americans go, and I guess George Bellows and Thomas Hart Benton are OK," he says. "But this guy here, from this town, Rembrandt, is one of my two favorite painters. I like his work because it's rough, crude and beautiful. Caravaggio's the other one. I'd probably go a hundred miles for a chance to see a Caravaggio painting or a Bernini sculpture. You know who I like a lot is [J.M.W.] Turner, the English painter. Art is artillery. And those guys, especially Caravaggio and Rembrandt, used it in its most effective manner. After seeing their work, I'm not even so sure how I feel about Picasso, to tell you the truth."

"Why's that?" I ask.

"Lots of reasons," he says. "He was a renegade painter. He just painted what he wanted. He didn't have anybody over him. I don't think he was ever pushed to the degree that those other guys were. I don't feel Picasso's paintings like I feel the other work I just mentioned. I like Jacques-Louis David a lot, too, although he was a propagandist painter. David's the artist who did the emblematic painting of 'Napoleon at the Saint-Bernard Pass' and 'The Death of Marat.'" As for Andy Warhol, Dylan glares at me for bringing his name into the heavyweight mix. "Only as a cultural figure," he says. "Not as an artist."

After that evening's show at the Heineken Music Hall—at around 11:30 p.m.—I interview Dylan again. Because it is Easter weekend, I decide to push him on the importance of Christian Scripture in his life. "Well, sure," he says, "that and those other first books I read were really biblical stuff. *Uncle Tom's Cabin* and *Ben-Hur*. Those were the books that I remembered reading and finding religion in. Later on, I started reading over and over again Plutarch and his *Roman Lives*. And the writers Cicero, Tacitus and Marcus Aurelius . . . I like the morality thing. People talk about it all the time. Some say you can't legislate morality. Well, maybe not. But morality has gotten kind of a bad rap. In Roman thought, morality is broken down into basically four things. Wisdom, Justice, Moderation and Courage. All of these are the elements that would make up the depth of a person's morality. And then that would dictate the types of behavior patterns you'd use to respond in any given situation. I don't look at morality as a religious thing."

But to Dylan, morality is often about holding firm to personal principles. We talk about his refusal to capitulate to CBS censors back in 1963 when he was to appear on *The Ed Sullivan Show* for the first time. The network had wanted Dylan to play a Clancy Brothers song, even though he had rehearsed "Talkin' John Birch Paranoid Blues." The censors refused to allow a so-called "commie" protest song into America's Cold War living rooms. Dylan wouldn't give in. He now views the walk-off as a seminal event in his early career. "Ed [Sullivan] was behind me, but the censors came down, and they didn't want me to play that particular song," he says. "I just had it in my mind to do that particular song. I'd rehearsed it, and it went down well. And I knew everybody back home would be watching me on *The Ed Sullivan Show*. But then I walked off *The Ed Sullivan Show*, and they couldn't have a chance to see me. So I don't know what that says about me as a person. That was the biggest TV show ever at that time, and it was broadcast on Sunday night. Millions of people watched from coast to coast. It was a dream come true just to be on that stage. Everybody knew that."

Bolting from *The Ed Sullivan Show* was the true turning point in Dylan's life script, even more significant than going electric at Newport. From that moment onward, Dylan would only play by his rules. His spine stiffened. When a recording artist blew off Ed Sullivan . . . well, the James Dean outsider avenue was the only option left. But how did Dylan's mother and father back in Minnesota feel about little Bobby stiffing Mr. Sullivan? "Well, we grew up without TV, really," Dylan explains. "TV came in when I was maybe 16. We didn't get the network shows up north. We only got TV from about 3:00 till 7:00 when it began to come in. We had no consciousness of TV. None. It was all live entertainment that would come through town. Those days are long gone. Even the memories have been obliterated. I think maybe I was in the last generation that grew up like that. We didn't see Dick Clark. I think *Ed Sullivan* came in the last year I was at home. Didn't see Elvis on *Ed Sullivan* because we didn't get that. It was a more innocent way of life. Imagination is what you had and maybe all you had."

More than any recent American artist, with the possible exception of the late collage painter Robert Rauschenberg, Dylan has repeatedly challenged his own intellect and faith. Nothing is ever fully settled. His mind is always crowded with future projects: a series of Brazil-inspired paintings, the next installment of *Chronicles*, a TV special, an orchestra playing new arrangements of his timeless standards, and the composition of more song-poems for the ages sometimes casually written on hotel letterhead. He is going out in life as a gnarled bluesman able to hold his head high, a tried-and-true folkloric figure who's outfoxed even B'rer Rabbit.

When President Sarkozy, looking to make small talk, asked Dylan, "Where do you live?" the quick response was a few simple words: "Right here. . . . No. I'm just joking. I'm from the Lone Star State." (Dylan ended by giving Sarkozy a Texas-style belt buckle as a gift.)

Technically, Dylan's answer wasn't true. Dylan belongs to no city or state. There is Dylan the family man who spends time in California with his children and grandchildren in Malibu, West Hollywood and Beverly Hills. Sometimes Dylan lingers in the Bay Area for weeks at a time, sketching fishmongers and longshoremen. As a New York Yankee fan, he can be found sitting behind first base in the Bronx on random autumnal nights, wishing Mickey Mantle were still batting cleanup. But it's Minnesota's north country, which seems to always lie just over the frozen brow of a long-remembered field, where the road still reaches into the void on below-zero blue winter days, that remains Dylan's touchstone place. That's the American landscape, which has influenced him most. The Great Lakes region is where he learned Mexican *conjunto* music by way of Polish polka bands. You can't find the real Dylan spirit in Greenwich Village or an L.A. studio, a Yazoo River juke joint or a Laredo cafe. For underneath all the mercurial antics and standing ovations, Dylan is so down-home that he considers the boondocks of Hibbing-Duluth to be far grander than Paris.

"The air is so pure there," he says. "And the brooks and rivers are still running. The forests are thick, and the landscape is brutal. And the sky is still blue up there. It is still pretty untarnished. It's still off the beaten path. But I hardly ever go back."

DYLAN ON

His Mainstream Music Contemporaries

"Those guys you are talking about all had conspicuous hits. They started out anti-establishment and now they are in charge of the world. Celebratory songs. Music for the grand dinner party. Mainstream stuff that played into the culture on a pervasive level. My stuff is different from those guys. It's more desperate. Daltrey, Townshend, McCartney, the Beach Boys, Elton, Billy Joel. They made perfect records, so they have to play them perfectly . . . exactly the way people remember them. My records were never perfect. So there is no point in trying to duplicate them. Anyway, I'm no mainstream artist."

—from interview with Bill Flanagan, HuffingtonPost.com, May 16, 2009

DYLAN ON

Receiving the Presidential Medal of Freedom

"Oh, of course it's a thrill! I mean, who wouldn't want to get a letter from the White House? And the kind of people they were putting me in the category with was just amazing. People like John Glenn and Madeleine Albright, Toni Morrison, and Pat Summitt, John Doer, William Foege, and some others, too. These people who have done incredible things and have outstanding achievements. Pat Summitt alone has won more basketball games with her teams than any NCAA coach. John Glenn, we all know what he did. And Toni Morrison is as good as it gets. I loved spending time with them. What's the alternative? Hanging around with hedge-fund hucksters or Hollywood gigolos?"

—from interview with Mikal Gilmore, *Rolling Stone*, September 27, 2012

DYLAN ON

Iron and Gates

"I've been around iron all my life, ever since I was a kid. I was born and raised in iron ore country—where you could breathe it and smell it every day. And I've always worked with it in one form or another. Gates appeal to me because of the negative space they allow. They can be closed but at the same time they allow the seasons and breezes to enter and flow. They can shut you out or shut you in. And in some ways there is no difference."

—from website of London's Halcyon Gallery,
which displayed Dylan's iron-gate creations in a show called
"Mood Swings" that ran from 2013 to 2014

DYLAN ON

The Basement Tapes

"I'd known I wasn't gonna write anything about myself. I didn't have nothin' to say about myself that I'd figure anybody else would be interested in, anyway. You kind of look for ideas . . . The TV would be on, like *As the World Turns* or *Dark Shadows* or somethin' and just any ol' thing would create a beginning to a song—names out of phone books and things. When China first exploded that hydrogen bomb, that just kind of flashed across the headlines in newspapers, so we just go in and write 'Tears of Rage'. Things were just happening, there was riots in the street, they were rioting in Rochester, New York, and that wasn't that far away, so we write 'Too Much of Nothin'. And just one thing led to another. You know, the human heart . . . that's the first time that anybody ever heard of a human heart being transplanted. That was incredible. It was a real breakthrough, so we came up with a song, and then after we got the lyrics down, we took the song to the basement."

—from *Lost Songs: The Basement Tapes Continued*,
Showtime TV network (US), November 21, 2014

BOB DYLAN: THE UNCUT INTERVIEW

Robert Love | February/March 2015 | *AARP The Magazine*

Bob Dylan's career has been loaded with unexpected ups, downs, twists, and turns. There was, for example, the shift to electric music in the mid '60s that led to boos and triumphs; the nod to country and the debut of a new voice on 1969's *Nashville Skyline*; the widely panned, covers-dominated *Self Portrait*; the resurgence that began with *Blood on the Tracks*; the detour into religious music on albums like *Saved*; and even a 2009 album called *Christmas in the Heart* that found Dylan working his way through "Here Comes Santa Claus" and "Winter Wonderland."

It's safe to say that by the time of that last release, most fans were ready for nearly anything. And sure enough, they got it, in the form of *Shadows in the Night*, a February 2015 CD that features Dylan's affecting albeit idiosyncratic readings of ten songs associated with Frank Sinatra.

Given the nature of the record—and the fact that Dylan himself was now seventy-three—it is probably not surprising that he chose to promote it by talking with AARP's magazine rather than with, say, *Rolling Stone*. "If it were up to me," Dylan told AARP's editor Robert Love during a long and fascinating, music-focused interview, "I'd give you the records for nothing, and you give them to every [reader of your] magazine. I think a lot of your readers will identify with these songs."

This would not be Dylan's last foray into the Great American Songbook. In May of 2016, he would follow *Shadows in the Night* with *Fallen Angels*, another collection of Sinatra-related standards; and in March 2017, he would issue his thirty-eighth studio album, *Triplicate*, a three-disc, thirty-track collection of standards such as "Stardust" and "Sentimental Journey."

Here is the introduction to the print version of Robert Love's interview with Dylan, followed by the intro and expanded Q&A that appeared online. —Ed.

For a man who has lived in the public eye for more than 50 years, Bob Dylan is fiercely private. When he's not on stage—since 1988, he's maintained a performance schedule so relentless it's known as the Never Ending Tour—he slips back into anonymity. But early last summer, Dylan's representatives reached out and told me he wanted to speak to *AARP The Magazine* about his new project. "I don't work at *Rolling Stone* anymore," I told them, thinking it was a case of crossed wires, since I put in 20 years there. No, they said, there's no mistake; he wants to talk to your readers.

And now, after five months of negotiation, a cross-country flight and days of waiting, it is less than an hour until our interview, and I still don't know exactly where I will meet the reclusive artist. Driving down into the late October sun from the hills of Berkeley, California, toward the San Francisco Bay, I wait for a phone call with directions to a certain floor of a hotel. Then I'll be given the room number, told to knock, and wait.

We shake hands. Dylan is wearing a close-fitting black-and-white leather jacket that ends at his waist, black jeans and boots. The 73-year-old singer is not wearing his trademark sunglasses, and his blue eyes are startling. We are here to talk about *Shadows in the Night*, an album of 10 beloved songs from the 1920s to the 1960s. These are not his compositions—they are part of what is often called the Great American Songbook: familiar standards like "Autumn Leaves," "That Lucky Old Sun" and "Some Enchanted Evening," along with others, like 1957's hymnlike "Stay With Me," that are a bit obscure. In his 36th studio album, Dylan leads a five-piece band including two guitars, bass and pedal steel, and occasional horns, in austere and beautiful arrangements that were recorded live. It is a quiet, moody record with "no heavy drums and no piano," he says more than once.

As the afternoon deepens, Dylan talks about youth and aging, songwriting, friends and enemies. He recalls with unvarnished affection the performers who shaped his musical DNA, from gospel singer Mavis Staples to rocker Jerry Lee Lewis. Sitting on the edge of a low-slung couch in a dimly lit hotel suite, coiled and fully present—but in good humor—he seems anxious to begin this, his one and only interview for the new album.

The Songs

"I've always been drawn to spiritual songs," Bob Dylan tells me. "In 'Amazing Grace,' that line —'that saved a wretch like me'—isn't that something we could all say if we were honest enough?" At 73, Dylan is still in the game, still brutally honest and authentically himself, as you will see in this extended version of the exclusive interview that appeared in the February/March issue of *AARP The Magazine*.

In the 9,000 or so words that follow, Dylan goes where he has rarely gone before in public conversation: He explores his creative process and offers his insights on songwriting, performing, recording, and the creative destruction unleashed by rock and roll. For fun, perhaps, he tosses us a few pointed asides on contemporaries like Elton John, Rod Stewart and Eric Clapton, but reserves his undiluted praise for Chuck Berry's poetry and Billy Graham's soul-searing hellfire.

You may be struck, as I was time and again, at just how powerful a force music has played in Dylan's life. At various times he was *hypnotized, spellbound, lifted, knocked out* by what he'd heard. Listening to the Staple Singers for the first time at 14, he said, he couldn't sleep that night. "It just went through me like my body was invisible." From the moment he stumbled upon blues, country and gospel at the nether end of the radio dial, he never stopped listening closely, absorbing the best. A student and professor of America's truest music, he begins our conversation by explaining his decision to record ten beloved standards for *Shadows in the Night*.

Q: After several critically acclaimed records of original songs, why did you make this record now?

A: Now is the right time. I've been thinking about it for a while, ever since I heard Willie [Nelson]'s *Stardust* record in the late '70s. I thought I could do that, too. So I went to see Walter Yetnikoff, he was the president of Columbia Records. I told him I wanted to make a record of standards, like Willie's record. What he said was, "You can go ahead and make that record, but we won't pay for it, and we won't release it. But go ahead and make it if you want to." So I went and made *Street-Legal* instead.

In retrospect, Yetnikoff was probably right. It was most likely too soon for me to make a record of standards.

All through the years, I've heard these songs being recorded by other people and I've always wanted to do that. And I wondered if anybody else saw it the way I did. I was looking forward to hearing Rod [Stewart]'s records of standards. I thought if anybody could bring something different to these songs, Rod certainly could. But the records were disappointing. Rod's a great singer. He's got a great voice, but there's no point to put a 30-piece orchestra behind him. I'm not going to knock anybody's right to make a living but you can always tell if somebody's heart and soul is into something, and I didn't think Rod was into it in that way. It sounds like so many records where the vocals are overdubbed and these kind of songs don't come off well if you use modern recording techniques.

To those of us who grew up with these kinds of songs and didn't think much of it, these are the same songs that rock 'n' roll came to destroy—music hall, tangos, pop songs from the '40s, fox-trots, rumbas, Irving Berlin, Gershwin, Harold Arlen, Hammerstein. Composers of great renown. It's hard for modern singers to connect with that kind of music and song. When we finally went to record, I had about 30 songs, and these 10 fall together to create a certain kind of drama. They all seem connected in one way or another. We were playing a lot of these songs at sound checks on stages around the world without a vocal mic, and you could hear everything pretty well. You usually hear these songs with a full-out orchestra. But I was playing them with a five-piece band and didn't miss the orchestra. Of course, a producer would have come in and said, "Let's put strings here and a horn section there." But I wasn't going to do that. I wasn't even going to use keyboards or a grand piano. The piano covers too much territory and can dominate songs like this in ways you don't want them to. One of the keys to making this record was to get the piano right off the floor and not be influenced by it in any way.

Q: It's going to be something of a surprise to your traditional fans, don't you think?

A: Well, they shouldn't be surprised. There's a lot of types of songs I've sung over the years, and they definitely have heard me sing standards before.

Q: Did you know many of these songs from your childhood? Some of them are pretty old.

A: Yeah, I did. I don't usually forget songs if I like them. It could be 30 years ago or something.

Q: What was your process like?

A: Once you think you know the song, then you have to go and see how other people have done it. One version led to another until we were starting to assimilate even Harry James' arrangements. Or even Pérez Prado's. My pedal steel player is a genius at that. He can play anything from hillbilly to bebop. There are only two guitars in there, and one is just playing the pulse. Stand-up bass is playing orchestrated moving lines. It's almost like folk music in a way. I mean, there are no drums in a Bill Monroe band. Hank Williams didn't use them either. Sometimes the beat takes the mystery out of the rhythm. Maybe all the time. I could only record these songs one way, and that was live on the floor with a very small number of mics. No headphones, no overdubs, no vocal booth, no separate tracking. I know it's the old-fashioned way, but to me it's the only way that would have worked for songs like this. Vocally, I think I sang about 6 inches away from the mic. It's a board mix, for the most part, mixed as it was recorded. We played the song a few times for the engineer. He put a few microphones around. I told him we would play it as many times as he wanted. That's the way each song was done.

Q: It sounds like the microphone was right in your face.

A: Yeah, yeah.

Q: It is a very intimate rendering of this material. I assume that's what you wanted.

A: Exactly. We recorded it in the Capitol studios, which is good for a record like this. But we didn't use any of the new equipment. The engineer had his own equipment left over from bygone days, and he brought all that in. Like I said before, I rehearsed the band all last fall in a tour we were doing over in Europe. We rehearsed a whole bunch of things on the stage, with no microphones so we could play at the right volume. By the time we went in to make this record, it was almost like we'd done it already.

Q: Beautiful horns. Really low-key. Atmospheric almost.

A: Yeah, but there are only a few. French horn, a trumpet, a trombone, all played in harmony. Together they make a beautiful sound.

Q: Did you do the arrangements?

A: No. The original arrangements were for up to 30 pieces. We couldn't match that and didn't even try. What we had to do was fundamentally get to the bottom of what makes these songs alive. We took only the necessary parts to make that happen. In a case like this, you have to trust your own instincts.

Q: Did you listen to multiple versions and then throw them away, cleanse your palate and come up with your own version?

A: Well, a lot of these songs, you know, have been pounded into the ground over the years. I wanted to use songs that everybody knows or thinks they know. I wanted to show them a different side of it and opened up that world in a more unique way. You have to believe what the words are saying and the words are as important as the melody. Unless you believe the song and have lived it, there's little sense in performing it. "Some Enchanted Evening"—that would be one. Another one would be "Autumn Leaves." That's a song that's been done to death. I mean, who hasn't done that song? You sing "Autumn Leaves" and you have to know something about love and loss and feel it just as much, or there's no point in doing it. It's too deep a song. A schoolboy could never do it convincingly. People talk about Frank [Sinatra] all the time—and they should talk about Frank—but he had the greatest arrangers. And not only that, but he brought out the best in these guys. Billy May and Nelson Riddle or Gordon Jenkins. Whoever they were. They worked for him in a different kind of way than they worked for other people. They gave him arrangements that are just sublime on every level. And he, of course, could match that because he had this ability to get inside of the song in a sort of a conversational way. Frank sang to you, not at you, like so many pop singers today. Even singers of standards. I never wanted to be a singer that sings at somebody. I've always wanted to sing to somebody. I would have gotten that subliminally from Frank many years ago. Hank Williams did that, too. He sang to you.

Q: This is a wide-ranging curation of songs from what people call the American Songbook. But I noticed Frank recorded all 10 of them. Was he on your mind?

A: You know, when you start doing these songs, Frank's got to be on your mind. Because he is the mountain. That's the mountain you have to climb even if you only get part of the way there. And it's hard to find a song he did not do. He'd be the guy you got to check with. I particularly like Nancy, too! I think Nancy is head and shoulders above most of these girl singers today. She's so soulful also in a conversational way. And where'd she get that? Well, she's Frank's daughter, right? Just naturally. Frank Jr. can sing, too. Just the same way, if you want to do a Woody Guthrie song, you have to go past Bruce Springsteen and get to Jack Elliott. Eventually, you'll get to Woody, but it might be a long process.

Q: You've written about how Frank's version of the classic song "Ebb Tide" knocked you back on your heels in the '60s. But you said, "I couldn't listen to the stuff now. It wasn't the right time."

A: Totally. . . . Yeah. Really. There are a lot of things like that in my past that I've had to let be and keep moving in my own direction. It would overwhelm me at times, because that's a world that is not your world. "Ebb Tide" was a song that I kind of grew up with. I don't know exactly when it was. But it was a hit song, a pop song. Roy Hamilton did it and he was a fantastic singer, and he did it in a grandiose way. And I thought I knew it. Then I was at somebody's house, and they had one of Frank's records, and "Ebb Tide" was on it. I must have listened to that thing 100 times. I realized then that I didn't know it. I still don't know it to this day. I don't know how he did it. The performance hypnotizes you. It's a spellbinding performance. I never heard anything so supreme—on every single level.

Q: Maybe that music was just too square to admit to liking back then?

A: Square? I don't think anybody would have been bold enough to call Frank Sinatra square. Kerouac listened to him, along with Bird [Charlie

Parker] and Dizzy [Gillespie]. But I myself never bought any Frank Sinatra records back then, if that's what you mean. I never listened to Frank as an influence. All I had to go on were records, and they were all over the place, orchestrated in one way or another. Swing music, Count Basie, romantic ballads, jazz bands—it was hard to get a fix on him. But like I say, you'd hear him anyway. You'd hear him in a car or a jukebox. You were conscious of Frank Sinatra no matter what age you were. Certainly nobody worshipped Frank Sinatra in the '60s like they did in the '40s. But he never went away. All those other things that we thought were here to stay, they did go away. But he never did.

Q: Do you think of this album as risky? These songs have fans who will say you can't touch Sinatra's version.

A: Risky? Like walking across a field laced with land mines? Or working in a poison gas factory? There's nothing risky about making records. Comparing me with Frank Sinatra? You must be joking. To be mentioned in the same breath as him must be some sort of high compliment. As far as touching him goes, nobody touches him. Not me or anyone else.

Q: What do you think Frank would make of this album?

A: I think first of all he'd be amazed I did these songs with a five-piece band. I think he'd be proud in a certain way.

The History

Q: What other kinds of music did you listen to growing up?

A: Early on, before rock 'n' roll, I listened to big band music: Harry James, Russ Columbo, Glenn Miller. Singers like Jo Stafford, Kay Starr, Dick Haymes. Anything that came over the radio and music played by bands in hotels that our parents could dance to. We had a big radio that looked like a jukebox, with a record player on the top.

All the furniture had been left in the house by the previous owners, including a piano. The radio/record player played 78-rpm records. And when we moved to that house, there was a record on there. The record had a red label, and I think it was a Columbia record. It was Bill Monroe sing-ing, or maybe it was the Stanley Brothers. And they were singing "Drifting Too Far From Shore." I'd never heard anything like that before. Ever. And it moved me away from all the conventional music that I was hearing.

To understand that, you'd have to understand where I came from. I come from way north. We'd listen to radio shows all the time. I think I was the last generation, or pretty close to the last one, that grew up without TV. So we listened to the radio a lot. Most of these shows were theatrical radio dramas. For us, this was like our TV. Everything you heard, you could imagine what it looked like. Even singers that I would hear on the radio, I couldn't see what they looked like, so I imagined what they looked like. What they were wearing. What their instruments were. Gene Vincent? When I first pictured him, he was a tall, lanky blond-haired guy.

Q: Did it make you a better listener?

A: It made me the listener that I am today. It made me listen for little things: the slamming of the door, the jingling of car keys. The wind blowing through trees, the songs of birds, footsteps, a hammer hitting a nail. Just random sounds. Cows mooing. I could string all that together and make that a song. It made me listen to life in a different way. I still listen to some of those old radio shows, and most of them still hold up. I mean, the jokes might be a little outdated, but the situations seem to be about the same. I don't listen to The Fat Man or Superman or Inner Sanctum in any way you could call nostalgic. They don't bring back any memories. I just like them.

Q: What did you listen to besides the radio dramas?

A: Up north, at night, you could find these radio stations with no name on the dials, you know, that played pre-rock 'n' roll things—country blues. We would hear Slim Harpo or Lightnin' Slim and gospel groups, the Dixie Hummingbirds, the Five Blind Boys of Alabama. I was so far north, I didn't even know where Alabama was. And then there'd be at a different hours the blues — you could hear Jimmy Reed, Wynonie Har-ris and Little Walter. Then there was a station out of Chicago. WSM? Is that the one I'm thinking of? Played all hillbilly stuff. Riley Puckett, Uncle

Dave Macon, the Delmore Brothers. We also heard the Grand Ole Opry from Nashville every Saturday night. I heard Hank Williams way early, when he was still alive. A lot of those Opry stars, except for Hank, of course, came through the town I lived in and played at the armory building. Webb Pierce, Hank Snow, Carl Smith, Porter Wagoner. I saw all those country stars growing up.

One night I was lying in bed and listening to the radio. I think it was a station out of Shreveport, Louisiana. I wasn't sure where Louisiana was either. I remember listening to the Staple Singers' "Uncloudy Day." And it was the most mysterious thing I'd ever heard. It was like the fog rolling in. I heard it again, maybe the next night, and its mystery had even deepened. What was that? How do you make that? It just went through me like my body was invisible. What is that? A tremolo guitar? What's a tremolo guitar? I had no idea, I'd never seen one. And what kind of clapping is that? And that singer is pulling things out of my soul that I never knew were there. After hearing "Uncloudy Day" for the second time, I don't think I could even sleep that night. I knew these Staple Singers were different than any other gospel group. But who were they anyway?

I'd think about them even at my school desk. I managed to get down to the Twin Cities and get my hands on an LP of the Staple Singers, and one of the songs on it was "Uncloudy Day." And I'm like, "Man!" I looked at the cover and studied it, like people used to do with covers of records. I knew who Mavis was without having to be told. I knew it was she who was singing the lead part. I knew who Pops was. All the information was on the back of the record. Not much, but enough to let me in just a little ways. Mavis looked to be about the same age as me in her picture. Her singing just knocked me out. I listened to the Staple Singers a lot. Certainly more than any other gospel group. I like spiritual songs. They struck me as truthful and serious. They brought me down to earth and they lifted me up all in the same moment. And Mavis was a great singer—deep and mysterious. And even at the young age, I felt that life itself was a mystery.

This was before folk music had ever entered my life. I was still an aspiring rock 'n' roller, the descendant, if you will, of the first generation of guys who played rock 'n' roll—who were thrown down. Buddy

Holly, Little Richard, Chuck Berry, Carl Perkins, Gene Vincent, Jerry Lee Lewis. They played this type of music that was black and white. Extremely incendiary. Your clothes could catch fire. It was a mixture of black culture and hillbilly culture. When I first heard Chuck Berry, I didn't consider that he was black. I thought he was a white hillbilly. Little did I know, he was a great poet, too. "Flying across the desert in a TWA, I saw a woman walking 'cross the sand. She been walking 30 miles en route to Bombay to meet a brown-eyed handsome man." I didn't think about poetry at that time—those words just flew by. Only later did I realize how hard it is to write those kind of lyrics.

Chuck Berry could have been anything in the music business. He stopped where he was, but he could have been a jazz singer, a ballad singer, a guitar virtuoso. He could have been a lot of things. But there's a spiritual aspect to him, too. In 50 or 100 years he might even be thought of as a religious icon. There's only one him, and what he does physically is even hard to do. If you see him in person, you know he goes out of tune a lot. But who wouldn't? He has to constantly be playing eighth notes on his guitar and sing at the same time, plus play fills and sing. People think that singing and playing is easy. It's not. It's easy to strum along with yourself, as you are singing a song and that's OK, but if you actually want to really play, where it's important, that's a hard thing and not too many people are good at it.

Q: And he was always the main guitar player in his band.

A: He was the only guitar player. Yeah. And there was Jerry Lee [Lewis], his counterpart, and people like that. There must have been some elitist power that had to get rid of all these guys, to strike down rock 'n' roll for what it was and what it represented—not least of all it being a black-and-white thing. Tied together and welded shut. If you separate the pieces, you're killing it.

Q: Do you mean it's musical race-mixing, and that's what made it dangerous?

A: Well, racial prejudice has been around a while, so yeah. And that was extremely threatening for the city fathers, I would think. When they finally recognized what it was, they had to dismantle it, which they did, starting with payola scandals and things like that. The black element was turned into soul music and the white element was turned into English pop. They separated it. I think of rock 'n' roll as a combination of country blues and swing band music, not Chicago blues, and modern pop. Real rock 'n' roll hasn't existed since when? 1961, 1962? Well, it was a part of my DNA, so it never disappeared from me. I just incorporated it into other aspects of what I was doing. I don't know if this is answering the question. [Laughs.] I can't remember what the question was.

Q: We were talking about your influences and your crush on Mavis Staples.

A: Oh, the Staple Singers! Mavis! So I had seen this picture of the Staple Singers. And I said to myself, "You know, one day you'll be standing there with your arm around that girl." I remember thinking that. Ten years later, there I was—with my arm around her. But it felt so natural. Felt like I'd been there before, many times. Well I was, in my mind.

Q: Did you recall your original thought?

A: No! I was moving too fast. Not until 10 years more beyond that did I remember anything about it.

Q: I was thinking how important it was to you when you were young to chase down those Woody Guthrie records. And I was thinking about how Mick [Jagger] and Keith [Richards] ran all over London to get blues records, and how Neil Young pumped quarters into the jukebox to hear Ian and Sylvia. And now the Internet has all of it—you can just touch a button and hear almost anything in the history of recorded music. Has it made music better? Or worse? More valued or less valued?

A: Well, if you're just a member of the general public, and you have all this music available to you, what do you listen to? How many of these things are you going to listen to at the same time? Your head is just going to get jammed—it's all going to become a blur, I would think. Back in the day, if you wanted to hear Memphis Minnie, you had to seek a compilation record, which would have a Memphis Minnie song on it. And if you heard Memphis Minnie back then, you would just accidentally discover her on a record that also had Son House and Skip James and the Memphis Jug Band. And then maybe you'd seek Memphis Minnie in some other places—a song here, a song there. You'd try to find out who she was. Is she still alive? Does she play? Can she teach me anything? Can I hang out with her? Can I do anything for her? Does she need anything? But now, if you want to hear Memphis Minnie, you can go hear a thousand songs. Likewise, all the rest of those performers, like Blind Lemon [Jefferson]. In the old days, maybe you'd hear "Matchbox" and "Prison Cell Blues." That would be all you would hear, so those songs would be prominent in your mind. But when you hear an onslaught of 100 more songs of Blind Lemon, then it's like, "Oh man! This is overkill!" It's so easy you might appreciate it a lot less.

The Album

Q: Are the songs on this album laid down in the order you would like people to listen to them? Or do you care whether Apple sells them one by one?

A: The business end of the record—it's none of my business. I sure hope it sells, and I would like people to listen to it. But the way people listen to music has changed, and I hope they get a chance to hear all the songs in one way or another. But! I did record those songs, believe it or not, in that same order that you hear them. Not that it matters, really. I didn't pay any attention to the sequencing like on other records. We would usually get one song done in three hours. There's no mixing. That's just the way it sounded. No dials, nothing enhanced, nothing—that's it. Capitol's got those big echo chambers. So some of that was probably used. We used as little technology as possible. It's been done wrong too many other times. I wanted to do it rightly.

Q: Was this recording an experiment?

A: It was more than an experiment. Because we had played these songs, we were dead sure that we could do them. It's just a question of could it be recorded right. We did it the old-fashioned way, I guess you would say. That's the way I used to make records anyway. I never did use earphones up until into the '80s or '90s. I don't like to use earphones.

Q: You feel that's a distancing thing?

A: Yeah. There's a complete disconnect. You can overwhelm yourself in your own head. I've never heard anybody sing with those things in their ears effectively. They just give you a false sense of security. A lot of us don't need earphones. I don't think Springsteen does. I know Mick doesn't. I don't think he does. But other people you see, more or less have given in. They just do it. But they ought not to do it. They don't need to. Especially if they have a good band.

Recording studios are filled with technology. They are set in their ways. And to update them means you'd have to change them back. That would be my idea of upgrading. And this will never happen. As far as I know, recording studios are booked all the time. So obviously people like all the improvements. The more technically advanced they are, the more in demand they become. The corporations have taken over. Even in the recording studio. Actually, the corporate companies have taken over American life most everywhere. Go coast to coast and you will see people all wearing the same clothes, thinking the same thoughts and eating the same food. Everything is processed.

Q: Let's talk about the first song on the album, "I'm a Fool To Want You." I'm interested in how you put across the heartbreak that's on this record. It's believed that Frank Sinatra wrote it for Ava Gardner, his great love. You wrote once that the performer, the artist transmits emotion via alchemy. "I'm not feeling this," you're saying. "What I'm doing is I'm putting it across." Is that right?

A: You're right, but you don't want to overstate that. Look, it all has to do with technique. Every singer has three or four or five techniques, and you can force them together in different combinations. Some of the techniques you discard along the way, and pick up others. But you do need them. It's just like anything. You have to know certain things about what you're doing that other people don't know. Singing has to do with techniques and how many you use at the same time. One alone doesn't work. There's no point to going over three. But you might interchange them whenever you feel like it. So yes, it's a bit like alchemy. It's different than being an actor where you call up sources from your own experience that you can apply to whatever Shakespeare drama you're in or whatever television show. With a song it's not quite the same way. An actor is pretending to be somebody, but a singer isn't. He's not hiding behind anything. And that's the difference. Singers today have to sing songs where there's very little emotion involved. That and the fact that they have to sing hit records from years gone by doesn't leave a lot of room for any kind of intelligent creativity. In a way, having hits buries a singer in the past. A lot of singers hide in the past because it's safer back there. If you've ever heard today's country music, you'll know what I'm talking about. Why do all these songs fall flat? I think technology has a lot to do with it. Technology is mechanical and contrary to the emotions that inform a person's life. The country music field has especially been hit hard by this turn of events.

These songs [on my album] have been written by people who went out of fashion years ago. I'm probably someone who helped put them out of fashion. But what they did is a lost art form. Just like da Vinci and Renoir and van Gogh. Nobody paints like that anymore either. But it can't be wrong to try.

So a song like "I'm a Fool to Want You"—I know that song. I can sing that song. I've felt every word in that song. I mean, I know that song. It's like I wrote it. It's easier for me to sing that song than it is to sing, "Won't you come see me, Queen Jane." At one time that wouldn't have been so. But now it is. Because "Queen Jane" might be a little bit outdated. It can't be outrun. But this song is not outdated. It has to do with human emotion, which is a constant thing. There's nothing contrived in these songs. There's not one false word in any of them. They're eternal, lyrically and musically.

Q: Do you wish you wrote them?

A: In a way I'm glad I didn't write any of them. I'm good with songs that I haven't written, if I like them. I already know how the song goes, so I have more freedom with it. I understand these songs. I've known them for 40 years, 50 years, maybe longer, and they make a lot of sense. So I'm not coming to them like a stranger. I've written all the songs that I feel are . . . I don't know how to put this . . . You travel the world, you go see different things. I like to see Shakespeare plays, so I'll go—I mean, even if it's in a different language. I don't care, I just like Shakespeare, you know. I've seen Othello and Hamlet and Merchant of Venice over the years, and some versions are better than others. Way better. It's like hearing a bad version of a song. But then somewhere else somebody has a great version.

Q: I like your version of "Lucky Old Sun." Can you talk about what drew you to this one in particular? Did you have a memory of it?

A: Oh, I've never not known that song. I don't think anybody my age can tell you that they ever remember not knowing that song. I mean, it's been recorded hundreds of times. I've sung it in concert.

Q: Have you?

A: Yeah. But I never really got to the heart of the song until recently.

Q: So how do you do that?

A: Well, you cut the song down to the bone and see if it's really there for you to do. Most songs have bridges in them. A bridge is something that distracts a listener from the main verses of a song so the listener doesn't get repetitively bored. My songs don't have a lot of bridges because lyric poetry never had them. But when a song like "Autumn Leaves" presents itself, you have to decide what's real about it and what's not. Listen to how Eric Clapton does it. He sings the song, and then he plays the guitar for 10 minutes and then he sings the song again. He might even play the guitar again, I can't remember. But when you listen to his version, where do you think the importance is? Well obviously, it's in the guitar playing. He sings the song twice both the same way. And there's really no reason to do that unless you're singing the song in a different way. It's OK for Eric because he's a master guitar player and, of course, that's what he wants to feature on any song he records. But other people couldn't do it and get away with it. It's not exactly getting to the heart of what "Autumn Leaves" is about. And as a performer, you don't get many chances to do that. And when you get the opportunity, you don't want to blow it. With all these songs you have to study the lyrics. You have to look at every one of these songs and be able to identify with them in a meaningful way. You can hardly sing these songs unless you're in them. If you want to fake it, go ahead. Fake it if you want. But I'm not that kind of singer.

Q: Can we talk about some of the melodies of these songs?

A: Yeah, they're incredible, aren't they? All these songs have classical music under-themes. Why? Because all these composers learned from classical music. They were composers who understood music theory, and they went to music academies. It could be a little piece of Mozart, Bach—Paul Simon did an entire song using a Bach melody—or it could be a piece of Beethoven or Liszt, Chopin, Rachmaninoff, or Stravinsky or Tchaikovsky. You can get a lot of great melodies listening to Tchaikovsky if you're a commercial songwriter or composer, and these guys did that. Not that I myself recognize where these melodies and parts came from, but I know they came from somewhere in that direction. Most of these songs are written by two people, one for the music and one for the words.

There's only one guy that I know of who did it all, and that was Irving Berlin. He wrote the melody and the lyrics. This guy was a flat-out genius. I mean, he had a gift, like, it just wouldn't stop giving, classical themes notwithstanding, because I don't think he used any. But everyone else who wrote lyrics had to depend on a piece of music. Lyricists themselves, they were a funny breed. They are not who you would think they would be. They came from all walks of life. Highbrow, lowbrow. Could be a telephone repairman, a typesetter, insurance salesman. One was a house painter, another a car mechanic. Jimmy Van Heusen was a stunt pilot. All these people knew how to keep it simple and understood ordinary daily existence, common life. And they did good.

Q: Who could speak the vernacular.

A: Who spoke the vernacular. Exactly. So there's nothing contrived about these songs. There's not one false word in any of them.

Q: Do you like Johnny Mercer?

A: I love Johnny Mercer. Yeah. I love . . .

Q: He did the English lyrics for "Autumn Leaves."

A: Yeah, he did. Well it doesn't surprise me. I love all of his stuff—one of the most gifted lyricists. Yeah. "Jeepers Creepers." "Lazy Bones." "Blues in the Night." We do a lot of his songs at sound checks. If he was around now, I'd like to give him some of my instrumental tapes. See what he could do with them. But they might be beneath him.

Q: Your renditions and these arrangements are very respectful. The arrangements are almost austere, but your renditions are very respectful of these melodies—more than you are of your own songs when you perform.

A: Well, I love these songs, and I'm not going to bring any disrespect to them or treat them irreverently. To trash those songs would be sacrilegious. We've all heard those songs being trashed, and we're used to it. They go by without even being heard. In some kind of ways you want to right the wrong, maybe unconsciously. But I'm not on a crusade. I think if others want to pick it up, they can and should. But if not, that's OK, too. I don't think of these songs as covers. I think of them as songs that have all been done before in many ways. The word "covers" has crept into the musical vernacular. Nobody would have understood it in the '50s or '60s. It's kind of a belittling term. What does it mean when you cover something up? You hide it. I've never understood that term. Am I doing a bunch of covers? Well, yeah, if you say so.

Q: So you're really uncovering.

A: Exactly. That's a good point.

The Fans

Q: These songs will have a different audience than they originally had. Do you feel like a musical archaeologist?

A: No. I just like these songs and feel I can connect with them. I would hope people will connect with them the same way that I do. I have no idea what people like or don't like. It would be presumptuous to think these songs are going to find some new audience as if they're going to appear out of nowhere. Certainly, the people who first heard these songs, like my parents and people like that, they're not with us anymore. I can't generalize who these songs are going to appeal to. Besides, when I look out from the stage, I see something different than maybe other performers do.

Q: What are you seeing from the stage?

A: Definitely not a sea of conformity. People I cannot categorize easily. I wouldn't say there is one type of fan. I see a guy dressed up in a suit and tie next to a guy in blue jeans. I see another guy in a sport coat next to another guy wearing a T-shirt and cowboy boots. I see women sometimes in evening gowns and I see punky-looking girls. Just all kinds of people. I can see that there's a difference in character, and it has nothing to do with age. I went to an Elton John show, and it was interesting. There must have been at least three generations of people there. But they were all the same. Even the little kids. They looked just like their grandparents. It was strange. People make a fuss about how many generations follow a certain type of performer. But what does it matter if all the generations are the same? I'm content to not see a certain type of person that could be easily tracked. I don't care about age, but the adolescent youth market, I think it goes without saying, might not have the experience it takes to understand these songs and appreciate them.

Q: So we at AARP represent people who are 50 and older. The magazine reaches 35 million readers.

A: Well, a lot of those readers are going to like this record. If it were up to me, I'd give you the records for nothing, and you give them to every [reader of your] magazine. I think a lot of your readers will identify with these songs.

Q: The songs on this album conjure a kind of romantic love that is nearly antique, because there's no longer much resistance in romance. People date and they climb into bed. That sweet, painful pining of the '40s and '50s doesn't exist anymore. Do you think these songs will fall on younger ears as corny?

A: You tell me. I mean, I don't know why they would, but what's the word "corny" mean exactly? I've heard it but don't use it much. It's like "tacky." I don't say that word either. There's just no power in those words. These songs, take 'em or leave 'em, if nothing else, are songs of great virtue. That's what they are. If they sound trite and corny to somebody, well so much for that. But people's lives today are filled on so many levels with vice and the trappings of it. Ambition, greed and selfishness all have to do with vice. Sooner or later, you have to see through it or you don't survive. We don't see the people that vice destroys. We just see the glamour of it on a daily basis—everywhere we look, from billboard signs to movies, to newspapers, to magazines. We see the destruction of human life and the mockery of it, everywhere we look. These songs are anything but that. Romance never does go out of fashion. It's radical. Maybe it's out of step with the current media culture. If it is, it is.

Q: What is the best song you've ever written about heartbreak and loss?

A: I think "Love Sick" [from 1997's *Time Out of Mind*].

Q: A fellow Minnesotan, F. Scott Fitzgerald, said famously, "There are no second acts in American life." You are a man who has probably had four or five second acts. Poet, Voice of a Generation, troubadour, rocker and now crooner!

A: Yeah [Laughs]. I know. Right. Well, look, he said that in a day and age where he was probably speaking the truth.

Q: You once said that as a folk artist you came into the music business through the side door.

A: I did?

Q: You did. And I think I know what you meant, because nobody thought folk music was going to amount to anything in the music business at the time. Now here you are with this grand parade of iconic American songs. Are you finally coming in through the front door?

A: I would say that's pretty right on. You just have to keep going to find that thing that lets you in the door, if you actually want to get in the door. Sometimes in life when that day comes and you're given the key, you throw it away. You find that whatever you were looking for your entire life isn't where you thought it was. Folk music came at exactly the right time in my life. It wouldn't have happened 10 years later, and 10 years earlier I wouldn't have known what kind of songs those were. They were just so different than popular music. But it came at the right time, so I went that way. Then folk music became relegated to the sidelines. It either became commercial or the Beatles killed it. Maybe it couldn't have gone on anyway. But actually, in this day and age, it still is a vibrant form of music, and many people sing and play it much better than we ever did. It's just not what you would call part of the pop realm. I had gotten in there at a time when nobody else was there or knew it even existed, so I had the whole landscape to myself. I went into songwriting. I figured I had to—I couldn't be that hellfire rock 'n' roller. But I could write hellfire lyrics.

When I was growing up, Billy Graham was very popular. He was the greatest preacher and evangelist of my time—that guy could save souls and did. I went to two or three of his rallies in the '50s or '60s. This guy was like rock 'n' roll personified—volatile, explosive. He had the hair, the tone, the elocution—when he spoke, he brought the storm down. Clouds parted. Souls got saved, sometimes 30- or 40,000 of them. If you ever went to a Billy Graham rally back then, you were changed forever. There's never been a preacher like him. He could fill football stadiums before anybody. He could fill Giants Stadium more than even the Giants football team. Seems like a long time ago. Long before Mick Jagger sang his first note or Bruce strapped on his first guitar—that's some of the part of rock 'n' roll that I retained. I had to. I saw Billy Graham in the flesh and heard him loud and clear.

The Process

Q: A lot of your newer songs deal with aging. You once said that people don't retire, they fade away, they run out of steam. And now you're 73, you're a great-grandfather.

A: Look, you get older. Passion is a young man's game, OK? Young people can be passionate. Older people gotta be more wise. I mean, you're around awhile, you leave certain things to the young and you don't try to act like you're young. You could really hurt yourself.

Q: In a period around 1966, you went into seclusion for more than a year, and there was much speculation about your motives. But it was to protect your family, wasn't it?

A: Totally. That's right.

Q: And I think that people didn't quite want to understand that, because your idiosyncratic view of the world as an artist made them think you were an idiosyncratic person, but in reality you were a typical dad who was trying to protect his kids.

A: Totally. I gave up my art to do that.

Q: And was that painful?

A: Totally frustrating and painful, of course, because that intuitive gift—which for me went musically—had carried me so far. I did do that, yeah, and it hurt to have to do it. But I didn't have a choice.

Q: Now your life is largely spent on the road: a hundred nights a year. I read that your grandmother once told you that happiness is not the road to anything. She said it is the road.

A: My grandmother was a wonderful lady.

Q: You obviously get great joy and connection from the people who come to see you.

A: It's not unlike a sportsman who's on the road a lot. Roger Federer, the tennis player, I mean, you know, he's working most of the year. Like maybe 250 days a year, every year, year in and year out. I mean, I think that's more than B.B. King does. So it's relative. I mean, yeah, you must go where the people are. You can't bring them to where you are unless you have a contract to play in Vegas. But happiness—are we talking about happiness?

Q: Yeah.

A: OK, a lot of people say there is no happiness in this life, and certainly there's no permanent happiness. But self-sufficiency creates happiness. Happiness is a state of bliss. Actually, it never crosses my mind. Just because you're satisfied one moment—saying yes, it's a good meal, makes me happy—well, that's not going to necessarily be true the next hour. Life has its ups and downs, and time has to be your partner, you know? Really, time is your soul mate. Children are happy. But they haven't really experienced ups and downs yet. I'm not exactly sure what happiness even means, to tell you the truth. I don't know if I personally could define it.

Q: Have you touched it?

A: Well, we all do.

Q: Held it?

A: We all do at certain points, but it's like water—it slips through your hands. As long as there's suffering, you can only be so happy. How can a person be happy if he has misfortune? Does money make a person happy? Some wealthy billionaire who can buy 30 cars and maybe buy a sports team, is that guy happy? What then would make him happier? Does it make him happy giving his money away to foreign countries? Is there more contentment in that than giving it here to the inner cities and creating jobs? Nowhere does it say that one of the government's responsibilities is to create jobs. That is a false premise. But if you like lies, go ahead and believe it. The government's not going to create jobs. It doesn't have to. People have to create jobs, and these big billionaires are the ones who can do it. We don't see that happening. We see crime and inner cities exploding, with people who have nothing to do but meander around, turning to drink and drugs, into killers and jailbirds. They could all have work created for them by all these hotshot billionaires. For sure, that would create a lot of happiness. Now, I'm not saying they have to—I'm not talking about communism—but what do they do with their money? Do they use it in virtuous ways? If you have no idea what virtue is all about, look it up in a Greek dictionary. There's nothing namby-pamby about it.

Q: So they should be moving their focus?

A: Well, I think they should, yeah, because there are a lot of things that are wrong in America and especially in the inner cities that they could solve. Those are dangerous grounds, and they don't have to be. There are good people there, but they've been oppressed by lack of work. Those people can all be working at something. These multibillionaires, and there seem to be more of them every day, can create industries right here in the inner cities of America. But no one can tell them what to do. God's got to lead them.

Q: And productive work is a kind of salvation in your view? To feel worth and pride in what you do?

A: Absolutely.

Q: Let me talk to you for a minute about your gift. There are artists like George Balanchine, the choreographer, who felt that he was a servant to his muse. Somebody else like Picasso felt that he was the boss in the creative process. How have you dealt with your own gift over the years? I mean your songwriting, your inspiration, your creativity.

A: [Laughter]

Q: That makes you laugh?

A: Well, I might trade places with Picasso if I could, creatively speaking. I'd like to think I was the boss of my creative process, too, and I could just do anything I wanted whenever I wanted and it would all be on a grand scale. But of course, that's not true. Like Sinatra, there was only one Picasso. As far as George the choreographer, I'm more inclined to feel the same way that he does about what I do. It's not easy to pin down the creative process.

Q: Is it elusive?

A: It totally is. It totally is. It's uncontrollable. It makes no sense in literal terms. I wish I could enlighten you, but I can't—just sound stupid trying. But I'll try. It starts like this. What kind of song do I need to play in my show? What don't I have? It always starts with what I don't have instead of doing more of the same. I need all kinds of songs—fast ones, slow ones, minor key, ballads, rumbas—and they all get juggled around during a live show. I've been trying for years to come up with songs that have the feeling of a Shakespearean drama, so I'm always starting with that. Once I can focus in on something, I just play it in my mind until an idea comes from out of nowhere, and it's usually the key to the whole song. It's the idea that matters. The idea is floating around long before me. It's like electricity was around long before Edison harnessed it. Communism was around before Lenin took over. Pete Townshend thought about Tommy for years before he actually wrote any songs for it. So creativity has a lot to do with the main idea. Inspiration is what comes when you are dealing with the idea. But inspiration won't invite what's not there to begin with.

Q: You've been generous to take up all of these questions.

A: I found the questions really interesting. The last time I did an interview, the guy wanted to know about everything except the music. Man, I'm just a musician, you know? People have been doing that to me since the '60s—they ask questions like they would ask a medical doctor or a psychiatrist or a professor or a politician. Why? Why are you asking me these things?

Q: What do you ask a musician about?

A: Music! Exactly.

DYLAN ON

Critics' Reaction to His Vocals

"Some of the music critics say I can't sing. I croak. Sound like a frog. Why don't these same critics say similar things about Tom Waits? They say my voice is shot. That I have no voice. Why don't they say those things about Leonard Cohen? Why do I get special treatment? Critics say I can't carry a tune and I talk my way through a song. Really? I've never heard that said about Lou Reed. Why does he get to go scot-free? What have I done to deserve this special treatment? Why me, Lord? No vocal range? When's the last time you've read that about Dr. John? Why don't they say that about him? Slur my words, got no diction. You have to wonder if these critics have ever heard Charley Patton or Son House or [Howlin'] Wolf. Talk about slurred words and no diction. Why don't they say those same things about them? Why me, Lord?"

—from Musicares Person of the Year acceptance speech,
Los Angeles, February 6, 2015

DYLAN ON

His Limitations

"There's a lot of things I'd like to do. I'd like to drive a race car on the Indianapolis track. I'd like to kick a field goal in an NFL football game. I'd like to be able to hit a hundred-mile-an-hour baseball. But you have to know your place. There might be some things that are beyond your talents. . . . Everything worth doing takes time. You have to write a hundred bad songs before you write one good one. And you have to sacrifice a lot of things that you might not be prepared for. Like it or not, you are in this alone and have to follow your own star."

—from interview with Edna Gundersen, *Telegraph* (UK), October 29, 2016

NOBEL PRIZE BANQUET SPEECH

Bob Dylan (presented by Azita Raji) | December 10, 2016 | Stockholm, Sweden

On October 13, 2016, word came that Bob Dylan had been awarded the Nobel Prize in Literature "for having created new poetic expressions within the great American song tradition." Around the world, critics and columnists weighed in on the news about the award, which had been given only once before to a songwriter (Rabindranath Tagore, who won in 1913). Some said the prize should have gone to a novelist, but many others—particularly fans and fellow musicians—asked the same question as *New York Times* critic Jon Pareles: "What took them so long?"

Dylan himself responded at first with silence. Someone posted an announcement of the award on his website, but the notice was deleted within a day. For weeks, meanwhile, Dylan issued no public statement and failed to respond to messages from the Nobel Committee regarding his possible attendance at the prize ceremony in Stockholm, Sweden.

This prompted criticism, but some observers pointed out that Dylan's nonresponse was not exactly out of the ordinary. "He's behaved so strangely for so many years that if he would show up now and be cheerful and pleased, you'd be surprised," said Daniel Sandstrom, the literary director at the publisher Albert Bonniers.

Finally, in an October 29 interview for the UK newspaper the *Telegraph*, he did comment, telling journalist Edna Gundersen that the award was "amazing, incredible. Whoever dreams about something like that?"

Would he attend the Nobel Prize banquet? "Absolutely," he said. "If it's at all possible."

In the end, though, it apparently wasn't. Dylan—who had clearly been uncomfortable receiving such earlier recognition as an honorary degree from Princeton University and a Grammy Lifetime Achievement Award—said he wouldn't be able to make it to the Nobel Prize banquet due to unspecified "pre-existing commitments." However, he did ultimately accept his award in a small private ceremony on April 1, 2017, in Stockholm. As for the banquet the previous December, he sent the following gracious speech, which US ambassador to Sweden Azita Raji delivered on his behalf. —Ed.

Good evening, everyone. I extend my warmest greetings to the members of the Swedish Academy and to all of the other distinguished guests in attendance tonight.

I'm sorry I can't be with you in person, but please know that I am most definitely with you in spirit and honored to be receiving such a prestigious prize. Being awarded the Nobel Prize for Literature is something I never could have imagined or seen coming. From an early age, I've been familiar with and reading and absorbing the works of those who were deemed worthy of such a distinction: Kipling, Shaw, Thomas Mann, Pearl Buck, Albert Camus, Hemingway. These giants of literature whose works are taught in the schoolroom, housed in libraries around the world and spoken of in reverent tones have always made a deep impression. That I now join the names on such a list is truly beyond words.

I don't know if these men and women ever thought of the Nobel honor for themselves, but I suppose that anyone writing a book, or a poem, or a play anywhere in the world might harbor that secret dream deep down inside. It's probably buried so deep that they don't even know it's there.

If someone had ever told me that I had the slightest chance of winning the Nobel Prize, I would have to think that I'd have about the same odds as standing on the moon. In fact, during the year I was born and for a few years after, there wasn't anyone in the *world* who was considered good enough to win this Nobel Prize. So, I recognize that I am in very rare company, to say the least.

I was out on the road when I received this surprising news, and it took me more than a few minutes to properly process it. I began to think about William Shakespeare, the great literary figure. I would reckon he thought of himself as a dramatist. The thought that he was writing literature couldn't have entered his head. His words were written for the stage. Meant to be spoken, not read. When he was writing Hamlet, I'm sure he was thinking about a lot of different things: "Who're the right actors for these roles?" "How should this be staged?" "Do I really want to set this in Denmark?" His creative vision and ambitions were no doubt at the forefront of his mind, but there were also more mundane matters to consider and deal with. "Is the financing in place?" "Are there enough good seats for my patrons?" "Where am I going to get a human skull?" I would bet that the farthest thing from Shakespeare's mind was the question "Is this *literature*?"

When I started writing songs as a teenager, and even as I started to achieve some renown for my abilities, my aspirations for these songs only went so far. I thought they could be heard in coffee houses or bars, maybe later in places like Carnegie Hall, the London Palladium. If I was really dreaming big, maybe I could imagine getting to make a record and then hearing my songs on the radio. That was really the big prize in my mind. Making records and hearing your songs on the radio meant that you were reaching a big audience and that you might get to keep doing what you had set out to do.

Well, I've been doing what I set out to do for a long time, now. I've made dozens of records and played thousands of concerts all around the world. But it's my songs that are at the vital center of almost everything I do. They seemed to have found a place in the lives of many people throughout many different cultures and I'm grateful for that.

But there's one thing I must say. As a performer, I've played for 50,000 people and I've played for 50 people and I can tell you that it is harder to play for 50 people. 50,000 people have a singular persona, not so with 50. Each person has an individual, separate identity, a world unto themselves. They can perceive things more clearly. Your honesty and how it relates to the depth of your talent is tried. The fact that the Nobel committee is so small is not lost on me.

But, like Shakespeare, I too am often occupied with the pursuit of my creative endeavors and dealing with all aspects of life's mundane matters. "Who are the best musicians for these songs?" "Am I recording in the right studio?" "Is this song in the right key?" Some things never change, even in 400 years.

Not once have I ever had the time to ask myself, "Are my songs *literature*?"

So, I do thank the Swedish Academy, both for taking the time to consider that very question, and, ultimately, for providing such a wonderful answer.

My best wishes to you all,

Bob Dylan

ABOUT THE CONTRIBUTORS

Randy Anderson wrote for the arts-and-leisure section of *Minnesota Daily* in the late 1970s and, later, for *Minneapolis City Pages.*

After covering the end of the Vietnam War and the White House, **Ed Bradley** spent twenty-six years as a correspondent for CBS News's *60 Minutes* program. The winner of nineteen Emmy Awards, he died in November 2006, less than two years after conducting the Dylan interview that appears in this book.

Douglas Brinkley has been a professor of history at Rice University in Houston since 2007. He is the author of *The Great Deluge: Hurricane Katrina, New Orleans and the Mississippi Gulf Coast* and the coeditor of Woody Guthrie's novel *House of Earth*; and he has written, coauthored, or edited about two dozen other books. Brinkley is CNN's presidential historian and a contributing editor at *Vanity Fair*. In 2017, he won a Grammy for coproducing *Presidential Suite with Jazz at Lincoln Center.*

Born in London in 1950, **Mick Brown** has contributed to such publications as the *Sunday Times*, the *Guardian*, *Esquire*, and *Rolling Stone*. He now writes on cultural subjects for the *Daily Telegraph* magazine. He is the author of six books, including *American Heartbeat: Travels from Woodstock to San Jose by Song Title*, *The Spiritual Tourist*, *The Dance of 17 Lives*, and *Tearing Down the Wall of Sound: The Rise and Fall of Phil Spector.*

When pirate radio stations shut down in 1961, the Swedish Broadcasting Corporation decided to set up a channel to provide a legal alternative, and **Klas Burling** was in the forefront of this process. Burling, who was born in 1941, subsequently interviewed the Beatles, the Rolling Stones, Jimi Hendrix, the Beach Boys, Johnny Cash, Carl Perkins, and many other British and American pop stars.

Bob Coburn was a disc jockey at Los Angeles-area radio station KLOS-FM from 1980 until his death in 2016. For most of that time, he hosted the nationally syndicated *Rockline*, a call-in program that Wikipedia has labeled the longest-running radio program in rock history.

John "Jay" Cocks was a film critic for such magazines as *Rolling Stone*, *Newsweek*, and *Time* before becoming a screenwriter. His scripts for Martin Scorsese's *The Age of Innocence* and *Gangs of New York* both received Academy Award nominations.

Musician, filmmaker, photographer, and musicologist **John Cohen** cofounded the New Lost City Ramblers, a traditional string band that played a key role in the folk revival during the 1960s. His other work includes *High Lonesome Sound*, a highly regarded film about old-time Appalachian music; and *Young Bob: John Cohen's Early Photographs of Bob Dylan*. Cohen, who was born in 1932, served as a professor of visual arts at the State University of New York's Purchase College from 1972 to 1997.

Sis Cunningham (1909–2004) was a folksinger and the founding editor of *Broadside* magazine.

John Dolen is a Florida-based journalist. A graduate of the University of Maryland, he spent twenty-seven years at the *SunSentinel* in Fort Lauderdale, including thirteen as the newspaper's arts and features editor. He is working on a memoir about his days following his "graduation" from the Summer of Love in Haight-Ashbury and then Woodstock.

Susan Edmiston, who has been an editor at *Redbook* and *Glamour*, has written for such publications as *New York*, the *New York Times Magazine*, *Esquire*, the *San Francisco Chronicle*, and *Women's Day*. She coauthored *Literary New York: A History and Guide* and *The Cow in the Parking Lot: A Zen Approach to Overcoming Anger*.

Nora Ephron, who died in 2012, wrote the scripts for such popular films as *Silkwood, Heartburn, When Harry Met Sally . . ., Sleepless in Seattle,* and *Julie & Julia.* She was also a producer, director, essayist, novelist, playwright, and journalist. In 1966, while working as a reporter at the *New York Post,* she broke the news that Bob Dylan had married Sara Lownds.

Bob Fass, who was born in 1933, has been a fixture on New York's listener-sponsored WBAI-FM for more than half a century. His late-night *Radio Unnameable* program was the subject of a 2012 documentary of the same name. In addition to Bob Dylan, the program has featured such musical and countercultural figures as Allen Ginsberg, Abbie Hoffman, Timothy Leary, Phil Ochs, and Arlo Guthrie.

Paul Gambaccini, who was born in New York in 1949, is a radio and television personality in the UK. He was a BBC Radio 1 presenter for sixteen years, including eleven years on a *Billboard* Top 30 countdown show, and he has hosted such other BBC programs as *America's Greatest Hits* and *Pick of the Pops.* He coauthored *The Guinness Book of British Hit Singles* and has written more than a dozen other books, including *Radio Boy* and *Track Record.*

Mikal Gilmore, one of America's leading music journalists, has written for *Rolling Stone* since the 1970s. He is the author of *Night Beat: A Shadow History of Rock and Roll* and *Stories Done: Writings on the 1960s and Its Discontents.* His 1995 memoir, *Shot in the Heart,* recounts his destructive childhood and relationship with his older brother Gary, who in 1977 became the first person to be executed in the US after restoration of the death penalty. It won the *Los Angeles Times* book prize and the National Book Critics Circle Award.

Cynthia Gooding, who died of cancer in 1988 at age sixty-three, was a folksinger and the host of the 1960s radio program *Folksinger's Choice,* which aired on WBAI-FM in New York.

Nat Hentoff was the jazz critic for New York's *Village Voice* from 1958 to 2009, and for the *Wall Street Journal* from 2009 until his death in 2017 at age ninety-one. His distinguished career also embraced authorship of numerous nonfiction books and novels, stints as a staff writer at the *New Yorker* and an editor and columnist at *Down Beat*, the hosting of several radio programs, columns for the *Washington Post*, and articles for such publications as the *New York Times* and the *Atlantic*.

As editorial director of EMAP Magazines in the 1980s and 1990s, British journalist **David Hepworth** was involved in editing, launching, or directing such leading magazines as *Q* and *Mojo*. He has been a presenter on BBC's *Whistle Test* and, in 1985, was an anchor of Live Aid. His writing has appeared in the *Guardian*, the *Times*, the *Independent*, and *Marie Claire*. His books include *1971: Never a Dull Moment* and *Uncommon People: The Rise and Fall of the Rock Stars*.

Neil Hickey is an adjunct professor at the Columbia University Graduate School of Journalism and a former editor at large of the *Columbia Journalism Review*. He was the longtime New York bureau chief of the original *TV Guide*. He has published hundreds of articles on subjects ranging from the Vietnam War and the first Persian Gulf War to glasnost and the 1968 Democratic convention; and he has interviewed presidents Johnson, Nixon, Ford, Carter, and Clinton. He has won the Country Music Association's Journalist of the Year Award and the Everett C. Parker Award for Lifetime Achievement for his coverage of telecommunications. His latest book, *Adventures in the Scribblers Trade*, includes the Dylan piece featured here as well as interview-based features on Johnny Cash, Kurt Vonnegut, Bobby Fischer, Willie Nelson, Henry Kissinger, and other cultural and political figures.

Bert Kleinman has been a radio consultant for decades. Since 2001, he has been an adviser to Radio Sawa, which broadcasts in Arabic in the Middle East, as well as to Radio Free Europe and the Voice of America.

Jonathan Lethem, a Brooklyn native who was born in 1964, is a novelist and the author of numerous essays and short stories. He first achieved mainstream success with 1999's *Motherless Brooklyn*, which won a National Book Critics Circle Award, and 2003's bestselling *The Fortress of Solitude*. His latest novel, *A Gambler's Anatomy*, appeared in 2016.

Robert Love is editor in chief of *AARP The Magazine*, the world's largest-circulation periodical. He previously spent twenty years in senior editorial positions at *Rolling Stone* and eleven years as an adjunct professor at Columbia Graduate School of Journalism. Love has also been an editor at such publications as *Playboy, Reader's Digest*, and *The Week*.

Don McLeese, a journalism professor at the University of Iowa, has been a columnist for the *Chicago Sun-Times* and *Austin American Statesman* and a senior editor at *No Depression*. He has written for *Rolling Stone*, the *New York Times Book Review*, the *Washington Post*, the *Chicago Tribune*, *Entertainment Weekly*, and dozens of other publications. His work has been anthologized in *The Best of No Depression: Writing About American Music*, *Rolling Stone: The Decades of Rock & Roll*, *Racing in the Street: The Bruce Springsteen Reader*, *Rockin' Out: Popular Music in the U.S.A.*, *33 1/3 Greatest Hits, Vol. 2*, and *Springsteen on Springsteen: Interviews, Speeches, and Encounters*. He is the author of *Dwight Yoakam: A Thousand Miles from Nowhere*, *The New York Times Arts and Culture Reader*, and *Kick Out the Jams*.

Elliot Mintz began hosting a radio talk show on KPFK-FM in Los Angeles in 1966, when he was twenty-one, and subsequently worked at several other Southern California radio and TV stations. According to Wikipedia, he interviewed more than two thousand luminaries during his broadcasting career. Mintz entered the public relations field during the 1970s. Besides Bob Dylan, his clients have included Christie Brinkley; Crosby, Stills, and Nash; and Paris Hilton. He was a friend and spokesperson for John Lennon and Yoko Ono throughout the 1970s and continues to represent Lennon's estate and Ono.

Artie Mogull, who died in 2004 at age seventy-seven, was an A&R executive who discovered or signed such acts as Laura Nyro, Bill Cosby, Olivia Newton-John, Wilson Phillips, and Hootie and the Blowfish. He worked for such record labels as Warner Bros., Capitol, and MCA, and served as president and then co-owner of United Artists Records. In 1962, he signed Bob Dylan to his first music-publishing contract.

Paul Jay Robbins appears to have maintained a low profile since the 1960s, when he published short fiction; worked as a film critic for Los

Angeles's KPFK-FM; sang in a choir on Van Dyke Parks's *Song Cycle*; and contributed articles about Bob Dylan, Andy Warhol, and others to the *Los Angeles Free Press*.

Pete Seeger (1919–2014), one of the giants of American folk music and political activism, was a member of the popular vocal group the Weavers in the early '50s. He authored or coauthored such now-standard songs as "Where Have All the Flowers Gone?" and "If I Had a Hammer." One of Bob Dylan's earliest supporters, he urged John Hammond to produce Dylan's first LP and invited him to perform at the Newport Folk Festival, for which Seeger was a board member.

Folk musician **Happy Traum**, a former editor of *Sing Out!*, has recorded numerous solo albums and recordings with his brother Artie. He has also recorded with many luminous folk and rock artists. He first collaborated with Bob Dylan in 1962 on the now-classic *Broadside Ballads, Vol. 1*, and he also appeared on such Dylan recordings as *Greatest Hits Vol. II* and *The Bootleg Series Vol. 10—Another Self Portrait (1969–1971)*. In early 1963, Traum's New World Singers released what was reportedly the first recorded version of Dylan's "Blowin' in the Wind."

Mary Travers (1936–2009) was a member of the pioneering folk group Peter, Paul, and Mary, which performed and recorded from 1961 to 1970 and again from 1978 to 2009. The trio—which, like Dylan, were managed by Albert Grossman—recorded such hits as "Leavin' on a Jet Plane," "Puff the Magic Dragon," and "Where Have All the Flowers Gone?" Their 1963 recordings of Dylan's "Don't Think Twice, It's All Right" and "Blowin' in the Wind," both Top 10 hits, played a big role in popularizing his early work.

A singer/songwriter and political activist, **Gil Turner** (1933–1974) was a key figure in the Greenwich Village folk scene in the early '60s. He was the first person to publicly perform Dylan's "Blowin' in the Wind" (on April 16, 1962, the night Dylan completed it), and, with the New World Singers, the first to record it.

At the time of his Dylan interview, **Paul Vincent** was music director and an afternoon DJ at San Francisco's KMEL-FM. In addition to Dylan,

Vincent's guests on the show included such artists as Peter Gabriel, Van Morrison, and the Grateful Dead's Bob Weir and Mickey Hart.

Peter Wilmoth is a Melbourne, Australia–based journalist who spent many years writing for the *Age* and the *Sunday Age* on everything from sports and politics to food and the arts. He covered the end of the Ceausescu regime in Romania and the civil war between Ethiopia and Eritrea. His interview subjects have included Woody Allen, Yusuf Islam (Cat Stevens), Christopher Hitchens, Rachel Ward, Leo Sayer, and Robert Altman. He has written for *Rolling Stone* (Australia) and the *Sydney Morning Herald* and has authored and coauthored several books, including *Glad All Over: The Countdown Years 1974–1987*. Since 2010, he has written an interview column for Melbourne's *Weekly Review* magazine.

Izzy Young, who was born in 1928, owned and operated Greenwich Village's Folklore Center (the subject of Bob Dylan's "Talking Folklore Center") from 1957 until the early 1970s, when he moved to Sweden and opened a similar store in Stockholm. Besides selling folk-related books and records, the New York store became a hangout for musicians such as Dylan, who reportedly met folksinger Dave Van Ronk there. Young— who wrote a column for *Sing Out!* from 1959 to 1969—produced Dylan's first concert at New York's Carnegie Chapter Hall on November 4, 1961.

Paul Zollo is a songwriter, music journalist, and author of several books, including *Songwriters on Songwriting, More Songwriters on Songwriting, Conversations with Tom Petty, Hollywood Remembered,* and *Matisyahu: King without a Crown.* A senior editor of *American Songwriter* magazine, he's also a recording artist with two solo albums to his credit, *Universal Cure* and *Orange Avenue.* As a songwriter, he has collaborated with many artists, including the late Steve Allen, Art Garfunkel, Dan Bern, Darryl Purpose, Stephen Kalinich, and Neil Rosengarden. He lives with his son and cats in Hollywood, California.

ABOUT THE EDITOR

Jeff Burger edited *Lennon on Lennon: Conversations with John Lennon* (2016), *Leonard Cohen on Leonard Cohen: Interviews and Encounters* (2014), and *Springsteen on Springsteen: Interviews, Speeches, and Encounters* (2013), all published in North America by Chicago Review Press. He has been a writer and editor for more than four decades and has covered popular music throughout his journalism career.

His reviews, essays, and reportage on that and many other subjects have appeared in more than seventy-five magazines, newspapers, and books, including *All Music Guide, Barron's, Circus, Creem, Family Circle, Gentlemen's Quarterly, High Fidelity,* the *Los Angeles Times, Melody Maker, No Depression,* and *Reader's Digest.* He has published interviews with many leading musicians, including Tommy James, Billy Joel, Foreigner's Mick Jones, Roger McGuinn, the Righteous Brothers, Bruce Springsteen, the members of Steely Dan, and Tom Waits; and with such public figures as F. Lee Bailey, Sir Richard Branson, James Carville, Daymond John, Suze Orman, Sydney Pollack, Cliff Robertson, Donald Trump, and Wolfman Jack.

Burger has been editor of several periodicals, including *Phoenix* magazine in Arizona, and he spent fourteen years in senior positions at *Medical Economics,* America's leading business magazine for doctors. A former consulting editor at Time Inc., he currently serves as editor of *Business Jet Traveler,* which was named one of the country's best business magazines in 2011, 2013, and 2016 in the American Society of Business Publication Editors' Azbee Awards competition.

Burger—whose website, byjeffburger.com, collects more than forty years' worth of his music reviews and commentary—lives in Ridgewood, New Jersey. His wife, Madeleine Beresford, is a preschool director and teacher, and a puppeteer. The couple have a son, Andre, and a daughter, Myriam.

CREDITS

I gratefully acknowledge the help of everyone who gave permission for material to appear in this book. I have made every reasonable effort to contact copyright holders. If an error or omission has been made, please bring it to the attention of the publisher.

Izzy Young's Notebook, by Izzy Young. Copyright © 1961–1962 by Izzy Young. Reprinted by permission.

Interview with Cynthia Gooding. Broadcast March 1962, WBAI-FM. Copyright © 1962 by Pacifica Radio Archives. Printed by permission.

Conversation with Izzy Young, Pete Seeger, Sis Cunningham, and Gil Turner. Copyright © 1962 by Pacifica Radio Archives. Printed by permission.

"A Day with Bob Dylan," by John Cocks. Published November 20, 1964 in the *Kenyon Collegian*. Copyright © 1964 by the *Kenyon Collegian*. Reprinted by permission.

"Bob Dylan as Bob Dylan," by Paul Jay Robbins. Published September 10, 17, and 24, 1965 in the *Los Angeles Free Press*. Copyright © 1965 by the *Los Angeles Free Press*. Reprinted by permission.

Interview with Nora Ephron and Susan Edmiston. Copyright © 1965. Reprinted by permission of Susan Edmiston and ICM Partners.

"*Playboy* Interview: Bob Dylan," by Nat Hentoff. Published March 1996 in *Playboy*. Copyright © 1966 by Nat Hentoff. Reprinted by permission of Margot Hentoff and *Playboy*.

Conversation with Bob Fass. Broadcast January 26, 1966 on WBAI-FM. Copyright © 1966 by Pacifica Radio Archives. Printed by permission.

Interview with Klas Burling. Broadcast April 28, 1966 on Swedish Radio Corporation's Radio 3. Copyright © 1966 by Klas Burling. Printed by permission.

"Conversations with Bob Dylan," by John Cohen and Happy Traum. Published October/ November 1968 in *Sing Out!* Copyright © 1968 by *Sing Out!* Reprinted by permission.

Interview with Mary Travers. Broadcast April 20, 1975 on *Mary Travers and Friend* on KNX-FM (and syndicated). Copyright © 1975 by CBS Radio. Printed by permission.

"Bob Dylan: '. . . A Sailing Ship to the Moon'," by Neil Hickey. Published March 4, 2015 in *Adventures in the Scribblers Trade.* Copyright © 2015 by Neil Hickey. Reprinted by permission.

"An Interview with Dylan," by Randy Anderson. Published February 17, 1978 in *Minnesota Daily*. Copyright © 1978 by *Minnesota Daily*. Reprinted by permission.

Interview with Paul Vincent. Broadcast November 19, 1980 on KMEL-FM. Copyright © 1980. Printed by permission of iHeart Media.

Interview with Paul Gambaccini. Broadcast June 20, 1981 on BBC Radio 1. Copyright © 1981 by Paul Gambaccini. Printed by permission.

"Jesus, Who's Got Time to Keep Up with the Times?," by Mick Brown. Published July 1, 1984, the *Sunday Times* (UK). Copyright © 1984 by Mick Brown. Reprinted by permission.

Interview with Bert Kleinman and Artie Mogull. Broadcast November 13, 1984 on Westwood One radio network. Copyright © 1984 by Westwood One. Printed by permission.

Interview with Bob Coburn. Broadcast June 17, 1985 on *Rockline*. Copyright © 1985 by *Rockline*. Printed by permission.

"Bob Dylan—After All These Years in the Spotlight, the Elusive Star Is at the Crossroads Again," by Mikal Gilmore. Published October 13, 1985 in the *Los Angeles Herald-Examiner*. Copyright © 1985 by Mikal Gilmore. Reprinted by permission.

"Ask Him Something, and a Sincere Dylan Will Tell You the Truth," by Don McLeese. Published January 26, 1986 in the *Chicago Sun-Times*. Copyright © 1986 by Don McLeese. Reprinted by permission.

"The Invisible Man," by David Hepworth. Published October 1986 in Q magazine. Copyright © 1986 by David Hepworth. Reprinted by permission.

Interview with Elliot Mintz. Broadcast May 1991 on Westwood One radio network. Copyright © 1991 by Westwood One. Printed by permission.

Interview with Paul Zollo. Published November 1991 in *SongTalk*. Copyright © 1991 by Paul Zollo. Reprinted by permission.

"Dylan: Jokes, Laughter, and a Series of Dreams," by Peter Wilmoth. Published April 3, 1992 in the *Age*. Copyright © 1992 by Peter Wilmoth. Reprinted by permission.

"A Midnight Chat with Dylan," by John Dolen. Published September 28, 1995 in the *Sun-Sentinel*. Copyright © 1995 by the *SunSentinel*. Reprinted by permission.

No Direction Home outtakes. Copyright © 2000 by Pacifica Radio Archives. Printed by permission.

Interview with Ed Bradley. Broadcast December 5, 2004 on *60 Minutes*, CBS-TV. Copyright © 2004 by CBS News. Printed by permission.

"The Genius and Modern Times of Bob Dylan," by Jonathan Lethem. Published September 7, 2006 in *Rolling Stone*. Copyright © 2006 by Jonathan Lethem. Reprinted by permission.

"Bob Dylan's Late-Era, Old-Style American Individualism," by Douglas Brinkley. Published May 14, 2009 in *Rolling Stone*. Copyright © 2009 by Douglas Brinkley. Reprinted by permission.

"Bob Dylan: The Uncut Interview," by Robert Love. Published February/March 2015 in *AARP The Magazine* (portions of intro) and aarp.org. Copyright © 2015 by AARP. Reprinted by permission. Permission conveyed through Copyright Clearance Center, Inc.

Nobel Prize banquet speech, by Bob Dylan. Delivered December 10, 2016 in Stockholm, Sweden by Azita Raji. Copyright © 2016 by the Nobel Foundation. Printed by permission.

Press conferences are in the public domain.

INDEX